THE
LOVE LETTERS
OF
Mark Twain

THE
LOVE LETTERS
OF
MARK TWAIN

EDITED
AND WITH AN INTRODUCTION BY
DIXON WECTER

Literary Editor of
The Mark Twain Estate

PUBLISHERS NEW YORK
HARPER & BROTHERS
MCMXLIX

TABLE OF CONTENTS

THE
LOVE LETTERS
OF
Mark Twain

Introduction

IN THE spring of 1867 Samuel Langhorne Clemens—already becoming a household word for American humor under his pseudonym Mark Twain—impulsively booked passage with a shipload of pilgrims bound for the Holy Land on the steamship *Quaker City*. It was the first transatlantic pleasure cruise. A majority of the passengers were prosperous, pious Congregationalists, for whom the destination of biblical lands justified the junket.

Without this voyage, Sam Clemens' path and that of a sheltered, semi-invalid girl in Elmira, New York, named Olivia Langdon, would never have crossed. A modern poet writes of

> . . . a mermaid and a saint
> Testing each other's existence with a kiss.

The meeting of these diverse lives seems as improbable. Born ten years and a thousand miles apart, with vast differences in upbringing, experience, and temperament, they had birthdays that fell within three days of each other in late November. On one such anniversary he was led to ponder this "event which was happening when I was a giddy school-boy . . . unconscious that on that day, two journeys were begun, wide as the poles apart, two paths marked out, which, wandering & wandering, now far & now near, were still narrowing, always narrowing toward one point & one blessed consummation."

Olivia, called Livy by family and friends, had a junior brother Charles, a harum-scarum buck of eighteen. In accord with old-fashioned notions that the chaperoned Grand Tour was the best specific for prodigal sons, he was shipped aboard the *Quaker City* by his rich Congregationalist parents. Clemens was Charles Langdon's senior by thirteen years and large segments of experience. But the pair quickly found themselves drawn together, along with two or three other young men, against the oppressive respectability of the mass, whose chief amusements were prayers, dominoes, and backbiting. The Solon Severances from Cleveland, a friendly and youthful couple, and the plain but kindly wife of a newspaper editor in that city, "Mother" Fairbanks, soon proved sympathetic enough to win the good will of these "Quaker City night-hawks" and share some of their forays ashore. Mary Mason Fairbanks continued a warm friend for life, and presently found herself chief confidante in Mark's siege to the heart of Charles Langdon's sister.

For, as almost everybody knows, Charles had in his cabin a miniature of his sister, and on seeing it one day in the Bay of Smyrna Mark grew interested in meeting the original. His *Autobiography* speaks explicitly of "an ivory miniature." Although the official biographer Albert Bigelow Paine reproduces as the famous keepsake a sepia-and-white porcelaintype owned by the Langdons and supposed by them to be the authentic article, he is almost certainly wrong. The only known ivory miniature of Livy as a young woman is one painted in delicate colors by S. R. Fanshaw in 1864, now owned by her daughter Clara Clemens Samossoud. To the average eye, neither likeness seems so ravishing as to extort love at first sight—as Mark always insisted, saying forty years later that "from that day to this she has never been out of my mind." Sweet, demure, conventional, the face lacks that charm of personality supplied by later and better portraits of Livy, with her features of cameo clarity, gentle musing smile, black hair, and large dark eyes warming to lapis lazuli.

In those days Sam Clemens was probably in love with love. His long bachelorhood was no testament to misogyny. He had had sweethearts in Hannibal schooldays, in printing-shop days at Keokuk, and pilot days on the Mississippi, and in his silver-mining and newspaper phase in Nevada and California was certainly interested in the local belles. Yet the life of a river man. prospector, roving correspondent or lecturer offered scant security for either homekeeping or steady support. Clemens' stout sense of the financial obligations of marriage, and his pride in meeting them adequately, are clear in the letters that follow. But now in his thirty-second year, he could command a hundred dollars a night on lecture tour, up to sixteen hundred in a friendly city like San Francisco—though a big slice of the take was sent home to help his mother and widowed sister with her two children. Unlike many a poor boy beginning to make good, he was and always remained an easy spender, generous, careless, often extravagant. His first slender book, *The Jumping Frog*, had appeared in the spring of 1867, and even though the contract was so sloppy as to yield its author no profit, sales augured success for later offerings. Furthermore, the best newspapers of New York and California stood ready to pay his passage almost anywhere for the sake of humorous travel letters. Cash in hand remained small, but expectations great. To a bachelor, therefore, with proud notions, marriage within the next few years looked at last feasible.

Also his itinerant life since boyhood had left its residue of weariness. "I am like an old, burnt-out crater," he told Mrs. Fairbanks on the voyage, with a touch of theatricality, "the fires of my life are all dead within me." And in his shipboard notebook, under the caption "Questions for Debate" he jotted the query, "Which is the most desirable—the single or the married state?"

He was not only in love with love, but with ideal womanhood —the exquisite purity, sweetness, and nobility which both Victorianism and the American tradition exalted as a mystery, transcending the moral quality of the male.

Young Clemens must certainly have encountered other sorts and conditions of women, in the cribs of ante-bellum New Orleans, those floating brothels the packets, and in Virginia City in the flush times, when its favorite toast was a "miscegen" prostitute with heart of gold named Julie Bulette (Mark witnessed the hanging of the Frenchman who robbed and strangled her). But as if shielded by that curious sexual taboo that runs through his writings—stemming probably from boyhood inhibitions lying deep in his nature and from personal fastidiousness— he seems to have escaped unscathed. Almost incredible as it appears, the known facts suggest that he entered into marriage as a virgin of thirty-four.

Woman he tended to regard always as the object of reverential chivalry. The assumption that women ought to exert a gentle tyranny over their menfolk for the latter's good, appealed to one who subscribed cheerfully to the Victorian theory that his own sex was coarser clay. All his life Mark invited women to reform him, "civilize" him, improve his taste and manners—whether they were his seniors like "Mother" Fairbanks or very much his juniors, like his own three daughters or that circle of little girls, the "angel fish" of Bermuda and New York who brightened his last years of widowerhood. And save for an occasional brief encounter with literary gold-diggers in those late lonely days, Mark was singularly lucky in the women whose serving cavalier he became.

It was inevitable that Clemens should fall in love with a girl who satisfied his deepest aspirations—not a fire-engine tomboy growing into sportswoman of gun and saddle like Lily Hitchcock, a platonic friend of San Francisco days described to Livy in a letter here published. His ideal had to be gentle, lovely, essentially serious, somewhat conventional and domestic, able to elicit the protective instincts gratifying to a suitor of rather slight physique (her "little man," in Livy's endearing phrase). And she must represent the leisure-class culture, that genteel Eastern tradition upon which this self-made provincial set much store. Whether in time he could kindle such a person into physical passion, and also lend her some of his own vitality and venturesomeness of mind, or the sense of playfulness and irony by which he lived—these adjustments seemingly required for perfect marriage might well have looked problematical at the start.

II

Back from his cruise with "those venerable fossils" and his few shipboard friends in late November 1867, Clemens headed for Washington. He took a job briefly as private secretary to a pompous senator from Nevada, William M. Stewart, but they soon quarreled. Mark's chief interest, however, lay in supplying

Capitol Hill letters to various newspapers and planning a book about his late adventures that became *The Innocents Abroad.* Christmas Day drew him back to New York to spend a fortnight with his roommate on the *Quaker City,* Dan Slote. As it happened, Charles Langdon's family had also come to town for the holidays, and there at the St. Nicholas Hotel on December 27 Clemens called and met the original of the ivory miniature.

The circuitous chain of coincidence had at last brought them together. Here was "the wild humorist of the Sage Brush hills" as San Francisco had first hailed him, this ex-printer and steamboat pilot now rising in the world by his quick wit and slow drawl, with piercing blue-green eyes under brows so thick and fierce that to one observer they resembled "a sort of plumage," russet hair and mustache, hawk nose, and sensitive nervous hands missing the perennial cigar they dared not bring forth in the presence of unfamiliar ladies. And facing him in the parlors of the St. Nicholas was the wealthy coal dealer's only daughter, a slender figure, pale and lovely, with great sweetness and dignity, her eyes peering with a tender myopic vagueness, her black tresses combed severely back from a high white forehead.

At the age of sixteen a fall on the ice had left her with partial paralysis, costing her two years of constant pain and nervous depletion. At last an osteopathic faith-healer named Newton brought the breath of self-confidence into that darkened bedroom where she lay under a tackle sometimes used to lift her to a sitting posture, though an access of fatigue and nausea had always come quickly. Then, by prayer and the laying on of hands Doctor Newton taught her in one morning to take a few steps, and sent the Langdons a bill for fifteen hundred dollars, which they paid gladly. Now aged twenty-two, Livy could walk a few blocks without exhaustion but was still unsure of her physical powers.

The cosseting of her family—an adoring father and brother and adopted sister Susan, and a mother whose preoccupation with her own ill-health verged upon the neurotic—had probably slowed Livy's recovery with unwise solicitude, as did the whole philosophy about the genteel girl of the period. In the courtship days ahead, Livy's misgivings about ever being "a healthy wife"

Mark affected to brush off lightly, as in one of two letters he wrote her on March 6, 1869, with a full understanding of her sensitiveness on that score. But to Mrs. Fairbanks he revealed now and then his secret anxieties about the slow pace of her improvement. Livy never grew robust, but the therapy of love rescued her from the abysses of timorous living and gave her an immeasurable gift of self-reliance.

His first glimpse of her led Mark four days later to pay a call on New Year's Day—that social custom he had learned in San Francisco, and mildly satirized for its bacchanalian progresses from house to house. The present stimulus was not notably alcoholic. Indeed the Langdons had helped to found a Congregational church in Elmira whose charter pledged that "no intoxicating liquors shall be used by the members"—a fact not to be forgotten in observing the new sobriety which hereafter settled upon Livy's suitor, a drinking man from the frontier West. With her Hartford chum Alice Hooker, niece of the Langdons' pastor, Livy was receiving New Year callers at the Manhattan house of their friend Mrs. Berry. Forty years later in his *Autobiography* Mark remembered that he arrived at ten in the morning and stayed thirteen hours. Clearly the visit left a vivid impression upon both, as he disclosed a year afterward in writing to her on January 6, 1869, in a letter here first published.

The biographer Paine states that on the night Mark and Livy first met, he dined with the Langdons at their hotel and then accompanied them to hear Charles Dickens read in Steinway Hall. No doubt that was the way Clemens recollected it. But his letter to the *Alta California*, dated January 11 after his return to Washington, begins by speaking of the British novelist: "I only heard him read once. It was in New York, last week. I had a seat about the middle of Steinway Hall . . . I am proud to observe that there was a beautiful young lady with me—a highly respectable young white woman." If these statements are true, then Mark's first date with Livy was to hear Dickens read on either January 2 or 3, 1868, since those are the only New York appearances of Charles Dickens that fit the calendar.

"I have just arrived from New York—been there ever since Christmas day staying at Dan Slote's house," Mark wrote his mother and sister from the capital on January 8, informing them that on New Year's Day "I anchored for the day at the first house I came to—Charlie Langdon's sister was there (beautiful girl) & Miss Alice Hooker, another beautiful girl, a niece of Henry Ward Beecher's. We sent the old folks home early, with instructions not to send the carriage till midnight, & then I just staid there & deviled the life out of those girls. I am going to spend a few days with the Langdon's in Elmira, New York, as soon as I get time. . ."

That invitation was a long time in getting filled. Mark had newspaper letters to write, a book to begin, and speeches to make at stag dinners—one of them on January 11, a toast to "Woman," flippantly observing that "she gives us good advice, and plenty of it: she soothes our aching brows: she bears our children—ours as a general thing," which when printed in the papers quickly brought a blistering reproof from Mrs. Fairbanks. His love of shocking, within carefully defined limits, was already well developed. In March Clemens dashed off for California via the Isthmus, to protect his interests in the *Alta* letters, and lingered to lecture on the coast, not returning to New York until the end of July. His Hartford editors, the Blisses of the American Publishing Company, gave him a room in their house and kept him at the grindstone over his manuscript of *The Innocents* until the third week in August. Then at last he was free to accept the hospitality of Elmira.

III

According to Langdon tradition the wild humorist arrived by train in "a yellow duster and a very dirty old straw hat," to the distress of young Charles, who met him on the way and smuggled him into the house by night, so that he could change to better garb before seeing the family. Perhaps Mark was practicing thrift by roughing it when he traveled. Certainly most of the evidence even in these youthful days suggests a scrupulous if not dandiacal touch in dress, as well as a love for dramatic clothes—the white waistcoats he affected for summer, and for winter the sealskin coat and cap with the fur out—presaging the later white serge suits and socks of green, pink, and lavender. But this and similar anecdotes suggest that by Langdon standards Mark Twain (in the phrase of Charles' son, the second Jervis) was "a rather rough diamond." Were the Langdon diamonds—derived, a wag might add, from the latter stages of coal—of a more prim and prismatic conventionality?

In weighing this question we find Van Wyck Brooks on the one hand describing the "stagnant fresh-water aristocracy" of Elmira in which the Langdons were obviously the biggest frogs. On the other hand Max Eastman, whose parents were Congregational preachers in the Langdon church, and whose father buried both Livy and Mark, sees the community in general and the Langdons in particular as blithe, progressive, even iconoclastic in their outlook on life, theology, and social attitudes—so that Elmira and the Langdons emancipated rather than fettered the suitor from Hannibal.

The truth lies somewhere between these two camps. In some of their social sympathies the Langdons were distinctly liberal—as in their strong ante-bellum stand for abolition, participation in the underground railway, hospitality toward such firebrands as Gerrit Smith, William Lloyd Garrison, and the Negro orator Frederick Douglass, and after the war gifts of thousands of dollars to educate poor whites and blacks down South. Although the family was never so gaily debonair as Eastman imagines, Jervis Langdon clearly owned a sense of humor, as his letters reveal. A strong and affectionate *esprit de corps* between the Langdons is one of their most characteristic and attractive traits. But by worldly standards the pattern of their daily life, which included rather marked prejudices against alcohol and tobacco, a Congregational minister or two at dinner almost every Sunday, and an earnest devotion to prayers and Bible reading, might have been classified as pious-provincial. Jervis Langdon was strictly a self-made man, who had risen from clerk in a country store; his prosperity in the coal business was barely twenty years old, and his solidified wealth scarcely ten, when Clemens arrived on the scene. Yet the Langdons were gentlefolk, who were neither spoiled by affluence nor ill at ease under the new amenities it made possible.

Mark Twain's impact upon this household is best told by the letters that follow—the first misgivings with which they regarded the invader, his bold yet deferential siege of the whole family, and their eventual surrender.

Livy's attempt to "civilize" him, about which so much has been said, clearly began early, and her effort to Christianize him still earlier. Max Eastman has written: "And if she suspected that Mark Twain had unorthodox views about religion, that could only have helped him to fit into the environment in which she had been born and reared." This statement is mostly nonsense, as applied to the Langdons of Livy's girlhood, whatever its relation may be to the later social gospel preached at Elmira's Park Church under the waning moon of orthodox Congregationalism. For the letters printed here, and others too verbose to include, are filled with the language of an old-fashioned evangelical faith—of sin and punishment, the vicarious atonement, conversion, grace, personal immortality. Whatever may have been the "radical" social implications of the Reverend Thomas Beecher's preaching, Livy herself at this time held firmly to a conventional middle-of-the-road piety, while Mark was and always remained a skeptic, whose true affinities were Paine and Ingersoll.

Yet in the beginning, probably with full sincerity, Mark invited her to convert him. A young man in love will do some extraordinary things. And so this Southwesterner who had absorbed some of his father's agnosticism along with the notions of a freethinking Scot in Cincinnati, and lately written several mocking articles from the Holy Land, soon found himself reading Henry Ward Beecher's *Plymouth Pulpit* with Livy's underscorings for his benefit, conning hotel Bibles for his nightly lesson, plumping to his knees to pray with clergymen, and all the while answering his little mentor in a tone of garrulous piety so uncharacteristic of either his past or future as to verge upon the ludicrous. "Turn toward the Cross & be comforted—I turn with you—What would you more?" he writes on December 23, 1868, assuaging her fears that she will be homesick if she leaves the Langdons. "Good-bye—with a kiss of reverent honor & another of deathless affection—and—Hebrews XIII, 20, 21," is a sample valedictory, in his letter of March 12, 1869.

No better lover's gambit could have been devised. Interest in his soul quickly spread to the whole man. Thus the heathen lured

this zealous little missionary armed with tracts and prayers deeper
and deeper into the forest—with designs connubial rather than
cannibal. The result, as he had clearly foreseen, was that she
ended by "tumbling" into the "matrimonial pit" he had dug.

To one of Mark's impulsiveness, it was easy to feel the glow
of godliness by radiation, from two such engaging Christians as
the girl he loved and a new friend made during early courtship
days and constantly mentioned in the letters below, the Reverend
Joseph Twichell. Pastor of Hartford's Asylum Hill Congregational Church, he took a prompt and hearty liking to Mark during
the latter's repeated visits there to see the Blisses about his book.
Twichell immediately became the chief male confidant of Mark's
courtship in Elmira, and recipient of letters from Mark which
are included here as an integral part of the story. Yale oarsman,
Union Army chaplain, handsome and friendly extrovert, con-
triver of absurd situations and the perfect teller of them, preacher
of a sunny, untheological religion, Joe Twichell added the in-
gredient of virility to those persuasions which Livy was exerting
upon Mark. "Rev. Mr. Twichell may be justly described without
flattery to be a bully boy with a glass eye (as the lamented
Josephus phrases it in his Decline & Fall of the Roman Empire)—
so is his wife," Mark wrote his brother Orion Clemens. To Livy
on December 19, 1868, he confessed: "I do not & *shall* not neglect
my prayers, Livy, but somehow they do not seem as full of life
as when you or Twichell are by." All his life Mark had a predi-
lection for preachers, from Jesuits to Unitarians, to "chin" and
"swap lies with," but Twichell led all the rest.

Nevertheless those who dwell upon Mark Twain's submissive-
ness to his wife or his so-called pastor must look beyond these
impressionable days to the return of Mark's habitual freethinking and the ultimate conversion of Livy herself. This process is
disclosed at an early stage in her wistful letter to him on December 2, 1871, given below, admitting that she has grown sadly
cold and indifferent to the church, and upon searching her heart
finds that she worships her husband far better than she loves her
God. According to Paine, Twichell's patient hopes of converting
Mark were finally ended during their tramp through the Black
Forest in 1878, when Mark told him frankly that he was not and
never could be a believer. Howells recalled how Livy once said

to Mark, "Well, if you are to be lost, I want to be lost with you."
A certain regret lingered in the air, for the solaces that had
vanished. The cycle of persuasion at last returned upon itself
when Mark reproached his wife on May 8, 1893: "Livy darling,
it broke my heart—what you wrote to Sue [Crane] about immortality. Let us believe in it! I will believe in it with you." But
the hour was late to recapture by act of pure reason the conventional faith that had fled long ago, and the touching sequel
can be read below in their exchange of letters on the soul's sur-
vival in late September 1903, a few months before her death. In
gravely dismissing this subject—which they both decided would
"take care of itself"—Livy wrote to her husband in words as
tender as a benediction: "How sweet & fine you are! How much
of immortality you have in your dear blessed self."

IV

These letters should go far to refute certain misconceptions
that have sprung up about Mark's relations with Livy. For example, by a legend of Mark's own creation, Livy was supposed
to play the heavy domestic tyrant—vetoing his pet schemes, and
upon the mildest remonstrance flying into volcanic rages—as
reflected particularly in the letters Mark wrote the husband of
another gentle and semi-invalid wife, William Dean Howells,
who enjoyed fabricating for himself a similar henpecked rôle. It
was their private little joke which a few other friends shared, and
was good for a laugh precisely on the score of its improbability.
As his betrothed, she had tried to "cure" him of minor vices like
whisky, cigars, and sparing but memorable resorts to profanity—
with only temporary success, as it turned out—and as his wife she
did exercise pressures now and then by tactful suggestion, nudg-
ing, patient domestic lobbying, and on rare occasions a mingling
of affectionate scolding with prideful concern that he do and say
his best before the public. But she also spoiled, petted, shielded
him, drudged over his correspondence while he was on lecture
tour, surrounded him with a gracious social life in which he was
always cast as the prima donna, worshiped his wit and creative
genius with well-grounded confidence and also his business judgment with a faith much less deserved.

Critics who see Livy only through Mark's lens of playful refraction have formed some curious ideas of her dominion. They might as well have drawn inferences of her refinement from an undated note of the 1880's in Hartford days, written by Mark to the Langdons: "Livy wants Sue & Mother to excuse her from writing, because she is 'gutting the house.' I wish to God she wouldn't use such language." Livy's own letters, in the selections given below from various stages of her life, are undeniable witnesses to her warm, gentle, loving heart. Whatever the prim, self-conscious face she had turned toward him in their early courtship days, Livy's true nature quickly bloomed under the confident warmth of love—finding in her "Youth" a comrade, protector, and hero whom she adored increasingly with the passing years. One difference between them was that he never criticized her, or sought to change or "reform" her in any way, but actually believed her to be the image of perfection avowed in his earliest letters to her, while Livy gave more thought to the probable readjustments required by their life together—assuming at first that Mark would make most of them, and ending quietly by making the greater number herself.

"She thinks a humorist is something perfectly awful. I never put a joke in a letter to her without feeling a pang. Best girl in the world," he wrote to Mrs. Fairbanks, early in the engagement. Her misgivings were sharpened by her sheltered conventional life and the sobriety that belonged to her by nature. But this disparity could also be adjusted. Mark's association with her, as can be surmised in their letters, gradually developed in Livy a sense of fun that never matched his own but was a fair derivative product. At first her gravity offered constant provocation to what he termed "loving badinage." While they were still writing each other as "brother and sister," on October 30, 1868, he reflected: "I would tease you only you take everything in such dreadful earnest, it beats my conscience. I never could venture farther than to convince you I act like a cabbage-head that hadn't anything in it." And on December 23, after their engagement began, he applauded a mild joke by warning her: "Look out—you are on dangerous ground—be careful, or you will blossom into a humorist when you least expect it, & so distress yourself beyond measure!" Or a few weeks later, "The ring continuing to be 'the

largest piece of furniture in the house' is a burst of humor worthy
of your affianced husband, Livy, you dear little Gravity." This
tutelage proceeded through the years.

But teasing her he could never resist. Sometimes he inked out
passages in his own or others' letters just to pique her curiosity,
or scissored away portions. At times he delighted to shock her by
little jokes or "dreadful speeches," such as one described below
to his sister in mid-April 1869, with the remark that "sometimes
her simplicity is so tempting that I can't resist the inclination."
He had chaffed his mother ever since boyhood, and speedily fell
into the same habit with Mrs. Fairbanks. That the literal-minded
Livy should be his next victim was inevitable.

Her spelling offered another obvious target. For, although
Mark's grammar in those days was still a trifle shaky (witness his
confusion of "who" with "whom," his vacillation between "you
& I" and "you & me"), he was a born speller, and knew it. The
perversities of a "natural misspeller" as he called Livy, in her
struggles with a word like scissors, often provoked his hilarity.
She seems never to have taken offense, but struggled valiantly to
mend her ways by every device, as he later remarked, save that of
looking into the dictionary. Such banter is a healthy admixture
to the idealization of these courtship letters.

His earliest letters to her, written under what might be described as the greensickness of love, are important revelations of
Clemens' mind and temperament—his self-distrust, his moods of
exuberance and depression, his almost feminine sensitivity and
solicitude for others—but they are intrinsically less attractive than
the later ones, when he was less introspective, more serene and
relaxed. Mark Twain, however, rarely wrote a dull letter. Almost
invariably the personal charm, the gleam of playfulness, the twist
of the unexpected, redeem even his routine letters from the commonplace. And the love letters, presenting an aspect of his nature
almost wholly unfamiliar to readers of his books, often touch high
levels of sensibility and eloquence.

The eldest daughter of Mark and Livy, Susy Clemens, began
at the age of thirteen a biography of her father, and in it she
observes: "Papa wrote mamma a great many beautiful love letters
when he was engaged to mamma, but mamma says I am too young

to see them yet; I asked papa what I should do for I didn't [know] how I could write a Biography of him without his love letters, papa said that I could write mamma's opinion of them, and that would do just as well. So I'll do as papa says, and mamma says she thinks they are the loveliest love letters that ever were written, she says that Hawthorne's love letters to Mrs. Hawthorne are far inferior to these." Those manuscripts, kept by the family in "the sacred green box," are an essential part of his biography, as Susy with precocious insight guessed. Hitherto they have been unknown save for excerpts quoted in Clara Clemens' *My Father Mark Twain*. Livy's answering letters in the earliest courtship days have unfortunately been lost, but in the later courtship and through the years ahead a sufficient number survive to indicate their tone and quality. Somewhat vague in continuity as in punctuation, they are of course inferior as literature to the letters of her famous husband, but reveal sources of integrity, sympathy, shrewd observation and intuitive wisdom that cannot be overlooked.

Above all, these letters demonstrate beyond any doubt that Clemens and his wife fell deeply and physically in love with each other. In the beginning he seemed bolder, but the pair embarked upon this correspondence as shy, reticent people unaccustomed to avowals of passion. "She isn't demonstrative a bit (who ever supposed she would be?)" Mark wrote Mrs. Fairbanks two weeks after Livy accepted him, "but she sticks like a good girl, & answers every letter just as soon as she has read it—& lectures me like smoke, too. But I like it." Two months later, in writing to Livy on February 17, 1869, he mentioned her prejudice against the name "Sam" and also the timidity she confessed in using it, quoting from her last letter: " 'It does not even now come quite easily from either tongue or pen, but it is sacred to me, & I shall soon grow familiar with it—' When you say that, I understand my own case without another word. I *know* you love me—& yet I see that the peculiar & especial language of this love seems awkward to your unaccustomed tongue. Thank you, Livy."

Sam Clemens' own family had been curiously undemonstrative, and their neighborhood likewise. "Our village was not a kissing community," he once wrote, while clearly implying that its folk practices called for courtship without consummation before mar-

riage, consummation without courtship afterward. He never saw
his own parents kiss each other, sensing that theirs was a loveless
union of two proud people joined by accident and pique. The
only family kiss Sam ever witnessed was when the father John
Marshall Clemens lay dying, and beckoned his daughter Pamela
to his bedside.

Sam Clemens could not help contrasting this coldness with the
ardor that Livy brought into his life: "She poured out her prodigal affections in kisses and caresses, and in a vocabulary of endearments whose profusion was always an astonishment to me. I was
born *reserved* as to endearments of speech, and caresses, and hers
broke upon me as the summer waves break upon Gibraltar." A
passage comes to mind from that enchanting little book *Eve's
Diary*—epitome of all that Livy in thirty-six years had taught him
about women—whose heroine muses, "He loves me as well as he
can; I love him with all the strength of my passionate nature, and
this, I think, is proper to my youth and sex." Indubitably he was
her first love, and in the deeper sense she was his.

The true perspective of this devotion can be seen only through
the arches of the years—their love-notes exchanged on birthdays
and anniversaries, missives sent and received during the enforced
absence of lecture tours, the impatient separations of travel abroad,
triumphs and disasters, bankruptcy and grief. About mid-January
1894, while Livy and the girls were living in France for economy's
sake while Mark labored in New York to disentangle their desperate finances, in his journal he reflected: "Love seems the
swiftest, but it is the slowest of all growths. No man or woman
really knows what perfect love is until they have been married a
quarter of a century." Near the end, ten years later, we come upon
those gay pathetic billets-doux with which he serenaded her sickroom during the months of her mortal illness.

At the grave of Eve, Mark Twain's Adam utters her epitaph:
"Where she was, *there* was Eden."

CHAPTER ONE

To the Dark Tower

ABOUT August 24, 1868, young Clemens arrived for the first time in Elmira, and approached the Langdons' big mansion. A rather grim triumph of the Brown Decades, it lay embowered in elms and encircled by gardens that occupied the whole city block. The choicest blooms, however, were glassed in a hothouse whose chief mission, as Clemens remarked in a later letter, seemed to be the supplying of local funerals. The interior of the house was somber—with narrow windows, heavy curtains, a sweeping mahogany staircase, and deep upholstery—and exhaled a characteristic odor, at once rich, aristocratic and a trifle awesome, indescribably redolent of solidity and depressed health, of costly perfume and *sal volatile.*

The best account of Mark's incursion into this household is a hitherto unpublished manuscript called "What I know about Mark Twain," written by Livy's first cousin Hattie Lewis, who later became Mrs. Paff. Her role in the courtship that followed is unknown to biographers, though not unimportant. Hattie, a lively fun-loving girl from Illinois, had come to stay with her aunt Olivia Lewis Langdon, and in the generous style of hospitality common in days when a visit was a visit, remained a year. Through the kindness of Hattie's niece Mrs. Ruth Wilcox Wheeler of Beverly Hills, California, her narrative is here excerpted:

Our branch of the Lewis family moved from New York state to Illinois in the 40's, and we cousins saw very little of each other, as travel was very difficult in those days.

At about the time when my Cousin Olivia Langdon and I were young ladies, just at the age to enjoy life to the full, an invitation came to me to spend a year at the Langdon home, and this happened to be the year that Mr. Clemens first visited them. Therefore my acquaintance with Mr. C. began during the last half of the 19th cent. My cousin Charles L. met the famous humorist at the time the Quaker City made its expedition to Europe. They were both in the party. This acquaintance ripened into a warm friendship, though there was more than 15 yrs. difference in their ages. After their return from the trip, Chas. invited Mr C. to visit him, at his home in Elmira, N. Y. and he accepted.

My cousin Olivia and myself felt a little nervous about entertaining an unmarried man, who had written a book! At this time he had written The Jumping Frog. We wondered how he would look: how he would act: would he be funny all the time? and must we try to be? etc. as young ladies will. I really felt that I had one advantage over my cousin, but only one. She was rich, beautiful and intellectual, but she could not see through a joke, or see anything to laugh at in the wittiest sayings unless explained in detail—I could.

The day came for his arrival—Whatever opinion we had formed of his appearance, at least we were not overawed by his presence, or greeting. He said, "How do you do," just as any one would, except with that lazy drawl which has added much flavor to his wit and humor. It has been my good fortune to meet & know a number of noted men & women and I have found that they speak and act just like other folks. Of course all have eccentricities of genius that crop out occasionally but have we not all of us peculiarities.

Our acquaintance progressed to our mutual enjoyment. We rode, walked, talked & sang together, for Mr. C. had a very sweet tenor voice. But alas—I soon discovered that my quickness at seeing the point of a joke and the witty sayings that I had considered almost irresistible were simply nothing in comparison to my cousin's gifts. Mr. C. evidently greatly preferred her sense to my nonsense. I told him later that I should never understand why he did. I think I discovered the fact almost as soon as he did, himself, and I thought it would be a most suitable match for both, and anything I could do to help them along should be done. I had been intending to go to N. Y. for a visit, but had postponed it on account of Mr. C. coming. I now decided to go, thinking the courtship might progress better if I were out of the way. Olivia was very unsuspicious, therefore, before leaving I gave her a hint of what I thought Mr. C. had in his mind & heart and said that on my return I should ask a question, in regard to a question I was quite sure would be asked her, and I wanted a favorable answer to both.

Before Sam Clemens left, after a two-week visit that ended about September 8, he did ask the question foreseen by Hattie—and was rejected. That the door was allowed to remain open a crack, however, is clear from the first letter that he ever wrote to Livy, just before his departure. Obviously she had consented to be his "sister" and occasionally to write to him on such terms.

This letter is endorsed by Livy "Sept 1868/1st," and was almost certainly written the first Monday in the month, on the eve of Mark's going from "within the shadow of this roof." Two business letters from Elmira on September 3 conclusively show Mark's whereabouts at that date.

[ELMIRA] MONDAY, MIDNIGHT [*September 7, 1868*]

MY HONORED "SISTER"—The impulse is strong upon me to say to you how grateful I am to you and to all of you, for the patience, the consideration & the unfailing kindness which has been shown me ever since I came within the shadow of this roof, and which has made the past fortnight the sole period of my life unmarred by a regret. Unmarred by a regret. I say it deliberately. For I do not regret that I have loved you, still love & shall always love you. I accept the situation, uncomplainingly, hard as it is. Of old I am acquainted with grief, disaster & disappointment, & have borne these troubles as became a man. So, also, I shall bear this last & bitterest, even though it break my heart. I would not dishonor this worthiest love that has yet been born within me by any puerile thought, or word, or deed. It is better to have loved & lost you than that my life should have remained forever the blank it was before. For once, at least, in the idle years that have drifted over me, I have seen the world all beautiful, & known what it was to hope. For once I have known what it was to feel my sluggish pulses stir with a living ambition. The world that was so beautiful, is dark again; the hope that shone as the sun is gone; the brave ambition is dead. Yet I say again, it is better for me that I have loved & do love you; that with more than Eastern devotion I worship you; that I lay down all of my life that is worth the living, upon this hopeless altar where no fires of love shall descend to consume it. If you *could* but—

But no more of this. I have said it only from that impulse which *drives* men to speak of great calamities which have befallen them, & so seek relief. I could not say it to give you pain. The words are spoken, & they have fallen upon forgiving ears. For your dear sake my tongue & my pen are now forbidden to repeat them ever again.

And so, hence forward, I claim only that you will let me freight my speeches to you with simply the sacred love a brother bears to a sister. I ask that you will write to me sometimes, as to a friend whom you feel will do all that a man may to be worthy of your friendship—or as to a brother whom you know will hold his sister's honor as dearly as his own, her wishes as his law, her pure judgments above his blinded worldly wisdom. Being adrift, now, & rudderless, my voyage promises ill; but while the friendly beacon of your sisterly love beams though never so faintly through the fogs & the mists, I cannot be hopelessly wrecked. I shall not shame your confidence by speaking to you in future letters of this dead love whose requiem I have been chanting. No, I will not offend. I will not misunderstand you.

My honored sister, you are *so* good & so beautiful—& I am so proud of you! Give me a little room in that great heart of yours —only the little you have promised me—& if I fail to deserve it may I remain forever the homeless vagabond I am! If you & mother Fairbanks will only scold me & upbraid me now and then, I shall fight my way through the world, never fear. Write me *something* from time to time—texts from the New Testament, if nothing else occurs to you—or dissertations on [the sin of]* smoking—or extracts from your Book of Sermons—*anything*, whatever —the reflection that my matchless sister wrote it will be sufficient.

* Words canceled apparently by Clemens are enclosed in brackets throughout these letters. When used internally in a word, brackets denote a missing letter or syllable supplied by the editor; dates deduced from postmarks and other circumstantial evidence are likewise bracketed.

If it be a suggestion, I will entertain it; if it be an injunction, I will honor it; if it be a command I will obey it or [break my loyal neck] exhaust my energies trying.

And now, good-bye, my precious sister—& may all the sorrows which fate has ordained for you fall upon this foolish head of mine, which would be so glad & so proud to suffer them in your stead. I leave you to the ministering angels—for, daughter of earth as you are, they throng the air about you—they are with you, & such as you always.

Sincerely & affectionately
SAML. CLEMENS

With affairs at this pass, Sam Clemens left Elmira for Cleveland, accompanied by Livy's brother Charlie, to visit their Ohio "mother," Mary Mason Fairbanks. Then traveling alone, Clemens went on to St. Louis—where his family seem to have learned little or nothing of his inner thoughts, save what could be guessed from his gloomy preoccupation, as he confessed in a later letter to his sister Pamela. Meanwhile he took new heart after getting an answer to his first from Livy, along with her picture. He was shrewd enough to scent ultimate victory.

St Louis, Sept. 21, 1868

MY HONORED SISTER: I cannot frame language so that it will express to you how grateful I am for that large charity & thoughtful consideration which prompted you to speak so gently when you could have wounded so deeply. I had wished ever so much to receive a reply from you, & yet dreaded it—for I could not believe it possible, under the circumstances, that you could write a letter that would not give me pain, no matter how hard you might try to avoid it. But you did.—It was almost a miracle. Therefore, is it strange that I am grateful?

And I thank you for the happy surprise the picture brought—I thank you more than I can tell—though I never blamed you in the least for withholding it [before] formerly. I never dreampt of such a thing—for I believed then, & still believe, that whatever you do is right. And so, now that you have set aside that just & proper rule of conduct to give me this gratification, I know that you have done it with a free will, & that the gift is sent without reluctance or distrust. You know too well the high honor & respect I hold you in, my sister, to fear that you can ever have cause to repent your transgressed law.

You say to me: "I shall pray for you daily." Not any words that ever were spoken to me have touched me like these. They have recurred to my mind often & again—& so I have been thinking, thinking, thinking—& what I have arrived at, is the conviction that I would be less than a man if I went on in my old careless way while you were praying for me—if I showed lack of respect, worthiness, reverence, while the needs of one like me were being voiced in the august presence of God. [I had not thought of this before] I beg that you will continue to pray for me—for I have a vague, far-away sort of idea that it may not be wholly in vain. In one respect, at least, it *shall* not be in vain—for I will so mend my conduct that I shall grow *worthier* of your prayers, & your good will & sisterly solicitude, as the days go by. Furthermore (—it has taken me long to make up my mind to say these grave words, which, once said, cannot be recalled) I *will* "pray with you," as you ask: and with such faith & such encouragement withal, as are in me, though feeble & of little worth I feel they must be. It seems strange enough to me—this reverence, this solemnity, this supplication—& yet, you must surely have some faith that it will not necessarily be useless, else you would not have suggested it. *You* do not speak carelessly. (You perceive that I do *not* think you have written "too earnestly.")

I was so sorry Charlie could not come further West with me, for he is a good traveling comrade, & if he has any unworthy traits in his nature the partiality born of old companionship has blinded me to them—Mrs. Fairbanks was very proud of him that night of the reception at her house. But I am glad, now, that he did not come to St. Louis. He would have had no rest here—I have none —& it is a muddy, smoky, mean city to run about in. I am called East—Must finish my visit here in January. I leave Thursday —24th. I shall rest in Chicago & in Cleveland, & I desire also to tarry a day & a night in Elmira (Monday 28th) if your doors are still open to me & you have not reconsidered your kind invitation.

I fear you did not expect to hear from me so soon—but still

you will forgive this letter, will you not? Consider, my indulgent sister, that after all it is only I that so offend. Good-night. The peace that belongeth unto the good, the just & the beautiful, abide with you alway!

—Which is the prayer of him who is proud to write himself—

Your affectionate Brother

SAML. L. CLEMENS

He actually left St. Louis on Saturday the twenty-sixth, paid the Fairbankses another brief visit, and then set out for Elmira, where he spent the night of Tuesday the twenty-ninth. On the evening of the next day, as Sam and Charlie were climbing into the wagon to catch a train to New York, the horse started suddenly and pitched the two young men out on their heads. "We went over backwards," wrote Clemens to Mrs. Fairbanks, "Charley falling in all sorts of ways & I lighting exactly on my head in the gutter & breaking my neck in eleven different places. . . . The seat followed Charley out & split his head wide open, so that you could look through it just as if you were looking through a gorge in a mountain. There wasn't anything to intercept the view—which was curious, because his brains hadn't been knocked out. . . . But seriously, it came very near being a fatal mishap to both of us . . ."

This jolt delayed Mark's departure a day or two and evoked sympathetic nursing, of which he cheerfully made the most. But his continued failure to press beyond the brother-sister threshold is shown by two letters he wrote Livy from Hartford, on October 18th and 30th—the first one acknowledging the justice of a "rebuke" she had dealt him for sending her a letter of "hotblooded heedlessness" that seems to have perished.

More happily he observed: "Set a white stone—for I have made a friend. It is the Rev. J. H. Twichell. . . . I met him at a church sociable." Already he had gone to tea at the Twichells, and with Mark's genius for prolonging visits when he struck good company, remained until eleven o'clock. The next day being Sunday, Mark "went with him to the alms house & helped him preach & sing to the inmates (I helped in the singing, anyhow). Heaven & earth, what a sight it was! Cripples, jibbering idiots, raving madmen;

thieves, rowdies, paupers; little children stone blind; blind men & women; old, old men & women, with that sad absent look in their faces that tells of thoughts, that are busy with 'the days that are no more.' I have not had anything touch me so since I saw the leper hospitals of Honolulu & Damascus."

Clemens began a heavy lecture tour in early November, but contrived to reach Elmira on the morning of Saturday the twenty-first, announcing himself at the Langdons' door with the ingratiating words, "The calf has returned; may the prodigal have some breakfast?"

He had a lecture to give in town, but his more serious concern was a private one. "She felt the first faint symptom *Sunday*, & the lecture *Monday* night brought the disease to the surface," he reported to Mrs. Fairbanks on November 26. "Tuesday & Tuesday night she avoided me and would not do more than be simply polite to me because her parents said NO absolutely (almost)," he continued to Twichell on the twenty-eighth. "Wednesday they capitulated & marched out with their side-arms—Wednesday night she said over & over & over again that she loved me but was sorry she did & hoped it would yet pass away—Thursday . . . said he was *glad* & *proud* she loved me!—& Friday night I left, to save her sacred name from the tongues of the gossips . . ."

Reaching New York, he wrote immediately to the girl so constantly in his thoughts.

Please address "Everett House, Union Square, New York"
Nov. 28 [1868]

My dear, dear Livy: When I found myself comfortably on board the cars last night (I see Dan[1] has just come in from breakfast, & he will be back here, within five minutes & interrupt me) —when I found myself comfortably on board the cars, I said to myself: "Now whatever others may think, it is *my* opinion that I am blessed above all other men that live; I have known supreme happiness for two whole days, & now I ought to be ready & willing to pay a little attention to necessary duties, & do it cheerfully." Therefore I resolved to go deliberately through that lecture, without notes, & so impress it upon my memory & my understanding

[1] Dan Slote.

as to secure myself against any such lame delivery of it in future as *I* thought characterized it in Elmira. But I had little calculated the cost of such a resolution. Never was a lecture so full of parentheses before. It was Livy, Livy, Livy, Livy, all the way through! It was one sentence of Vandal[2] to ten sentences about *you*. The insignificant lecture was hidden, lost, overwhelmed & buried under a boundless universe of Livy! I was sorry I had ever made so reckless a resolve, for its accomplishment seemed entirely hopeless. Still, having *made* it, I *would* stick to it till it was finished, & I *did*—but it was rather late at night. Then, having a clear conscience, I prayed, & with good heart—but it was only when I prayed for you that my tongue was touched with inspiration. You will smile at the idea of *my* praying for *you*—I, who so need the prayers of all good friends, praying for you who surely need the prayers of none. But never mind, Livy, the prayer was honest & sincere—it was *that*, at least—& I know it was heard.

I slept *well*—& when I woke my first thought was of you, of course, & I was so sorry I was not going to see you at breakfast. I hope & believe you slept well, also, for you were restful & at peace, darling, when I saw you last. You needed rest, & you still need it, for you have been so harassed, & so persecuted with conflicting thoughts of late—*I* could see it, dear, though I tried so hard to think my anxiety might be misleading my eyes. *Do* put all perplexing reflections, all doubts & fears, far from you for a little while, Livy, for I dread, dread, *dread* to hear you are sick. No mere ordinary tax upon your powers is likely to make you ill, but you must remember that even the most robust nature could hardly hold out against the siege of foodless, sleepless days & nights which you have just sustained. I am not talking to you as if you were a feeble little child, for on the contrary you are a brave, strong-willed *woman*, with no nonsense & no childishness about you—but what I am providing against is your liability to indulge in troubled thoughts & forebodings. Such thoughts *must* come, for they are *natural* to people who have brains & feelings & a just appreciation of the responsibilities which God places before them, & so *you* must have them—but as I said before, my

[2] "The American Vandal Abroad" was the title of his lecture about the cruise of the Innocents.

dearest Livy, temper them, *temper* them, & be *you* the mistress & not *they*. Be cheerful—always cheerful—you can *think* more coolly, & calmly, & justly for it. I leave my fate, my weal, my woe, my *life*, in your hands & at your mercy, with a trust, & a confidence & an abiding sense of security which nothing can shake. I have no fears—none. I believe in you, even as I believe in the Savior in whose hands our destinies are. I have faith in you—a faith which is as simple & unquestioning as the faith of a devotee in the idol he worships. For I know that in their own good time your doubts & troubles will pass away, & then you will give to me your *whole* heart & I shall have nothing more to wish for on earth. This day I prize above every earthly gift so much of your precious love as I *do* possess, & so am satisfied & happy. I feel no exacting spirit— I am grateful, grateful, unspeakably grateful for the love you have already given me. I am crowned—I am throned—I am sceptred. I sit with Kings.

I do love, love, *love* you, Livy! My whole being is permeated, is renewed, is leavened with this love, & with every breath I draw its noble influence makes of me a better man. And I shall yet be *worthy* of your priceless love, Livy. It is the glad task of my life —it is the purest ambition & the most exalted, that ever I have known, & I shall never, never swerve from the path it has marked out for me, while the goal & *you* are before me. Livy, I could not tell your honored father & mother how deeply I felt for them, & how heartless it seemed in me to come, under cover of their trusting, generous hospitality, & try to steal away the sun out of their domestic firmament & rob their fireside heaven of its angel. I could not tell them in what large degree (& yet how feebly in comparison with the reality) I appreciated & do still appreciate the tremendous boon I was asking at their hands. I could not tell them how grateful I was, & how I loved them for pausing to listen to my appeals when they could have upbraided me for my treachery & turned me out of doors in deserved disgrace. I call these things by their right names, Livy, because I *know* I ought to have spoken to them long before I spoke to you—& yet there was nothing criminal in my *intent*, Livy—nothing wilfully & deliberately underhanded & dishonorable—I could say it in the high court of Heaven. *You* know I would scorn to do a shameful act, my darling—you know it & will maintain it—for never yet had any friend a stauncher, braver defender than *you*—you—you Perfection! Ah, how "deluded" I am, & how I do love to be so "deluded"! I could not tell them those things, Livy, but if it shall seem necessary, I know that *you* can. And moreover you can always say, with every confidence, that I have been through the world's "mill"—I have traversed its ramifications from end to end —I have searched it, & probed it, & put it under the microscope & I *know* it, through & through, & from back to back—its follies, its frauds & its vanities—all by personal *experience* & not through dainty *theories* culled from nice moral books in luxurious parlors where temptation never comes & it is easy to be good & keep the heart warm & one's [generous] best impulses fresh & strong & uncontaminated—& now I know *how* to be a better man, & the *value* of so being, & when I say that I *shall* be, it is just the same as if I *swore* it! *Now!*

Good-bye, Livy. You are so pure, so great, so good, so beautiful. *How* can I help loving you? Say, rather, how can I keep from *worshipping* you, you dear little paragon? *If* I could only see you! I do *wish* I could. Write me im-*mediately*. Don't wait a minute. You are never out of my waking thoughts for a single fraction of a second, & I do so want to hear from you. Ah, well, I suppose I shall lecture to those Rondout[3] pirates about *you*, & yet, poor con- fiding creatures, they think I am going to talk about the Vandal. But such is life. And mind you just keep on writing until you begin to feel tired—but not a moment afterward, my peerless Livy, for I love you too dearly to wish to have you [tire yourself] do irksome things, even to gratify me.

Tell me the name of that book you were going to lend me, Livy, so that I can get it. I shall send *those* books by Ed,[4] if I can find him.

I saw an old friend of mine at breakfast awhile ago (ex-Gov. Fuller) & he gave me a lot of notices of my New York lecture delivered 18 months ago. I inflict them on you—for why *shouldn't* I? The house was crowded, on that occasion, but it was not my popularity that crowded it. The exertions of my friends did *that*.

[3] A Hudson valley town, place of his next engagement.
[4] Probably Ed Bement, an Elmira neighbor of the Langdons.

They got up the whole thing—suggested it, engineered it, & carried it through successfully. If any man has a right to be proud of his friends, it is I, thy servant. The *Tribune* notice is by Ned House, who ranks as the most eminent dramatic critic in the Union.

Good-bye, Livy. All this time I have felt just as if you were here with me, almost—& part of the time as if I could *see* you standing by me. But you are vanished! I miss a gracious presence—a glory is gone from about me. I listen for a dear voice, I look for a darling face, I caress the empty air! God bless you, my idol. Good-bye—& I send a thousand kisses—pray send *me* some.

Most lovingly, Yours
Forever—SAMUEL

P. S. I do LOVE you, Livy!

P. P. S.—I enclose a [melain(otype)] ferrotype—don't you see how soft, rich, expressive, the lights & shades are, & how *human* the whole picture is? If you can't get me the porcelain picture, Livy, do please have a ferrotype taken for me. This pretty little sixteen-year-old school-girl is Gov. Fuller's daughter—Fuller gave it to me this morning. I never saw the young lady but once—at a party in Brooklyn a short time ago—& then I petrified her by proposing with frozen gravity (just after introduction) to kiss her *because I was acquainted with her father. He* enjoyed the joke immensely (because he had known me so long & intimately,) but *she* didn't.

P.P.P.S.—I do love, *love*, LOVE you, Livy, darling. Write immediately—*do*.

If any of the family inquire of me, remember me kindly to them —& please convey to Mr. & Mrs. Langdon my love & respectful duty. They know *that* is sincere enough, no matter what may befal you & I. I *love* you, Livy!

Livy, shan't you come to New York this winter?

I love, love, *love* you, Livy!

PPPPP.S. I *do* love you, Livy!

To his widowed sister in St. Louis, Pamela Clemens Moffett, Sam wrote about this time to break the news. His remark that Livy's parents "are not *very* much concerned about my past" is not wholly borne out by an earnest letter that Mrs. Jervis Langdon was writing on December 1 to Mrs. Fairbanks, almost the only friend that Clemens and the Langdons had in common: "I cannot, and need not, detail to you the utter surprise and almost astonishment with which Mr. Langdon and myself listened to Mr. Clemens' declaration to us, of his love for our precious child, and how at first our parental hearts said no, to the bare thought of such a stranger mining in our hearts for the possession of one of the few jewels we have. . . . The question, the answer to which, would settle a most wearing anxiety, is—from what habitual life, did this change, or improvement, or reformation, commence? Does this change, so desirably commenced, make of an immoral man a moral one, as the World looks at men?"

Sam's letter to his sister is imperfect, with the top of page one missing, and with it, the date and beginning, but page three bears the New York business letterhead of Dan Slote.

[NEW YORK, *circa December* 1, 1868]

. . . [Rondout &] Newark [& one or two] other places, I go West to deliver 21 lectures at $100 a piece—beginning at Detroit, Michigan Dec. 23, & ending at some Wisconsin town, Jan. 18— after which I have promised to preach in New York City for the Fireman's Fund. I would send Ma some money but Dan has gone home (he is my banker).

Now—*Private*—Keep it to yourself, my sister—do not even *hint* it, to *any* one—I make no exceptions. I can trust you. I love —I *worship*—Olivia L. Langdon, of Elmira—& she loves me. When I am permanently *settled*—& when I am a Christian—& when I have *demonstrated* that I have a good, steady, reliable character, her parents will withdraw their objections, & she *may* marry me—*I* say she *will*—I intend she *shall*—the earth will cease to turn round & the sun to traverse his accustomed courses when I give it up. Cool, deliberate, critical Mrs. Fairbanks says her peer does not exist upon earth—& cool, deliberate, critical Mrs. Brooks of New York, says the same, & I endorse it with all my heart. Both have informed me frankly that neither I nor any other man is worthy of her & that I can never get her. What will they say *now*, I wonder? Her parents have refused to permit the attentions of *any body*, before, but I was mean enough to steal a march on them. They are not *very* much concerned about my past, but they simply demand that I shall prove my *future* before I take the sunshine out of their house. I have made that household spend several sleepless nights lately. But they all like me, & they can't help it. *Now* you know why I was so savage & crazy in St Louis. I had just been *refused* by my idol a few days before—was refused again afterward—was warned to *quit* after that—& have won the fight at last & am the happiest man alive. If I were in St Louis *now* you would see me in my *natural* character, & love me. I drink no spirituous liquors any more—I do nothing that is not thoroughly *right*—I am *rising*. I think Mrs. Fairbanks (who loves me like a son) will go beside herself for joy when she hears of my good fortune. For in her eyes & mine, Livy Langdon is *perfection* itself. Mind—*no word of this to any body*. The above is my address for ten days.

Affectionat[el]y

SAM

In a mingled vein of jest, sentiment, and concern over the already emergent problem of supporting the bride in her accustomed style, Clemens addressed his future father-in-law.

A.M.

EVERETT HOUSE, N. YORK, *Dec.* 2 [1868]

DEAR MR. LANGDON—I wish I hadn't come away, now. I might just as well have spent two or three days persuading Mrs. Langdon to let me stay longer. I don't know what I could have been thinking about, that I hadn't sagacity enough to think of that. However, during the last day or two I suppose my head was so full of lecturing, & writing for newspapers, & other matters of a [strictly] business nature, that I couldn't think of *anything* I *ought* to have thought of. You may have noticed that I was a good deal absorbed —in business. You may have noticed that I hadn't much time to be around with family.—Well, it was because I had to get off in the drawing-room by myself, so I could think about those lectures & things. I can always think better when I get off in a drawing-room by myself. So you see that was how it was. I thought I ought to make this explanation, because, latterly, you know, I was not

as sociable as I might have been. I meant to be very sociable with
all the family. And I *did* make as fair a start for it as I could—
But I never got very far—I never finished the list.

But notwithstanding all this pretended cheerfulness, I am not
boisterously cheerful. I know from what Miss Langdon said the
night I left, that she would have answered my letter yesterday if
she had been well. There is nothing tranquilizing about that
reflection. I—— ——however, I will not try to wet-blanket *your*
spirits. You will need all your hopefulness & all your cheer when
Mrs. Crane[5] goes from you—when every heart in your household
shall yield up a sunbeam & take to itself a shadow. Even the dumb
brutes will know that a friend is gone from among them. And the
flowers will, I am sure—& if they exhale a sweeter incense that
day, you may know it for a prayer they are sending up for their
lost mistress. Everything & everybody will miss her, from Mrs.
Ford[6] down to the captive birds in the cages—& missing her will
grieve that she is gone. Without knowing Mrs. Crane very well
—certainly not as well as I wish to—I know how you all regard
her & how keenly her going forth from your midst is going to
be felt.

But I am not cheering you up as much as I meant to when I
sat down. Dan & I had conspired to get Jack[7] over to my Newark
lecture [ten] 7 days hence, & I was to tell the "Moses Who?" story
in most elaborate detail & enlarge on Jack's peculiarities un-
stintedly—but I fear the scheme must fail, because Dan cannot
get any tickets. They have used the plan of reserving seats at an
extra price, & that has persuaded the people that I am a prodigy
of some kind—a gorilla maybe—& so the seats are all sold. (The
truth is, it is not my popularity that has caused this, I think, but
the fact that I am to lecture for an energetic, well-organized Association.) Dan says that he wishes he was out of the blank-book
business, because he believes it is more respectable to be a fraud
& go around deluding the ignorant, like me! But Dan's an old

[5] Susan Langdon, Mrs. Theodore Crane, Livy's sister by adoption. Chronic throat
trouble sent her south in winter.
[6] Eunice Ford, mother of Jervis Langdon, who lived in this household. Thrice
married, she died in 1873 in her 91st year.
[7] Jack Van Nostrand, youthful fellow-traveler of the Innocents, whose alleged
ignorance about Moses furnished Clemens with an anecdote told often from the
lecture platform and set down in *Roughing It*, I, vi.

fool—I mentioned it to him. I am invited back to Pittsburgh to repeat—& by people of standing, too—& by the same lecture committee, also—& that shows that when I delude people they don't *know* it—& consequently it is no sin.

John Russell Young (the Managing Editor) tells me that the price of *Tribune* shares is $7,000 each, & none in market just now. There are 100 shares, altogether, & a share yields $1,000 a year—sometimes as high as $2,000. He wants me to buy—told him I would take as many shares as I could mortgage my book for, and as many more as I could pay for with labor of hand & brain. I shan't make up my mind in indecent haste (because I haven't heard from Cleveland & am waiting) [but if I do make it up in that direction I will own in that high-toned stuck-up institution yet. But in . . .] but if I *do* buy, I shall retain Horace Greeley on the paper.

Chase of the Herald says Frank Leslie wishes to see me—thinks he wants me to edit a new paper he designs issuing, but don't know. *I* can't make pictures. However, I will go & see him.

If you hear that I didn't get away in the 11:30 train this morning, & didn't lecture in Rondout to-night, you will know that the reason was because I was writing to you, & so you will be responsible for the damage done to my pocket—but you can come back on the Rondouters, you know, for the damage you have saved *them*.

If you please, I wish you would say to Mrs. Langdon that I wish to go back to Elmira—for a little while—*only* a little while—only just long enough to say to Miss Langdon a few things which I hadn't quite finished telling her—it will only take a couple of weeks, or a couple of months, or such a matter? Will she let me? —But really, I suppose I *could* get along with just one evening— or just one *hour*—if I couldn't do any better. Now be *good*—you are the splendidest man in the *world*!—be generous, now—be merciful—*do* ask her, please? I'll call you all the nice names I can think of if you will enter into this little conspir——

Time's up—good-bye—love to all—Yrs ever

SAM'L L. CLEMENS

Please don't let Miss L. hear the first part of this letter—she won't like to be w. . . .

On December 4 her suitor wrote Livy two letters. The first has been published in part in Clara Clemens' *My Father Mark Twain*, p. 13; the second, "a mangled letter" written in "a mangled mood," as he later alluded to it, is exceedingly long, despite proof that he cut out all or parts of five pages before sending it to her. Some of it mirrors the badinage of love, such as his accusation that she has four "faults": "They are—1. The using of slang (but you didn't know it was slang, my little angel by brevet, else you wouldn't have used it); 2. The leaving off of blue ribbons at times (which is unconstitutional & unsustained by law); 3. The appearing five minutes late at breakfast, every morning when I have been watching the door for ages & ages to see you enter, radiant & beautiful, & fill all the dull air with sunshine; 4. But your most heinous fault is in loving *me*—& I pray that it may grow, & grow, & grow, till it shall usurp all your being & leave you nothing but one stately, magnificent, concentrated, sublimated, overwhelming Fault, for all Time!" And with a touch of that feudalism so dear to one who had been Tom Sawyer as a boy and hereafter would write *The Prince and The Pauper* and *Joan*, he pledged himself "leal & true subject of thine, O loved & honored liege!"

A tincture of sentimentalism, the fret and fever of awakening love, makes this garrulous letter not a little boring in its entirety. Also characteristic is the emotional spectrum it traverses, from rose to indigo. It begins with boyish jubilance, but slides at last into a mood of introspection and despair, a "hatred of myself for my clinging wickedness—& contempt for myself for putting such easy faith in these aspirations after better things." In thought, word, or deed he has lately done nothing unworthy of Livy, and yet "forth I drift again into the moonless night of despondency." And he quotes, then cancels lest it make Livy "unhappy," a scrap of sentimental poetry:

> My Mother, would I might
> But be your little child tonight
> And feel your arms about me fold
> Against this loneliness & cold.

More happily he quotes from Twichell's reply to Mark's confidential news of the betrothal:

Receive my benediction, Mark—my very choicest! I breathe it
toward you—that particular doxologic & hallelujah formula
thereof which I use on occasions which but for the sake of propriety I should celebrate by a smiting of my thigh, a grand *pas
seul* & three cheers with a tiger!—a style of Te Deum which somehow I never *could* manage to execute successfully in the pulpit.
Bless you, my son!—yea, Bless you, my children both!!

A few days later on lecture tour Mark reported further to his
new found but trusted friend. The reference in this letter to a
cousin is probably to Andrew Atwater. Later, in the spring, Mark
wrote to Livy alluding to some "trial" which had tested her love:
"Do you mean your cousin Andrew Atwater? *Whoever* it is, I wish
to hold him in grateful remembrance if he did that which made
it possible for you & me to become all in all to each other."

NORWICH, N.Y., *Dec.* 12 [1868]

DEAR TWICHELL—Hip-hip-Hurrah! She just goes on "accepting the situation" in the most [natural] innocent, easy-going way
in the world. She writes as if the whole thing were perfectly understood, & would no doubt be unpleasantly astonished [to find] if she
only knew I had been regarding it differently & had been ass
enough to worry about a cousin whom she merely gives the passing mention accorded to the humblest guests. *She* don't know
anything about beating the devil around the bush—she has never
been used to it. She simply calls things by their right names & goes
straight at the appalling subject of matrimony with the most
amazing effrontery. I am in honor bound to regard her grave,
philosophical dissertations as *love letters*, because they probe the
very marrow of that passion, but there isn't a bit of romance in
them, no poetical repining, no endearments, no adjectives, no
flowers of speech, no nonsense, no bosh. Nothing but solid chunks
of wisdom, my boy—love letters gotten up on the square, flat-
footed, cast-iron, inexorable plan of the most approved commercial correspondence, & signed with stately & exasperating decorum.
"Lovingly, *Livy L. Langdon*"—*in full*, by the Ghost of Caesar!
They are more precious to me than whole reams of affectionate
superlatives would be, coming from any other woman, but they

are the darlingest funniest *love* letters that ever were written, I do suppose. She gets her stateliness of [English] epistolary composition from her native dignity, & she gets that from her mother, who was born for a countess.

Hip-hip-Hurrah! I have badgered them & persecuted them until they have yielded, & I am to stop there for one day & night on Dec. 17!

I am full of gratitude to God this day, & my prayers will be sincere. Now write me a letter which I can read to her, & let it reach Elmira a day or so before I get there—enclose it in an envelope directed to *"Chas. J. Langdon, Elmira, N.Y."* Good-bye. My love to you *all*.

Yrs always
MARK

P.S. She knows you & Mrs. T. know all about it.—She likes that.

Letters to Livy during the weeks that followed, written regularly every other day and sometimes daily—usually late at night in his hotel room, after a lecture in towns of upstate New York, Michigan, Ohio, Indiana, and Illinois—are filled with tender love-making, gentle banter, biblical texts, and comments on reading. He admires Coventry Patmore's *The Angel in the House*, finds Elizabeth Barrett Browning's *Aurora Leigh* a trifle obscure and turns to Livy for explanations, praises the "Recording Angel" passage in Sterne's *Tristram Shandy* but asserts that as a whole "the book is coarse, & I would not have you soil your pure mind with it."

CHAPTER TWO

The Langdons Capitulate

JERVIS LANGDON'S wide and aggressive jaw, mutton-chop whiskers, and mouth with down-turned corners, "the quivering of one lip with passion while the other was firm and thin with will," as a friend described him, marked a man who could be equally formidable as foe or champion. With the not uncommon dualism of the competitive businessman in America, he proved himself a frank and fair associate, a stout friend, and a thoughtful, humorous, devoted father. His lawyer later said incredulously, "He would tell everything and conceal nothing—blurt the truth right out." Langdon once collected all the evidence he could find in a suit brought against him, and sent it along to the plaintiff, remarking that he wanted the case decided on merit.

The Langdons were no Victorian ogres like the Barretts of Wimpole Street, seeking to keep their daughter captive to prolong the dependence wrought by years of invalidism. But beyond question they had lapped her in a rather heavy mantle of petting and devotion. "To think of having them grow used to my being absent," wrote Livy to her lover in mid-December 1868, "so that at last they would cease to miss me, made me feel as if I wanted father to put his arms about me and keep me near him always. . . . He said last night that if he could live as long as I did, he would never let any man take me away from him; and he said that when I left home he was going to sell out—he is good at making threats." This last comment from Livy is no less reassuring than are passages in Mark's letters to Mrs. Fairbanks describing Jervis Langdon's friendly teasing of the newly engaged couple. But the Langdons could not help being startled by Mark's impetuous wooing. Nor were they wholly reconciled at first to seeing her spirited away by this raider from the wild West—who, with that unsparing directness about himself which was a lifelong trait, stood self-accused of having picked up some frontier vices, but pledged reform.

In early December, Jervis Langdon wrote his prospective son-in-law a letter that is no longer preserved, but seemingly in his usual blunt style he requested Mark to proceed more slowly with the courtship until Langdon had satisfied himself by consulting character witnesses from Mark's Western days. This letter did not overtake the itinerant lecturer for almost three weeks, when he was in Cleveland staying at the home of the Cleveland *Herald's* proprietor. But at last it came to hand and met a prompt and equally direct answer.

CLEVELAND, *Dec.* 29. [1868]

DEAR MR. LANGDON—I wrote to the Metropolitan Hotel for your letter (of Dec. 8) & it overtook me two or three days ago at Charlotte, Mich. I will not deny that the first paragraph hurt me a little—hurt me a good deal—for when you speak of what I said of the drawing-room, I see that you mistook the harmless overflow of a happy frame of mind for criminal frivolity. This is a little unjust—for although what I said may have been unbecoming, it surely was no worse. The subject of the drawing-room cannot be more serious to you than it is to me. But I accept the rebuke, freely & without offer of defence, & am as sorry I offended as if I had *intended* offense.

All the rest of your letter is just as it should be. The language is as plain as ever language was in the world, but I like it all the better for that. I don't like to mince matters myself or have them minced for me. I think I am safely past that tender age when one cannot take his food save that it be masticated for him beforehand —& I would much prefer to suffer from the clean incision of an honest lancet than from a sweetened poison. Therefore it is even as you say: I have "too much good sense" to blame you for that part of the letter. Plain speaking [only increases one's esteem & respect for the speaker] does not hurt one.

I am not hurrying my love—it is my love that is hurrying *me* —& surely no one is better able to comprehend that than you. I fancy that Mrs. Langdon was the counter part of her daughter at the age of twenty-three—& so I refer you to the past for explanation & for pardon of my conduct. At your time of life, & being, like you, the object of an assured regard, I shall be able to [talk] urge moderation upon younger people, & shall do it relentlessly —but now I feel a larger charity for such. Your heart is big enough to feel all the force of that remark—& so believing, you will not be surprised to find me thus boldly knocking at it. It does not seem to me that I am otherwise than moderate—it cannot seem so from my point of view—& so while I continue as moderate as I am now & have been, I think it is fair to hope that you will not turn away from me your countenance or deny me your friendly toleration, even though it be under a mild protest.

It is my desire as truly as yours, that sufficient time shall elapse to show you, beyond all possible question, what I *have been*, *what I am*, & what I am *likely to be*. Otherwise you could not be satisfied with me, nor I with myself. I think that much of my conduct on the Pacific Coast was not of a character to recommend me to the respectful regard of a high eastern civilization, but it was not considered blameworthy there, perhaps. We go according to our lights. I was just what Charlie would have been, similarly circumstanced, & deprived of home influences. I think all my references can say I never did anything mean, false or criminal. They can say that the same doors that were open to me seven years ago are open to me yet; that *all* the friends I made in seven years, are still my friends; that wherever I have been I can go again—& enter in the light of day & hold my head up; that I never deceived or defrauded anybody, & don't owe a cent. And they can say that I attended to my business with due diligence, & made my own living, & never asked anybody to help me do it, either. All the rest they can say about me will be *bad*. I can tell the whole story myself, without mincing it, & will if they refuse.

I wish to add to the references I gave Mrs. Langdon, the following: Hon. J. Neely Johnson, Carson City, Nevada. He was Governor of California some ten years ago, & is now Chief Justice of the Supreme Court of Nevada, if my memory serves me. He has known me about seven years—he & his wife—we were next door neighbors—& his house is always my home, now-a-days when I am in Carson, & has been for a year or two past. Then there is the

present Governor of Nevada, H. G. Blaisdel—he has known me
four or five years—don't know whether he has known any good
of me or not. He is a thoroughly pure & upright man, & a most
excellent. And I give you, also, Joseph T. Goodman (reared in
Elmira, I believe) proprietor & chief editor of the "Daily Enterprise," Virginia City, Nevada & C. A. V. Putnam, his News-editor
—the first of whom has known me six years (I was his City editor
3 years without losing a day) & the latter five years & neither of
whom would say a damaging word against me for love or money
or hesitate to throttle anybody else who ventured to do it—& so
you will perceive at once that they are not the [best people] most
promising sources to refer you to for information. Those two
fellows are just the salt of the earth, in my estimation. Now, however, being appealed to seriously, in so grave a matter as this, it is
very possible—even likely—that they would override their ancient
friendship for me, & speak the whole truth. I shall not write to
them—or to any of these references, of course—& so their testimony will be unbiased. Then there is A. J. Marsh, who is a
Phonographic Reporter, in San Francisco, my close friend for five
or six years—he & his wife & family are utterly without reproach,
& would be in *any* community. And Frank Gross & wife (of the
San Francisco "Bulletin")—& Sam Williams & Rev. Mr. Bartlett
of the same editorial staff. (—The two latter don't know me so
intimately as the other.) There is Lewis Leland (I think he is
proprietor of the Metropolitan Hotel in New York—& if he is
not now he soon is to be, if I understand the matter rightly). He
has known me intimately for 3 or 4 years—I boarded at his Occidental Hotel 2 or 3 years—& he will surely know my general
character & standing in San Francisco. And R. B. Swain & family,
San Francisco. Mr. Swain is Superintendent of the U. S. Mint, &
is also one of the "merchant princes" there. He is the Schuyler
Colfax of the Pacific Coast—being regarded by high & low, rich
& poor, Tom, Dick & Harry, as a man against whose pure reputation *nothing* can be said. He don't know much about me, *himself*
maybe, though we were pretty intimate latterly, but he ought to
know a good deal through his Secretary Frank B. Harte (editor
of the Overland Monthly & [one of] the finest writer[s] out there)

for *we* have been very intimate for several years.[1] This morning I received from Mr. Swain a letter which has been following me some time. I think a great deal of him else I wouldn't write to him. You have no antipathy to thoroughly good men, & so I beg that you will give his picture a place on the mantelpiece.

As to what I am *going to be*, henceforth, it is a thing which must be *proven* & established. I am upon the right path—I shall succeed, I hope. Men as lost as I, have found a Savior, & why not I? I have hope—an earnest hope—a long-lived hope.

I wrote you & Mrs. Langdon a letter from Lansing, which will offend again, I fear—& yet, no harm was meant, no undue levity, no disrespect, no lack of reverence. The intent was blameless—& it is the *intent*, & not the *act* that should be judged, after all. Even men who take life are judged by this rule only.

They say the desire is so general, here, to have this public distressed again by a repetition of my lecture, that Mr. Fairbanks offers me $150 to repeat it the third week in January, & Mrs. Fairbanks offers to let me repeat it for the benefit of the Orphan's Home at a dollar a head & pay me nothing for it. I have accepted the latter proposition. I have received a second invitation from the Association I lectured for in Pittsburgh to come there & talk again. They have gotten up some little feeling there because of an unjust & angry criticism upon the lecture (it appeared in the "Dispatch") & that I think maybe is the cause of these calls. I shall try to go, though really I am not disposed to quarrel with the Dispatch's opinion or make myself sad about it, either. I always like to express my opinions freely in print, & I suppose the Dispatch people have a taste that runs in a similar direction.

The folks here are all well, & we are having a very pleasant time of it. I shall lecture in Akron tomorrow night, & then return here & spend New Year's.

I like the Herald as an anchorage for me, better than any paper in the Union—its location, politics, present business & prospects, all are suitable. Fairbanks says the concern (with its lot & building) inventories $212,000; its earnings were $42,000 for the past year, which is a good percentage for such safe & lasting property as a newspaper. He owns half & the Benedicts the other half. He

---

[1] Better known as Bret Harte.

wants me in very much—wants me to buy an eighth from the Benedicts, so that the control would rest with him when I gave my vote so—price about $25,000. He says if I can get it he will be my security until I can pay it all by the labor of my tongue & hands, & that I shall not be hurried. That suits me, just exactly. It couldn't be better. He says the salaries of himself & the elder Benedict are $3,000—& mine would be $3,000. Yet he would *hire* me & pay me more. I don't understand these things—It is a slim salary—& so I should *have* to make the paper make money, to save myself. However, I shall see Mr. Benedict & try to make the arrangement.

I believe I have nothing further to say, except to ask pardon for past offenses against yourself, they having been heedless, & not deliberate; & that you will

(Mrs. Fairbanks has just come in & she says: "For shame! cut that letter short—do you want to wear out what endurance the poor man has left after his siege of illness?" This is a woman, Sir, whose commands are not to be trifled with—& so I desist.)

With reverent love & respect

I am
Sincerely
SAML. L. CLEMENS

As Mark remembered it many years later in dictating his *Autobiography*, he gave Mr. Langdon as character witnesses the names of "six prominent men, among them two clergymen," in the far West. Despite the evidence of the letter above, Mark thought he had hesitated to invoke his best friends like Joe Goodman, lest they lie for him out of loyalty. Goodman's name at least was absent from the earlier list with which Mrs. Langdon had been supplied. Clearly enough, in an access of fanatic honesty, he entrusted his reputation too largely to clerical and civic stuffed shirts, as the sequel showed—men who remembered his hard swearing and hard drinking, or had heard of those fabulous sessions with newspaper cronies in the midnight bars of Virginia City and San Francisco.

Now in some respects he was a new man. Even in a literary sense the influences of "refinement" were at work, at least temporarily, upon the Wild Humorist of the Pacific Slope. In Mark's letter to Livy on the last day of the year 1868 he besought: "Don't read a word in that Jumping Frog book, Livy—don't. I hate to hear that infamous volume mentioned. I would be glad to know that every copy of it was burned, & gone forever. I'll never write another like it." But interestingly enough a year later, under appreciation from his lecture audiences, his confidence in the yarn had revived notably. On December 14, 1869, he wrote Livy in a different vein: "The other night at Meriden I struck upon an entirely new *manner* of telling a favorite anecdote of mine,—& now, without altering a single word, it shortly becomes so absurd that I have to laugh, myself. Last night I got to one particular point in it 3 different times before I could get by it & go on. Every time I lifted my hand aloft & took up the thread of the narrative in the same old place the audience exploded again & so did I— But I got through at last, & it was very funny. This teaches me that a man might tell that Jumping Frog story fifty times without knowing *how* to tell it—but between you & I, privately Livy dear, it is the best humorous sketch America has produced, yet, & I must read it in public some day, in order that people may know what there is in it."

While spending New Year's, 1869, with the hospitable Fairbankses, Mark found time to dash off another note to Joe Twichell, informing him of the progress being made in this courtship by correspondence. His confidence in the Langdons' continued good will is also worthy of remark.

CLEVELAND, *New Year's* [1869]

DEAR J. H.—While they get the carriage ready (for I am with my dear old Quaker City adopted mother)—for we are going out to pay New Year's calls, I will snatch a moment to say I have just received yours. And along with it a handful of dainty letters from that wonderful miracle of humanity, little Miss Livy. She has a most engaging commercial reliability & promptness allied to her stately commercial style of correspondence. I can always depend on an 8-page letter, every day. Never any whining in it, or any nonsense, but wisdom till you can't rest. Never any foolishness— but whenever she *does* miss fire & drop *herself* into her epistle accidentally, it is perfectly gorgeous. She thinks about me all the time, & informs me of it with Miltonic ponderosity of diction.

She loves me, & conveys the fact with the awful dignity of an Ambassador construing an article of international law. But in her *sermons* she excels. They are full of a simple trust & confidence, & touched with a natural pathos that would win a savage. Ours is a funny correspondence, & a mighty satisfactory one, altogether. My letters are an ocean of love in a storm—hers an ocean of love in the majestic repose of a great calm. But the waters are the same —just the same, my boy.

And I have delightful Christmas letters, this morning, from her mother & father—full of love & trust—Lo! the world is very beautiful—very beautiful—& *there is a God*. I seem to be shaking off the drowsiness of centuries & looking about me half bewildered at the light just bursting above the horizon of an unfamiliar world.

The carriage waits! Good-bye—love to you both—God send you a happy New Year that shall continue happy until the year is old again—& forever more.

Yrs. always
MARK

Setting out once more on the Midwest lecture circuit, he sent frequent letters to Livy such as this one.

ROCKFORD [ILL.], *Midnight, Jan. 6./69*

MY DEAREST LIVY—I was just delighted with your letter received to-day. We forgot the extract, but I have just written to Mrs. Fairbanks, & she will send it to me to be prepared for publication.[2] —Your letter was so natural, Livy, & so like yourself—I do *wish* I could see you! I scold you as bitterly as I can for daring to sit up & write after midnight. *Now* you have it, at last. And I forgive you & bless you in the same moment! (Oh, you are so *present* to me at this moment, Livy, that it seems absurd to be *writing* to you when I almost seem to touch your forehead with my lips.) I thank you with all my heart for your warm New Year wishes— & you know that you have mine. I naturally thought of you all the day long, that day—as I do every day—& a dozen times I

[2] An excerpt from his Christmas letter to Mrs. Fairbanks, which she wished to publish in the *Cleveland Herald*.

recalled our New Year at Mr. Berry's. I remembered it perfectly well, & spoke of it to Mrs. Fairbanks—& the Moorish architecture, too. And I remembered perfectly well that I didn't rightly know where the charm was, that night, until you were gone. And I did have such a struggle, the first day I saw you at the St Nicholas, to keep from loving you with *all* my heart! But you seemed to my bewildered vision, a visiting *Spirit* from the upper air—a something to *worship*, reverently & at a distance—& *not* a creature of common human clay, to be profaned by the *love* of such as I. Maybe it was a little extravagant, Livy, but I am honestly setting down my thought, just as it flitted through my brain. *Now* you can understand why I offend so much with praises—for to me you are *still* so far above all created things that I cannot speak of you in tame commonplace language—I *must* reserve that for tame commonplace people. Don't scold me, Livy—let me pay my due homage to your worth; let me honor you above all women; let me love you with a love that knows no doubt, no question—for you are my *world*, my life, my pride, my all of earth that is worth the having. Develop your faults, if you have them—they have no terrors for me—nothing shall tear you out of my heart. Livy, if you only *knew* how much I love you! But I couldn't make you comprehend it, though I wrote a year. God keep you from suffering & sorrow always, my honored Livy!—& spare you to me till many & many a peaceful New Year shall wax and wane & crown & re-crown us with their blessings.

My heart warms to good old Charlie, whenever I think of him —& more than ever when he crosses my plane of vision, now, doing thoughtful kindnesses for *you*. He loves you, Livy, as very, very few brothers love their sisters. And you deserve it, you dear good girl, if ever sister did in the world.

"People" made you cross? I wonder what they did. Come to the deserted confessional, Livy—what was it?

Ah, I thought I was going to get a *dreadful* scolding!—I began to wish I had risen earlier, latterly—I was commencing to feel twinges of guilt tugging at my heart—but I turned the page & presto! you were a brave defender of the worn & weary instead! You were my champion, as it were, & not my censurer. And your mother took the same view of the case—& Mr Beecher also, in his miscellany.[3] I felt ever so much better. And I did love your generous indignation against that outrage, Livy! And well I might —for several times, lately, when I have gone to bed completely tired out, I have fallen asleep fancying that I would sleep *late*, & breakfast with *you* alone—a thing so pleasant to think about— & behold, here was tacit permission for some future day when I may come to you wearied out with these wanderings, & longing for rest. But a plague take that fellow, for an idiot!—to put off his marriage for so silly a thing—to put it off at *all*! even for a day, if she is ready & he has his home prepared.—What can compensate him for three long years of happiness spurned?—a "splurge?" Verily it *is* a funny world, even as you say. Make some more pictures of our own wedded happiness, Livy—with the bay window (which you shall have) & the grate in the living-room— (which you shall have, likewise,) & flowers, & pictures & books (which we will read together)—pictures of our future home—a home whose patron saint shall be Love—a home with a tranquil "home atmosphere" about it—such a home as "our hearts & our God shall approve." And Livy, *don't* say at the bottom of it, "How absurd, perhaps wrong, I am to write of these things which are so uncertain." Don't, Livy, it spoils everything—& sounds so chilly. Let us think these things, & believe them—it is no wrong—let us believe that God has destined us for each other, & be happy in the belief—it will be time enough to doubt it when His hand shall separate us, if it ever does—a calamity, I humbly & beseech-ingly pray He will spare us in His great mercy. Let us hope & believe that we shall walk hand in hand down the lengthening highway of life, one in heart, one in impulse & one in love & worship of Him—bearing each other's burdens, sharing each other's joys, soothing each other's griefs—&, so linked together— & so journeying, pass at last the shadowed boundaries of Time & stand redeemed & saved, beyond the threshold & within the light [that beams] of that Land whose Prince is the Lord of rest eternal. Picture it, Livy—cherish it, think of it. It is no wrong —we are privileged to do it by the blameless love we bear each

[3] Thomas K. Beecher, the Langdons' pastor in Elmira, for many years edited a weekly "Miscellany" in the local *Advertiser* and later *Gazette*.

other. God will bless you in it—will bless us both, I fervently believe.

When I get starved & find that I have a little wife that knows nothing about cooking, and—Oh, my prophetic soul! *you* know anything about cookery! I would as soon think of your knowing the science of sawing wood! We shall have some peculiarly awful dinners, I make no manner of doubt, but I guess *we* can eat them, & other people who don't like them need not favor us with their company. That is a fair & proper way to look at it, I think.

You are such a darling faithful little correspondent, Livy. I can depend on you all the time, & I do enjoy your letters so much. And every time I come to the last page & find a blank area on it I want to take you in my arms & kiss you & wheedle you into sitting down & filling it up—& right away my conscience pricks me for wanting to make you go to work again when you have already patiently & faithfully wrought more than I deserve, & until your hand is cramped & tired, no doubt, & your body weary of its one position.

I bless you for your religious counsel, Livy—& more & more every day, for with every passing day I understand it better & appreciate it more. I am "dark" yet—I see I am still depending on my own strength to lift myself up, & upon my own sense of what is right to guide me in the Way—but not always, Livy, not always. I see the Savior dimly at times, & at intervals, *very near* —would that the intervals were not so sad a length apart! Sometimes it is a *pleasure* to me to pray, night & morning, in cars & everywhere, twenty times a day—& then again the whole spirit of religion is motionless (not dead) within me from the rising clear to the setting of the sun. I can only say, Be of good heart, my Livy—I am slow to move, & I bear upon my head a deadly weight of sin—a weight such as you cannot comprehend—*thirty-three years* of ill-doing & wrongful speech—but I have hope— hope—*hope*. It will all be well. Dare I to say [it]—to say—& why not, since it is the truth? Only this: I *fear* I would distrust a religious faith that came upon me suddenly—that came upon me otherwise than deliberately, & *proven*, step by step as it came. You will blame me for this, Livy—but be lenient with me, for you know I grope blindly as yet.

I am all impatience to see the picture—& I do hope it will be a good one, this time. I want it to be *more* than a painted iron plate—I want it to be yourself, Livy—I want the eyes to tell me what is passing in the heart, & the hair & the vesture & the attitude to bring to me the vivid presentment of the grace that now is only vaguely glimpsed to me in dreams of you at night when I & the world sleep.

I shudder to think what time it may be! All the sounds are such *late* sounds! But though you were *here* to scold me, darling, I would *not* put this pen down till I had written I *love you, Livy!*

Good-bye—Lovingly now & forever & forever

SAML. L. C.

P. S. Can't stop to correct the letter, Livy.

Hattie Lewis Paff's narrative, "What I Know about Mark Twain," explains the background of the next letter—how, as a perennial visitor in the Langdon household, she submitted to the role of romantic decoy before the engagement of Mark and Livy was ripe for announcement:

"O. had felt sensitive all the time about the public knowing that she was the object of Mr. C's attentions and would be until she could come to a decision, therefore when guests came or when we were out together Mr. C. and I appeared to be devoted to each other, and unlikely as it may seem, we did succeed in deceiving people, much to the amusement of us all. A friend had written me from Chicago asking if the report was true that was in one of the daily papers—that Mr. C. & I were engaged. I read the letter to O. and said I believed I would write Mr. C. about the reports and the remarks that had been made because of his attentions to me, and how badly I felt that he had already written 20 letters to her and not one to me—that I was getting pale and emaciated etc. So we wrote the letter and received a reply . . ."

GALESBURG [ILL.], *Jan.* 10. [1869]

MISS HARRIET LEWIS—[No, that is too cold for a breaking heart—]

DEAR HATTIE—It cannot but be painful, I may even go so far as to say harrowing, to me, to say that which I am about to say. And yet the words must be spoken. I feel that it would be criminal to remain longer silent. And yet I come to the task with deep humiliation. I would avoid it if I could. Or if you were an unprotected female. But it must out. I grieve to say there has been a mistake. I did not know my own heart. After following you like your shadow for weeks—after sighing at you, driving out with you, looking unutterable things at you—after dreaming about you, night after night, & playing solitary cribbage with you day after day—after rejoicing in your coming & grieving at your going, since all sunshine seemed to go with you—after hungering for you to that degree that for two days I ate nothing at all but you—after longing for you & yearning for you, & taking little delight in any presence but yours—& after writing all those twenty double-postage letters to you, lo! at last I wake up & find it was not you after all! I never was so surprised at anything in all my life. You never will be able to believe that it *is Miss Langdon* instead of you—& yet upon my word & honor it is.—I am not joking with you, my late idol—I am serious. These words will break your heart—I feel they will—alas! I *know* they will—but if they don't damage your appetite, Mr. Langdon is the one to grieve, not *you*. A broken heart won't set you back any.

Try to bear up under this calamity. O [grieving] sad heart, there is a great community of generous souls in good Elmira, & you shall not sorrow all in vain. Trot out your "wasted form" & plead for sympathy. And if this fail, the dining-room is left. Wend thither, weeping mourner, & augment the butcher's bills as in the good old happy time. Bail out your tears & smile again. Don't pass any more sleepy days & nights on my account—it isn't complimentary to me. And you were *unusually* distraught & sleepy of late, I take it, for you dated your letter "December" 4, instead of January. I know what that indicates. If you will look through those twenty letters you will find that I was in a perfectly awful state of mind whenever I dated one of them as insanely as that.

It grieves me to the heart to be compelled to inflict pain, but there is no help for it, & so you will have to go to Mr. Langdon & explain to him frankly what I meant by such conduct as those—& confess to him, for me, that it was the other young lady instead

of you. And I wish you would tell *her*, also, for otherwise she
will never suspect it, all my conversations with her having been
strictly devoted to the weather. Come—move along lively, now!

But do you know, I can't account for Charley's reticence? He
used to write to me very faithfully. But really & truly he never
has answered one of those twenty letters.[4] Never. However, hard-
heartedness does not affect me. I am so forgiving. Many people
would feel hurt, & break off the correspondence—but I forgive
him—I forgive him, & shall go on writing to him every day just
the same. I shall move him after a while, no doubt. If these
letters have grown monotonous to Charley & have ceased to
interest him, I am grieved, & I am truly grieved—for I do not
know any other way to write "Miss Olivia L. Langdon—Present"
but just that way. If I *could* write it in any other way so as to
thrill him with enthusiasm, I certainly would.

Are you well, my poor Victim? How is your haggard face?
What do you take for it? Try "S. T.—1860—X" And have you
hollow eyes, too?—or is most of the holler in your mouth? I am
sorry for *you*, my wilted geranium.

And next you'll *fade*, I suppose—they all do, that get in your
fix—& then you'll pass out, along with Sweet Lily Dale, & Sweet
Belle Mahone, & the rest of the tribe—& there'll be some ghastly
old sea-sickening sentimental songs ground out about you & about
the place where you prefer to be planted, & all that sort of bosh.
Do be sensible & *don't*.

But deserted & broken-hearted mourner as you are, you are a
good girl; & you are with those who love you & would make your
life peaceful & happy though your heart were really torn & bleed-
ing, & freighted with griefs that were no counterfeit. You are
where you deserve to be—beyond the reach & lawful jurisdiction
of wasting sadnesses & heart aches, and where no trouble graver
than a passing, fancied ill, is like to come to you. And there I
hope to find you when I come again, you well-balanced, pleasant-

---

[4] The love letters were sent in an outer envelope addressed to Charles Langdon,
to allay local suspicion. The inner envelope—often inscribed with a facetious message like "Cart it home, Charley, please," or "Courtesy of His Holiness Bishop
Langdon,"—is often preserved with the letter itself. These friendly relations go far
to disprove the idea set forth by Paine and others that for some time Charles
looked with hostility upon the "rough" Missourian's courtship of his sister.

spirited, excellent girl, whom I love to hold in warm & honest friendship.

Sincerely,

SAML. L. CLEMENS

P. S.—This is No. 22. Don't be foolish, now, & silent, merely because I believe that the other young lady is without her peer in all the world, but write again, please. Tell me more of your wretchedness. I can make you *perfectly* miserable, & then you'll feel splendid. I am equal to a good many correspondences.

The trials of an itinerant lecturer invite Livy's sympathy in the next letter.

OTTAWA, ILL., *Jan.* 13 [1869]

MY DEAREST LIVY—Another botch of a lecture!—even worse than Elmira, I think. And it was such a pity—for we had a beautiful church *entirely full* of handsome, well-dressed, intellectual ladies & gentlemen. They say I *didn't* botch it, but I should think *I* ought to know. I closed with a fervent apology for my failure, just as I did in Elmira—& the apology was the only thing in the lecture that had any life or any feeling in it. It cuts me to the very quick to make a failure. I did feel so ashamed of myself. I even distressed the committee—I touched their hearts with my genuine suffering, & real good fellows as they are, they came up to my room to comfort me. The failure was chiefly owing to an idiot president, who insisted on introducing me while the people were still pouring in—& they kept on coming in till one-fourth of the lecture had been delivered to an audience who were exclusive engaged in watching the newcomers to their seats—it seemed that I *never* would get their attention. I grew so exasperated at last, that I shouted to the doorkeeper to close the doors & not open them again on *any* account. But my confidence was gone. The church was harder to speak in than an empty barrel would have been, I was angry, wearied to death with travel, & I just hobbled miserably through, apologized, bade the house good-night, & then gave the President a piece of my mind, without any butter or sugar on it. And now I have to pray for forgiveness for these things—

& unprepared, Livy, for the bitterness is not all out of my bad, foolish heart yet.

Took tea with Mr. Lewis—like him ever so much.—If you remember, he is like Twichell, you are acquainted with him as soon as you take him by the hand. It would take some time to get acquainted with his wife, though.

Lost my baggage somewhere, day before yesterday—heard of it to-day, but can't get it before I arrive in Toledo—am lecturing in my bob-tail coat & that makes me feel awkward & uncomfortable before an audience.

Livy, dear, I am instructed to appear & lecture in New York City Feb. 15. It is the most aggravating thing. I have to miss the re-union after all, I suppose, for no doubt I shall have to go on lecturing just the same, after that. But you must write me all that the happy re-unionists do & say, & I shall be with you all in spirit, at least, if not in the flesh.[5] And I shall keep a sharp look-out & see if I can't get a day or two to myself between Jan. 22 & Feb. 13, because I do so long to see you, Livy dear. So far there are only five applications in my agent's hands for lectures during that interval, I think. You were right not to send the picture if it slandered you like the other, but it does seem to me sometimes that *any* new picture of you would be a comfort to me—one that had seen your face lately. The old photograph is a dear old picture to me, & I love it; but still it isn't as beautiful as you are, Livy, & I want a picture that is. I am not so absurd as to love you simply for your beauty—I trust you know *that* well enough—but I *do* love your beauty, & am naturally proud of it & I don't want the picture to mar it.

Poor Lily Hitchcock! see how they talk about her in print— just as generous & warm-hearted a girl as you ever saw, Livy, & her mother is such a rare gem of a woman. The family are old, old friends of mine & I think ever so much of them. That girl, many & many & many a time, has waited till nearly noon to breakfast with me, when we all lived at the Occidental Hotel & I was on a morning paper & could not go to bed till 2 or 3 in the

[5] A reunion of *Quaker City* pilgrims had been proposed for February 18, with the Langdons as hosts, but did not take place. From a later letter it is clear that Livy assured him that such a gathering lacking Mark would be *Hamlet* without the Prince.

morning. She is a brilliant talker. They live half of every year in Paris—& the hearts that rascal has broken, on both sides of the water! It always seemed funny to me, that she & I could be friends, but we *were*—I suppose it was because under all her wild & repulsive foolery, that warm heart of hers *would* show. When I saw the family in Paris, Lily had just delivered the mitten to a wealthy Italian Count, at her mother's request (Mrs. H. said Lily loved him)—but ah me! it was only going from bad to worse to jilt *any*body to marry Howard Coit. *I* know him, a dissipated spendthrift, son of a deceased, wealthy eminent physician, a most worthy man. Howard "went through" the property in an incredibly short time. And this poor little numbscull Lily's last act was to mortgage her property for $20,000, gold, & give the money to that calf. He will squander it in six months if he has not mended greatly. (The above was told me in Chicago by a confidante of Lily's who was simply under promise to keep the matter from her parents.) Until that moment I said the whole affair must be untrue, because, as detestable as some of Lily's freaks were she could not be capable of deceiving her mother & father & marrying secretly. And to tell the plain truth I don't really believe it yet. She is an *awful* girl (the newspaper article is written by somebody who knows whom he is talking about), but she isn't *that* awful. She moves in the best society in San F. Does that horrify you, Livy? But remember, there never was so much as a whisper against her good name. I am so sorry for that girl, & so very, very sorry for her good kind mother. I hold both of them in [grateful remembrance because they said in their] happy remembrance always—for they were your brave, outspoken sort of friends, & just as loyal to you behind your back as before your face.

Well—I simply meant to enclose the slip, with a line of explanation—I think I rather overdid it.

Tell Miss Lewis that I think the answer is *"Considerable."* What is her notion? I have told her brother all *I* knew about her, & a mighty sight that I didn't know.—I always like to give good measure.

The passage from the "exquisite" struck me at the time as a vivid echo of my own sentiments—I *knew* it would be of yours, without your mentioning it, dear Livy. No, you wouldn't ask me to go to prayer meeting if you fancied I was tired, & I am sure I would always try to be as thoughtful of you, & as watchful for your happiness. I think our very chiefest pleasure would (*will*, Livy,) consist in planning & scheming each for the other's happiness. Livy, I cannot conceive of such a thing as my failing in deference to you, either now or when you are my wife (for I will not think of your being any one else's wife, Livy) or even conducting myself toward you in a manner unbecoming to your dignity. Why *did* you talk of not sending "this half sheet"? It delighted *me* more than I can tell.—I like all you say about marriage, for it shows that you appreciate the tremendous step it is, & are looking at it in all its parts, & *not* simply seek flaws in it.

After some little delay, I am back & ready to go on answering your letter—but alas! it is 1 A M, I am tired to death & *so* sleepy—

And so I press this loving kiss upon your lips, my darling Livy & waft you a fond Good-night.

SAML. L. C.

[CHICAGO] *Sunday Jan.* 16. 1869.

MY DEAREST LIVY—I am uncomfortably lame this morning. I slipped on the ice & fell, yesterday, in Iowa City, just as I was stepping into an omnibus. I landed with all my weight on my left hip, & so the joint is rather stiff & sore this morning.

I have just been doing that thing which is some times so hard to do—making an apology. Yesterday morning, at the hotel in Iowa City, the landlord called me at 9 o'clock, & it made me so mad I stormed at him with some little violence. I tried for an hour to go to sleep again & couldn't—I wanted that sleep particularly, because I wanted to write a certain thing that would require a clear head & choice language. Finally I thought a cup of coffee might help the matter, & was going to ring for it—no *bell*. I was mad again. When I *did* get the landlord up there at last, by slamming the door till I annoyed everybody on my floor, I showed temper again—*& he didn't*. See the advantage it gave him. His mild replies shamed me into silence, but I was still too obstinate, too proud, to ask his pardon. But last night, in the cars, the more I thought of it the more I repented & the more ashamed I was; & so resolved to make the repentance good by apologizing—which I have done, in the most ample & unmincing form, by letter, this morning. I feel satisfied & jolly, now.

"Sicisiors" don't spell *scissors*, you funny little orthographist. But *I* don't care how you spell, Livy darling—your words are always dear to me, no matter how they are spelt. And if I fancied you were taking pains, or putting yourself to trouble to spell them right, I shouldn't like it at all. If your spelling is never criticised till *I* criticise it, it will never be criticised at all. I do wish I could have been at the birthday dinner. All that, & the paragraphs about your conversations were just as pleasant as they could be—& yet you thought it was foolish to write them. I am glad enough that you didn't mark them out. It was a good, long, pleasant letter, & I thank you ever so much for it. I can easily see that Mr. Beecher was preaching upon a subject that was near his heart. *People can always talk well when they are talking what they feel.* This is the secret of eloquence—I wish you could hear my mother, sometimes. In the cars, the other day I bought a volume of remarkable sermons—they are from the pen & pulpit of Rev. Geo. Collyer, of Chicago. I like them very much. One or two of them will easily explain the Christian history of the sea-Captain's wife of whom you wrote me. These sermons lack the profundity, the microscopic insight into the secret springs & impulses of the human heart, & the searching analysis of text & subject which distinguish Henry Ward Beecher's wonderful sermons,[6] but they are more polished, more poetical, more elegant, more rhetorical, & more dainty & felicitous in wording than those. I will send you the book before long.

Now am I not going to get a letter at Norwalk, Ohio (Jan. 21) nor Cleveland (Jan. 22)? I do hope I wrote you of those appointments, but I am a little afraid I didn't.

Your Iowa City letter came near missing—it arrived in the same train with me.

It was just like Mr. Langdon in his most facetious mood, to say he would kill me if I wasn't good to you—& it was just like

[6] Livy was sending him regularly Beecher's sermon leaflets called *Plymouth Pulpit*.

you, you dear true girl, to say you'd never tell—for I believe you *would* go bravely on, suffering in secret from ill-treatment, till your great heart broke. But we shall circumvent Mr. Langdon, utterly—he never will have the satisfaction of killing me—because you & I will live together always in closest love & harmony, & I shall be *always* good to you, Livy dear—*always*. And whenever he needs a model married couple to copy after, he will only have to come & spend a few weeks at our home & we will educate him. He will see me honor you above all women, & he will also see us love each other to the utmost of human capability. So he can just put up his tomahawk & wash off his war-paint. He won't have to kill me—*will* he, Livy?

So I am to be three days without a letter. I don't like that much. It comes so natural to get a letter from you every two days that I shall feel odd without one this evening. I am so bound up in you, & you are in my thoughts so constantly by day & in my dreams by night, & you have become so completely a part of my life—of my very flesh & blood & bone, as it were—that I shall feel lost, to-day while this temporary interruption of communication lasts—I shall feel as if the currents of life have ceased to flow in some part of my frame, having been checked in some mysterious way. Oh, I do *love* you, Livy! You are so unspeakably dear to me, Livy.

I am to start for Sparta, Wisconsin, at 4 P.M., to-day. And I am to talk in Franklin, Pa., Feb. 14, & in Titusville, (Pa., I suppose) Feb. 15—the New York appointment is changed.

Give my loving duty to your father & mother, please, & tender my savage regards to Miss Lewis & Charlie. And I wish that you would remember me most kindly to Mr. & Mrs. Crane when you write. I like Mr. Crane—I never have seen anything whatever about him to dislike—& you know one can't help liking Mrs. Crane.

Have you got a good picture, yet, Livy?—because I want it so badly. Good-bye. Reverently & lovingly I kiss your forehead & your lips, my darling Livy, & wish you rest, & peace, & happy dreams.

For all time, devotedly,

SAML. L. C.

[The following on a separate sheet:]
Miss Olivia L. Langdon—Present.
Politeness of the Right Reverend Bishop Chas. J. Langdon.

Charlie, this makes about twenty-five letters I have directed to you—& you have been faithful in answering in the same way—that is, in directing letters to me written by other people—& a little more interesting than if you had written them yourself, my boy.

CLEVELAND, *Jan.* 19 [1869]

I reached here at daylight yesterday morning, Livy dear, pretty well tired out with railroading—& they called me at 8 o'clock, this morning. It was a great mistake. They ought to have let me sleep longer. I did not try to get to Sparta, because I found it could not be done. I found a Plymouth Pulpit here postmarked *Dec. 30*—a sermon on self-culture & self-denial—& read it through in bed last night. "*Man is a tease.*" You marked that for *me*, you little rascal—what do you mean by such conduct as those? But I like the sermon, notwithstanding it was below Mr. Beecher's average. You found little in it to mark, but what there was, was Truth, & came home to me.

I find the family well & happy. But I meet with one disappointment—Mr. Benedict[7] is sick & very low, & so I cannot talk business with him. All yesterday afternoon I played cribbage with Miss Allie[8]—everybody else was gone up town. I worried her considerably, in a good-natured way. Occasionally I would say, absently, "Well I wish I were in Elmira"—& she would retort very sharply.—"Indeed? well why don't you start?—*I'm* not keeping you." And sometimes I would observe, politely, "I wish you were Livy—then I would take more interest in this game—I *love* to play cribbage with Livy." We had a very pleasant time of it. She beat four games out of eleven. Charlie Stillwell is in Indiana—she says she writes to him every night, the last thing before she goes to bed; & he writes her every day. It is true—& if you had less to fatigue you, & more leisure, Livy darling, I would beg you to write me every day. Still, if you did, I am afraid you wouldn't write as long a letter as you do now,

---

[7] George Benedict, co-owner of the Cleveland *Herald.*
[8] Alice Fairbanks.

& so I am not sure I would be better off. I ought to be grateful enough—& am—that you write me every two days.

Although they called me so early this morning, and ruined my sleep, for good, they didn't get me up till 10 o'clock & after—& so Mr. & Mrs. F. were gone up town. Miss Allie set the table for me & kept me company—& I *did* wish it were your dear little self instead, but I didn't *say* it until I had got my second cup of coffee. She says the servant girls are never good-natured about late breakfasts, except for *me*—& that they say they are glad to hear I am coming, & glad to do anything for me at any time. Isn't that splendid? Because you know when good-will is shown me by servants, it is a patient, much-suffering sincere good-will, for I am necessarily a nuisance to them with my rascally irregular ways. But you will break up all my irregularities when we are married, & *civilize* me, & make of me a model husband & an ornament to society—won't you, you dear matchless little woman? And you'll be the dearest, best little wife in all the world, & we shall be happier than ever any condition of single life can experience. May the day come soon!—Amen.

I haven't been shaved for three days—& when Mrs. Fairbanks kissed me this morning, she said I looked like the moss-covered bucket. Livy dear, be sure & tell Charlie that his letter came this morning, & it shall all be just as he says—& I would write him a line & shake him by the hand if I had a moment of time to spare. But I haven't even the time to write *you* only these 3 or 4 pages (there goes the dinner-bell) & I'll hear from Mrs. F. in a minute. Must go up town right after dinner. We are going to write you all a family letter.

Good-bye—& take this loving kiss—& this—& this—my darling Livy—& God bless you.

SAML. L. C.

They are hurrying me—Fairbanks called upstairs to know what part of the chicken I wanted—told him to give me the port side, for'rard of the wheel.

The birth of Julia Twichell, first daughter and second child of his Hartford friend, on January 9, gave Mark the opportunity of sending both congratulations and a fresh bulletin on his own courtship.

CLEVELAND, Jan. 23, 1869

DEAR J. H. & TRIBE—Hurrah!—because you *do* rise to the dignity of a Tribe, now, since this last accident. I am *glad* to hear it—don't see why I should be glad, but I *am*—I should actually be appalled if *I* were to have a baby. But I know *you* are glad, & so I go it blind. That you are glad, is enough for me—count me in. I am *mighty* glad, Twichell. I am, indeed. It must be awful—I mean it must be splendid—but then the whole subject is a little confusing & bewildering to me, & I don't really know whether this ecstasy of mine is gratitude or consternation—because—well, *you* know how it is with us fellows who have never had any experience—we *mean* well, but then we are so dreadfully off-soundings in *these* waters. But I *am* glad, if I bust. And I'll stick to it & take the chances.

I'll scratch out a suggestive sentence or two & send your letter to Livy—maybe she can raise a hurrah & have sense enough to know what she means by it—She must learn to rejoice when we rejoice, whether she knows what she is rejoicing about or not, because we can't have any member of the family hanging fire & interrupting the grand salute merely because they *don't know*. By *George*, I'm mighty glad. I wish there'd been six or seven. Wouldn't we have had a time, though? You hear *me*.

Elmira? Why it just goes on like clock-work. Every other day, without fail, & sometimes *every* day, comes one of those darling 8-page commercial miracles; & I bless the girl, & bow my grateful head before the throne of God & let the unspoken thanks *flow* out that never human speech could fetter into words.

If you could only see her picture! It came last night. She sat six times for a ferrotype—taking 3 weeks to it—& every picture was a slander & I gently said so—very gently—& at last she tried a porcelain type—& [presto] when I opened the little velvet case last night, lo! a messenger-angel out of upper Heaven was roosting there! I give you my word of honor that it is a very marvel of beauty—the expression is sweet, & patient, & *so* far-away & dreamy. What respect, what reverent honor it compels! *Any* man's un-

conscious impulse would be to take his hat off in its presence.
And if he had not the impulse, I would give it him.

I have lectured about 30 times, so far, & from the way the
invitations keep coming in, I believe I could stay in the West.
I never miss a night during the entire season. But I *must* close
with the West Feb. 13 & go forward to fill eastern engagements.
I *repeated* here, last night & cleared for the Orphan Asylum
807.00, over & above everything. That is as far as heard from—it
may reach $1,000.

Shall be in Hartford about March—& then make a flying trip
to California. I swept Nasby's dung hill (Toledo) like a Besom of
Destruction—don't know what a Besom of Destruction is, but it
is a noble sort of expression. Came off with flying colors. Print
the notices for me.
Love to all four of you.

Yrs. always,

MARK

Now the Langdons began to get replies from Mark's character
witnesses in California—from some of the "friends" who felt
obliged to tell all, and more than the facts warranted. Some
months later, on August 25, 1869, Mark disclosed to his one-time
San Francisco comrade Charles Warren Stoddard: "Mr. Stebbins
[a clergyman of that city] . . . came within an ace of breaking off
my marriage by saying, 'Clemens is a humbug . . . a man who
has talent, no doubt, but will make a trivial use of it.' " Stebbins
seems also to have shared the opinion of an ex-Sunday-school
superintendent from Elmira now in the West, that Sam Clemens
"would fill a drunkard's grave."

That, by more worldly standards, the issue at stake was not
too grave, can be surmised from Mark's bold statement to Livy
on January 22, 1869: "I care nothing about the California letters
—being conscious that if they have said any permanent or important blemish rests upon either my private character or public
reputation they have simply stated that which is *false*—but the
thought of their causing you distress, will *not* let me rest—& I
have *no* peace. . . . I have sinned, in the dead past—& now my
punishment is come—but *you* should not suffer."

But while Mr. Langdon mulled gravely over these reports, Livy reasured her lover by writing him that her trust remained unshaken. This letter missed him at Sparta, Wisconsin, but overtook him a week later in Cleveland.

CLEVELAND, *Jan.* 24 [1869]

My Dearest Livy—It has come at last—the Sparta letter. And like [all] most hidden terrors, I find myself reassured as soon as it is uncurtained, and ready to cope with it. I sought eagerly for just one thing—if I could find that, I was safe. I did find it—*You still have faith in me*. That was enough—it is all I ask. While you stand by me, no task that is set me will be [too] so hard but that my heart & hands & brain will perform it—slowly, maybe, & discour- agingly to your *sometimes* impetuous nature, but *surely*. By your two later letters I saw that you had faith in me, & that you wrote them was evidence that you still love me—but what I yearned for at this particular moment was the evidence that your faith re- mained at its post when the storm swept over your heart. I believed I should find that evidence, for I did not think that your faith was the child of a passing fancy, a creature of the sunshine & destined to perish with it. The belief was well grounded, & I am satisfied. I have been, in times past, that which would be hateful in your eyes, provided you simply viewed me from a distance, without knowing my secret heart—but I have lived that life, & it is of the past. I do not live backwards. God does not ask of the returning sinner what he *has* been, but what he *is* & what he *will* be. And this is what you ask of me. If I must show what I am & prove what I *shall* be, I am content. As far as what I *have* been is concerned, I am only sorry that I did not tell all of that, in full & relentless detail, to your father & your mother, & to *you*, Livy— for it would be all the better that you knew it also. I would not seem to have been that which I was not. If I am speaking care- lessly or untruly now, I am doing a fearful thing, for before I began this letter I offered up that prayer which has passed my lips many & many a time during these latter months: that I might be guarded from ever unconsciously or unwittingly saying anything to you which you might misconstrue & be thereby *deceived*—& that I might not be guilty of any taint or shadow of *hypocrisy*, however refined, in my dealings with you—that I might be *wholly* true & frank & open with you, even though it cost me your priceless love, & the life that is now so inestimably valuable to me become in that moment a blank & hated captivity. Wherefore I now speak to you standing in the presence of God. And I say that what I have been I am not now; that I am striving & shall strive to reach the highest altitude of worth, the highest Christian excellence; that I know of *nothing* in my past career that I would conceal from your parents, howsoever I might blush to speak the words; & that it is my *strong conviction* that, married to you, I would never desire to roam again while I lived. The circumstances under which I say these things, make the statements as grave & weighty as if I endorsed them with an oath.

Your father & mother are overlooking one thing, Livy—that I have been a wanderer from necessity [four-fif], three-fourths of my time—a wanderer from choice only one-fourth. During these later years my profession (of correspondent) made wandering a necessity—& *all* men know that few things that are done from necessity have much fascination about them. Wandering is not a *habit* with me—for that word implies an enslaved fondness for the thing. And I could most freely take an oath that all fondness for roaming is dead within me. I could take that oath with an undisturbed conscience before any magistrate in the land. Why, a year ago, in Washington, when Mr. Conness, one of our Senators, [urged] counseled me to take the post of United States Minister to China, when Mr. Burlingame resigned (the place was chiefly in Mr. C.'s gift) I said that even if I could feel thoroughly fitted for the place, I had at last become able to make a living at home & wished to settle down—& that if I roamed more, it must be in pursuit of my regular calling & to further my advancement in my legitimate [calling] profession. And then I went at 11 at night & pledged our delegations to support me for Postmaster of San Francisco, but gave up *that s*cheme as soon as I found that the place, honorably conducted, was only worth $4,000 a year & was too confining to allow me much time to write for newspapers. (My office-seeking instincts were born & murdered all in one night, & I hope they will never be resurrected again—a winter spent in Washington is calculated to make a man *above* mere ordinary office-holding.)

Wandering is *not* my habit, nor my proclivity. Does a man, five years galley-slave, get in a habit of it & yearn to be a galley-slave always? Does a horse in a tread-mill get infatuated with his profession & long to continue in it? Does the sewing-girl, building shirts at sixpence apiece grow fascinated with the habit of it at last & find it impossible to break herself without signing the pledge? And being pushed from pillar to post & compelled so long to roam, against my will, is it reasonable to think that I am really fond of it & wedded to it? I think not.

I am very tired & drowsy, & *must* lie down. If I could only *see* you, love, I could satisfy you—satisfy you that I am earnest in my determination to be *everything* you would have me be—& that I bring to this resolve the consciousness of that faith & strength & steady purpose which has enabled me to cast off as many slavish habits & utterly lose all taste or desire for them—some of them dating back ten years now. Once a Christian, & invested with *that* strength, what should I fear? I pray you be patient with me a little while, till I see you—& hold fast your faith in me & let your dear love still be mine. The Sparta letter was a blessing to me, not a trouble.

With a loving kiss, dear Livy.

Always,

SAML

Mark's fleeting interest in his Washington newspaper days, in the post of American minister to China, as mentioned in the above letter, is unknown to any of his biographers. More familiar is his brief dalliance, also recalled here, with the postmastership of San Francisco. In a letter still unpublished to Elisha Bliss, Mark wrote on February 4, 1868: "One of our Senators suggested that I apply for the San Francisco postmastership, because in case I got it I could perform its duties by Deputy, & then in receipt of a large salary & perquisites, I could give myself up exclusively to scribbling. So I went to work & have eternally ruined the chances of the most prominent of a swarm of candidates." But in a post-script two days later he added: "I have thrown away that office, when I had it in my grasp, because it was plain enough that I could not be postmaster & write the book [*The Innocents Abroad*], too. . . . But it was worth from ten to twelve thousand a year." That he escaped such inducements is undoubtedly the gain of American literature.

The more urgent issue, in January 1869, concerned Samuel Clemens' moral worth as suitor for Livy Langdon's hand. The Langdons, moving in circles of small-town Protestant temperance —Thomas Beecher's parishioners having all covenanted solemnly to that end—and doubtless prone to conjure up visions of frontier debauchery, at first were puzzled and worried. But Livy's loyalty to her fiancé and Jervis Langdon's horse sense carried the day. Intuitively they knew this young man was no profligate at heart, and some of his letters filled with scriptural texts ("I have read VI Corinthians, Livy, & shall read more in the Bible before I go to bed," is a typical remark) now suggested an aspiration calculated to reassure even the most conventional.

At length, when Mark returned to Elmira, according to his recollection, Jervis Langdon showed him the evidence against him, inquired sadly if he had no friends, and then burst forth, "I'll be your friend, myself. Take the girl. I know you better than they do."

At all events, the day after Sam Clemens reached Elmira for a week's holiday from the rigors of lecturing, on February 4, the Langdons gave their assent to a formal engagement, which was announced soon afterward. The air was swept clean of misgiving and suspicion. Thereafter Mark and Livy planned for the future under smiles of generous trust and affection from the Langdons.

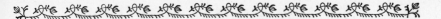

CHAPTER THREE

The Engaged Couple

JUST a year earlier, in February 1868, Mark had written a facetious piece about the marriage of a "homely old friend of mine" from the Pacific slope, a "wrinkled, aged, knock-kneed, ring-boned, and spavined old war-horse of the Plains" to "a handsome young Ohio widow worth $300,000." This coup led Mark to reflect: "I have always considered that I ought to fairly expect to marry about $17,000, but I think differently now. If McCorkle ranges at $300,000 in the market, I will raise my margin to about a million and a half." Now, finding himself engaged to a rich man's daughter—whose share in the fortune, though not astronomical, amounted at least to a quarter-million dollars—Mark felt a certain new diffidence upon the subject. To Livy herself he played down their domestic expectations to the level of his own unaided earning power, just as he entertained amusingly dismal notions of Livy's cookery. After talking with the Fairbankses about buying on credit into their *Herald*, he had written, December 30, 1868: "I think we'll live in Cleveland, Livy—& then we'll persuade Mr. Langdon to come & live in Euclid Avenue, so that we can have a place to go & get a *good* dinner occasionally when we have got so hungry we can't stand it any longer. But I don't think *we'll* live in the Avenue yet a while, Livy—we'll take a back seat with Mrs. Fairbanks, in St. Clair Street.—But then, what of it?—it will be a *pleasant* back seat, *won't* it? It couldn't well be otherwise, with you there." The first letters which follow bear witness rather bluntly to this spirit of pride, a self-reliance which he wanted to make clear to himself and others, including his own family and Livy's, lest the motive of marrying money be imputed.

He wrote first to St. Louis, where now lived his mother, his brother Orion, his sister Pamela Moffett and sister-in-law Mollie Clemens (Orion's wife), his young nephew Sam Moffett and niece Annie Moffett. All are addressed in the salutation of the next letter, along with their servant Margaret, who for years had been accepted as one of the family.

ELMIRA, N.Y., *Feb.* 5, 1869

MY DEAR MOTHER & BROTHER
   & SISTERS & NEPHEW
   & NIECE, & MARGARET:

This is to inform you that on yesterday, the 4th of February, I was duly & solemnly & irrevocably engaged to be married to Miss Olivia Langdon, aged 23½, only daughter of Jervis and Olivia Langdon, of Elmira, New York. *Amen.* She is the best girl in all the world, & the most sensible, & I am just as proud of her as I can be.

It may be a good while before we are married, for I am not rich enough to give her a comfortable home right away, & I don't want *anybody's* help. I can get an eighth of the Cleveland Herald for $25,000, & have it so arranged that I can pay for it as I earn the money with my unaided hands. I shall look around a little more, & if I can do no better elsewhere, I shall take it.

I am not worrying about whether you will love my future wife or not—if you know her twenty-four hours & then don't love her, you will accomplish what nobody else has ever succeeded in doing since she was born. She just naturally drops into everybody's affections that comes across her. My prophecy was correct. She said she never could or would love me—but she set herself the task of making a Christian of me. I said she would succeed, but that in the meantime she would unwittingly dig a matrimonial pit & end by tumbling into it—& lo! the prophecy is fulfilled. She was in New York a day or two ago, & George Wiley & his wife & Clara know her now. Pump *them,* if you want to. You shall see her before *very* long. Love to all.

Affec'ly

SAM

P. S. Shall be here a week.

Resuming his travels on February 12, Clemens wrote back to Elmira from his first lecture stand, to reassure Livy's mother about his soundness in respect both to conduct and financial prospects. A certain mistrust he may have detected lingering in her mind, after it had been banished from that of her forthright husband.

[RAVENNA, OHIO] Feb. 13, [186]9

DEAR MRS. LANGDON—It is not altogether an easy thing for me to write bravely to you, in view of the fact that I am going to bring upon you such a calamity as the taking away from you your daughter, the nearest & dearest of all your household gods. —You might well ask, "Who are you that presumes to do this?" And it would be a hard question to answer. I could refer you to fifty friends, but they could only tell you (& very vaguely, too) what I *have* been—just as a forester might talk learnedly of a bush he had once known well, unwitting that it had stretched its branches upward & become a tree, since *he* saw it. It is a bold figure but not altogether an unapt one. For those friends of mine, who certainly knew little enough of me in the years that are gone, know nothing of me *now*. For instance, they knew me as a profane swearer; as a man of convivial ways & not averse to social drinking; as a man without religion; in a word, as a "wild" young man—though never as a dishonorable one, in the trite acceptation of that term. But now I never swear; I never taste wine or spirits upon *any* occasion whatsoever; I am orderly, & my conduct is above reproach in a worldly sense; & finally, I now claim that I am a Christian. I claim it, & it only remains to be seen if my bearing shall show that I am justly entitled to so name myself.

I beg, with justice, that you will make due allowance for the fact that I am in some sense a *public* man, in considering my character. You are aware that public men get ample credit for all the sins they commit, & for a multitude of other sins they never were guilty of. A private citizen escapes public scrutiny, & fares all the better for it—but my private character is hacked [scorched] & dissected, & mixed up with my public one, & both suffer the more in consequence. Every man in California could tell you something about me, but not five men in the whole community have really any right to speak *authoritatively* of my *private* character, for I have not *close* friendships with more than that number there, perhaps. I can state as an absolute *truth*, that only one person in all the world really *knows* me, & that is Miss Langdon. To her I must refer you. My own mother & sister do not know me half so well as she does. I never have been in entire sympathy with any one but her (except with a brother, now dead) —I never have given thorough & perfect trust & confidence to any one in these latter years but her, & so there has always been a secret chamber or so in my being which no friend has entered before. But I have no secrets from her—no locked closets, no hidden places, no disguised phases of character or disposition. And so, only she really knows me.

I do not wish to marry Miss Langdon for her wealth, & she knows that perfectly well. As far as I am concerned, Mr. Langdon can cut her off with a shilling—or the half of it. To use a homely phrase, I have paddled my own canoe since I was thirteen, *wholly* without encouragement or assistance from any-one, & am fully competent to so paddle it the rest of the voyage, & take a passenger along, beside. While I have health & strength, & the high hope & confidence that God gave me in my nature, I will look to it that we always have a comfortable living, & that is all (of a purely worldly nature) that either of us will care a great deal about. Neither of us are much afflicted with a mania for money-getting, I fancy. She thinks we *might* live on two thousand a year (& you know she is an able & experienced housekeeper & has a sound judgment in such matters,) but if I thought I couldn't earn more than that, I would not be depraved enough to ask her to marry me yet awhile. No, we can make the canoe go, & we shall not care a straw for the world's opinion about it if the world chooses to think otherwise. This is *our* funeral, & we are proud enough & independent enough to think we can take care of it right. If we get in trouble we will sell our point lace & eat our shucks in a foreign land, & *fight it out*, but we won't come back & billet our-selves on the old home, & have Charley charging us for board "on the European plan" as he is always threatening to do with me when I linger there a few days. There's a shot for Charley! I propose to earn money enough some way or other, to buy a remunerative share in a newspaper of high standing, & then instruct & elevate & civilize the public through its columns, & my wife (to be) will superintend the domestic economy, furnish ideas & sense, erase improprieties from the manuscript, & read proof. That is all she will have to do. Mere pastime for a person of her calibre.

Now if anybody wants to ask questions, you can read them any or all of the above & say with perfect confidence, that it is the *truth*. I don't know whether it is what you wanted or not, but I judged that the best way, after all, to write the letter, was to do exactly as I do when I wish to write a newspaper article—that is, sit down & let it *write itself*.—This letter has written itself—& you have the result. There is no restraint in it, no expediency, no policy, no diplomacy. It simply means what it says—nothing more, & nothing less.

I tender my loving duty to you & to Mr. Langdon, & wish you all possible happiness & content, most cordially—& likewise the cheerfulness & peace of mind which were yours before your proud & happy prospective son came to disturb it.

Sincerely
Saml L. Clemens

Once more swinging back from the Middle West, Mark revisited Elmira from February 19 until 22, then departed for New York City in company with Mr. Langdon, before lecturing in Trenton and provincial New York towns, such as Lockport.

Lockport, *Feb.* 27. [1869]

Livy dear, it does seem that I am doomed never to get a satisfactory chance to write you again. They gave me no opportunity at Mr. Nevins's,[1] & so I traveled all night last night, purposely that I might have plenty of time to-day. But now the day is nearly gone & I have only just gotten rid of an old California friend or

---

[1] The clergyman who had been his host in Stuyvesant, N. Y.

two & the inevitable "committee." And I have raced my feet off in the storm trying to find the villain (of the "Committee") who has got your letter—but of course I have failed, so far. If it were not wicked, I could cordially wish his funeral might occur to-morrow. However, I have bribed a man to find & bring me his body, dead or alive—& that letter. I *know* it is from you—there is no question about that.

We did not see Mrs. Brooks, my love. As I wrote you from Stuyvesant, she was out. We drove out there in the evening. I was not so very sorry she was absent, because I preferred to talk to Mr. Langdon, anyhow—for I love him, & I only *like* Mrs. Brooks. Having made the call, my conscience was clear, because my Livy's orders had been obeyed—& without orders from you, & *only* you of all people in the world, I wouldn't have gone—for you know I wouldn't be likely to forget that neither she nor her husband invited me to come back when I was there last. But I would go there fifty times if you desired it. Mr. Langdon acted very badly—& that was one reason why I didn't grieve when we found her absent. He *persisted* in getting shaved before starting, & for no other reason than that he wanted to "show off." He wanted to appear better looking than me. That was pure vanity. I cannot approve of such conduct as those.

I could not get much of Mr. Langdon's company (except his Coal company). I hardly like to tell on him—but Livy you ought to have seen what sort of characters he was associating with. He had his room full of them all the time. He had two abandoned coal-heavers there from Scranton, & two or three suspicious look-ing pirates from other districts, & that dissolute Mr. Frisbie from Elmira, & a notorious character by the name of Slee, from Buffalo. But it was pleasant. The subject of coal is very thrilling. I listened to it for an hour—till my blood curdled in my veins, I may say. And what do you suppose they are going to do? Why they are going to take the Captain's case into consideration. The Captain lives at Buffalo, you know. The Captain is all very well, but he don't suit the Company. He wants his salary raised to three thousand. He says he can't live on less. Simply because he has a large family to support—as if the coal company was responsible

for his family—or any of his other crimes, for that matter. No—
the Captain will find the large-family dodge won't answer. It is
too old. We want something fresh. He lives in a twelve thousand
dollar house, you know, & his lease is about out, & they are going
to raise the rent on him from $500 to $800 a year—& just on that
pretense he wants his wages advanced $600, per annum. . . . The
Captain is all very well, you know, but he is altogether too valuable. He not only transacts all the duties that belong in his
department, but he transacts a little of everything that comes
along. And maybe you won't believe it, but he has actually been
selling hundreds of dollars worth of coal on *tickets*—(hence the
term "on tick").—He sold a lot of Demurrage & other stuff on
tickets to a Canadian mining company years ago, & they have
got that [coal] plunder yet. Think of selling coal for *tickets*, Livy
—when *you* know, & *I* know that tickets are not good for anything but bread, & to travel on railroads with. But hereafter the
notorious Slee will have to take charge of everything in Buffalo
himself—& the Head Centre (I mean the Head Salesman) will
hire & discharge the men under him to suit himself, & be personally responsible to Mr. Slee—& the Captain will have to keep
his fingers out of that pie, & go remarkably slow on the Ticket
system, too. And his wages will not be raised, either, unless Mr.
Slee thinks fit. The Captain's salary *isn't* high enough, according
to the size of his family as it now stands, & so it is plain enough
to *any* noodle that that family has got to be reconstructed. Therefore, the salary will remain just as it is, & Mr. Slee will proceed
to cut down the Captain's family to fit it. Business is business,
you know.[2]

Mr. Slee gave me a very cordial invitation to visit his home in
Buffalo, & I shall do it, some day. I like him first-rate.

(Livy, they spell Plymouth without the u—take courage, my
darling.)[3]

Mr. Langdon thought of going up to Hartford about to-day, to
see the Hookers; & you may well be glad of it, for he would wear

[2] For Mark's later reflections on the ruthlessness of the coal business in Buffalo,
see "Letter from the Recording Angel," ed. Bernard De Voto, *Harper's Magazine*,
February 1946.
[3] Alluding probably to coal from the anthracite district of that name near
Wilkesbarre, Pa., another jest doubtless at Livy's unsure spelling.

himself out with business in New York in another week. He was at it all the time. However, he was in good spirits, & apparently in excellent health.

When I read your Stuyvesant letter I was inclined to be angry with Bement, at first, for writing you a note that made you downhearted, but upon reflection I felt more charitable. He *couldn't* write you a cordial letter, dear—it wouldn't be human nature—for he loves you himself. Don't talk back Livy! He *does* love you—& so how *could* he rejoice that you are lost to him?

I am glad I marked those books for you, since the marking gives you pleasure, but I remember that the pencilings are very meagre—for which I am sorry. I have marked many a book for you, in the cars—& thrown them away afterward, not appreciating that I was taking a pleasure of any great moment from you. I will do better hereafter, my precious little wife.

And so *you* have been having visions of our future home, too, Livy? I have such visions every day of my life, now. And they always take one favorite shape—peace, & quiet—rest, & seclusion from the rush & roar & discord of the world.—You & I apart from the jangling elements of the outside world, reading & studying together when the day's duties are done—in our own castle, by our own fireside, blessed in each other's unwavering love & confidence. But it makes me ever so restive, Livy!—& impatient to throw off these wandering duties that thrall me now, & take you to my arms, never to miss your dear presence again. Speed the day! How I dread the California trip.[4] Three awful months without seeing Livy once—it weakens my resolution to think of it. It is not a week since I saw you, & yet it seems already an age, & I would walk twenty miles through this snow-storm to kiss you, Livy. How will three months seem to me? A century.

Livy, darling, I see by your letter that you are not sleeping enough. Do you want to break this old heart of mine? But I was ever so glad to hear that when your father left, that morning, at 9 o'clock, you were still in bed. What I do *long* to hear, Livy, is that you lie abed *late* in the morning—that you don't get up until your dear eyes *refuse* to stay shut any longer. An hour of

---

[4] A lecture trip to the West, projected for the spring of 1869, was finally abandoned largely at Livy's desire.

it is worth any other *three* hours. *Please* sleep later, Livy. I have talked it over with your father, & he is ready to miss the blessing of your presence at breakfast in order that you may become more than ever a blessing to him by building up your strength through late sleeping. I want to see you looking strong and healthy when I take you in my arms on the 17th of March, Livy—& I *can* see you so if you will only listen to my pleadings & sleep till ten o'clock every morning. Please, Livy darling.

Your new letter is come! No, Livy, Livy, Livy, I *can't* see that you are in constant danger of pursuing your own tastes & pleasures instead of giving up your life for others. What I *do* see, though, is that you are always sacrificing yourself for other peoples' benefit. I *know* it, Livy. You are doing enough. You are doing *all* that God has given you strength to do, & I tremble every time I detect a disposition in you to tax that strength further. Livy, the sweet spirit that goes out from you carries a constant blessing to every member of the little circle you inhabit. You bless *many* persons by your beautiful life, while most people bless only one or two or three, by theirs—& therefore, why not be content? No, no, darling, it makes me uneasy, these thinkings, these longings & aspirings after a broader field of usefulness. It is because such thoughts & such broodings have their effect upon your physical strength—they waste it, they burn it out—& I so long to see you have a strength-restoring season of calm, of contentment, of tranquillity, both of mind & body—for then I *know* you would grow strong & cheery & happy. *Then* you could think of others' weal as much as you wished, Livy, & I would gladly help you scheme & plan & execute. Don't be hurt at my solicitude, & my anxiety about your health, darling, for it is born of my strong, deep, deathless love for you, my worshipped idol.

I will send Hattie a photograph of the old pattern, & when I sit again, I will send her a new one. (I talk of sitting, as complacently as if I were an old hen, & used to it.) And this reminds me that I told Mrs. Fairbanks you would sit for a large photograph for her (like mine that hangs in the library) as a companion to the one I gave her. She said she wanted her son & her daughter *both*, where she could look at them when she pleased. But you needn't hurry,

Livy—in the spring will do. I will take you to the photographer's
& "fix" you, to suit myself.

The ring continuing to be "the largest piece of furniture in
the house" is a burst of humor worthy of your affianced husband,
Livy, you dear little Gravity. How I envy you your multiplicity
of cousins!—for I can hardly claim a relative in the world outside
our own family. I suppose it *will* be hard to write that letter to
the Chicago cousin, under the circumstances, but then you are
the brave girl that can do it.[5]

I did not try to get the porcelain picture taken in New York
because I would have no chance to examine "proofs" of it, having
only half a day to spare there—but I will sit for it in Hartford.
Which reminds me, honey, that you must direct your letters
henceforward to "Saml. L. Clemens, 148 Asylum St., Hartford,"
& thus oblige the man who loves, *loves*, LOVES you, Livy!

I kiss you, my own darling, on lip & cheek & brow, & bid you
good-night, & pray that the ministering spirits of God will have
you in their keeping & shield you from all harm.

Tell your mother that her eldest son is well, & sends his love.

Thine, until Death doth us part.

SAML

The next letter, an engaging revelation of Clemens' remorse at
having dismissed a shade brusquely a flock of his young admirers,
to get some needed rest, and then of calling them back to surrender his whole evening and the next day to them, is as characteristic as his earlier repentance over scolding the landlord in
Iowa City. "I never did a thing in all my life, virtuous or otherwise," he once told the public, "that I didn't repent of within
twenty-four hours."

ROCHESTER, *March* 1. [1869]

I love you, Livy. That is not what I sat down especially to say,
if it were I might continue to write, now that I am at it, & never
stop again. No—I wished to say, *particularly*, Be sure & send
my first Geneseo letter (I mean the one *you* first wrote me, to that

---

[5] Another fancied rival for Livy's hand, probably related to her mother's family,
the Lewises of Illinois.

point) to Hartford. Do I make myself understood? Don't you see, Livy, I was so bewitched by you, there in Elmira, that I could think of nothing connectedly & collectedly *but* you, & so I forgot to telegraph those Geneseo folks to retain your letter till I came— & I wrote them from New York, too late—& so *of course* they had no better sense than to send the letter back to Elmira, directed to Mr. Langdon. Now Livy, please don't tear it up, but forward it to me at Hartford, there's a darling.

And the next thing I wish to say, is, please tell Charlie to tell those tailors to make my coat nearly or full three-quarters of an inch higher in the back of the neck than this one. This one gives me the lockjaw every time I look in the glass. The collar is an unmitigated atrocity. I want the collar of the new coat to be five inches higher than the collar of this one. Tell Charlie, please.

In Geneseo yesterday I got your letter of the 25th. And so you are writing me every day? That is right, you dear little Livy— only, don't you write me or anybody else when you are tired or are hurried by company. I shall write you every chance I get, just the same, & any time that a letter is due from you & it don't come, I shall feel satisfied that you needed rest, or something interfered, & so I shall be content. I am at rest & peace in you now, my Livy, & I know perfectly well that when no obstacles intervene, you will be sure to write me regularly—but not a great many weeks ago, the failure of one of your letters to arrive when it was expected, would have terrified me.

You have been writing every day, & I only every other day. But my reason was that I had no opportunity to write oftener. I was in Geneseo thirty hours, & ought to have been permitted to write from there, but wasn't. Half a dozen young gentlemen [of Charlie's] 20 to 25 years of age, received me at the depot with a handsome open sleigh, & drove me to the hotel in style—& then *took possession of my room*, & invited a dozen more in, & ordered cigars, & made themselves entirely happy & contented. But they were hard to entertain, for they took me for a lion, & [were ludicrously] I had to carry the bulk of the conversation myself, which is a thing that presently grows wearisome. At dinner I begged off from going sleigh-riding, & said I wanted to go to bed in about an hour. After dinner they came up again. Pretty soon I spoke once more of retiring. It produced no effect. Then I rose & said, "Boys, I shall have to bid you a good-afternoon, for I am stupid & sleepy—& you must pardon my bluntness, but I *must* go to bed." Poor fellows, they were stricken speechless—they looked mortified, & went blundering out like a flock of sheep, treading on each other's heels in their confusion. I undressed & went to bed, & *tried* to go to sleep—but again & again my conscience smote me—again & again I thought of how mean & how shameful a return I had made for their well-meant & whole-hearted friendliness to me a stranger within their gates—& how puppyish it was in me to be angered instead of gladdened by that gushing cordiality of youth, a thing which ought to have won me by its very *naivete* & its rare honesty. And then I said to myself, I'll make amends for this—& so got up & dressed & gave the boys *all* of my time till midnight—& also from this noon till I left at four this afternoon. And so, if any man is thoroughly popular with the young people of Geneseo to-day, it is I. We had a full house last night, & a fine success. I just *love* boys of their age with all my heart—& I don't see how I ever could have treated them discourteously. (Yes I do, too. I know the secret of it. I *wanted to read your letter*—& if they had only just allowed me an hour of privacy for that, I would have been with them heart & hand from that time forth.) Some of those boys came fourteen miles, from a college at Lima, & were splendid young scalawags. The whole tribe came to the hotel after the lecture, & entertained me with vocal & piano music in the parlor, & with cider & whole worlds of tobacco smoke—but *they* drank a little of everything, & made music which you might have heard a mile. I played sedate old gentleman, but never reproved them once, for I couldn't help saying to myself, You'll be all the better men for sowing your wild oats while you are *young*—*I*'ll go your security.[6] They assembled in the street before the hotel, shortly after I had retired, & gave me three ter-

---

[6] Moved by her dissent, he changed his opinion on March 8: "No, Livy, I yield in the matter of sowing the wild oats. I have thought it over—& I have also talked it over with Twichell, the other night, & I fear I have been in the wrong. Twichell says, 'Don't *sow* wild oats, but *burn* them . . .' I only thought of sowing them being the surest way to make the future man a steady, reliable, *wise* man, thoroughly fitted for this life . . . But there is a deeper question—whether it be advisable or justifiable to trample the laws of God under foot at *any* time in our lives?"

rific cheers—which was rather more honor than I desired. Of course I *half* promised to lecture in Genêseo *in the middle of August,* at which time they propose to give me a ball & a concert —& I also *half*-promised to spend my summer vacation there—& I have made that *half* promise in a good many places (but always with the thought in my mind, "It will depend entirely upon where *Livy* is going to spend her vacation"—for I don't propose to be very far from *you,* my dear, when *vacations* fall to my good fortune).

Now if you have kept up your letter a day, I ought to find a perfect feast awaiting me at Hartford—& I do hope it is the case. Remember, "148 Asylum Street," Livy dear. But since you have a house full of company to entertain, I am a little afraid you won't have time to write, except after your bed-time—& you must not do that, Livy. If either of us must suffer, let it be me.

Bless you I am glad to be in your apple sauce—or even in your soup, Livy—for it is a sign that I am in your thoughts, & therefore in your heart, the daintiest mansion that ever *I* inhabited, my darling.—And I pray that its doors may never be closed against me until one or the other of us shall go forth forever from among the living. You were brave, Livy—it was like you to come out & acknowledge what was in your mind, without adopting one of those false little subterfuges usual in such circumstances & commonly regarded as permissible.

I still look among the faces in my audiences for one like yours —for one that shall give token of a nature like yours—& I still look in vain. And so I grow prouder & prouder of you day by day, as each new evidence comes that there is none like you in all the world. If ever a man had reason to be grateful to Divine Providence, it is I. And often & often again I sit & think of the wonder, the curious mystery, the *strangeness* of it, that there should be only *one* woman among the hundreds & hundreds of thousands whose features I have critically scanned, & whose characters I have read in their faces—only *one* woman among them all whom I could love with all my whole heart, & that it should be my amazing good fortune to secure that woman's love. And more, that it should be revealed to me in a single *instant* of time, when I first saw you, that you were that woman. It passes my comprehension.

I have stated the case truly—& I can swear to it as I have stated it. I have known many, very many estimable & lovely women, but they all betrayed one or more unpleasant qualities—& all this time, twelve long years, I have been growing naturally more & more critical & hard to please, as is the way of old bachelors—but behold, I have found you at last, & in you I can discover *no* blemish. It is strange, it is very strange. The hand of Providence is in it. When I cease to be grateful, deeply grateful to you for your priceless love, my honored Livy, I shall be—dead. Never before, Livy—never before.

I have been reading—I *am* reading—Gulliver's Travels, & am much more charmed with it than I was when I read it last, in boyhood—for now I can see what a scathing satire it is upon the English government, whereas, before I only gloated over its prodigies & its marvels. Poor Swift—under the placid surface of this simply-worded book flows the full tide of his venom—the turbid sea of his matchless hate. You would not like the volume, Livy— that is, a part of it. Some of it you would. If you would like to read it, though, I will mark it & tear it until it is fit for your eyes —for portions of it are very coarse & indelicate. I am sorry enough that I didn't ask you to let me prepare Don Quixote for your perusal, in the same way. It pains me to think of your reading that book just as it stands. I have thought of it with regret, time & again. If you haven't finished it, Livy, don't do it. You are as pure as snow, & I would have you always so—untainted, untouched even by the impure thoughts of others. You are the purest woman that ever I knew—& your purity is your most uncommon & most precious ornament. Preserve it, Livy.—Read nothing that is not *perfectly* pure. I had rather you read fifty "Jumping Frogs" than one Don Quixote. Don Quixote is one of the most exquisite books that was ever written, & to lose it from the world's literature would be as the wresting of a constellation from the symmetry & perfection of the firmament—but neither it nor Shakespeare are proper books for virgins to read until some hand has culled them of their grossness. No gross speech is ever harmless. "A man cannot handle pitch & escape defilement," saith the proverb. I did not mean to write a sermon, but still I have done it.—However, it is good sense, & it was a matter that lay near my heart; & so I am not sorry that it is written.

It is high time you were in bed, Livy—& so if you will put your arms about my neck & kiss me, while I look for a moment into the eyes that are dearer to me than the light that streams out of the Heavens, you may go. And take you these two kisses & place them as I would if I were there—& so, Good night, & God bless you always, my own darling.

Till death,
SAM

Envelope:
Politeness of the Hardware Cub.

Charles Langdon was serving a brief apprenticeship to the hardware business. Moreover his addiction to a style of men's hat in fashion called a "nail keg" re-enforced such joking asides (for example, letters of Dec. 21 and 23, 1868).

Mark's lecture season finished, he settled down at Hartford in early March as a guest of the Blisses, of the American Publishing Company, who were now supplying proof of *The Innocents Abroad.* Spring and summer saw him commuting frequently between Hartford, where his professional interests now centered, and Elmira, where his heart lay.

New names and personalities begin to appear in these letters. In addition to the Twichells, his Hartford acquaintance now widened to include the whole suburban circle of Nook Farm. On that tract of woodland and rolling hills inside the bend of Park River, a colony of Hookers, Gillettes, Burtons, Days, Hawleys, Stowes, and Warners had all settled within the past fifteen years —a remarkably tight little coterie of brains, bookishness, and bank accounts, a nest of liberal Congregationalism.

In Mark's early letters from the land of steady habits the Hookers figure most prominently. With them Mark had stayed on his first visit to this community early in 1868. "I am in Hartford," he informed the readers of the *Alta California* of March 3, 1868. "At the hospitable mansion where I am a guest, I have to smoke surreptitiously when all are in bed, to save my reputation, and then draw suspicion upon the cat when the family detect the unfamiliar odor. . . . So far, I am safe; but I am sorry to say that the cat has lost caste." More seriously, as his letters to Livy make plain, something done or said by the Hookers "humiliated" him, and on his return to town he regarded them suspiciously.

Yet they were great friends of the Langdons, thanks partly to the fact that Mrs. Hooker's brother, Thomas K. Beecher, was the pastor in Elmira. Mrs. Langdon and Mrs. Hooker counted themselves close friends, while Livy held in special devotion the daughter, Alice Hooker, to whose approaching wedding on June 17, 1869 she would come as bridesmaid. Another daughter, Mary Beecher Hooker, in 1866 had married Eugene Burton, brother of the noted Congregational divine Dr. Nathaniel J. Burton, and had set up housekeeping near her parents.

Livy's desire for a rapprochement between Mark and the Hookers was therefore strong. But as a highly sensitive man he found it hard to overlook this rebuff or offense they had inflicted apparently at the time of his earlier visit. In the first of two letters written to Livy on March 6, 1869, he observed: "Since you speak of it, I propose to call on the Hookers to-night—not *the* Hookers exactly, but the Burton branch, & then if the original branch will invite me, I will visit there also. I am afraid I never shall feel right in that house, though I let my trust & confidence go out to them as I seldom do with new acquaintances, & they responded by misunderstanding me. If I had given them *all* of my trust & confidence, they never *could* have humiliated me by any ordinary slight, because then, not expecting such things I would have been stupidly blind to them. I like them pretty well, but I believe it is more because you like them than for any other reason. And for the same reason I shall choke down my gorge & do the *very best* I can to like them well—always provided, that they will give me a chance—can't *seek* it, though, Livy darling."

As the following letter and others make plain, Mark found the Hookers singularly hard to take. The trouble evidently did not lie with John Hooker, lean and bearded descendant of that great Puritan divine Thomas Hooker—John being a minor lawyer always yearning uncomforted to sit on the State supreme bench—but with his wife.

Isabella Beecher Hooker was a phenomenon of nature. Strong of will and temper, a lover of publicity like all the Beechers, feminist and spiritualist, she believed intermittently in her destiny, under God and "my adorable brother Jesus," to be grand matriarch of the world in a new apocalypse. Even in the somewhat neurotic atmosphere of Nook Farm as it developed over the years —where mediums and faith healers drove a considerable traffic, and Isabella's brother-in-law Calvin Stowe rejoiced in an invisible companion named Harvey who had been his playmate since early childhood—the Hookers stood pre-eminent. In these early letters Mark was only beginning to feel their quality.

9 P.M.

HARTFORD, *March* 6 [1869]

Livy dear, I have already mailed to-day's letter, but I am so proud of my privilege of writing the dearest girl in the world whenever I please, that I must add a few lines if only to say *I love you*, Livy. For I *do* love you, Livy—as the dew loves the flowers; as the birds love the sunshine; as the wavelets love the breeze; as mothers love their first-born; as memory loves old faces; as the yearning tides love the moon; as the angels love the pure in heart. I so love you that if you were taken from me it seems as if all my love would follow after you & leave my heart a dull & vacant ruin forever & forever. And so loving you I do also honor you, as never vassal, leal & true, honored sceptred king since this good world of ours began. And now that is honest, & I think you ought to reach up & give me a kiss, Livy. (Or I will stoop down to your dainty little altitude, very willingly, for such a guerdon.)

I suppose I have been foolish, Livy dear, but I couldn't help it. I have walked all the way out to Nook Farm from this hotel (the Allyn House) this bitter-cold stormy night—& then concluded I would call on the Hookers *another time*. Now hold on, Livy dear —don't ruffle your feathers too soon—don't "fly off the handle," as we say in Paris—but hear me out. I was going to call on the Burtons, you know. Well, it's an awful night outside—& breasting the blinding gusts of snow (for the wind was lifting it out of the streets & blowing it in clouds that made the gas lamps loom vaguely, as in a fog), it took me half an hour to walk there, & then

—why *then*, the depraved & unreliable Burtons were *not at home.*
Johnny (I think that is Mr. Hooker's boy's name) was there, &
said *his* folks were all at home & he thought they would be glad
to see me—& that there was a young lady there from somewhere
—& so forth & so on. But I was justly incensed at the unaccount-
able conduct of those Burtons in being out on such a night; &
I—I—I—I—I—

Well, I thought I had a splendid excuse to give you, & so escape
a scolding, but I don't know what the mischief has become of it.
There wasn't fire enough to get right warm by, & I thought I had
better get back into the cold quick, while I was used to it—so I
left my card, & said that as it was nearly 9 o'clock & consequently
too late for visiting, in this land of steady habits, I would not go
to Mr. Hooker's now, but would come again at a more proper
time—& then went away, thinking to myself, "What a *mercy* it is
that I am alone—if Livy were here I should 'catch it' for just such
conduct as these." I struggled against it, Livy, but I couldn't help
it—I *couldn't help* it. Scold away, you darling little rascal sweetheart—because I just *know* you will.—And I expect I deserve it,
maybe. (But I wanted to come back & go on writing to you, Livy
dear, I guess *that* was the reason—now *can't* you let that appease
you? [honey?] there's a dear sweet, precious, good Livy. I'm *bound*
to call on the Hooker's! E pluribus Unum! I do not know what
E pluribus Unum means, but it is a good word, anyway.) [Let's]
Now we will kiss & make friends, Livy. [How's this? . . .] You
mustn't enclose other people's letters in yours—put them in
another envelop. Here I thought I had a good long letter from
you to-day, & behold, half of it was from my sister. What do you
want to disappoint me so, for?

She has read the letter to Vanderbilt[7] in a Western paper, & says
—however, it is too much trouble to copy the passage—I will send
the whole letter—there are no secrets in it, & besides it refers to
my princess in one place, anyhow. She naturally feels drawn
toward you, & has asked, in her diffident way, about the propriety
of writing a line to you.

[7] His "Open letter to Commodore Vanderbilt," in which Mark advised him to
"go and surprise the whole country by doing something right," appeared in
Packard's Monthly, March, 1869.

I guess I will tell her to bang away. (Because, you know, you like to write to strangers, & it will just be fun for you to acknowledge the receipt of her letter & say a pleasant word in reply.) All that ever you will need to say will be to tell her that I am earnestly seeking a Christian life, & no letter that ever fell under her eye will seem so beautiful to her. My sister is a good woman, familiar with grief, though bearing it bravely & giving no sign upon the surface; & she is kind-hearted, void of folly or vanity, perfectly unacquainted with deceit or dissimulation, diffident about her own faults, & slow to discover those of others. She isn't such a gem as you; [by a long shot] & neither is any other woman, but then she is a very, very excellent woman anyway. You'll like her, Livy —she don't seem to spell worth a cent. You see she spells cow with a k. And she has spelled "tripped" with only one p, & she puts only one t in "delighted," & only two s's in "expression." I can stand those little blunders well enough, but I do hate to see anybody spell John with a G. I look upon that as perfectly awful. I notice that you always spell John with a G.—(Now forgive me, Livy darling—you *know* I wouldn't poke fun at you to save a man's life if I thought it would wound you. *I* don't care a straw *how* you spell, Livy dear—I hardly ever notice when you make a mistake—& bless you I am just as proud of you as if you could beat the Unabridged Dictionary spelling. It would be a pity indeed if *I* presumed to criticize your spelling—I who am sown as thick with faults as you are with merits, & shining virtues, & beautiful traits of character; & yet you have found it in your heart to take me just as I am & lift me up & bless me with your priceless love—*I* never can be *your* critic, my loved & honored Livy.)

I called at the Courant office yesterday, but Gov. Hawley was absent in Washington. They said he would arrive in town to-night & call on me at the hotel.

George Francis Train is here, lecturing to-night at Allyn Hall, about Ireland. I have not called on the distinguished jailbird— I don't like him. He may have some little reason to dislike me, but none to like me. I black-guarded him like everything in a newspaper letter once, which was pretty widely copied. I would like to trot him out again, ever so well—(excuse that slangy language, Livy—I am on a slangy subject). He is lecturing to the Irish, to-night, & lying like all possessed, I make no manner of doubt—(excuse *that*, too, Livy—I guess I had better get off of this subject).

Yes, Livy, as you say, I suspect that if you write me every second day it will be as much as I ought to expect of you—& as much as your various taxes upon your time, & your frequent company interruptions, will allow you to do. I must beware how I run the risk of being a burden to you, in either great or small things, instead of a help.—Therefore, make sunshine for me—make me glad & happy, & generous toward the world & its ills, with one of those prized little missives signed "Your Livy" only when you have plenty of time at hand or when desire prompts you. (You compel yourself to write sometimes when you simply feel that you *ought* to write—& then it is a hardship to you.) Never mind me —see that you make yourself contented & happy—for that is what *I* want to see, my dear.

Well, some things *can't* be done as well as others, do you know that? I have been trying my very best, for two days, to answer your letters received yesterday & to-day—& the first letter I wrote, yesterday, I laid yours on the table by me & got ready—but I wrote about twenty pages of stuff & *never* got to it. This evening I laid your *two* letters by me & began again—& wrote fifteen or sixteen pages of rubbish & never once got to *them*. And now to-night I place them by me once more, determined to answer them this time, anyway—& here I am. The fact is, I think to myself, every time, "Now I will just chat a little with Livy about one thing or another, & then after that I will read her letters over again & answer them." But then I chat *too long*—& so the answering has to be deferred. I guess I'll accomplish it tomorrow, Livy —be patient, my little treasure. To think that within the last twenty-four hours I should have written fifty mortal pages of manuscript to you, & yet am obliged at last to beg further time wherein to answer your two letters. I am acting a good deal like a "Committee of the Whole" in one of these one-horse State Legislatures, early in the Session when they keep sounding the lobby's financial pulse on certain bills, by "reporting progress" and "asking leave to sit again" till the lobby grows frantic & disgusted.[8]

Goodnight & God bless you, my darling.—Take my kiss & my benediction, & try to be reconciled to the fact that I am

Yours, forever & always.

SAM

P. S.—I have read this letter over & it is flippant, & foolish & puppyish. I wish I had gone to bed when I got back, without writing. You said I must never tear up a letter after writing it to you—& so I send it. Burn it, Livy—I did not think I was writing so clownishly & shabbily. I was in much too good a humor for sensible letter writing.

[*Envelope:*] Cart it home, Charlie, please.

His next letter, two days later, reported that he had just encountered Mrs. Burton on the street, "was approaching her from behind, & arrived just in time to receive her in my arms as she lost her balance & fell backwards when climbing into her carriage. She was surprised to find it was not a stranger. She invited me to come up to dinner at 6. . . . And I'll call on the Hookers or die. . . . I *like* [Mr. Hooker], in spite of prejudice & everything else." Still later, on March 13, he reported that, buttressed by Twichell's company, he had achieved the promised call. After a long evening's talk Mark pronounced John Hooker "splendid," although Isabella "startled" Mark and "distressed" Twichell by airing some extraordinary ideas about Christ's continuous preaching to sinners in purgatory.

On March 12 he wrote to tell Livy of a dream in which *she* had appeared to snub him. He thought he saw her sitting in the Langdon drawing room discussing "the properties of light, & heat, & bugs" with Elmira's local savant Professor Ford, while a maid sternly barred the lover from interrupting "the philosophy lesson." "But upon my word I was only disappointed—not hurt, not offended . . ." he wrote humbly. "It simply brought back to me my desperate temerity in venturing to locate myself for two weeks in a house where I was a stranger—& in what strong anxiety and dread I was some times, that some humiliation might visit me in

[8] As journalist Mark had covered the Nevada Territorial legislature from 1862 to 1864.

my defenceless position. But *you* were the magnet, & I could not depart from the influence."

These words and the dream itself were inspired not only by Mark's uneasy relations with the Hookers, but also by a chance disclosure Livy had recently made to her fiancé, with something less than her usual thoughtfulness. It was that on his first two-weeks' visit to the Langdons he had come perilously close to wearing out his welcome. For several days he brooded over this candid revelation. "Why it even touches my pride yet to think of it!— What did you go & tell us that, for, you dear little persecutor?" he wrote in one letter, and after her slightly aggrieved response to that query, ended the matter on March 12 by apologizing himself: "But for that remark of yours, I would always have fancied I was quite a pleasant addition to the family circle at that time! And but for *my* stupid remark *about* your remark, my own precious Livy would have been spared her temporary distress of mind on her first page. So *I* apologize Livy—*you* are not to do it. . . . I will make it my business to forget that [first visit] ever caused you uneasiness, & remember only that it gave me my darling, my matchless, my beautiful Livy—my best friend, my wise helpmeet, my teacher of the Better Way—my wife."

Such talk belongs no doubt to the dialectic of courtship, its small misunderstandings, teasings, rifts and questionings, for the sake of the ultimate apology and kiss of reconciliation. But beyond much question it also discloses the pride, hypersensitiveness, self-distrust, and masochism that lay deep within Samuel Clemens' nature. He was a man of feeling, as though he had come out of the eighteenth century.

Leaving Hartford in mid-March, he visited his fellow-humorist Petroleum V. Nasby in Boston to meet "the literary lions of the 'Hub,'" as he told Livy, then passed through New York City, and arrived once more at the Langdons on March 17. There he settled, as if secure of a more durable welcome, until the first week in May, reading proof with Livy in the intervals of courting. A one-page fragment to the Clemens family, on letter paper with an embossed "L," was certainly written in Elmira during this visit, and probably on the day before a letter to Pamela Moffett which follows it here.

[ELMIRA, *circa mid-April*, 1869]

. . . Orion on the same paper, of it, for you know it is not good judgment & then we could be all come-atable.

My head is so busted up with endeavors to get my own plans straight, that I am hardly in a condition to fix up anybody else's. [Livy and I sit for hours] I don't know whether I am going to California in May—I don't know whether I want to lecture next season or not—I don't know whether I want to yield to Nasby's persuasions & go with him on the Toledo Blade—I don't know *any* thing. And I don't care a dam. I mean a mill dam, of course —for I have not been a profane man for 2 years—(but between you & I, I put that "don't care a dam" in, solely for Livy's benefit, for I knew perfectly well that she had crept up behind me at that moment & was looking over my shoulder—but you bet you she's gone off, now). I ought not to tease her & "sell" her so much, but I can't easily help it, & she is as long-suffering & patient as any Job. She is *almost* perfection—I solemnly swear to that. I never have discovered a fault in her yet, or any sign or shadow of a blemish. And I must inform you that I sing her praises in a weaker key than any other friend she has.

> Good-bye. Love to you all.
> Affectionately
> SAM

About the same time he wrote to Pamela, largely upon the subject of Livy's provocative "simplicity."

ELMIRA, *Apl Something*, 1869

MY DEAR SISTER—I wrote yesterday & I surely did not expect to write again to-day—but Livy is taking a nap & I have an hour to myself.—She is wise. We are going out to dinner, & it's a fearful bore & she is getting up strength for the occasion, through sleep. I have been outraging her feelings again. She is trying to cure me of making "dreadful" speeches as she calls them. In the middle of winter when I was here, we had a "run" on the hot house for a day or two—which is to say, an unusual lot of people died & their friends came to get roses & things to decorate the coffins with, & at the end of a week there was hardly a dozen flowers of any

kind left. Charley & I made a good many jokes about it, & thus
horrified Livy. But a while ago I came in with a first-rate air of
dejection on, & heaved a vast sigh. It trapped Livy into a burst
of anxious solicitude, & she wanted to know what the matter was.
I said, "I have been in the conservatory, & there is a perfect *world*
of flowers in bloom—& we haven't a confounded corpse!" I guess
Orion will appreciate that. I don't like to fool Livy this way, &
don't do it often, but sometimes her simplicity is so tempting I
can't resist the inclination. I wish you could see that girl—the first
time I ever saw her I said she was the most beautiful creature in
the world, & I haven't altered my opinion yet. I take as much
pride in her brains as I do in her beauty, & as much pride in her
happy & equable disposition as I do in her brains.

Haven't got anything to write about, so I will enclose one of
Livy's letters—don't read it to anybody but the family & Margaret
—but M. *is* one of the family, I suppose. Livy is a sensible girl,
& don't go into any hysterics in her letters—but I do when I write
her. Her letter will help you to know her.

Affectionately
SAM

Mr. and Mrs. Langdon ask me to send their regards—& Livy also.

CHAPTER FOUR

Proofreading and Pining

AFTER remaining about six weeks in Elmira, Clemens went down to New York at the end of the first week in May and a day or so later settled down at Hartford once more. Again he lodged at the Blisses, and spent most of his time working over the book and yearning for his beloved.

Despite his early misgivings about some denizens of Nook Farm —abetted by passing moods of depression when he succumbed to a cold and nostalgia, lying wretchedly abed listening to "the eternal miserere of the rain"—these repeated visits to Hartford wrought their decisive effect upon Mark Twain's future. They fixed his attachment to this little city and its townspeople, and eventually led him and his bride to find here the only stable home they ever possessed.

HARTFORD, *May 12th* [1869]
Wednesday Eve

Was there *ever* such a darling as Livy? I *know* there never was. She fills *my* ideal of what a woman should be in order to be enchantingly lovable. And so, what wonder is it that I love her so? And what wonder is it that I am deeply grateful for permission to love her? Oh you are such an exquisite little concentration of loveliness, Livy! I am not saying these things because I am stricken in a new place, dearie—no, they are simply the things that are always in my mind—only they are demanding expression more imperiously than usual, maybe, because (9:30 P.M.,) I am just in from one of those prodigious walks I am so fond of taking in these solemn & silent streets by night, & these pilgrimages are pretty thoroughly devoted to thinking of you, my dainty little idol. How *could* I walk these sombre avenues at night *without* think-

87

ing of you? For their very associations would invoke you—every flagstone for many a mile is overlaid thick with an invisible fabric of thoughts of you—longings & yearnings & vain caressings of the empty air for you when you were sleeping peacefully & dreaming of other things than *me*, darling. And so now, & always hereafter, when I tread these stones, these sad phantoms of a time that is gone (thank God!) will rise about me to claim kinship with these new *living* thoughts of you that are all radiant with hope, & requited love, & happiness. God bless & keep you always, my Livy!

I am in the same house (but not in the same room—thanks!) where I spent three awful weeks last fall, worshipping you, & writing letters to you, some of which I mailed in the wastepaper basket & the others never passed from brain to paper. But I don't like to think of those days, or speak of them.

Now that I am well again, dearie, I am not afraid to tell you that I have been sick for a day or two. It was of no particular consequence (I worked nearly all the time), & it was useless to make you uneasy. This morning I felt almost persuaded that I was going to have a severe attack—but it is all gone, now, & I am well & cheery, & am enjoying the warm night & writing you in my night-clothes for comfort—& smoking. The good God that is above us all is merciful to me—from Whom came your precious love— from Whom cometh all good gifts—& I am grateful.

(Lucky I am, now, to be able to write with two pictures of you before me—& one of dear old Hat (tie)). Give me a kiss, please.

I guess I'll have to have a letter every day, dearie. Except, of course, when it would be too much of a hardship.—I did not hear from you to-day [& I confess] & do assure I *wanted* to. However, this is all pure selfishness & I will not be guilty of it. Write every other day—that is work enough for such a dear little body as you.

I expect to scribble very meagre letters to you, because I confess that I use you as a sort of prize for good behavior—that is when I transact all my duties, my abundant & ample reward is the luxury of writing to you—& when I fail to finish up my duties, Jack must go without his supper which is to say, I must lose the luxury of writing you. But the other night I did a vast deal of work, keeping myself to it with the encouraging assurance that I might talk to Livy when it was all done—& so at last I worried through—but alas for my reward, I could hardly sit up, & so I had to go to bed & lose all I had worked for so well. *Now* I have reached my goal for to-day, for I finished my work before supper.

(The picture of you with Hattie strikes me a little better now, but it still looks a little thin, & I am haunted with the fear that you are not as well as usual. Am I right?—Excuse this solicitude —for you are very dear to me, Livy—dearer than all things else on earth combined.)[1]

Walking, to-night, I heard the voices of ten million frogs warbling their melancholy dirge on the still air. I wished Mrs. Langdon were there to enjoy the plaintive concert. I mean to catch two or three hundred of them & take them home to Elmira. We can keep some of them in the cage with the mocking-bird, & colonize the rest in the conservatory. They made good music to-night, especially when it was very still & lonely & a long-drawn dog-howl swelled up out of the far distance & blended with it. The shadows seemed to grow more sombre, then, & the stillness more solemn, & the whispering foliage more spiritual, & the mysterious murmur of the night-wind more freighted with the moanings of shrouded wanderers from the [grave] tombs. The "voices of the night" are always eloquent.

I suppose you are having summer weather, now.—We are—& it is perfectly magnificent. I do *love* the hot summer weather. If I had had my darling here to-day, & Jim & "our" buggy, we would have had a royal drive. The town is budding out, now—the grass & foliage are, at least—& again Hartford is becoming the pleasantest city, to the eye, that America can show.—The park & the little river look beautiful—& yesterday as the sun went down, & flung long shafts of golden light athwart its grassy slopes & among its shrubs & stately elms & bridges, & gilded the graceful church spires beyond, it was a feast to look upon. But it was only a half-way sort of feast, after all, without Livy—a banquet of one cover, as one might say.

Oh you darling little speller!—you spell "terrible" right, this time. And I won't have it—it is un-Livy-ish. Spell it wrong, next time, for I love everything that is like Livy. Maybe it is wrong for

[1] To Mrs. Fairbanks two days earlier he wrote: "I have no news to tell you, except that Livy is no stronger than she was six months ago—& it seems hard & grieves me to have to say it. I cannot talk about it with her, though, for she is as sensitive about it as I am about my drawling speech & stammerers of *their* infirmity. She turns crimson when it is mentioned, & it hurts her worse than a blow."

me to put a premium on bad spelling, but I can't help it if it is. Some how I love it in you—I have grown used to it, accustomed to expect it, & I honestly believe that if, all of a sudden, you fell to spelling every word right, I should feel a pain, as if something very dear to me had been mysteriously spirited away & lost to me. I am not poking fun at you, little sweetheart.

Livy, you must not let Mr. Beecher beat you more than one game in five—you must do credit to your teacher. But you did everlastingly slaughter him on the first game, & *that* was doing credit to your teacher. It was about the way I beat *you*, my love.

From the stillness that reigns in the house, I fancy that I must be the only person up, though I know it is not late. However, the very dearest girl in the wide world has given me strict orders to go to bed early & take care of myself, & I will obey, though I had rather write to her than sleep—for, writing to her, it is as if I were *talking* to her—& to talk to her so, is in fancy to hold her tiny hand, & look into her dear eyes, & hear her voice that is sweet as an answered prayer to me, & clasp her pigmy foot, & hold her dainty form in my arms, & kiss her lips & cheeks, & hair & eyes for love, & her sacred forehead in honor, in reverent respect, in gratitude & blessing. Out of the depths of my happy heart wells a great tide of love & prayer for this priceless treasure that is confided to my life-long keeping. You cannot see its intangible waves as they flow toward you, darling, but in these lines you will hear, as it were, the distant beating of its surf.

I leave you with the ministering spirits that are in the air about you always. Good-night, with a kiss & a blessing, Livy darling.

SAM

The next letter is written in his happiest manner, with gusto and humor describing a soaking he received on a rainy afternoon —whose results were far less comic, in laying him low with a very heavy cold.

HARTFORD, *Saturday Night*
[*May 15, 1869*]

Livy dear, only let me say Good-night—that is all. Just as I expected, & just as I said in your mother's letter, Mr. Bliss forgot to mail that letter to you, & I discovered the fact an hour after supper & took it & cleared out for the post office—it was raining like sixty. I grabbed a seedy old umbrella in the hall & hurried. But that umbrella appeared to go up too much & sloped the wrong way—it was like a funnel—& Livy, would you believe it, before I had walked three blocks it had conveyed more than eighteen tons of rain-water down the back of my neck. Why, I was ringing wet. And I had my thin shoes on, & I began to *soak up*, you know. Barrels & barrels I soaked up—& that water rose in me, & rose in me, higher & higher, till it issued from my mouth, & then my nose, & presently I began to cry—part from grief & part from overflow —because I thought I was going to be drowned, you know—& I said I was a *fool* to go out without a life-preserver, which Livy always told me never to do it, & now what would become of *her*?

Well, you know I live half way from Hooker's to the post office, & it is six miles by the watch, & I only got there just in the nick of time to mail my letter three hours & a half before the mail closed, & I tell *you* I was glad, & felt smart—& then I bought 4 new numbers of Appleton's Journal & went up town & called on Billy Gross a minute, & went away from there & left my Appletons—& went down to the photographers & ordered a lot of pictures from the negative of the porcelain I gave you, & came away from there & forgot my umbrella—& then rushed back to Gross's & got my Appleton's—& crossed over & started home & got about 3 miles & a half & recollected the umbrella, & said "All right, never had a seeming misfortune yet that wasn't a blessing in disguise," & so, turned & tramped back again, damp but cheerful—twice three & a half is nine miles—& *got* my umbrella, & started out & a fellow said, "Oh, good, it's you, is it?—you've got my umbrella—funny I should find you *here*." And it *was* funny. We had unconsciously swapped umbrellas at the post office, or up a tree, or somewhere, & here, ever so long afterward & ever so far away, I find him standing unwittingly by his own umbrella looking at those pictures, with my old funnel in his hand. But the moment I picked his property up he recognized it—splendid umbrella, magic case, chronometer balance—he paid a thousand dollars for it in Paris —& it was unquestionably my umbrella that he had, because what was left of his paper collar was washed down around the small of his back & he had come just in an ace of being drowned before he noticed the little peculiarity of my property—& you know he had made a pass at that daguerrean shop & climbed in there just in time to save his life,—& *he* was wet, Livy, you better believe. He was very glad to see me. And I went away cheerful, & said "I *never* had a seeming misfortune yet that wasn't a blessing in disguise—& it holds good yet, & it was a blessing this time, too—for that other fellow." And then I came home, you know. And since then I have written a beautiful little romance about a nigger which was stolen out of Africa which was a prince—& sold into American slavery, & discovered, 30 years afterward & purchased of his master by the American public & sent home to Timbuctoo—& it is a *true story*, too, & Rev. Trumbull told me all about it—& his father had seen this poor devil with his own eyes—& T. showed me his majesty's portrait (original) painted by *Inman*.[2] And if you were here you could *read* this stirring romance, darling, & make out all the marginal poetry—& mark out all the jokes you didn't understand—& all the—well *every* thing—you should mark it *all* out, if you wanted to, for if Livy didn't like it nobody else should have a *chance* to like it—& since then—it is just "midnight—& All's well!"

A thousand blessings on your honored head & kisses on your precious lips, my own darling.

Good-night.

SAM

Ill and probably a little feverish from the cold that followed, he wrote with less than his usual equanimity—scolding Livy for neglect of her health, criticizing her pastor Thomas Beecher for his egotism, and then making rather savage sport of a little memoir or poetic tribute that the Langdons and their neighbors evidently planned in honor of a young man who had died not long before. Although Mark could not have known him, the saccharine obitu-

[2] Mark's "letter" in the *Weekly Alta* for August 7, 1869, relates this story and adds flippantly, "I, for one, sincerely hope that after all his trials he is now . . . eating and relishing unsaleable niggers from neighboring tribes that fall into his hands." According to Mark, Henry Inman painted this portrait from life in Hartford in 1822, shortly before the prince's return, aged sixty, to Timbuctoo. His name was Abduhl Rahhaman, and a factual account will be found in *The Literary Register* (Oxford, Ohio), September 15, 1828.

ary muse always filled him with derisive glee—as any reader of the Emmeline Grangerford passages in *Huckleberry Finn* will remember.

HARTFORD, *Monday Night* [*May* 17, 1869]

I can't resist the temptation to write you a line or two even though I sneeze myself to death before I get through with it.— What a bewitching little darling you are, Livy. You were going to come. It seems almost a misfortune that I *wasn't* dangerously sick, so that I might see the dear face again.—I used to think of sickness with dread—for I always had visions of dreary hospitals —solitude—shut out from friends & the great world—dragging, unevently minutes, hours, weeks—hated faces of hired nurses and harsh physicians—& then an unmourned death, a dog's burial, and—dissection by the doctors! But with *you* at the bedside—it seems to me that sickness would be luxury! You *are* a noble, true-hearted little darling, Livy. And I *love* you.

The printing is proceeding, & the bright, clean pages look hand-some. I sent you to-day a duplicate of the only proofs I have had since those I read when I first arrived here (except one little trifle of a few pages).

No, I haven't seen Mr. Beecher. As I passed up the street yester-day, John Day[3] bowed to me from the Allyn House steps, & I returned his salutation, though I did not remember who he was, at first. I didn't feel like crossing over, & he didn't either, & so we both of us didn't cross over at all, neither of us which. Somehow that sentence don't sound right, but I guess you can make it out. Colds always make me stupid & blundersome.

"The little throat trouble that you have is nothing at all seri-ous." Oh, *Livy*! You are not doing anything at all for that throat. Now why *will* you distress me so? That dreaded disease. Livy, do please doctor it until it is *entirely* cured, just to please me. It is not a trifling sore throat that lasts *two weeks*. It is the first foothold of that awful disease that lasts *for life*. I lay this thing up against Mrs. Corey & I never *will* forgive her for it, if one sign or symptom of it is left four days after you get this. It can be cured in that time, with care & attention, if it is not that frightful permanent

[3] Fiancé of Livy's friend Alice Hooker.

disease. Up to this time I have prayed night & day like a hypocrite & a liar—for I have thought of that trip every day, & always with a spasm of anger against that woman. I wish she had been in Jericho before she took it into her head to drag you out to that dismal valley & leave you to stare at vacancy & freeze yourself to death for an hour & a quarter while she cavorted through the woods, never caring two cents *how* you put in the dreary time. Livy I am *angry* (but not at *you*, my precious). You are all good, & true, & generous & forgiving & unselfish—all things that are a glory to womanhood meet & blend themselves together in the matchless mosaic of your character—& a single day's health to you is worth more than the eternal salvation of——I am just running away with myself. Livy, your inoffensive sore throat is nothing to you, & you can afford to be indifferent about it—but is *misery & death* to *me*—& so, *won't* you make a sacrifice for me & doctor it night & day faithfully & without shirking, till it is entirely cured, so that I can breathe again & be at rest? Livy, if you knew how this spectre goads me, tortures me, you would not be so thoughtless as to be indifferent to it. There—have I hurt her? God forbid that I should ever by word or deed, hurt you Livy, my beautiful, my pride, my darling. But I am distressed. I never, never will leave you again when you are not well. My conscience upbraided me cruelly when I *did* leave you so. But you said it was nothing—& you thought it, else you would not have said it; & I believed it, because I would believe your simple word against the oaths of the world. But my mind was full of bodings.

Later in the Evening.—If I can keep that torturing subject out of my mind, I shall remain in the good humor I am now in. Theodore was just *right* in that fight, & I am glad he won. We cannot have Mrs. Sue running around town acting Florence Nightingale in a hospital for decayed carpets. (Except it be at the request of Mrs. Corey.)

Mr. Beecher robs himself of the best happiness of his life when he enjoys his pleasures in solitude. What is a splendid sunset worth when there is nobody to see it with you—no sympathetic ear to pour your raptures into? And what is *any* joy (except the miser's) without companionship? And then the glaring *wrong* of the thing: for Mrs. Beecher shares his sorrows, & this earns the *right* to share his pleasures. But it seems that when the two are done carrying all the *burdens* of the day, he has no more use for her—she may sit down in sadness & weariness, while he loses the memory of the drudgery in the happy relief of pleasure. It is selfish—though, superbly gifted as he is, let us charitably try to fancy that he don't know it. Only, my dear, I will suggest that his heart & his brain would not have been so dull in these matters *with his first wife.* I think he possesses a very good *brotherly* love for his present wife —& you furnish me ample proofs that he possesses nothing more. Therefore, with such a love, let us not expect of him the noble things that are born only of a far higher & sublimer passion. It is the native *instinct* of *our* love to have no secrets, no concealments —therefore it is no merit in us to avoid this misfortune of his— we never will have to *reason* ourselves into doing a thing that necessarily comes natural to us. We shan't be able to *comprehend* this thing of having secrets. But the brotherly instinct is to conceal more things than it reveals—nothing but the cold, dismal *reasoning faculty* can enable Mr. Beecher to change this—& then he will have the *corpse* of the marital love—but with no pulse in its temples, no light in its eyes, no tenderness in its heart.

You little rascal, you *slurred over* Noyes's name, because you knew very well you didn't know how to spell it! Never mind, Livy darling, you know your spelling is perfectly safe in my "deluded" eyes, because I love everything you do, whether it be good, bad, or indifferent. Let Mrs. Sue be troubled no more about her memoir. *I* will write it—(with pleasure, I came near saying, but it seems like rather a doubtful compliment, & so I withhold the words). I will write it, & I will do it with such grace & such felicity that the ghost of the late William Lord Noyes[4] shall tear its filmy garments with envy & chagrin. I will put in tasty congratulations from each member of the family, & from all the admirals & brigadier generals, & even from the President, the Emperor of the French & Queen Victoria—for *both* of you—both of you in the same volume—& I will write all these felicitations myself—every *one* of them—so that I shall know that they are just exactly as they ought to be. And I'll have some poetry in—some of those sublime

[4] Son of the Langdon's neighbor, Henry Babcock Noyes of Big Flats. He had died in 1866, at the age of twenty.

conundrums from Young's Night Thoughts which only Livy can cipher out the meaning of, & some dark & bloody mystery out of the Widow Browning—& also some poetry of my own composition—& between the three I guess we'll "hive" the gentle reader. And I shall have in a lot of smart remarks made by both of you when you were teething (after the "load of hay" pattern) & I shall get up these remarks myself, so as to be sure that they are not insipid like the late Wm. L.'s (which I regard as altogether "too thin"). And I will put speeches into your maturer mouths which shall astonish the nations—profound remarks upon agriculture, commerce, diplomacy, war, chemistry, afghans for babies at $15 a day, geology, theology, cut-throat, painting, sculpture, niggers, poetry, politics—*every thing* that erudition loves & intellectuality revels in. And there shall be a picture of you two & Jim for a frontispiece, with your autographs underneath, which I will write myself, so that people can *read* them. And I will have pictures of the Spaulding girls (together with *their* regrets,) & pictures of Mr. & Mrs. Langdon & Hattie & the mocking-bird in a group, & a portrait of the late Jep engaged in his favorite study (landscape gardening)—& toward the end a handsome likeness of your grandmother, along with *her* letter announcing her exasperation at the said news. And away over at the extreme back-end of the book I shall wind up with a weeping & disconsolate picture of Theodore's friend with a basket, going for flying arbutus—& *"hoofing it,"* as Charley says.

There you are. *I'm* no compiler of Wm Lord Noyes bosh. When *I* get up memoirs I make the deceased get up too—at least turn over. How many copies do you want issued, young woman?

But my dears, it is my present hope that I shall be spared the sad office I have so banteringly assumed, by being already dust & ashes when "memoirs" of you shall have become possible & proper.

"Lovingly *your* Livy"—the very dearest words to me that ever illuminated paper & gave it a glory as of a vision. How the words seem to *nestle up* to me!—& put arms about me, & a loved head upon my shoulder, & the hymning of the angels in my heart! You *are* my Livy—& I am grateful that it is so, beyond all power of speech to express—& I pray God you may remain my Livy *always.*

I secured the rooms for you[5]—& felt all the time that I was doing a thing that somehow would prevent my seeing you. And so I was not cheerful over it. But I *must* see you. There are only one or two suits of rooms on the second (all stores on first, you know) & those are occupied by permanent families; but they will dig out a family, or, failing that, give you their best on the 3d floor.

I haven't half finished my letter, darling, but I suppose I ought to quit for to-night & snort & sneeze a while.

Give my love to all the household gods & goddesses. Good-night, little darling—blessings, & kisses & pleasant dreams.

Saml

Livy, I *love* you! And I've got a perfectly *awful* cold. Took to my bed in pure desperation, to-day. I was afraid to stay there, though —had to get up, & attend to business, anyhow. I am not going to take the slightest care of this cold till your throat is *well*. So there now! I shall take off my underclothes to-night; & to-morrow I shall not wear any socks. I will *not* get well till you do. So there now, again! I *love* you, Livy.

Chafing under his confinement and fretted by introspection, he wrote her in a self-tormenting mood—imagining that she was ordering him off to California on his long-projected trip, without a farewell visit to Elmira. As a matter of fact, he never saw California again, and it was largely her persuasion which caused the journey to be abandoned.

Wednesday Afternoon [*May* 19, 1869]

Livy dear, I *think* it is Wednesday, & yet I feel almost certain that it is as much as *Thursday*—though lying in bed the last day or two being a thing I have never been used to—& being alone, also, & the rain seeming never to cease its dreary dirges day or night—the time has so dragged, dragged, *dragged*, that when the lagging sun goes down at last it seems as if I cannot *remember* when it rose, it was such an age ago. So I try to *think* it is only Wednesday, though a *month* has surely drifted by in these long-drawn hours. I am tired of fretting & chafing. I will leave this bed

---

[5] Probably lodgings for the Langdons a month hence, for the Day-Hooker wedding.

to-morrow, sick or well. I am *not* sick enough to deem it impru-
dent, else I would not make so decided a determination.

If I am writing a foolish low-spirited letter, remember it is to
you *only*, & you will not betray me—you will not reveal its con-
tents. Otherwise I would deny myself the relief of writing, while
I am in such a depressed state. I expected to be in Elmira to-day
(or is it to-morrow?) but the first mention you made of my intended return was a little discouraging, & so I did not know what
to say, & said nothing, meaning to judge by subsequent events
whether—Well, somehow I can't get my thoughts straight—I am
all confused & blundering—I only know that in your last letter
there seems an intimation that I am not to see you before I go to
California—& yet I was counting so entirely upon the reverse of
this. Why Livy, I *can't* go away without seeing you. I am only
flesh & blood—I cannot do impossibilities. Livy dear, do not be
conventional with *me*—I am not with you. You manifest reserve.
Don't do that. Tell me whatever is in your mind, freely—& let it
be in your mind, above all things, that I am to see you before I go.
Livy, I am not prying into your secrets—I know you would not
accuse me of that—but it *did* seem uncharacteristic of you to
imply that I was coming & yet never once say "Come!" So I——I
thought upon the matter, & put myself in your place, & fancied
whether I would use decided language or not—& I knew I *would*!
Wherefore it seemed plain that Livy had something to say to me
which she did not say—& it was naughty, Livy darling, very
naughty. I thought when I first left that the same reasons which
made it proper & best for me to go would hold good longer than
an absence of two weeks; but still, in my selfish disregard of expediency & my longing to see you, I would have marched back at
the end of the fortnight, but that there was such an appalling
[reserve] lack of heartiness in your subsequent references to that
matter! Forgive me, Livy, if I hurt you—for you hurt *me* dreadfully. And we must give & take, dearie. Only I want to have the
most of the taking to do. But bless you, darling, I knew you had
reasons, & I accepted my fate with a fair degree of cheerfulness,
because of that full confidence & trust which I had & shall always
have in you. But I said, "She might *tell* me—for I am sure I can
bear Livy's decrees handsomely if she will only *trust* me." But this

last one I don't get over so easily. This thing of my going to California without seeing you, goes clear beyond my capabilities. *Entirely.* I honored your other implied wish—& it was no small sacrifice either—but this time, Livy, *what* am I to do? I surely thought I would be *rewarded* for this fortitude of mine, & I know I *deserve* it—but instead of rewarding me, you just as good as threaten me with a greater punishment! "Be good, sweet child"— remove this [negative] disability—tell me I may see you—& tell me *when*—for if I see California before I see you, I will see it not a day earlier than the millennium.—There, now!

Don't scold me, Livy dear. I am weak, & savage, & foolish by turns—& I chafe like any prisoner—& it is night, at last, & there is the eternal miserere of the rain. I'll get up & march down town tomorrow *sure*—for I *must* have somebody to talk to—I'm *full* of talk. I never wanted to hear Bliss talk till to-day—for he is worse than a clatter-mill when he gets started. But he brought my tea up himself a while ago (*tea*—that spoon-victuals for infants) & I thought I could listen to him forever. And now *he* is gone, sorrow catch him, & left me only the melancholy music of the rain. You will laugh at this, Livy, but I am not used to confinement, & it seems to make a baby of me. If my memory serves me I have been bedridden only [once] twice before in 23 years—cholera in St Louis 16 years ago—& 20 hours in Damascus 2 years ago. But I'll be out of this tomorrow, I'm pretty sure—I am *sure*. I would not be here now, but that I have achieved such a ghastly accession to my cold every time I have ventured out. Well, *I* never had such a cold before—& in strict confidence, between you & me, I never want another one like it. I haven't done anything for it, because Bliss isn't worth a cent for a nurse, & his wife is away on a visit. But when she comes home, in a day or two I—shall be well by that time.

Livy, in one of the first violences of this distemper, I abused Mrs. Corey in a letter to you, & now I beg your pardon for it—& I beg it in *earnest*, too. I ought to have been too thoughtful of your feelings to say harsh things to you about your friends—for it is a beautiful trait in your character that you love them so & stand up for them so loyally; & it seems strange to me that I who am so proud of you for it am yet capable of wounding you through that very trait.—I am a brute. I am very, very sorry, Livy, to have shown you this lack of respect, this want of deference. It has been in my mind very often, since. It is a pity that I cannot think harsh things of people without saying them to you, & so offending a heart that I would so much rather fill with happiness. Forgive me, Livy darling.

You see I am not trying to answer your letters (3 yesterday and to-day, thank you with all my heart, Livy)—I have no ability to write. You will let me wait till this exasperation of trying to scribble on a book in bed is no longer necessary—I know you will.

But here—this is all wrong. And from this moment I will not chafe any more—not *once*. I will accept the situation, & in the spirit of the sermon you sent me, say, "God's will be done." An easy thing to say, about such a trifle—but could I say it about things of real moment? I hope so. I do not know. One cannot tell till he is tried.

Good-night Livy. I am glad I warned you to keep this foolish screed to yourself, dearie. It has been better than medicine to me to write it—& the reason I don't tear it up is because I think we know each other well enough to not misunderstand each other dreadfully; & love each other well enough to bear with weaknesses & foolishnesses, & even wickednesses (of mine). (I could not apply those harsh terms to *you*, because it did not seem natural—& so my sentence broke down awkwardly.) (But I *do* love you well enough to bear with those things in you, if I saw them.)

And without any misgivings I mail this letter, which I would tear up if it were written to anybody else. You will not scoff, or get angry at any thing my disordered head has framed among its half-coherencies. Thanks for the book, the sermon & the Bible notes.

Good-night. God & his good angels keep you, darling.

SAM

Morning

I am up—& shall go down town [before I go back to bed—shall stay up] My cold is worse. Never mind—it will break today, maybe.

SAM

Some four days later Mark went into the country and paid a brief visit to East Windsor Hill, as guest of the aged novelist A. S.

Roe, whose son he had known in the Western years. His cold cured, Mark then set out for Elmira. He remained there until mid-June, when he accompanied the Langdons to Hartford for the wedding of Alice Hooker and John Day, with Livy in the rôle of bridesmaid. Afterwards, he lingered there briefly before following her to New York, and thence escorting her home to Elmira.

HARTFORD, *June* 21 [1869]

By the almanac, darling, this is the longest day in the year—& since you are gone from me I would know it to be the longest day without having to refer to the almanac. For I do miss you so much. "Old" Bliss says you are the prettiest girl he has seen for 2 years —& thinks he could venture to say longer, but he can't recollect further back than that. Young Bliss says it is his usual luck—when he finds a girl he wants, somebody else has already got her. He thinks there can't be any more like you—& I *know* it. You are the Ninth Statue—the Jim of the Ocean—you are the dearest, & the loveliest, & the *best* girl in all the world.

I don't think I shall accomplish anything by tarrying here, & so I shall be in New York tomorrow evening. Warner[6] says he wishes he could effect a copartnership with me but he doubts the possibility of doing it—will write me if anything turns up. Bromley of the Post[7] says the 5 owners of that paper are so well satisfied with the progress the paper is making that they would be loth to sell. He wants to talk with me again tomorrow morning. However, I am not anxious, for the Post is not quite as desirable property in my eyes as it is in theirs.

P.S. However, I believe I'll run out now & fill an appointment. Good-bye—in haste, my darling.

SAM

[6] Charles Dudley Warner, co-editor of the *Hartford Courant.*
[7] The *Hartford Post,* another prospect for Clemens's editorial ambitions. See his letter to Mrs. Langdon of [June] 23 in S. C. Webster, *Mark Twain, Business Man,* p. 105.

CHAPTER FIVE

Newspaper Days in Buffalo

SAMUEL CLEMENS spent most of the summer of 1869 with the Langdons. Before the end of July *The Innocents Abroad* was published, and by early autumn had advanced well along the road to best-sellerdom. Meanwhile near the beginning of August, Mark took Jervis Langdon's advice and his loan of $12,500, and bought a partnership in the *Buffalo Express*, thus canceling his earlier schemes respecting other newspapers in Cleveland, New York, or Hartford. On August 14 he took possession, with a certain satisfaction in returning to journalism at the top level of ownership, and in offering his fiancée and her family the hallmark of a career seemingly more substantial than that of lecturer and fledgling author.

He returned frequently from Buffalo to Elmira, and in the intervals sent a steady stream of letters to Livy.

[Buffalo Express] Office
7:30 A. M. *Thursday [August 19, 1869]*

My child, I believe you'll have to be obeyed at last—I don't see any easy way around it without having your fingers in my hair. And so at this moment I slash from this morning's paper everything of mine that is in it. Of course it don't take ten or twelve hours to write those twenty or thirty pages of MS., dearie, but it takes a deal of time to skim through a large pile of exchanges, because one gets interested every now & then & stops to read a while if the article looks as if it might be a good thing to copy. And then one is interrupted a good deal by visitors—& there is proof-reading to do & a great many little things that use up time—but it is an easy, pleasant, *delightful* situation, & I never liked anything better. I am grateful to Mr. Langdon for thinking of

Buffalo with his cool head when we couldn't think of any place but Cleveland with our hot ones. (Before I forget it, tell [him] I got his dispatch yesterday, but of course I never could have needed it, for I think She would not dare to write & print articles over his name, and I am particularly sure *I* wouldn't.) So you see, with all my work I do very little that is visible to the naked eye, & certainly not enough, visible or invisible, to hurt me. I am simply [running] working late at night in these first days until I get the reporters accustomed & habituated to doing things my way,—after that a very little watching will keep them up to the mark. I simply want to educate them to modify the adjectives, curtail their philosophical reflections & leave out the slang. I have been consulting with the foreman of the news room for two days, & getting *him* drilled as to how I want the type-setting done—& this morning he has got my plan into full operation, & the paper is vastly improved in appearance. I have annihilated all the glaring thunder-&-lightning headings over the telegraphic news & made that department look quiet & respectable. Once in two months, hereafter, when anything astounding *does* happen, a grand display of headings will attract immediate attention to it—but where one uses them *every day*, they soon cease to have any force. We are not astonished to hear a drunken rowdy swear, because he does it on great & trivial occasions alike—but when we hear a staid clergyman rip out an oath, we know it *means* something.

My own little darling, I clear forgot to write with a pen—forgive me this time & I will be more careful hereafter—I will, Livy.

Tell Charlie I am very grateful for his cordial family invitation to come, from the head even unto the tail of it—but I cannot tell, until tomorrow, whether I can do it or not.

Your little head is *always* right, honey. I *do* find it nearly impossible to keep my newspaper thoughts still on Sunday. But I will try to do better, darling.

I still don't know whether you get the paper or not—but I know it is sent. I have instructed them to send the Weekly to Hattie Lewis, also.

Good bye, my darling Livy, whom I love with all my whole heart, & whose spirit presence is never absent from my thoughts, but is the dear companion of my communings morning, noon & night. Peace & blessings & kisses, little sweetheart.

SAM

To Olivia Langdon

BUFFALO, *Aug.* 21, P.M. 1869

Darling, it is 9 o'clock, now, & you are aware that there are no kisses for us to-night. I feel more than half sorry I did not go to you, for I have not succeeded in doing the mass of work I had laid out for myself, for sitting up so late last night has kept me stupified all day. It is the last time I shall be out of bed at midnight. And this night I mean to catch up. I shall be in bed, Puss, before your dainty little figure is tucked between your sheets, this evening. Bless your precious heart, I wish I could see you. I am afraid this is going to be a pretty long week, without a glimpse of my darling. But then (D.V.) I shall put my arms about you next Friday evening & stay till Monday morning. You see I ought to be at my post by 8 o'clock every morning, & *fresh*—so I would have to return on Saturday night—& that was partly why I put off my visit this week. But Larned[1] says don't bother about that—he will do the work of both of us from 3 P.M. Friday till Monday noon whenever I want to go to Elmira—which is equivalent to getting out two editions of the paper alone. He is not a very bad fellow.

McWilliams[2] & I went down to the Lake after supper & had a row. I needed the exercise.

His wife sorts out my soiled linen, takes a list of it, delivers it to the washerwoman in my absence, returns it again & attends to the settlement of the bill—& Mac tells me she will cheerfully do any mending I may need. She is a very excellent young lady, & I like her very much.—Thanks to my darling's busy fingers, however, I haven't any mending to do, at present.

Among the books sent us to review was one called "Wedlock,"[3] which I siezed & read, intending to mark it & take it to you, but it was nothing but a mass of threadbare old platitudes & maudlin

---

[1] J. N. Larned, co-owner of the *Express*.

[2] Mark boarded with this family during his brief bachelorhood in Buffalo. McWilliams was also connected with the paper.

[3] S. R. Wells, *Wedlock; or, The Right Relation of the Sexes* (1869).

advice shoveled together without rhyme or reason, & so I threw it away & told Larned to embody that opinion in his notice (he was reviewing the books).

I wrote Redpath today, asking him to let me off entirely from lecturing in New England this season, for I would rather scribble, now, while I take a genuine interest in it, & I am *so* tired of wandering, & want to be still & rest.

That thief that wrote about the dead canary & sends me so much execrable music has found me out & is publishing extravagant puffs of me & mailing the papers to me, only marked, as usual. I shall offer a bounty for his scalp, yet. He is one of the most persistent & exasperating acquaintances I was ever afflicted with.[4]

Larned & I sit upon opposite sides of the same table & it is exceedingly convenient—for if you will remember, you sometimes write till you reach the middle of a subject & then run hard aground—you know what you *want* to say, but for the life of you you can't say—your ideas & your words get thick & sluggish & you are vanquished. So occasionally, after biting our nails & scratching our heads awhile we just reach over & *swap manuscript*—& then we scribble away without the least trouble, he finishing my article & I his. Some of our patchwork editorials of this kind are all the better for the new life they get by crossing the breed.

Little dearie, little darling, in a few minutes, after I shall have read a Testament lesson & prayed for us both, as usual, I shall be in bed. And I shall dream, both before & after I go to sleep, of the little flower that has sprung up in the desert beside me & shed its fragrance over my life & made its ways attractive with its beauty and turned its weariness to contentment with its sweet spirit. And I shall bless you, my darling, out of the fulness of a heart that knows your worth beyond the ken of any, even those that have been with you always; & out of the depths of a gratitude that owes to you the knowledge of what light is, where darkness was, & peace where turbulence reigned, & the beauty & majesty of love where a loveless soul sat in its rags before & held out its unheeded hand for charity.—Better than all others I understand you & ap-

---

[4] George W. Elliott, editor of the *Mohawk Valley Register*, author of "Bonny Eloise, the Belle of the Mohawk Vale," and other plaintive songs. He had been Mark's host at Fort Plain, N. Y., in December 1868, but his sentimental lyrics soon outraged Mark's sensibilities.

preciate you, for this it is the prerogative of love to attain to alone,
& therefore better than all others I can love you, & *do* love you, &
shall love you, always, my Livy.

Good night darling—& peaceful slumbers refresh you & ministering angels attend you.

SAM

"I'll *learn* to like button-hole flowers because Livy does," he
wrote her on September 2, after refusing on his last Elmira visit
to wear a boutonnière of tuberoses she had made for him. Characteristic is Mark's mingling of bland irony with tenderness in the
letter that follows:

BUFFALO, *Friday Eveg* [*September* 3], 1869

Oh no, my darling, you are making a wild mistake—I *do* love
to wear a button-hole bouquet, Livy, about the house, especially
& particularly when you make it for me. [I like them well] I do
not think I ever wore one until you taught me to like them, but
now, under your instructions I have learned to like them well
enough to make them for myself when I get a chance & you are
not by to do it for me.—At the Press Dinner out at Mr. Jewell's
a fortnight ago I decorated myself with a delicate & beautiful panzy
or two, & first one admired & followed suit & then another, until
presently every individual present had flowers in his button-hole,
& we wore them all the afternoon. And seeing how our tastes ran,
Mr. J. set his gardener quietly to work, & when we were ready to
leave, at night we were each presented with an elaborate bouquet.
No, dearie, I have such an invincible repugnance to show or display in a man's dress, or anything that has a snobbish air about it,
that I can't wear flowers in the street yet, but what I meant you
to understand, was, that I would break down my prejudice &
learn to do it to please *you*, dearie. That was all. Livy, in all my
experience I never saw an American in the street with flowers in
his button-hole but he happened to be a fellow who had a weak
spot about his head somewhere. Now you know, dearie, that that
will give a man a prejudice, bye-&-bye. It always brings San Francisco to my mind, & Geo. Ensign & Emperor Norton, who have

just about monopolized bouquet wearing in that city. If my memory serves me I did what I could to paint Ensign's portrait in my book—maybe as "M'sieu Gor-r-dong," but I am not sure. Any way, it closes by saying he does all he can to inspire the idea that he looks like Napoleon "& with an amount of gratitude entirely disproportioned to the favor done him, he *thanks* his Maker that he is *as* he is, & goes on enjoying his little life just the same as if he *had* really been deliberately designed & erected by the great Architect of the Universe!"[5] That is meant for Geo. Ensign & when I uttered it in a lecture on Venice in San Francisco there was a perceptible flutter all over the house, because they recognized the portrait—& poor George was present, though I didn't know he was there—only thought it likely he *would* be. He never appears anywhere, in the house or out of it, without his buttonhole bouquet—& so other people eschew them, to a great extent. Now darling, there are good, & great men, no doubt, who wear these flowers publicly, like George, but the awful majority are insufferable snobs. And there are good & great men, no doubt, who put an initial for their first name & spell their second out in full—but the awful majority of men who do that, will lie, & swindle & steal, just from a natural instinct. Livy dear, I am writing all this because it *is important*—it is not a trivial matter, in my eyes, that you should do anything for me & see me receive it tranquilly, or possibly shrinkingly, when my natural impulse ought to be to receive it with warm delight & gratitude, as another token of your love for me. I should not seem unenthusiastic at such a time without being able to give you a most ample & convincing reason for it.—And many a time I have remembered remorsefully how the knot of tube-roses which your loving fingers formed for me lay neglected on the library table simply because I had a silly prejudice against wearing them in the street—& I have been angry at myself & wished I could have the opportunity over again. My darling, I love the flowers as bouquets on the table, & am proud when I arrive at home & fancy they were put there for me, though

[5] "Emperor" Norton was a famous San Francisco eccentric with delusions of grandeur. In S. D. Woods, *Lights and Shadows of Life on the Pacific Coast* (1912), 128, Ensign is recalled as "the Beau Brummell of the town, the organizer of the Spring Valley Water Company." The satiric portrayal to which Mark here refers occurs in *The Innocents*, chap. xxiii.

I would never dare to *say* a word or seem to notice them lest I might discover to my chagrin that my vanity had led me astray & attributed to me an honor not intended for me. And I love the button-hole bouquets in the house, honestly—better than in the street, you will readily believe, by this time. Livy dear, you will hurt me if you neglect to decorate my button-hole hereafter—& I will do penance & wear a sunflower down street if you say so.

I am so disappointed. Redpath says he *can't* get me free from Boston & 2 or 3 other places—& so I submit, & have written him to let me out to lyceums far & near, & for half the winter or all of it—do with me as he chooses while the lecture season lasts. There was no way that was better. It isn't worth the bother of getting well familiarized with a lecture & then deliver it only half a dozen times. I considered the matter well, & concluded that I ought to have some money to commence married life with, & if I tried to take it out of the office I might fail to be able to pay the first note that falls due next August. And yet the distress of it is, that the paper will suffer by my absence, & at the very time that it ought to keep up its best gait & not lose the start we have just given it & have the long, hard pull of giving it a *new* start after a while. I feel sure that the money I make lecturing, the paper will lose while I am gone—but you see how I am situated. When I once start in lecturing I might as well consent to be banged about from town to town while the lecture season lasts, for it would take that shape anyhow.

But our marriage! That is where the shoe pinches *hard*, dearie. It will just suit *you* to put it off till spring, but it don't suit me. [I oppose more] However, I don't really think I shall have to talk any to speak of after the first of February, & so I shan't be delayed more than a month, after all. Last year I hadn't a great many appointments in February, & if the same is to be the case this time I won't talk *at all* in that month. I shall know about this matter shortly, through Redpath. Livy dear, have I done wisely, or foolishly? Two things demand that the season shall stop as early as possible—my desire to bring you home as my wife; & the interest of the paper. Both touch me as being urgent. Tell me all you think, Livy darling.

Another of those anti-monopoly thieves sent in a long gratuitous advertisement to-night, about coal "for the people" at $5.50 a ton—& I have deposited it under the table. The effrontery of these people transcends everything I ever heard of. Do they suppose we print a paper for the fun of it? This man Denther sent in just such a thing the other day, & I left that out. The other papers insert both of them for nothing. Day before yesterday there was a sneaking little communication in one of the other papers wondering why the Express had become so docile & quiet about the great coal monopoly question. If Mr Denther don't go mighty slow I will let off a blast at him some day that will lift the hair off his head & loosen some of his teeth. Good-bye little sweetheart—I've lost my temper, now.

SAM

The obvious inference of his fellow-journalists in Buffalo, as he implies in the last paragraph of the letter above, was that Mark had given hostages to fortune. For the Anthracite Coal Association, a kind of regional cartel for keeping up the price of coal, consisted of J. Langdon & Company and the Delaware, Lackawanna & Western railway. Mark's loyalty to persons always transcended his comprehension of business principles, as he demonstrated many years later in defending Standard Oil against all comers because its ruthless Henry H. Rogers had befriended him in an hour of need.

BUFFALO, *Sept.* 8, 1869

Livy, my precious little darling, I am as happy as a king, now that it is settled & I can count the exact number of days that are to intervene before we are married. I am full of thankfulness, & the world looks bright & happy ahead. On the fourth day of February, one year after the date of our engagement, we shall step together out into the broad world to tread its devious paths together till the journey of life is done & the great peace of eternity descends upon us like a benediction. We shall never be separated on earth, Livy; & let us pray that we may not in Heaven. This 4th of February will be the mightiest day in the history of our lives, the holiest, & the most generous toward us both—for it makes of two fractional lives a whole; it gives to two purposeless lives a work, & doubles the strength of each [to do] whereby to perform it; it gives to two questioning natures a reason for living, & something to live for; it will give a new gladness to the sunshine, a new fragrance to the flowers, a new beauty to the earth, a new mystery to life; & Livy it will give a new revelation to love, a new depth to sorrow, a new impulse to worship. In that day the scales will fall from our eyes & we shall look upon a new world. Speed it!

I have written to Redpath that my lecture-tour must come to a permanent close a week or ten days before the end of January, & when I hear from him, if he has made no appointments after Jan. 15, I will not let him make any. I ought to have the whole month, if I can get it. I am booked for Newark, N.J., Dec. 29.

It seems a dreadfully long time till Feb. 4, dearie, but I am glad we are to have that day, for it will always be pleasant to keep our engagement & wedding anniversaries together. I would rather have that day than any in the 365, for it will be doubly dear to me, & be always looked forward to as one peculiarly & sacredly blessed—the day about which the most precious memories of my life have been concentrated. We can always prepare for it weeks ahead & keep it in state.

Livy darling, I ought not to have told you about Charlie's trip,[6] maybe, & yet after all, I ought, for we *must* begin to do something for that boy. It is nearly time for him to have finished his wild oats (though he will *not* cease to sow them for six or eight years yet unless he gets married sooner). If he is to be married a year hence there is no great need of solicitude, but still there is some need. There is only one uncomfortable feature about him, & that is his disposition to dishonor his father's wishes under shelter of absence. Most boys do that, & so he is not worse than his race—but most boys *shouldn't* do it, for it is a bad foundation to build upon. I suspect that the most promising course will be to set Ida[7] to reforming him. Judging by my experience, you energetic & persistent little task-mistress, if any [thing] body can change his style of conduct, it is the darling that has her nest in

[6] On September 30, 1869 Charles Langdon commenced a trip around the world, via Utah, Nevada, and California. His companion was Professor D. R. Ford of Elmira College.

[7] Ida Clark, his fiancée, whom he eventually married, on October 12, 1870.

his heart. I gave Charlie a scorching lecture on this fault of his, two months ago, & he seriously promised reform—but he needs [a lecture] a reminder every day, or else he is sure to drift backward. I am sorry I made my darling sad about it. Don't be sad, dearie, Charlie will come out all right, yet. It would be an unnatural marvel if Charlie were a better boy than he is. Let us not expect extravagant things of the fellow. He is another sort better & manlier than ninety-nine out of a hundred boys in his situation in life. Now if you knew boys as well as I do, sweetheart, you would know that as well as I do. Let us do the rascal justice, Livy. I suppose *I* was a better boy at his age, but then you know I—well I was an exception, you understand—my kind don't turn up every day. We are very rare. We are a sort of human century plant, & we don't blossom in everybody's front yard.

*　　　*　　　*

Since I wrote that last line I have read column after column of proof, & now it is so late that I must stop talking with Livy & go home to bed. It has rained all day & I suppose is raining yet, & I told Jo. Larned to stay at home after supper & be a comfort to his wife & I would sit up & do the work for both—though there wasn't a great deal to do, for that fellow works straight along all day, day in & a day out, like an honest old treadmill horse. I tell him I wish I had his industry & he had my sense.

Good-night my darling little wife, idol of my homage & my worship, & the peace of the innocent abide with you.

SAM

In the morning—(got your letter)—O the darling little traducer!

. . . When I said "the country," I mean *America*. But it was natural for you to think I was malicious, but I wasn't, honey—I bear Ishmael not the least malice—certainly none that I would express in an undignified way. Now I kiss you & tell you the mistake you made was perfectly natural to one who knows Ishmael had abused me in print.

Darling, I propose to start to Elmira Friday night at 11—& start back at same hour on Monday night. Is my sweet heart answered. I kiss my darling good-bye, now, till Saturday morning.

CHAPTER SIX

To the Road Again

NEVER patient under routine, Clemens seems early to have grown bored with his editorial duties in Buffalo. In early October he finally solved the problem of divided interests by taking a leave of absence from the *Express*, to settle for almost a month in Elmira, absorbed in his love for Livy and in preparation for a grueling lecture season which he had undertaken under James Redpath's management. It opened in Pittsburgh, and from there he dispatched the next letter to Livy—written on twenty-one sheets torn from a small diary.

It is a long but blithe letter. His story of the unsuccessful lecturer is told in Mark's best manner, and his savage outburst against spoiled brats recalls the ferocity of one of his earliest San Francisco pieces, "Those Blasted Children."

11 P.M. PITTSBURGH *Oct.* 30 [1869]

LIVY DARLING—[We] I have just this moment returned & gone to bed.

We had a pleasant time of it. They came for me at 7:30, & we went to a private room in a restaurant & had an oyster supper in a quiet, comfortable, sensible way—no wine, no toasts, no speeches —nothing but conversation. (Though it *was* appalling to have 30 newspaper men lay down their napkins with the last course & gather their chairs together in front of me, a *silence* following— for that silence naturally had the effect of suggesting that I was expected to do the talking—a thing which was not meant at all. Still, it was a little startling.)

During the evening, a dry, sensible genius, a Mr. Smythe, told his experiences as a lecturer. He said:

"A year ago, I was ass enough to go to Europe. When I came back I was ass enough to think I was stocked with knowledge

about Europe that the public would like to hear. I expected they
would be calling on me for a lecture, & so hurried to get ready.
I wrote my lecture in the third story of a printing office in the
intervals between calls for "copy," & I judged it was a pretty
creditable effort. I said to myself, I can do this sort of thing just
as well as Mark Twain did—& if I had his house to hear me, I
could show them. Then I waited for the flood—the freshet of
calls from the lyceums. It was a good opportunity to wait—a
singularly good one—it never has ceased to be. I am still waiting.
I did not get any calls. I could not understand it. But I knew the
people were suffering for the lecture, & so I quit bothering about
calls, & went & took the Academy on my own hook. At the
appointed time I was on hand, & so were eleven other people.
At half past 8, observing that the rush had ceased & that the
audience were unquestionably assembled, I stepped on to the
stage with my MSS, & for an hour & a half I instructed those 11
people. I was "out" $75 on the experiment. A friend met me a
day or two afterward & said he had heard I had been out lecturing.
I said yes, I was out yet.

I waited again for calls. They did not come. I then cast my
eye upon East Liberty, a suburb of Pittsburgh, I knew they were
aching to have me there but daren't invite me. And so I went
there on my own hook. I paid $35 for the use of the theatre. At
half past 7 I took a retired stand opposite & watched. At 8 or a
little after, the first great wave of relief swept over my soul—I saw
a man enter the hall. I went into a saloon & drank to him. Bye
& bye I saw two men go in at once. I took a drink to them. After
a little a carriage drove up & the estimable Mrs. Swisshelm, of
whom you may have heard, went in. I drank to her. At 8.30
nobody else having come, I drank to the absent.

Then I went over & read my MSS. drearily, & was absolutely
happy, even cheerful, once—when I got through.

Then I rested for a while & at length determined to go up to
Steubenville, O., & give those people a taste of my quality. When
I got there I looked wistfully about the street corners for my
posters, but I did not see any. I hunted up the bill poster & he
explained that it had been rainy, & he had refrained from posting the bills because they would not stick. I went to the village

newspaper man who had been advertising me, & he encouraged me to believe there would be a slim attendance. He was a man of very good judgment. At 8:30 nobody had come, & for the sake of economy I discharged the doorkeeper, & went off with the journalist to take a drink. I could not get rid of him, somehow— on account of one of us being in the other's debt, I thought. At 9 we went back & found one man in the house. I felt a little cheered, for this was nearly as large an audience as I had ever had. I began my lecture but when I was half through a thought occurred to me & I asked that man who he was. He said he was the janitor. "Then I suppose you do not pay?"

"No."

So I closed the lecture at that point.

Subsequently I received my first invitation. This began to look like business. It was to go to Greensburg & lecture for the benefit of the Methodist Mite Society—$25 & expenses. I went with a light heart. Some newspaper friends volunteered to go with me— & they are a class of people who are given to drink. They were companionable, but expensive.

We arrived in a rain storm—& very dark. The Rev. Mr. Noble received me in considerable state & walked me to the Court House. At 8:30 an audience of nearly 13 persons had assembled— it seemed a sort of ovation—I was not accustomed to these multi- tudinous manifestations of popular favor. The Rev. Noble intro- duced me in a right pretty speech, & then I delivered my lecture. It was complimented a good deal, & the Rev. Noble was so kind as to say they might want me again in case the Society survived this ordeal. The Secretary then came forward & said there had not been as large an attendance as he had hoped for & so the finances were correspondingly meagre, but if five dollars would be any object to me, a draft for that amount—

I begged him to let the whole sum go into the coffers of the Mite Society, & I hope that in its sudden acquisition of wealth it would not grow proud, but would sometimes think of its benefactor.

Since then I have thought seriously of forsaking the lecture field, & will remark that my lecture, unmutilated, & with all the places for applause legibly marked in it, is for sale."

I walked all around town this morning with a young Mr. Dean, a cousin of Wm D. Howells, editor of the *Atlantic Monthly*. He kindly offered to give me a letter of introduction to Mr. Howells, but I thanked him sincerely & declined, saying I had a sort of delicacy about using letters of introduction, simply because they place the other party in the position of being obliged to take the stranger by the hand whether or not & show him civilities which he may not feel like showing him, or at least may not feel like it at that particular time. He may have engagements—business— the headache—twenty circumstances may conspire to make the entertainment of a guest a hardship. I prefer to be casually intro- duced, or to call ceremoniously with a friend—then the afflicted party is perfectly free to treat me precisely as he chooses, & no harm done.

Many gentlemen have called on me to-day. Mr. E. B. Coolidge, formerly of the Navy—met him once when I was visiting Admiral Thatcher on board his flagship, at San Francisco. W. A. Taylor, of the *Post*. Asa L. Wangaman (knew him in Nevada); A. H. Lane, Jno. G. Holmes, Wm L. Chalfant, Wm. C. Smythe of the *Dispatch;* W. W. Thomson; Wm. N. Howard; Geo. W. Dean; O. T. Bennett of the *Commercial*; & a number of gentlemen who came with one or another of the above & sent no cards. So they have dropped in one after another all day long & have made the time busy & pleasant. I am to go to church to-night with Mr. Chalfant.

Wangaman made me go to his house to see his wife. I knew her in Nevada, too. I staid 15 minutes, & would have remained to supper, for the table looked tempting, but their young boy of 7 is one of your petted smarties whose entire mind is given to climbing around & getting where he can intercept your vision & attract your attention—industriously watching your eye & chang- ing position so as to intercept it again if you change the direction of your glance—a child with a feverish desire to do something surprising & win the notice of the stranger—a creature that parades its toys & asks its mother questions concerning them which it is plain are merely asked to compel the stranger's attention to them & gouge a remark out of him—a soiled & nasty imp that sings nursery stuff in a loud & still louder & louder key as the conversation rises to meet the emergency, & does it all to win coveted admiration—a small whelp that says those ineffably [stupid] flat things which mothers treasure up & repeat & regard as "smart" things, purring & smiling blandly the while—a little pug-nosed, mop-headed, sore-toed, candy-smeared beast that paws after things at table, & & spills its coffee, & eats mashed potatoes with its fingers, & points & clamors for "some of that"—a sinful tiresome, homely, hateful, execrable *nuisance* at all times & in all places whatsoever!

I may be a brute. Doubtless I am. But such is my opinion of this breed of children, nevertheless. The "four-year-old" department at Harper's Monthly is written in vain for *me*.

Well, Livy dear, I was afraid that brat would be at supper— Mothers who rear such prodigies always like to have them on exhibition—& so I first started to *ask,* & then, recognizing that that would not be strictly polite, I simply declined supp & returned to the hotel.

One of the newspaper gentlemen who called today was Mr. Bennett of the *Commercial*, a good fellow, modest & pleasant. He wants to make a synopsis of my lecture tomorrow night, or report it in full. I told him a synopsis of a humorous lecture holds up all the jokes, in a crippled condition for the world to remember & so remembering them hate them if ever they hear that lecturer repeat them in solemn & excruciating succession one after the other.

And I said to take the points out of a humorous lecture was the same as taking the raisins out of a fruit cake—it left it but a *pretense* of a something it was *not,* for such as came after.

And further, the charm of a humorous remark or still more, an elaborate succession of humorous remarks, *cannot* be put upon paper—& whosoever reports a humorous lecture *verbatim*, necessarily leaves the *soul* out of it, & no more presents that lecture to the reader than a person presents a *man* to you when he ships you a corpse.

I said synopses injure—they do harm, because they travel ahead of the lecturer & give people a despicable opinion of him & his production.

I said my lecture was my property, & no man had a right to

take it from me & print it, any more than he would have a right to take away any other property of mine. I said "I showed you what time it was by my watch a while ago, & it never occurred to me that you might pull the hands off it so that it would be only a stupid blank to the next man that wanted the time—but yet I see you meditate pulling the hands off my lecture with your synopsis & making it a blank to future audiences. You see me sitting here perfectly serene although I know you could walk off with my valise while I am talking with these other gentlemen— but won't steal my valise because it is property—my property. Now *do* take the valise & let the lecture alone. I own both of them—I *alone*. Take the valise—it is only worth a hundred dollars—the lecture is worth ten thousand."

This was all perfectly friendly & good-natured, of course. I was trying to show him how in the wrong he was—I had no desire to offend him, & I didn't.

But Livy, if his chief orders him to report the lecture he can't help himself—for although the law protects rigidly the property a shoe maker contrives with his hands, it will not protect the property I create with my brain.

I went to church & heard a man from a distance preach a sermon without notes—which was well—but in a frozen, monotonous, precise & inflectionless way that showed that his discourse was a carefully memorized production. There was something exceedingly funny about this bald pretense of delivering an off-hand speech—& something exceedingly funny, too in a full grown man "speaking a piece" after the manner of a little schoolboy. His gestures were timid—never could finish one—always got scared & left it half made. He evidently had the places marked, & knew how he wanted to make them but he didn't dare.

Oh, the music was royal! It was superb! It was the very ecstasy of harmony! With the first grand explosion of rich sounds, I started from my reverie & thought, Heavens! What a choir we've got here! And I looked up, & there were only 4 singers! But how their voices did match & blend together & how they did peal out at times—& then languish & die—& then swell upward again & reel away through the charmed atmosphere in a drunken ecstasy of melody!

My! what a soprano singer! When I thought the very hair would stand up straight with delight, & looked again & wondered if that grand flood of mellow sound *did* issue from so small a constitution—& how it could come with such utter absence of effort.

And when they sang "O'er the Dark Waves of Galilee" I didn't feel as if I *could* sit still. What worship was in the music! How it preached, how it pleaded! And how earthy & merely human seemed the clergyman's poor, vapid declamation! *He* couldn't make us comprehend Christ desolate & forsaken, but the music did!

Oh, wouldn't Hattie Lewis have stood on her head if she had been there! Livy I never heard anything like it in all my life.

And do you know there are some people whose complacency *nothing* can subdue. In the midst of the beautiful music a skinny old cat sitting next me tuned her pipe & began to yowl. Well I came as near as anything to banging her over the head with a pew. Now *was* there ever such effrontery as that woman's.

The second tune was a little too complicated for her & I had a rest. On the third, I waited in pure torture all through the first verse, & felt happy, satisfied, safe—but on the second the venerable screech-owl came to the rescue again & filed her saw all through the hymn.

The young man who went with me got tired of the sermon early. He evidently was not used to going to church, though he talked as if he was. Toward the last he got himself down till he was resting on the end of his backbone; & then he propped his 2 knees high against the pew in front of him; he stroked his thighs reflectively with his palms; he yawned; he started twice to stretch, but cut it short & looked dejected & regretful; he looked at his watch 3 times; & at last he got to belching.* I then threw him out of the window. (1 P.M. Good night & God bless & preserve you, my own darling.)

SAM

The next is apparently the first love-letter from Livy to survive. It was addressed to Mark at Danvers, Massachusetts, in the thick of his New England itinerary.

*—'Tisn't elegant, but there isn't any other, Livy.

Some of it concerns the famed incubus of "the Tennessee land," bought by the father of Orion and Sam Clemens, in expectation of huge distant profit. It never proved more than a mirage to the family. But in 1869 the report of coal deposits on it led the Clemenses in St. Louis to hope that Jervis Langdon might buy or develop their interests. As a letter written by Sam to Pamela on November 9 shows, he renounced his stake in this venture in favor of Orion and their mother, but at the same time declined to put much pressure on his prospective father-in-law.

As Livy understood from Sam, Orion was equally conspicuous for high-mindedness and ineptitude. Without Sam's generous financial support, now and in the years ahead, his mother, Orion, and Orion's wife would have been gravely impoverished. It is good to find that Livy's spirit of openhandedness matched her future husband's.

Nov. 13th 1869—ELMIRA

My dear, I am sorry that there has gone no letter to you today, but it has been a very busy day and I could not find the time to write, and now I must send you only a few lines, as it is rather late—

Sunday morning—

I was too stupid to write last night after I had commenced so I put by the letter and went to bed—

I read Father what you wrote about the Tennessee land, he said, it was too bad for your brother to be such a drag to you, he did not make any remark about his working the land, and I did not like to press the matter because I know that he has a good deal on his hands—more than he ought to have, but if you think that I better bring it before him again, I will do so—I am very sorry that your brother is troubled, and very thankful that you are prospered, glad on your account and glad because you can help others—God gives diversities of gifts, he has not given to your brother money making wisdom, but from what you say, he has given him a beautiful spirit never the less—as God prospers us we will not forget Him and allow ourselves to blame those who seem to use less judgment in getting on in this world, but

will help just as many people to live their burdens as we are able
—You are a good youth to say what you have to your brother
about helping him to the money when he cannot get along
longer without it because I know that while you are in debt[1] you
do not know very well how to spare money, but it is the gifts
that really cost us something that are most valuable in Gods
sight—We will be the more economical in our way of living, I
will look out that I get our dresses and gloves and the like, and
we shall be able to help them on—I am glad that your work is
doing so well, for two very obvious reasons—

I am so happy so perfectly at rest in you, so proud of the true
nobility of your nature—it makes the whole world look so bright
to me that I cannot but have a great desire to do all I can to lift
the burdens from those who are carrying a heavy load—I feel
that I have no burden, that I am so richly cared for, that I cannot but have a tender yearning for those whose backs seem almost
broken with the heavy load under which it is bent—we are
happy, my dear, therefore we are the better able and must be the
more ready to help others—and I know that you are, I wakened
this morning, and looked out on the winter landscape which I
so dearly love, with the comfort and beauty of my home, with the
love of those here and yours which I know to be true and steady
even when separated from me, and I felt like dancing, that
seemed the most natural way to express it—I believe dancing
and singing is a true way to give *praise* to God—our whole
natures seem to enter in then—

It snowed nearly all night last night and this morning the
ground and trees were beautifully arrayed in their white garments—

We are all delighted that you are to be with us on New Year's
day, I trust that no adversity may come to you—

I was indeed proud and happy that you succeeded so well in
Boston[2] —

Don't let your sister stay away from our wedding because she
fancies her clothes are not fine enough—We want *her,* and her
daughter here we don't mind about their clothing.

[1] He still owed $12,500 on the Buffalo *Express* deal, along with other debts.
[2] He had sent her press reports of what he described confidentially as "a handsome success," on his first appearance in Boston, November 10.

I had a perfectly delightful letter yesterday from Mrs. Brooks she is as lovely and charming as ever—

I would like to write on but I must close this and get ready for Sunday school—

Now and always lovingly Livy

The tribulations of a visiting lion are amusingly set forth by Mark in his next letter.

CLINTON, MASS. *Nov.* 15 [1869]

LIVY DARLING—I had to submit to the customary & exasperating drive around town in a freezing open buggy this morning (at Norwich) to see the wonders of the village.

(Mem.—They always consist of the mayor's house; the ex-mayor's house; the house of a State Senator; house of an ex-governor; house of a former member of Congress; the public school with its infernal architecture; the female seminary; paper mill or factory of some kind or other; the cemetery; the court house; the plaza; the place where the park is going to be—& I must sit & shiver & stare at a melancholy grove of skeleton trees & listen while my friend gushes enthusiastic statistics & dimensions. All towns are alike—all have the same stupid trivialities to show, & all demand an impossible interest at the suffering stranger's hands. Why *won't* these insane persecutors believe me when I protest pleadingly that I *don't* care two cents for all the thrilling wonders the village can boast.—

(How I gloat in secret when one of those people regrets that I cannot "remain over" & see his accursed village! And how unblushingly I repeat the threadbare lie that I am sorry!

(After the natural wonders are all visited, then we have to call on other inanimated wonders with dull faces, but with legs to them that show them to be human: the mayor; the richest man; the wag of the village (who instantly assails me with old stale jokes & humorous profanity); the village editor—& a lot more of people I take no possible interest in & don't want to see. And when by some divine accident one of them isn't at home what a fervent prayer of thankfulness rises up in my heart!)

I only have to submit to these inflictions when I am the guest of somebody & cannot refuse to suffer in return for his hospitality. When I am paying my own bills at a hotel, I talk out & say No *Sir*—not any village wonders for the subscriber, if you please.

Here I am in a hotel—the Clinton House—& a villainous one it is—shabby bed, shabby room, shabby furniture, dim lights—everything shabby & disagreeable.

This message is unsigned. A short letter written the next day from Holyoke, of small intrinsic interest, seems to have been mailed with the above; a single valediction did for both.

HARTFORD, *Nov.* 24/69

I *am* perplexed—for I wonder where my darling is. She keeps writing me indefinitely about going to New York, this week, but I can't make out what part of this week she means. She is a dear little—rascal. But I love her—I love her with a stronger, prouder & profounder affection every day as the time goes by. One year ago, lacking a day, my life was glorified with the gladdest surprise that had ever burst upon it—since that moment my Livy has been all in all to me. I have now known almost ten months of restful happiness, a satisfied tranquillity, a broadening charity, a more generous view of men & motives, an unaccustomed stirring within me of religious impulses, not grand and strong, it is true, but steady & hopeful—the subdued & far-off cadences of approaching music, as it were. A new, strange, beautiful life these ten months have given me; a broadening & aspiring life, a life worth ages of the desert existences that went before it. And therefore how can I help loving the noble woman who has made this paradise for me & [beautified] adorned it with her enduring love & the gentle graces of her nature? I *do* love you, darling, with all the energy of a heart starved for love these many & many years. And its passion-torments are left behind, its rocks & shoals are passed, its restless rivulets are united, & so, in one stately river of Peace it holds its unvexed course to that sea whose further tides break upon the shores of eternity.

We have had a pleasant day & a pleasant evening, child. I called at Mr. Hooker's a moment & saw him—then went over to Warner's & visited with him & his wife an hour. She sent a world of love & loving messages to you which I ship to you in bulk to save port dues. I like her.

Warner soon talked himself into such a glow with the prospect of what we could do with the Courant now that I have achieved such a sudden & sweeping popularity in New England, that he forgot we had not yet come to any terms, & fell to appointing the work I should do on the paper. The same way this evening at Twichell's, in another long private conversation. I told him I would not leave the Express unless the boys were willing, & I felt sure they would not be—& that I would not ask them to give me as much for my interest as I gave for it, for they should not say I left without benefiting them by leaving—further, by his own showing, the only Courant fifth I could get they had foolishly bought from a partner & paid $4,000 more for it than they considered it worth, in order to get rid of him, & borrowed the money to do it with (unpaid yet—a hungry debt of near $30,000). I said it would be paying the Express $5,000 to let me go, & paying the Courant $29,000 for $25,000-interest to take me in— $9,000 altogether to get hold of an interest far less valuable & lucrative than my Express interest—& all I should get for it would be, the pleasure of living in Hartford among a most delightful society, & one in which you & I both would be supremely satisfied. I said if I were absolutely worth $35,000 I would pay $9,000 in a moment for the sake of getting ourselves comfortably situated, but unfortunately I wasn't worth any such sum. I said I would do nothing till I talked with you. He wanted me to talk with Mr. Langdon & write the result, & I said I would.

Three times I have met Sam Bowles, of the Springfield Republican, & notwithstanding he wrote me a note saying I must always sit at his table when in Springfield, I was ashamed to find myself calling him in my secret heart a born & bred *cur*, every time. And notwithstanding my shame, I could not help comforting myself with the reflection that my judgment of men was oftener right than wrong. The other day we met him, & afterward I said, "Nasby, I never have heard anybody say a word against Sam. Bowles, & he always treats me politely, but I cannot get rid of the conviction that he is a dog"—& Nasby said a very great many people had very convincing proofs that Mr. Bowles was exactly that. Then I remembered his treatment of Richardson, a circumstance I had forgotten, since Bliss told me the other day. And now it came out, confidentially, from Twichell to-night, that last June both Hawley & Warner were full of the idea of having me on the Courant, but ran to consult Bowles, the great journalistic oracle, & he advised them not to do it—& in their simplicity they took in good faith the word of a man who had just come from California & knew what a card I was there & consequently what a trump I could make myself here. Livy darling I guess we couldn't pull loose all the Buffalo anchors easily, & so we may as well give up Hartford—but my gracious, wouldn't I like to tilt that Courant against the complacent Springfield Republican & make that journal sick? I think so.

My pet, I had to give up Mrs. Perkins. I slopped out there in the mud to-day (it rained like all possessed, yesterday, but held up & did not interfere with my audience at night). When I reached her house she had been gone to the city about fifteen minutes. I was very sorry, but it couldn't be helped.

Didn't see Alice Day—am afraid I didn't right thoroughly want to, though maybe I might have been mistaken.

I have ordered Twichell to stand by & assist Mr. Beecher to marry us, & I told him you wanted it so. It's powerful expensive, but then we'll charge him for his board while he is there.

Bless your old heart I wish I could see you. Rather all you than anybody in the world. I *would*, Livy, old sweetheart. I would, indeed. Because I love you. I love you with *all* my heart, Livy darling.

Good-bye, & the peace of God rest upon you now & always, darling.

SAM

In the next letter, one of the tenderest passages concerns the eternal miracle of love—the seemingly improbable tangency of two diverse lives, that in boyhood and girlhood lay so far apart, unconscious of their future destiny. In a similar vein of sentiment he wrote Livy on January 10, 1870: "I shall love the silk quilt, not only because our mother gave it to you, but because it will always preserve that old dress that was so dear to me. And we never can sleep under it, darling, & forget the old pleasant days that were ours when it was still 'in the flesh,' if I may so speak. We will cherish the quilt well, & help it hoard its memory treasures. It must be sacred to our bed—guests cannot have it. And I am very glad, too, that it has in it something that knew you when you were a little girl—for I always feel a sense of loss, when I reflect that *I* never knew you when you were little."

Through an error, however, he wrote the following birthday letter to Livy one day after her real anniversary.

Boston, *Sunday M.* [November 28, 1869]

Livy darling, I thank dear Mrs. Susie very much for helping to get you ready to come to me. Anybody that helps in that is my good friend, & I in turn his humble servant. The day approaches, old fellow! Only nine weeks, & then—! Hurrah! Speed the day!

You are with Mrs. Brooks to-day, I suppose, & consequently happy. To-morrow morning I shall telegraph her to know where you will be on Wednesday. If at her house, I shall stop at the Everett (or may be at the Albemarle) & run up & see you till noon, & then bid you good-bye until next day, for you would all be in bed by the time I got back from Brooklyn.[3] But if you are at the St. Nicholas I shall stop there till 2 P M, & then you shall sit up & wait till I return from Brooklyn.

To-morrow evening at 6:30 I must run out to Newtonville, half an hour's journey by rail, & lecture, returning here at 10 P.M. Tuesday I shall run down to Thompsonville & talk till half past 8, & then trot along about [an hour] half an hour & sit up with Twichell at Hartford till after midnight, & then take a sleeping car for New York, arriving at 5 o'clock Wednesday morning.

This is your birthday darling, & you are 24. May you treble your age, in happiness & peace, & I be with you to love you & cherish you all the long procession of years! I have kept this day & honored this anniversary alone, in solitary state—the anniversary of an event which was happening when I was a giddy school-boy a thousand miles away, & played heedlessly all that day & slept heedlessly all that night unconscious that it was the mightiest day that had ever winged its viewless hours over my head—un-

[3] On December 1 he lectured for the Brooklyn Library Association.

conscious that on that day, two journeys were begun, wide as the poles apart, two paths marked out, which, wandering & wandering, now far & now near, were still narrowing, always narrowing toward one point & one blessed consummation, & these the goal of twenty-four years' marching!—unconscious I was, in that day of my heedless boyhood, that an event had just transpired, so tremendous that without it all my future life had been a sullen pilgrimage, but with it that same future was saved!—a sun had just peered above the horizon which should rise & shine out of the zenith upon those coming years & fill them with light & warmth, with peace & blessedness, for all time.

I have kept the day alone, my darling—we will keep it together hereafter, God willing. My own birthday comes Tuesday, & I must keep that alone also, but it don't matter—I have had considerable experience in that.

Twichell gave me one of Kingsley's most tiresomest books—"Hypatia"—& I have tried to read it & can't. I'll try no more. But he recommended Chas. Reade's "Hearth & Cloister" & I bought it & am enchanted. You shall have it if you have not read it. I read with a pencil by me, sweetheart, but the book is so uniformly good that I find nothing to mark. I simply have the inclination to scribble "I love you, Livy" in the margin, & keep on writing & re-writing "I love you Livy—I love my Livy—I worship my darling"—& bless your dear heart I *do* love you, love you, *love* you, Livy darling. Livy mine—but it won't do to write it in books where unsanctified eyes may profane it—& so, you see, sweetheart, there is nothing to mark.

Livy my precious sweetheart, I have received all your letters & my uneasiness is gone—got 4 in one day & what a blessed feast it was! I was glad that it had happened so, since it brought so ample a pleasure.

I remember Miss Bateman—she was a gentle-looking little school girl of 12 or 13 when I used to see her in her front yard playing, every day.

And now, if my child is tired reading this—which I am proud to say I don't believe she is—I will write some other letters. Thank goodness I shall kiss you, Wednesday, right on your

blessed little mouth. And so good-bye, my own loved & honored
Livy.

SAML

Mark stopped in New York City en route from a lecture at
Germantown on the 9th to one in Mount Vernon, New York,
on the 10th. There he had met the Langdons. To his family he
wrote on December 15: "I left Livy & the folks at the St. Nicholas,
where they will remain a week or so buying Livy's 'trowsers'
(trousseau) as Mr. Langdon calls it." Her father's solicitude on
these shopping trips pleased Livy, and in turn her fiancé. To Mrs.
Fairbanks Mark related that "when dresses arrived even at 11 at
night he would not go to bed till he had opened all the packages
& seen that everything was all right . . . & so touched Livy with
this loving unbending to her little womanly affairs that she could
not tell me of it without moistened eyes."

Mark meanwhile continued his swing back into New England.

PAWTUCKET, R.I., 14th [December, 1869]

My child, I was thunderstruck at getting no letter from you in
Boston to-day. It seemed to me that I had neither seen nor heard
from you for many a day—but now that I come to count up I am
astonished to find that I saw you, touched you, held you in my
arms, kissed you, only four days ago. This will give you an idea
of how immensely long a lecture season seems. A 3-month season
seems a year ordinarily—& when you come to add absence from
one's sweetheart, it becomes a sort of lifetime.

Had a talk with Fred Douglass, to-day, who seemed exceedingly
glad to see me—& I certainly was glad to see *him* for I do so admire
his "spunk." He told the history of his child's expulsion from
Miss Tracy's school, & his simple language was very effective. Miss
Tracy said the pupils did not want a colored child among them—
which he did not believe, & challenged the proof. She put it at
once to a vote of the school, and asked "How many of you are
willing to have this colored child be with you?" And they *all* held
up their hands! Douglass added: "The children's hearts were
right." There was pathos in the way he said it. I would like to
hear him make a speech. Has a grand face.

I have such a cold that I did not thoroughly please myself to-night though the audience seemed to like it.

I am writing in bed, now—which you write a breakfast. Take all the sleep you can, little rascal, it will do you more good than harm.

I did not write you to-day—my cold reduced me to a spiritless state. I wouldn't be writing you now, only I love you so, Livy, that I can't help it. I have to commune with you, even if it be in simply a few sentences scratched with a vile, blunt pencil. I was afraid something was the matter, but I am content, now that I have heard from my darling.

I bless you & kiss you, my precious Livy, & have prayed that God would fill your soul with peace & shelter you from harm.

SAM

Mark's sympathy with Frederick Douglass and the code of non-segregation of black and white suggests that he had come far since his Southern boyhood and brief service in the Confederate gray. And in 1881 he addressed a letter to President-elect Garfield requesting Douglass' retention as marshal of the District of Columbia, a reward for "his brave, long crusade for the liberties and elevation of his race."

BOSTON, *Dec.* 21, 1869

Little sweetheart, I have the advantage of you at last. Often & over again your letters for me have been accumulating at some point distant from me while I have been fidgetting & doing without. But now for a day or two I have been forwarding my remarks to Elmira while my darling has been still vegetating in New York. And this one goes to Elmira, too. But I sent your father a telegram a little while ago to let you know that Joe Goodman & Mr. Seeley are in New York on their way to Elmira. Seeley is after the comfortable berth of U. S. District Judge for the District of Nevada— an old friend of mine.

I do hope Joe won't get tight while he is here in the States, but I wouldn't be surprised if he did. But he is a splendid fellow, anyhow.

I have written my sister in such a way that she will be almost sure to come to our wedding. I have promised to send my mother $500—in a short time—& I will pay my sister's expenses too.

I talked last night in Canton, & had the hospitalities of Mr. Ames (son of Oakes Ames the P.R.R. Mogul) inflicted on me—& it is the last time I will stop in a New England private house. Their idea of hospitality is to make *themselves* comfortable *first*, & leave the guest to get along *if he can*. *No smoking allowed on the premises*. The next New Englander that receives me into his house will take me as I *am*, not as I ought to be. To curtail a guest's liberties & demand that he shall come up to the host's peculiar self-righteous ideas of virtue is simply pitiful & contemptible. I hate Mr. Ames with all my heart. I had no sleep last night, & must seek some rest, little sweetheart. Bless you my own darling, whom I love better & better & more & more tenderly every day.

SAM.

Haggling over lecture fees was an occasional habit among the provincial Yankees. It never failed to enrage Mark Twain, as the next letter bears witness.

BOSTON, *Dec.* 25, 1869

A happy Christmas to my darling, & to all that are dear to her! You are at home, now, Livy, & all your labors & vexations are over for a while. Poor child, I am afraid you are pretty well worn out. But you must be quiet, for a few days & recruit your strength, & then I shall find you restored & well when I see you a week hence.

I did not write you yesterday, sweetheart, & I suppose it was mutual, for you could have had no opportunity to write me. I called at Redpath's a while ago when I arrived in town, thinking I might hear from you, but I did not. I shall expect a letter in the loved & familiar hand in New Haven day after tomorrow, though—& a month after that, we shall close our long correspondence, & *tell* each other what our minds suggest, by word of mouth. Speed the day!

It is just a year to-day since I quit drinking all manner of tabooed beverages, & I cannot see but that I have fared considerably better in consequence, than I did formerly—& certainly I have not upon my soul the sin of leading others to dissipate. But all that goes to *your* credit, not mine. I did not originate the idea.

I had a delightful time of it last night, with the lecture (in Slatersville—the place was changed) & was *really* hospitably entertained in a private family—a rare thing in New England. The night before, the dog at whose house I staid took advantage of his hospitality (I was undressing & could not leave) to ask me to abate ten dollars on my lecture price—asked it as a *charity* to his society. I told him I wouldn't—that I hated the dishonored name of charity in the questionable shape it usually comes in. He said they had liked the lecture, & they wanted to keep the society alive so that they could hear me next winter. I said that when I jammed their hall full of people & then they had the cheek to ask me to abate my price, they hadn't money enough to hire me to talk in such a place again. In the morning he called me to breakfast, but I said as it was only 7 o'clock I would manage to do without breakfast until I could get it in some other town.—And when I went down stairs I said, "Doctor Sanborn, here are ten dollars for my night's lodging." He said he was much obliged, & would hand it to the committee. I said he would do nothing of the kind —I would not abate one cent on my price, & he must accept the ten dollars for his New England hospitality or not take it at all. He took it with a world of servile thanks. (He was the chief physician of Rockport & a very prominent citizen.)

Honey, I got the Jamaica Plains letter, & it did just as well as a new one would have done. It was from *you*, my darling, & that makes a letter always fresh & full of interest.

Mrs. Barstow has been trying to get a clerkship for her husband in the Treasury Department at Washington, so that he could support her & the children & let her get the rest & recreation her ill health demands, but she couldn't accomplish it right away. She did not want to bother me, she said, but it was no bother—I wrote to Senator Stewart, & he said he would put Barstow into a clerkship right away. So *that* is all right. I may write again, to-day, sweetheart, but just at present I will close & run down to breakfast. God's peace be with you my darling little wife.

SAM.

William H. Barstow had been Clemens' fellow-worker in 1862-64 on the Virginia City *Territorial Enterprise*. But while Clemens was steadily rising in the world, Barstow became a drifter and ne'er-do-well. His wife, with three small children, had written Mark from Fredericksburg, Virginia, soon after publication of *The Innocents*, requesting a local sales agency. Mark promptly recommended her to Bliss on September 9, 1869: "She is an educated, cultivated lady, & has a deal of vim & enterprise in her, if trouble hasn't broken her spirit." William M. Stewart, senator from Nevada, was Mark's former Washington employer.

Turning to the next letter, we find Mark exulting, with a very human satisfaction, in the courtship of those *Hartford Courant* people who had given him the genteel cold-shoulder before his book had become a best seller.

NEW HAVEN, *Dec.* 27 [1869]

Sweetheart, it is after supper, & I shall have a few minutes to spare before the committee come for me, I suppose.

I forgot to thank the man with the umbrella for assisting you to the street car, but I thank him now, sincerely, Livy darling.

I stopped two hours in Hartford to-day & Twichell & I bummed around together—(I had telegraphed him to be at the depot).—I told him he must come a day or two *before* the wedding, & he said he would arrive Tuesday evening, Feb. 1st, with Mrs. T. (leaving the children behind). I said we would have him at the *house* if we had any room—otherwise he would have to go to the hotel (which he said he would probably have to go there because we would be sure to be crowded). I said I meant to write you about it anyhow, before the house party should be permanently decided on.

You & I & the Twichells leave for the Adirondacks, old fellow, the first day of August (D.V.)—& if all the folks will go, so much the better. We spend the month there.

Twelve thousand copies of the book sold *this month*. This is perfectly enormous. Nothing like it since Uncle Tom's Cabin, I guess.

To-day we came upon a democrat wagon in Hartford with a cargo in it composed of Mrs. Hooker & Alice (who looks as

handsome as she ever did in her life) Mrs. Warner & another lady.
—They all assailed me violently on the Courant matter & said
it had ceased to be a private desire that we take an ownership in
that paper, & had become a public demand.—Mrs. H. said Warner
& Hawley would do anything to get me in there (this in presence
of Mrs. W. who did not deny it by any means) & Mrs. H. said she
had been writing to Mr. Langdon to make us sell out in Buffalo
& come here. (It afforded me a malicious satisfaction to hear all
this & contrast it with the insultingly contemptuous indifference
with which the very same matter was treated last June (*by every
one of them.*)

Revenge is wicked, & unchristian & in every way unbecoming,
& I am not the man to countenance it or show it any favor. (But
it is powerful sweet, anyway.)

I have read several books, lately, but none worth marking, &
so I have not marked any. I started to mark the Story of a Bad
Boy, but for the life of me I could not admire the volume much.
I am now reading Gil Blas, but am not marking it. If you have
not read it you need not. It would sadly offend your delicacy, &
I prefer not to have that dulled in you. It is a woman's chief
ornament.

Well, these people are a long time coming. The audience must
be assembling by this time—in Boston three-fourths of them
would be in the house at this hour.

Good-bye my loved & honored Livy, & peace be with you.

SAM.

An amateur in science, Clemens developed an early interest
in geology and astronomy which persisted into old age. The
puzzle of the cosmos, its age and its creation, always excited his
imagination.

TROY, *Saturday, Jan.* 8. [1870]

Sweetheart, this is the anniversary of the battle of New Orleans,
which was fought & bloodily won by Gen. Jackson, at a time when
England & America were at peace.

It is also the anniversary of other events, but I do not know
what they were, now.

I have been reading some new arguments to prove that the world is very old, & that the six days of creation were six immensely long periods. For instance, according to Genesis, the *stars* were made when the world was, yet this writer mentions the significant fact that there are stars within reach of our telescopes whose light requires 50,000 years to traverse the wastes of space & come to our earth. And so, if we made a tour through space ourselves, might we not, in some remote era of the future, meet & greet the first lagging rays of stars that started on their weary visit to us a million years ago?—rays that are outcast & homeless, now, their parent stars crumbled to nothingness & swept from the firmament five hundred thousand years after these journeying rays departed—stars whose peoples lived their little lives, & laughed & wept, hoped & feared, sinned & perished, bewildering ages since these vagrant twinklings went wandering through the solemn solitudes of space?

How insignificant we are, with our pigmy little world!—an atom glinting with uncounted myriads of other atom worlds in a broad shaft of light streaming from God's countenance—& yet prating complacently of our speck as the Great World, & regarding the other specks as pretty trifles made to steer our schooners by & inspire the reveries of "puppy" lovers. Did Christ live 33 years in each of the millions & millions of worlds that hold their majestic courses above our heads?[4] Or was *our* small globe the favored one of all? Does one apple in a vast orchard think as much of itself as we do? or one leaf in the forest—or one grain of sand upon the sea shore? Do the pismires argue upon vexed questions of pismire theology—& do they climb a molehill & look abroad over the grand universe of an acre of ground & say "Great is God, who created all things for Us?"

I do not see how astronomers can help feeling exquisitely insignificant, for every new page of the Book of the Heavens they open reveals to them more & more that the world we are so proud of is to the universe of careening globes as is one mosquito to the

---

[4] In *Captain Stormfield's Visit to Heaven*, published in 1907-08 but written years earlier, the celestial clerk is puzzled when Stormfield tries to identify his world as "the one the Saviour saved": "He bent his head at the Name. Then he says, gently —'The worlds He has saved are like to the gates of heaven in number—none can count them.' "

winged & hoofed flocks & herds that darken the air & populate the plains & forests of all the earth. If you killed the mosquito would it be missed? Verily, What is Man, that he should be considered of God?

One of these astronomers has been taking photographs of tongues of flame 17,000 miles high that shoot aloft from the surface of the sun, & waver, & sink, & rise again—all in two or three minutes—& sometimes in *one* minute swinging a banner of flame from left to right a distance of 5,000 miles—an inconceivable velocity! Think of the hurricanes that sweep the sun, to do such miracles as this! And other tongues of flame stream upward, bend & hang down again, forming a crimson arch 20,000 miles in height, through which our poor globe might be bowled as one bowls a football between a boy's legs.

But I must stop. I have concluded to stay here to-day & tomorrow, as this hotel suits me first-rate. I had the sagacity to enter my *nom de plume* on the register, & so they have made me very comfortable. (For I find that the landlord is a frantic admirer of mine.) He is a good fellow, too (naturally).

Go to bed, sweetheart. Go to bed, & sleep peacefully, & awake refreshed & happy, my darling.

SAM

In his next letter, written three weeks before their marriage, Mark summarized his lifelong progress toward "reform," under feminine dominion—first of his mother, then of Mrs. Fairbanks, and finally of Livy. But her last crusade, to end his smoking on the alleged grounds of health, he manfully resisted. Here he points out that his mother had smoked for thirty years and was hale enough, that he himself had indulged since the age of eight and was the picture of fitness—superior, he could not resist implying, to the abstemious but ailing Langdons, who, he surmised, were the real instigators of this anti-nicotine crusade. But even this innocent pleasure he offered to resign if it proved an obstacle to their perfect union.

CAMBRIDGE [NEW YORK], *Jan.* 13 [1870]

No, Livy dear, I shall treat smoking just exactly as I would treat the forefinger of my left hand: If you asked me in all seriousness to cut that finger off, & I saw that you really meant it, & believed that the finger marred my well-being in some mysterious way, & it was plain to me that you could not be entirely satisfied & happy while it remained, I give you my word that I would cut it off.— I might think what I pleased about it, & the world might *say* what it pleased—it should come off. There would be nothing foolish in the act—& all wordy *arguments* against it would sink to their proper insignificance in presence of the one *unanswerable* argument that *you desired it* & our married life could not be completely in unison while that bar remained.

Now there are *no* arguments that can convince me that *moderate* smoking is deleterious to me. I cannot attach any weight to either the arguments or the evidence of those who know nothing about the matter personally & so must simply theorize.—Theorizing has no effect on me. I have smoked habitually for 26 of my 34 years, & I am the only healthy member our family has. (What do mere theories amount to in the face of a *fact* like that.) My health is wholly faultless—& has been ever since I was 8 years old. My physical structure—lungs, kidneys, heart, brain—is without blemish. The Life insurance doctor pronounced me free from all disease & *remarkably* sound. Yet I am the victim of this fearfully destructive habit of smoking. My brother's health has gradually run *down* instead of *up*—yet he is a model of propriety, & has *no* bad habits. My mother smoked for 30 years, & yet has lived to the age of 67.

Livy dear, make no argument of the fact that you have seen me "nervous, irritable," &c., &c., for it happens to *be* no argument.— You can see your father nervous, worn, restless—you can see *any* anti-smoker affected just as you have seen me. It is not a condition confined to smokers—as you possibly know in your own experience.

There *is* no argument that can have even a feather's weight with me against smoking (in my case, at least) for I *know*, & others merely *suppose*.

But there is one thing that will make me quit smoking, & only one. I will lay down this habit which is so filled with harmless pleasure, just as soon as you write me or say to me that *you desire it*. It shall be a sacrifice—just the same as if I simply asked you to give up going to church, knowing that no *arguments* I offered could convince you that I was right. It will not be hard for me to do it. I stopped chewing tobacco because it was a mean habit, partly, & partly because my mother desired it. I ceased from profanity because Mrs. Fairbanks desired it. I stopped drinking strong liquors because you desired it. I stopped drinking all other liquors because it seemed plain that you desired it. I did what I could to learn to leave my hands out of my pantaloon pockets & quit lolling at full length in easy chairs, because you desired it. There was no sacrifice about any of these things. Discarding these habits curtailed none of my liberties—on the contrary the doing it released me from various forms of slavery. With smoking it is different. No argument against it is valid—& so to quit it I must do without other reason than that *you* desire it. The desires of [all] others have weight with me, but are not strong *enough* quite.

But even if you never *said* the words, if I saw that my smoking was a bar to our *perfect* wedded unity & happiness, it should go by the board—& pitilessly.

You seem to think it will be a Herculean task for me to suddenly cast out a loved habit of 26 years, Livy dear. Either you do not know me, or I do not know myself. I think differently about it.—Speak the words, Livy dear—unaccompanied by any of the hated arguments or theories—& you shall see that I love you well enough to follow your desires, even in *this* matter. Nothing shall stand in the way of our perfect accord, if I can help it.

If you had ever harried me, or persecuted me about this thing, I could not speak as I do—for persecution only hardens one in evil courses. But it is you, darling, that have suffered the persecution (& yet, being you, it has *seemed* to be me, & so I have resisted all along). You have had to listen to it all, & it grieves my heart to think of it. It has had its necessary effect in making me more loth to yield up this habit than I would have been otherwise. We do hate to be driven.

Ah, Livy, if the whole matter had been left solely in *your* hands, I would have been quit of the habit of smoking, long ago, & without a pang or a struggle. It was bad judgment to attack so strong a vice save through you. There could be little prospect that other means would succeed if your gentle ministrations failed.

It is about supper time, & some new friends are to come in after

supper & sit with me till lecture time. Just as usual, I am in splendid trim for this little country town—& just as usual I must get
up at 6 in the morning & be in a lifeless lethargy for the next large
city—Utica, & so make a botch of it.

I am so sorry I have been the prime cause of blasting a happy
Sunday for my darling—sorry & dejected—& resolved to make up
for it in some way. Poor child, nobody shall harass you when my
roof covers you. I won't even let Mr. Langdon do it, dear good
father though he is to both of us. I kiss you good night, darling.

SAM

TROY, *Jan.* 14 [1870]

Livy darling, I have been worrying sorely over the letter I wrote
you yesterday about smoking—& wondering what I said in it—
for as usual none of the language is left in my memory. I only
remember having in my mind a picture of your returning from
church all worn & unhappy, & a consciousness in my mind that
you had been wrongfully treated, & were blameless & should not
have been made to suffer for the sin of another. And I had upon
me a rasping, chafing sense of . . .

There, there, there—let us bother with the hateful subject no
more. I am sure it has caused us both more real suffering than
would accrue from smoking a million cigars.

And this is a bad time for me to write about exciting matters,
for my nerves, & my whole physical economy, are shattered with
the wear & tear of travel, lecturing, ten thousand petty annoyances
& vexations & an unusual loss of sleep. When things get to going
wrong, they keep it up. Yesterday afternoon I arrived at Cambridge & drove to the hotel through a driving storm of sleet—it
was dreary & cold. My spirits began to ebb. Then the Committee
(with customary brilliancy of judgment) informed me that the
Troy *Times* had published my entire lecture, praising it highly,
& using numberless dashes & hyphens to imitate my drawling
manner of speaking—& further informed me that the *Times* had
a large circulation in Cambridge.—My spirits fell lower—my
anger began to rise. I abused my informant in no minced language
for knowing no better than to *tell* me I was to talk to an audience
to whom my speech would be no news. Then he left (to return

after supper) & I was alone in my fury. I opened your letter, & lo, even the darling of my heart could not be spared! You had received another shot upon that old, old subject whose bare mention by any lips but yours is getting to be sufficient to make my hair rise. For I am a full grown man with gray hairs in my head, & have all a man's repugnance to being [per . . .]

There I go again. Well, I had but little time to spare, & so I must have written as I felt—I must have copied my condition. And it was not a happy condition. In due time the Chairman returned, & at 7 the fire bells rang, & he sprang to his feet, & exclaimed, "My God, there is the lecture-hall in flames!"

Mentally I uttered a Thanksgiving so fervent that if ever prayer of mine pierced the vault of Heaven that one did. I did not move from my chair, & so my wild excited chairman halted in his mad flight to the door. I said: "You can see by the blinding glare from the windows that nothing can save your hall—why need you rush there for nothing?"

He cooled a little & sat down—& as the fires glowed through those tall windows my spirits came up till I felt that all I needed to be entirely happy was to see the Troy Times editors & this chairman locked up in that burning building.

But my rising spirits were crushed to earth, & exasperation came again. The house was saved. It was burned a little, & flooded with water. But within the hour they scrubbed the floors, let out the smoke & warmed the place up again—& I lectured.

Of course, after the lecture, a lot of committeemen invited themselves to my room—although they knew I must rise at 7 in the morning—& presently I grew cheerful & kept them there till 12 o'clock.

This morning the porter failed to call me. I woke, surprised to see it so light, looked at my watch—14 minutes to 8—train leaves at 8.05—depot 4 or 5 blocks distant—no vehicle in sight. Inside of 4 minutes I was not only fully dressed, but down stairs making trouble. The landlord was crazy as a loon in 5 seconds—darted this way & that—yelled for a coach—tore his hair—swore at his porter, & was in despair—said the jig was up, & the best he could do was to take a buggy & drive me to Troy—30 miles—thermometer already below zero & growing steadily colder.

I said, "Collect your senses & don't go wild—we have still 6 minutes—show me to the depot—run!" And he did run—ran a tolerably good gate, but I beat him to the depot & jumped on the train—he arrived the next second with my hand-sachel & I was safe for Utica! Hurrah!

Don't grieve over anything I said about smoking, my poor child, but remember that in *all* moods I love you & honor you—no storm can [ruffle that] move the depths of that sea—& remember also, that whenever, unbiased by any influence but your own calm, just & charitable judgment, or your own dear, resistless desire, I am called upon to give up smoking or any other habit of mine, I stand ready to do it—not reluctantly or churlishly, but cheerfully & with a loving whole-heartedness & devotion to your happiness, my Livy.

Peace be with you my precious wife.

SAM

P. S. I talk in Fredonia, N.Y., Jan. 19.—(L. McKinstry.)

Although Mark never completely renounced smoking, early in their marriage he made large concessions to Livy's prejudice. To Twichell on December 19, 1870, he wrote that now he smoked solely "from 3 till 5 Sunday afternoon," to humor Livy, "just as I would deprive myself of sugar in my coffee if she wished it." Many years later, on March 14, 1882, in reply to a query from England, from A. Arthur Reade, who published his letter in *Study and Stimulants*, Clemens asserted: "When I was thirty-four . . . [I] ceased from smoking during a year and a half. My health did not improve, because it was not possible to improve health which was already perfect." But on beginning to write *Roughing It* he found it necessary in 1871 to resume his monthly quota of three hundred cigars. Henceforth Mark practiced no self-denial on this score, save by observing his well-known rule never to smoke more than one cigar at a time. And so he continued through a life preserved by some miraculous Providence from the constant hazard of smoking in bed and (as Howells remembered) falling asleep with the day's last cigar still smoldering between his fingers.

The next letter Livy has marked on the envelope, "184th—Last letter of a 17-months' correspondence."

HORNELLSVILLE [NEW YORK], 20*th* [*January*, 1870]

My child, I am within sixty miles of you, & so I *do* feel that your unseen presence is stronger about me than when you are away at the other side of a State—but further than this, your proximity does not benefit me, little one, but on the contrary is rather a matter to growl at, because it only makes me want the more to see you, without giving me the opportunity. I cannot right truly say I haven't the opportunity, either, for I *could* be with you at this moment, & remain with you half a day, & then run up here in time. But I am not going to have my jubilee of joy at having *finished* the lectures for good & all, & my other jubilee of joy in the reflection that I am with you never more to part again in life, marred & diluted by a little unsatisfying taste of the holiday & glimpse of you, my darling. No, sir—I want the enfranchisement from worry & work to be *complete*, & the joining company with you, my child, to be just as complete, perfect & lasting.

I left Buffalo at 4 P M yesterday, & went to Dunkirk, & thence out to Fredonia by horse-car (3 miles), rattled my lecture through, took horse-car again & just caught 9.45 P.M. train bound east— sat up & smoked to Salamanca (12:30) stripped & went to bed in a sleeping car two hours & a half, & then got up & came ashore here at 3 o'clock this morning—& had a strong temptation to lie still an hour or two longer & go to Elmira. But I resisted it. By coming through in the night, I saved myself 2 hours extra travel.

Sweetheart, tomorrow you must go into the wardrobe in my room & burrow into those pasteboard boxes & get out a new shirt, & an undershirt & drawers, & put them on the bed I am to sleep in when I get home—provided I am to stay in Charley's room or the front chamber. But if I am to occupy the room these clothes are now in, of course you need not bother with them. And before you go to bed tomorrow night you must write a note, telling me how to get into the house & what bed to take—& you must put that note in the newspaper box at the side gate, so that I can get it when I arrive. Those are your orders, Livy darling, & you will be court-martialed if you don't obey them.

We did have a most delightful audience at Fredonia, & I was just as happy as a lord from the first word of the lecture to the last. I thought it was about as good a lecture as I ever listened to —but some of the serious passages were impromptu—never been written.[5]

This, my precious Livy, is the last letter of a correspondence that has lasted seventeen months—the pleasantest correspondence I ever had a share in. For over two months of the time, we wrote every other day. During the succeeding twelve months we have written *every* day that we have been parted from each other. And no man ever did have a dearer, more faithful little correspondent than you have been to me, my heart's darling.—Your letters have made one ray of sunlight & created a thrill of pleasure in every one of these long-drawn days, howsoever dreary the day was otherwise. And so I thank you & bless you now, once more, as I have thanked you & blessed you all these days. And I pray for you, even as I have done with the closing in of each night, ever since you moved my spirit to prayer seventeen months ago. This is the last long correspondence we ever shall have, my Livy—& now on this day it passes forever from its honored place among our daily occupations, & becomes a *memory*. A memory to be laid reverently away in the holy of holies of our hearts & cherished as a sacred thing. A memory whose mementoes will be precious while we live, & sacred when either one shall die.

They have come for me, my sweet Livy.

Good-bye & God bless you,

SAM

[5] So pleasant was his memory of Fredonia and the intelligence of its audiences that he soon settled his mother, widowed sister, and niece there.

CHAPTER SEVEN

Honeymoon

SAMUEL CLEMENS reached Elmira on the night of January
21, and wedded Livy on the evening of February 2, with two
clergymen, Twichell and Thomas K. Beecher, officiating. The
next day, with greater tribal solidarity than romantic privacy, the
honeymoon couple left for Buffalo in a "palace car" festively filled
with all the Langdons, Clemenses, Beechers, and Fairbankses who
had rallied round for the wedding. The Langdon agent in Buffalo,
J. D. F. Slee, at Mark's request and in his absence from town,
supposedly had rented quarters for the newlyweds in a suitable
"boarding-house." Actually he entered into Langdon's benign
plot to surprise Mark with the gift of a house bought, paid for,
and furnished by the coal magnate. Mark's astonishment, in the
midst of the blue satin drawing room and the "sanctum" with
scarlet upholstery, was sufficient to gratify everybody, Livy included. "I have read those absurd fairy tales in my time," wrote
Mark to Dan De Quille, his crony of the Comstock Lode, "but I
never, never, never, expected to be the hero of a romance in real
life as unlooked for and unexpected as the wildest of them."
Hence his reference, in the first letter that follows, to "Little
Sammy in Fairy Land."

The story told by the love letters is best pieced out, during the
days that followed, by the joint messages written by this couple
to the Langdons—which Mark delighted to sprinkle with sly and
outrageous statements, aware that Livy was reading over his
shoulder and would exclaim or protest between the lines, as in
this sample:

[February 20, 1870] AT HOME, *Sunday* P.M.
Livy gets along better & better with her housekeeping, & indeed
she astonishes me sometimes by the insight she shows into things

one wouldn't suppose she knew anything about. But while she surprises me with her ability to follow the old beaten paths of housewifery, her achievements when she branches out of those beaten paths surprises me still more. Now this morning she had a mackerel fricaseed with pork & oysters [*Livy:* False] & I tell you it was a dish to stir the very depths of one's benevolence. We saved every single bit of it for the poor.

I never saw anybody look so unearthly wise as Livy does when she is ordering dinner; & I never saw anybody look so relieved as she does when she has completed her order, poor child. [*Livy:* This is false too, mother dear, prettie nearly.] (So you see she has come down from her roost for the afternoon & is prepared to look after me.)

You can't think what a carver I have become. I hardly ever have to take hold of a chicken by the leg, now. And I look mighty imposing, too, at the head of my table, with my big fork, & my carving-knife & my glove-stretcher about me. (I use the glove-stretcher to hold the chicken open while I get out the stuffing— Livy is keeping her eyes shut till I tell her she may look & see what I am to do with the glove-stretcher.)

[*Livy:* Isn't he a funny Youth?]

As a matter of fact, the role of Livy as cook, that favorite topic of foreboding in courtship letters, remained almost wholly a myth. For Mr. Langdon had engaged not only a cook named Ellen and a housemaid called Harriet but also a young coachman named Patrick, destined to spend a lifetime in the Clemens' livery. Livy's actual testing came largely upon the score of managerial rather than culinary skill.

"Livy discharged Harriet yesterday, after weeks of solemn & imposing preparation [wrote Mark on April 17], & I tell you I am glad the thing is done, for it hung over us like a pall & shadowed all our sunshine. Toward the last the mere mention of it was sufficient to make me shudder, & I came to regard it as an awful ordeal which we had got to pass through & which might let go in the midst & blow us to Jericho. But it is all over, now, & we still live. But I had rather discharge a perilous & unsound cannon than the soundest servant girl that ever was."

Through these letters runs the passionate adoration which

united Livy to "Mr. Clemens," as she sometimes styled her spouse, with Victorian formality, and at other times "Samuel," despite her inherent prejudice against that name, and still other times, with growing frequency, "Youth." This pet name, so happily chosen and persisting for life, epitomized the gaiety of spirit, impulsiveness, and boyishness which easily erased Mark's ten years' seniority, and served constantly to relax Livy's overserious disposition. "I wish that I could remember some of the funny things that Mr Clemens says and does," she wrote the Langdons on Sunday morning, February 6, in her first letter as bride, "and besides these funny things, he is so tender and considerate in every way." As for Mark's own felicity, on the afternoon of this same day he addressed a letter to his boyhood chum Will Bowen: "For behold I have at this moment the only sweetheart I ever *loved*, & bless her old heart she is lying asleep upstairs in a bed that I sleep in every night, & for four whole days she has been *Mrs. Samuel L. Clemens!*" A month later to a friend of his Nevada mining days, Bob Howland, Mark declared: "If all of one's married days are as happy as these new ones have been to me, I have deliberately fooled away 30 years of my life. If it were to do over again I would marry in early infancy instead of wasting time cutting teeth & breaking crockery."

A week after their wedding Mark wrote to the Langdons as follows:

AT HOME, *Noon, Feb.* 9. 1870

MY DEAR FATHER & MOTHER—Livy has gone shopping & to visit the Slees, & I remained at home to write a newspaper letter, but find after pacing the floor for an hour that I have no special interest in the subjects that present themselves. A man cannot do a thing well which his heart is not in, & so I have dropped the newspaper scribbling for to-day.

We have called upon the Slees once—*I* have called upon them once—*they* have called upon *us* once—& now *She* has gone to call upon *them*—so the lines of communication between these two households are unbroken, thus far, & are likely to remain so.

We telegraphed the Twichells to come, & they did—& remained twenty-four hours by the watch, & were happy, & so were we. They took full account of the house & all its belongings, partly because they vastly enjoyed doing it, & partly because they expect to have to tell, & retail, & iterate & reiterate the details of our grandeur to all them that be in Hartford (& who somehow of late appear to take an interest in us).

I went after them with the carriage at 3:40 PM day before yesterday, & from that till dinner time (at 5) we showed them elaborately over the house, & made Twichell wipe his feet & blow his nose before entering each apartment (so as to keep his respect up to an impressive altitude)—& we listened to their raptures & enjoyed the same—& I told them the story of what happened to Little Sammy in Fairy Land when he was hunting for a Boarding House, & they enjoyed *that*. But I never let them go near that drawing room till they thought they had seen all the glories of the palace—till after dinner, in fact, for I wanted to have the gas ablaze & the furniture covers removed. It looked magnificent! I think they will give a good account. Mrs. T. says Alice Day's house is vulgarly showy & out of taste. I am awful glad of it. (So is Livy, but she don't say so—at least she don't want it mentioned outside.)

[*Livy*: Its no such thing and Mrs. T. did not say so—ahem! naughty youth.]

Livy makes a most excellent little housekeeper, & I always knew she would. Everything goes on as smoothly as if it were worked by hidden machinery. The servants are willing & entirely respectful toward her (which they had *better* be).

Livy has a dreadful time making her cash account balance; & she has a dreadful time economising a turkey in such a way as to make him last a week; & she has a dreadful time making the servants comprehend that they must buy nothing whatever on credit & that whatever they buy they must make the butcher or the grocer set down in the pass-book to be critically scanned by her eagle eye. These are all the dreadful times she has *on the surface*. She naturally has her little sad moments within, & she confesses it—but you may take an honest man's word for it that I think she secretly reproaches herself for not being sad *oftener*, so as to show a proper grief at leaving so lovely & so dear a home. The plain fact of the matter is that she has undergone the most astounding change—for verily she is become so boisterous, so noisy, & so lawless in her cheery happiness that I, even I, am forced to put on an irksome gravity & decorum in order to uphold the dignity of the house. She pulls & hauls me around, & claws my hair, & bites my fingers, & laughs so that you might hear her across the street; & it does appear to me that I never saw anybody so happy as she is in all my life—except myself.

We entirely enjoy these glad days. We sit alone in the loveliest of libraries, in the evening, & I read poetry—& every now & then I come to a passage that brings the tears to my eyes, & I look up to her for loving sympathy, & she inquires whether they sell sirloin steaks by the pound or by the yard. Ah, the child's heart is in her housekeeping, not in the romance of life.

We are very regular in our habits. We get up at 6 o'clock every morning, & we go to bed at 10 every evening. We have three meals a day—breakfast at 10 o'clock, lunch at 1 PM & dinner at 5. The reason we get up at 6 in the morning is because we want to see what time it is. Partly this, & partly because we have heard that early rising is beneficial. We then go back to bed, & get up finally at half past 9. Lovingly Your Son

SAML. L. CLEMENS

I have returned from my shopping expedition and now Mr Clemens has gone down town—I purchased a clothes bar, a bread box a flat iron stand, a blower stand &c &c—

The names enclosed Mr C. wants after cards sent to—Annie will probably know if he has duplicated any—I would like it if Sue could find from Zippie, Hattie Marsh Tylers address and send after cards to her also to Lucy Gage Cursons—

We are as happy as two mortals can well be—

Lovingly LIVY—

Not all the financial incomprehensions belonged to the distaff side. To her mother on February 14 Livy wrote: "Mr Clemens says that I had presents and good times when I was married, and when I reached here people came to see me, but his first salutation was a paper enquiring about his income tax—That income tax has been a matter of most intense anxiety to him, he could not *possibly* comprehend it." This bewilderment he later invited the public to share, after a revenue assessor's call and (so Mark said) the boasting of affluence into which he was betrayed. Thus reported his article "A Mysterious Visit," in the *Buffalo Express* of March 19, 1870.

Among their wedding presents was a marble statuette, which failed to survive the first month of marriage. Its breakage left Livy on the verge of tears until the Langdons shipped a replacement, here acknowledged by Clemens to his father-in-law.

Polishing Irons

March 2, 1870

DEAR FATHER—Got your dispatch, & shall talk no business with my partners till Mr. Slee gets back.

The "Peace" has arrived, but Livy don't know it, for she has got some eternal company in the drawing-room & it is considerably after dinner-time. But I have spread the fringed red dinner-table spread over the big rocking-chair & set up the beautiful thing on it, in a prominent place, & it will be the first thing Livy sees when she comes in.

Later—She went into convulsions of delight when she entered. And I don't wonder, for we both so mourned the loss of the first Peace that it did not seem possible we could do without it—& for you to send another in this delightful & unexpected way was intensely gratifying. You have our most sincere gratitude—Livy's for the present, itself, & mine because I shall so much enjoy looking at it.

March 3

Your two letters came this morning, father, & your dispatch yesterday afternoon. (Mem.—Ellen's in the stable & the horse in the attic looking at the scenery.)[1]

---

[1] Livy's concern over moving the washtubs from the cellar inspired Mark to tell Mr. Langdon on February 26 that he had just exhorted his bride: ". . . it is not showing proper respect to a father who pulls *his* house to pieces all the time— Move the wash tubs into the wood house, Madam, pile the wood in the stable & put the horse in the laundry—I tell you something *must* be altered quick, or your father won't like it." Mr. Langdon promptly replied: "You may put the carriage in the cellar, the horse in the drawing room, & Ellen in the stable. Please your own tastes, my boy. . . . I am for liberty."

We think it cannot be worth while to enter into an explanation of the Express figures, for the reason that Mr. Slee must have arrived in Elmira after your letter was written, & he would explain them to you much more clearly & understandingly than I could.

I thank you ever so much for your offer to take my money & pay me interest on it until we decide whether to add it to the Kennett purchase or not. I was going to avail myself of it at once, but waited to see if Mr. Slee & Mac Williams couldn't make Selkirk's figures show a little more favorably. As I hoped, so it has resulted. And now, upon thorough conviction that the Express is not a swindle, I will pay some more on the Kennett indebtedness.[2]

I am very glad to begin to see my way through this business, for figures confuse & craze me in a little while. I haven't Livy's tranquil nerve in the presence of a financial complexity—when her cash account don't balance (which does not happen oftener than once [*Livy:* "false"] a day) she just increases the item of "Butter 78 cents" to "Butter 97 cents"—or reduces the item of "Gas, $6.45" to "Gas, $2.35" & *makes* that account balance.—She keeps books with the most inexorable accuracy that ever mortal man beheld.

[*Livy:* Father it is not true—Samuel slanders me—]

I wrote *Polishing Irons* at the head of this letter the other night to remind either Livy or me to write about them—didn't put it there for a text to preach from.

The report of my intending to leave Buffalo Livy & I have concluded emanates from Hartford, for the reason that it really started in the newspapers only a very little while after my last visit & your last letter to Hartford & has been afloat ever since.

Yr Son

SAMUEL

"Mr Clemens is very anxious to have the polishing irons come," Livy wrote her parents on this same date. "I should get some here but they do not seem to keep them, I could not get any—I do not

---

[2] Thomas A. Kennett was the co-owner of the Buffalo Express whose share Clemens had bought at an inflated figure; Col. George F. Selkirk was business manager.

know whether there is any way to hurry them, but the youth does not like to wear his shirts done up without them."

The date of Mark's next letter to the Langdons is somewhat puzzling. Though labeled "Sunday 26th," no Sunday fell on the 26th in their early Buffalo days prior to June. Internal evidence indicates Sunday, March 27, as the correct date.

AT HOME, *Sunday Afternoon*, 26th [*March*, 1870]

DEAR FATHER & MOTHER—It is snowing furiously, & has been, the most of the day & part of the night. We are glad that you are safe beyond its jurisdiction—for albeit snow is very beautiful when falling, its loveliness passes away very shortly afterward. The grand unpoetical result is merely chilblains & slush.

Cousin Anna is here—came last night. She enjoys the beautiful home, naturally. Livy has just gone to roost. Theodore's dispatch to inform us that Anna would arrive at *8:30* P.M. made a mistake & said *8* A.M. The consequence was that we were up at such a vile, inhuman hour in the morning that we shall be torpid & worthless for a day or two. Livy & I are delicate creatures & cannot stand dissipation.

Anna brought flowers from Sue, & Livy made some handsome bouquets, & immediately grew riotous & disorderly because, she said, "Nobody ever comes to call when we have fresh flowers." Well, somebody had *better* come—else I will take a club & go & invite half a dozen or so. Our flowers are not to go to waste *this* time. Merely for want of a little energetic affability.

The roof of the house on the corner right opposite Mr. Howells' (diagonally opposite Mr Lyon's), caught fire this morning & blazed pretty lively for a while—& but for the snow on the roof there would have been a conflagration—for when I discovered it from our bedroom window & went over there to stir up the family, there was but one man in sight anywhere, & he came to *help*, instead of going for the firemen. It burned so slowly that Patrick, who followed me, climbed out on the roof & put it half out with snow before we succeeded in getting buckets of water to him. After he had got it under complete control a couple of steam engines came, but the occupant of the house persuaded them to go away without damaging anything.

There, now—perhaps we need not go to explaining, now, why we have not written you before (still, if any letters have miscarried & you haven't received them we wish to be understood as having written those letters).—We need not, now, explain, perhaps, since it is so late in the day. I know it isn't Livy's fault. (Now if she stands by me faithfully & says as much for me, we are surely proven blameless.) Which I think she'll do it.

Yes, mother, whenever you issue your call, we stand ready to voyage over the ocean with you, right cheerfully.

Thank you for Charley's journals. I have given up Prof. Ford, & shall discontinue the "Round the World" letters—*have* done it. The Prof. has now been 6 months writing 2 little letters, & I ten —making 12 in all. If they continue their trip 18 months, as they propose, the Prof will succeed in grinding out a grand total of 6 letters, if he keeps up his present vigor. So I shall quietly drop the "Round the World" business & simply write (from Charley's journal) what shall seem to be simply a vagrant correspondence from some George M. Wagner or other person who writes letters when he happens to feel like it, & travels for the comfort of it.

I have taken the editorship of a department in the "Galaxy" magazine, New York, & am to furnish ten pages of matter every month (made up of my own writing & contributions together) for $2,000 a year, I to absolutely *own* the matter & print it in book form after they have used it, if I want to.[3] I shall write one or two sketches a month for the Express, & I have an idea that for a good while I shall do nothing else on the paper. Thus the Galaxy & the Express together will give me fully six days' work every month, & I positively need the rest of the time to admire the house in. Need it, too, to write a book in. The "Innocents" sells just as handsomely as ever. [9 to 10,000 copies a month] It is still netting me $1,400 a month.

But I must stop, & leave room for a line from Livy. And so, with all love & duty I am

Yr Son SAML

[3] His *Galaxy* connection, dropped in the following year after many harassments of family illness and depression, resulted in some of the mediocre pieces later collected in *Sketches New and Old* (1875).

MOTHER DEAR—Cousin Anna, Mr Clemens and I are sitting about the Library table, we have been having a pleasant visit— Now Samuel is speaking of Olive Logan—

Our house is just as prettie and pleasant as ever, perhaps a little more so, we want to see you and father here in it—I am sure you will think it a restful place—

I was out on two calling expeditions last week—I have rec'd about seventy calls—I had a very pleasant call at Mrs Wadsworths last week—I thought that I called there two weeks ago, but discovered that I went to the wrong home & left my card—Mrs. George Wadsworth has called too—she is also very attractive—Mr & Mrs Gray (he is the editor of the Courier) are attractive people, seem as if they might be friends—

Good night

Lovingly LIVY—

Plans mentioned above for Mark and Livy and the senior Langdons to join Charles and his tutor Professor Ford in Europe, as the latter came homeward from their global tour, soon were canceled by the illness of Jervis Langdon. In the late spring he failed rapidly, chronic indigestion forecasting cancer of the stomach. Hopefully Clemens wrote to him after a fancied improvement.

AT HOME, *May* 22 [1870]

DEAR FATHER—For several days the news from you has grown better & better, till at last I believe we hardly seem to feel that you are an invalid any longer. We are just as grateful as ever two people were in the world. Your case was looking very ominous when we came away, & if we had been called back within a day or two we could not have been surprised. Now we hope to see you up here with Mother, just as soon as you can come. Everything is lovely, here, & our home is as quiet & peaceful as a monastery, & yet as bright & cheerful as sunshine without & sunshine within can make it. We are burdened & bent with happiness, almost, & we do need to share it with somebody & so save the surplus. Come & partake freely.

I do not think we shall be easily able to go home when Anna

Dickinson visits you, & so it has not been right seriously in our minds, perhaps, as yet. We expect to spend a full month in the Adirondacks (August or Sept.), & I shall have to do all that amount of Galaxy & Express writing in advance, in order to secure the time. So I shall make myself right busy for a while now—shall write faithfully every day.

I want Theodore to send $150 to Charley for me, & I *never* shall think [to fix it] of it when down town. Can Theodore send the money & just charge it up against me with interest till I see Elmira again? I have asked Charley to get a fine microscope for me, & I guess he would like me to trot the money along.

We are offered $15,000 cash for the Tennessee Land.—Orion is in favor of taking it provided we can reserve 800 acres which he thinks contain an iron mine, & 200 acres of cannel coal. But inasmuch as the country is soon to be threaded with railways, the parties who are trying to buy (they are Chicago men) may very much prefer to have the iron & coal themselves.—So I advise Orion to offer them the entire tract of 30 or 40,000 acres of land at $30,000 without reserving anything; *or*, all except that 1,000 acres of coal & iron for $15,000. Our own agents have for two or three years been holding the tract complete, at $60,000, and have uniformly hooted at any smaller price.

My sister writes that the plants have not yet arrived from Elmira.

She also writes that she & Margaret have finished making & putting down the most of the carpets, though the one for the parlor has not transpired yet. (Transpired is no slouch of a word —it means that the parlor carpet has not *arrived* yet.) And she writes that the Kitten slept all the way from Buffalo to Dunkirk & then stretched & yawned, issuing much fishy breath in the operation, & said the Erie road was an *infernal* road to ride over. (The joke lies in the fact that the Kitten did not go over the Erie at all —it was the Lake-Shore.)[4]

Livy is sound asleep, I suppose, for she went to our room an hour ago & I have heard nothing from her since.

[4] After the wedding, Mark's mother, sister Pamela, and niece Annie settled in Fredonia (whose rail junction point with Buffalo was Dunkirk). They were accompanied by the faithful Margaret, and obviously by one of the cats in which Mark's life abounded.

Ma will go to Fredonia tomorrow to advise about the Tennessee land, but she may return, as my sister's house must be pretty well tumbled yet.

Mr. & Mrs. Slee are well. We saw them Friday evening.

We took dinner & spent yesterday evening most pleasantly with the Grays (editor Courier)—they are going to Addirawndix with us.

Must write the Twichells.

With very great love to all of you, including Mother, Sue, Theodore & Grandma—& in very great haste—

Yr Son SAML

Although the newlyweds were indeed "burdened & bent with happiness" in the fruition of their love, their first year together soon turned into a nightmare of illnesses, mishaps, and deaths among those close to them—a series of disasters under whose burden Mark Twain the writer ceased almost wholly to produce.

In June, Jervis Langdon failed rapidly, until his nourishment was reduced solely to "the foam of champagne." Livy, Susan Crane, and Mark nursed him devotedly through the hot summer in Elmira. Hope continued awhile, and on July 4 Mark wrote Bliss that "we have every reason to believe that he is going to get well & that speedily." In this sanguine mood he left Livy at her father's bedside and made a hasty trip to Washington on July 5.

This trip is unknown to his biographers, but his first letter to Livy from the national capital discloses that its purpose was to lobby for a bill of interest to "our Tennesseans." Mark apparently sought to bring pressure upon his old Nevada acquaintance and former boss, Senator William M. Stewart, to get the bill favorably reported from the Senate Judiciary Committee. *The Congressional Globe* for July 7, 1870, shows that this bill proposed "to divide the State of Tennessee into two judicial districts," but that it failed to pass. The source of Mark's concern—such, for example, as an oblique connection with the Clemens holdings in that state —remains unknown.

Mark's Washington visit, however, is of interest because during his stay he sat to Matthew Brady for his photograph. This photograph, showing Mark flanked by David Gray, his Buffalo friend, and George Alfred Townsend, another journalist, is in the Mark Twain Papers. He also dined in company with the corrupt Kansas senator who became the villain of *The Gilded Age*, and met President Grant under circumstances unlike those related by Mark's biographer Albert Bigelow Paine.

WASH. *July* 8 [1870]

Livy my Darling, the bill having been reported in the Senate last night, & not yet being printed—& the House proposing to take it up & in its original form & come snap judgment on the Senate, to-day (but never got to it) there was naturally nothing for me to do but *wait*—which I did. Borrowed $100 from Bennett[5] (having come off with only $50 or thereabouts, & I had ordered a suit of clothes for my friend Riley this morning[6]) & spent half the day in the House Gallery (after first giving an hour to Brady to take my picture in).

This evening dined with Ex-Vice-President Hamlin, Senator Pomeroy, Mr. Gardiner G. Hubbard & Mr. Richard B. Irwin, & had a good time. Hubbard wants to be remembered cordially to father, & Irwin spoke with great appreciation of how Charley wrote back from Japan to thank him for the pains he had taken to make him & the Prof. comfortable in the ship—a courtesy which Irwin said most people forgot after enjoying his hospitable services & reaching dry land where they no longer needed his attentions. I was glad to hear him compliment Charley so.

Drove up to the Senate & staid till now (10:30 P M) & came back to hotel. Oh, I have gathered material enough for a whole book! This is a perfect gold mine.

Called on the President in a quiet way this morning. I thought it would be the neat thing to show a little embarrassment when introduced, but something occurred to make me change my deportment to calm & dignified self-possession. It was this: *The General was fearfully embarrassed himself.*[7]

[5] David S. Bennett, congressman from Buffalo.

[6] J. H. Riley, crony of his earlier newspaper days, whom Mark soon sent, expenses paid, to the South African diamond fields to collect material for a book that never came to birth.

[7] Paine's biography, 360, relates the familiar story of Mark's breaking the ice by remarking, "General, I seem to be a little embarrassed. Are you?" but assigns it to the winter of 1867-68, apparently incorrectly.

I have promised to come down some time & go off with Gen. Dent on a "tear" for a whole day.[8]

I was sorry to hear that father was feebler, but very glad to know that it was nothing serious.

My precious child, I shall stop now, write a note to Twichell killing our trip, & then go to bed. God bless & angels keep my darling.

SAM

This last allusion was to a projected vacation in the Adirondacks. Jervis Langdon's death on August 6 brought an end to their long vigil, but left Livy—an expectant mother—careworn and exhausted.

When the Clemenses returned to Buffalo their state of mourning heightened the sense of isolation they always felt in that city. Their only close friends were David Gray, poet and editor of the Buffalo *Courier*, and his young wife. Shortly after her father's death Livy invited as her house guest a family friend named Emma Nye, a young schoolteacher whose parents were far away in South Carolina. Emma Nye sickened almost immediately with typhoid, and after a month's prostration died on September 29 in Mark and Livy's bedroom.

These tragic illnesses and the nursing demanded proved too much for Livy, and on November 7 she gave birth prematurely to a frail boy, christened Langdon, remaining herself an invalid all through the winter that followed.

Four days later Clemens wrote a letter purporting to be from little Langdon to his great-grandmother Eunice Ford, matriarch of the household at Elmira.

N O T I C E. Do not tell Grandma who the letter is from. Let her find out as she goes along.

BUFFALO, *Nov.* 11 [1870]

DEAR GRANDMA: I have waited with some impatience to hear from you or from some other member of the family, but up to this time, no letter has arrived for me. I have received enthusiastic

[8] General Frederick Dent, the President's brother-in-law, described as "companionable but useless" (Louis A. Coolidge, *Ulysses S. Grant* [1917], 390).

notice in telegrams from Cleveland & in congratulations from Mr. Brooks in New York—& the telegrams from Elmira have been gladly received & carefully preserved. But from you personally, I have not heard, at least in the shape of a letter, & I am obliged to say that I am hurt at it. Every now & then I think it all over & then I comprehend that you cannot write in these latter years without great difficulty. Of course that makes me feel better about it, but it does not last long. I soon get to worrying again & saying to myself that you might have written me one line at least. But never mind, I know it is all just as it should be, & that you have neglected me not because you *desired* to do it, but because you could not well *help* it. For I will not believe but that you love me. I am four days old to-day at eleven o'clock. Do you recollect when *you* were only 4 days old? I guess you don't. I am looking for Granny Fairbanks tomorrow, & will be glad to see her, too, but I shall be outrageously sorry to part with Aunt Susie Crane, for she was here when I first came, & I have come to like her society very much, & she knows my disposition better than anybody except Auntie Smith.

I *am* boarding with a strange young woman by the name of Brown, & *her* baby is boarding with my mother. I expect Mrs. Brown could take several more boarders like me, for I *am* not a very hearty eater. I don't understand this little game, but I guess it is all right. It is some little neat trick of my father's to save expense, I fancy.

I have a ridiculous time of it with clothes.—Except a shirt which aunt Hattie made for me I haven't a rag in the world that fits me. Everything is too large. You ought to see the things they call "slips." I am only 13 inches long, & these things are as much as 3 feet. Think of it. I trip & break my neck every time I make a step, for I can't think to gather up the surplus when I am in a hurry.

I tell you I am tired being bundled up head & ears nine-tenths of my time. And I don't like this thing of being stripped naked & washed. I *like* to be stripped & warmed at the stove—that is real bully—but I do despise this washing business. I believe it to be a gratuitous & unnecessary piece of meanness. I never see them wash the cat.

And I tell you it is dull, roosting around on pillows & rocking chairs & every body else spinning around town having a good time. Sometimes they let that other baby lie on the kitchen table & wink at the sun, but bless you *I* never get a show. Sometimes I get so mad that I can *not* keep my temper or my opinion. But it only makes things worse. They call it *colic*, & give me some execrable medicine.—*Colic*. Everything is *colic*. A baby can't·open its mouth about the simplest matter but up comes some wise body & says it is *wind in its bowels*. When I saw the dog the first time, I made a noise which was partly fright & partly admiration—but it cost me a double dose of medicine for wind in the bowels. Do these people take me for a balloon?

I am not entirely satisfied with my complexion. I am as red as a lobster. I am really ashamed to see company. But I am perfectly satisfied with my personal appearance, for I think I look just like Aunt Susie. They keep me on the shortest kind of rations, & that is one thing that don't suit the subscriber. My mother has mashed potatoes, & gruel, & tea, & toast, & all sorts of sumptuous fare, but she never gives *me* a bite—& you can risk your last dollar on it that I don't *ask* for it. It would only be another case of "wind in the bowels." You'll have to excuse *me*. I am learning to keep my remarks to myself. [But between you & I, Grandma, I get the advantage of them occasionaly—now last night I kept aunt Smith getting up every hour to feed me—and I wasn't hungry once.]

That doctor had just been here again. Come to play some fresh swindle on *me*, I suppose. He is the meanest looking white man I ever saw. Mind, now, this is not a splenetic & prejudiced outburst, but a calm & deliberate opinion formed & founded upon careful observation. Won't I "lay" for him when I get my teeth?

Good-bye Grandma, good-bye. Great love to you & grandma & all the whole household.

Your loving great grandson

LANGDON CLEMENS

With the coming of spring Livy was carried on a mattress to Elmira, where during the summer she began slowly to regain her strength at the Cranes' hilltop retreat called Quarry Farm—henceforth the Clemens' favorite spot for summer holidays. The baby continued sickly.

These disasters, joined to the social uncongeniality of Buffalo and the irksomeness of editorial work, led Mark to sell out his interests there in 1871. He prepared to move his little family to Hartford, and August went ahead to rent a house for the winter and consult with the Blisses about a new book he had been writing, *Roughing It*.

And from there he wrote Livy the following letter, of which only the third page survives.

[HARTFORD, *circa August* 9, 1871]

. . . it isn't worth while to think about it or talk about it.

Don't fear for us darling. If you are taken away I will love the baby & have a jealous care over him.—But let us hope & trust that both you & I shall tend him & watch over him till we are helped from our easy-chairs to the parlor to see his children married. Let us hope that way, sweetheart & try to trust that it will be so. In any case, you need not suffer any uneasiness about that influence you speak of. He shall never come under it. Better poison his body than his soul. Better make a corpse of him than a cur.

Livy dear, it is sad to think of your passing alone through these solemn anniversaries[9] that are so fraught with memories of a happy time & a gracious presence; a noble heart, a beautiful spirit, a love only less than divine; a protecting arm [never selfish] a courage that quieted fear & brought repose, a sympathy so broad & general, & withal so strong & warm, that to possess it is to be that rare thing, that jewel of price, a Comforter.

The absent-minded Orion and his aggressive wife Mary or Mollie, mentioned in the next letter, had lately moved to Hartford, where through Sam's influence Orion was made editor of a trade paper, *The Publisher*, put out by the Blisses. And the mother of Sam and Orion, Jane Clemens, accompanied by her granddaughter Annie Moffett, had just come from her new home in Fredonia to visit Orion's household, then established in a boarding house.

[9] The first anniversary of her father's death and burial.

HARTFORD, 10th [August, 1871]

Livy darling, the dispatch came, & I answered it right away.
Funny, ain't it, how the letters hang fire? I have written every day
but two, I believe—one day in N. Y., & one since I arrived here.
One day I wrote *two* letters—one of them brief. Shall do that
oftener hereafter.

Also the box of clothing came, & was welcome. It was thoughtful of you, my treasure. With this box came another from N. Y.
—for I bought two coats & five vests there. I am all right, now.
I didn't need five vests, but sent for them in a spurt of anger when
I found I had nothing with me but a lot of those hated old single
breasted atrocities that I have thrown away thirteen times, given
away six times, & burned up twice. Now I'll inflict them on Orion,
with the understanding that the next time I find them among my
traps again there shall be a permanent coolness in the Clemens
family here.

I wrote a splendid chapter to-day, for the middle of the book.[10]
I admire the book more & more the more I cut & slash & lick &
trim & revamp it. But you'll be getting impatient, now, & so I am
going to begin to-night & work day & night both till I get through.
It is a tedious, arduous job shaping such a mass of MS for the
press. It took me two months to do it for the Innocents. But this
is another sight easier job, because it is so much better literary
work—so much more acceptably written. It takes 1800 pages of
MS to make this book?—& that is just what I have got—or rather,
I have got 1,830. *I* thought that just a little over 1500 pages would
be enough & that I could leave off all the Overland trip—what a
pity I can't.

Ma bought a silk dress yesterday, for $24 & tired herself clear
out, to-day, helping Mary & Annie make it up. She looked fagged.
You see, they couldn't find a sempstress, & Ma absolutely needed
the dress to swell around in while she is here. Ma is a wonderfully
winning woman, with her gentle simplicity & her never-failing
goodness of heart & yearning interest in all creatures & their
smallest joys & sorrows. It is why she is such a good letter-writer—
this warm personal interest of hers in every thing that others have
at heart. Whatever is important to another is important to her.

[10] *Roughing It.*

Her letters treat of every body's affairs, & would make her [out] seem a mousing, meddling, uneasy devil of a gossip to a person who did not know her.

Annie is a very attractive & interesting girl, & your brown silk becomes her exceedingly, it is so modest & yet so dressy & handsome.

Mollie is *always* attractive & pleasant and interesting in company.

Orion is as queer & heedless a bird as ever. He met a strange young lady in the hall this evening; mistook her for the landlady's daughter (the resemblance being [similar] equal to that between a cameleopard & a kangaroo) & shouted: "Hello, you're back early!" She took him for a fugitive from the asylum & left without finishing her errand.

Night before last he was standing on the porch—absent minded, as usual—when a lady came out with the landlady—couldn't get the gate open—Orion said to the landlady, "Stay where you are— I'll open it for her"—which he did. Thought he knew her—which he didn't. Said: "It is getting late—I'm going to see you home." She said, "Oh, no, thank you—it isn't very far, & I'm not afraid." Said he, gaily: "Oh, you *ain't*! well if *you* ain't, *I* ain't either—so come along." What could the woman do, with so cheerful an infant? Why, simply let him go home with her—which she did. She took him a route he had never traveled before—finally stopped before a house he never had seen before—said: "This is my home; I am much obliged to you, sir: Good-night"—& left him standing there wondering whether his friend had moved her habitation within twenty-four hours, or whether he had been making an ass of himself again. The odds were in favor of the latter—& if he had bet with himself on it he might have made some money.

But *this* won't do.—Good night, my old darling & yours truly will go to work.

SAML

P.S. I bet Bliss is still carrying some of my letters in his pocket. That's why they don't go.

CHAPTER EIGHT

The Redpath Circuit

RENTING the John Hookers' house at Nook Farm, the Clemenses in the early autumn of 1871 cast anchor in that little Hartford community where they would soon build a roof of their own and remain for the twenty happiest years of their life together.

After getting his wife and baby settled there, Clemens struck out upon a rigorous lecture tour under the auspices of James Redpath of Boston. The sequence of letters that follows is the best disclosure of his ups and downs, joys and worries, and constant preoccupation with the response of his audiences. The first lecture for which he was billed bore the cumbersome title "Reminiscences of Some Un-Commonplace Characters I Have Chanced to Meet," featuring Artemus Ward, Dick Baker the quartz miner, Riley the journalist, the King of the Sandwich Islands, and others. When writing it in the summer of 1871 Mark judged it "tip-top," but under the test of performance quickly grew dissatisfied, as the next letter shows, and shifted to one about Artemus alone. This also palled, and in midseason he had the happy inspiration of drawing one from his new book and calling it by the same name, "Roughing It."

ALLENTOWN, *Tues.* P M [*October* 17, 1871]
Livy darling, this lecture will *never* do. I *hate* it & won't keep it. I can't even handle these chuckleheaded Dutch with it.

Have blocked out a lecture on Artemus Ward, & shall write it next Saturday & deliver it next Monday in Washington.

Poor child, I am so sorry you are so lonely & forlorn—but bear up—just think, you *don't have to lecture*! You ought to be in ecstasies. We'll come together again, & then we'll forget all our troubles.

With a world of love,

SAM

MILFORD, MASS., 31*st* [*October, 1871*]

Livy darling, the same old practising on audiences still goes on— the same old feeling of pulses & altering manner & matter to suit the symptoms. The very same lecture that *convulsed* Great Barrington was received with the gentlest & most well-bred smiles & rippling comfort by Milford. Now we'll see what *Boston* is going to do. Boston must sit up & behave, & do right by me. As Boston goes, so goes New England.[1]

I got no letters at Brattleboro. None had come. None in the post office, either. No proofs from Bliss. Brattleboro is unreliable, I guess.

I didn't write last night. Felt kind of beat out. To-day I traveled the entire day in piddling trains that stopped every four or five minutes. Am lazy, but not a bit tired—hot bath fetched me around handsomely. Saw Mrs. Lee's brother to-night (we saw *her* at Gov. Hawley's).

Read Eugene Aram[2] all day—found it tedious—skipped 4 pages out of 5. Skipped the corporal *all* the time. He don't amount to *anything*. World of love. Kiss mother & cubbie for Saml. Would the doctor's henchmen stand that? No.

I tell you Annie's & Sammy's fresh & genuine delight make squandering watches a coveted & delicious pleasure.[3] I don't know when I have enjoyed anything so really & so heartily as Annie's letter. I wish the watch had been seven times as large, & much more beautiful.

This printed joke is *splendid.* Oh I *would* love to see Sue & The & Clara in our dear, dear Nook Barn.[4] Hang it though, I'll miss

[1] From that city on November 1 he reported: "People say Boston audiences ain't responsive. People lie. Boston audiences get perfectly uproarious when they get started. *I* am satisfied with to-night."

[2] Bulwer Lytton's popular novel, published in 1832.

[3] Sam Moffett, then aged eleven, was Annie's younger brother and Samuel Clemens' namesake. Their uncle showered them with presents.

[4] That is, Susan and Theodore Crane, and Clara Spaulding, Livy's most intimate Elmira friend.

it all, just know. My darling, I deluge you now with all my love— bail it out on them second-hand when they come.

I know there are other things I ought to write, but it is so late & I am so sleepy.

Expect to put a check in this for $125—making $550 to you since (& including) Danville, Ill. Telegraph receipt, if I put in the check.

With a world of love. Oh, the letters! Never get done writing business letters till long past midnight.

Lovingly

SAML

P. S.—Me sick? The idea! I should as soon expect a wooden image to get sick. I don't know what sickness is.

HAVERHILL [MASS., *November* 16, 1871]
Livy darling, it was a dreadfully stormy night, the train was delayed a while, & when I got to the hall it was half an hour *after* the time for the lecture to begin. But not a soul had left the house. I went right through the audience in my overcoat & over-shoes with carpet bag in hand, & undressed on the stage in full view. It was no time to stand on ceremony. I told them I knew they were indignant with me, & righteously so—& that if any aggrieved gentleman would rise in his place & abuse me for 15 minutes, I would feel better, would take it as a great kindness, & would do as much for *him* some time. That broke the ice & we went through with colors flying & drums beating.

You sent the "Not a stage trick" (for which I am greatly obliged to Warner—it was copied in the Boston papers) but you didn't send the Brooklyn note you speak of. What was it about?

I am getting my lecture in better shape, now. I end it with the poetry, every time, & a description of Artemus's death in a foreign land.

Mighty glad to hear old Twichell is back. I want to hear him howl about the "strange, strange lands beyond the sea."

Confound the confounded cooks. Offer *five* dollars a week, & see if that won't fetch one. Advertise again.

I don't get a chance to read anything, my old darling—am patching at my lecture all the time—trying to weed Artemus out of it & work myself *in*. What *I* say, *fetches* 'em—but what *he* says —*don't*. But I'm *going* to mark Lowell for you—pity, too, to mar such dainty pages.

Bless your heart, *I* appreciate the cubbie—& shall, more & more as he develops & becomes vicious & interesting. To me he is a very very dear little rip. Kiss him for me, sweetheart. I have ordered the song book for him.

Since I wrote that last sentence, I have been studying the railway guide an hour, my dearie, & I think I can reach home some time Saturday afternoon or evening, & stay till after midnight, & then go on to New York, where I can rest all day Sunday & half of Monday—or possibly there may be a *day light* train on Sunday from Hartford to New York. I'll find out. I want to see my darling I do assure you.

Sleepy!
Lovingly
SAML

Love to Mr. & Ce.

This last cryptic postscript surely means "Mother and Cubbie." Four days later Livy wrote to him as follows, on the heels of a flying visit to Hartford.

HARTFORD Monday Eve [November 20, 1871]

MY DARLING—Last night you were here and how much nicer it was than it is tonight when you are away—Didn't we have a good visit together? I do hope that this will be the last season that it will be necessary for you to lecture, it is not the way for a husband and wife to live if they can possibly avoid it, is it? Separation comes soon enough—The Pottier and Stymas bill has come, it is $128.00, I thought it would probably be 150.00 at least— Then the bill on the insurance of our goods against accident $60.00—so it is well that you left me the additional $150.00 if you had not I should have run ashore—

I answered all your letters today except the one from Meline that I could not find, if I do not find it I will get his address in some way and write him.[5] It was a pleasure to be writing letters for you, it is a pleasure to do *any* thing for you—

[5] James P. Meline had written Mark six months earlier, asking his influence in persuading the Blisses to publish his book on New Mexico.

As soon as I had the baby washed and dressed this forenoon I went up in the guest room lay down and slept until two o'clock.

I am going over to the "the club"[6] now in a few minutes I wish you were going with me I rather dread it—I want you along to protect me.

The baby is so sweet and dear, I know as he grows older you and he will love each other like *every thing* What a wonderful thing love is, I do trust that we shall be a *thoroughly united loving family*—it certainly is the heaven here below—

Youth in certain things you must teach me a "don't care" spirit, as regards cooks and the like, and I too will endevour to teach myself—I believe there is nothing that sooner ruins the happiness of a family than a worrying woman—

Cubbie is very anxious to have you get home Sat. he hopes that you will not fail us on any account—

I hope it is a pleasant evening in Phila. it is rainy and unpleasant here. I have not been out today, I have slept and visited with the baby most of the day—

Mother sits near me at work on her silk quilt I will try to add a line to this when I come home from Mr Warners

Send Annie's and Sammy's watches to me, so that I can send them with the other gifts—Am home from Mr Ws, will write about it tomorrow—too sleepy tonight

With never ending love

Your Livy

Mark's next letter is interesting for its proof that he had long contemplated a book about his Mississippi pilot memories— although to Howells on October 24, 1874, he credited Joe Twichell with having just planted the idea in his mind during "a long walk in the woods."

BENNINGTON [Vt.], *Monday* p m [*November 27, 1871*]
Livy darling, good house, but they laughed too much.—A great fault with this lecture is that I have no way of turning it into a serious & instructive vein at will. *Any* lecture of mine ought to be a running narrative-plank, with square holes in it, six inches

---

[6] Probably the ladies' auxiliary of the Monday Evening Club of Hartford, a locally famous discussion group to which Mark belonged.

apart, all the length of it, & then in my mental shop I ought to have plugs (half marked "serious" & the other marked "humorous") to select from & jam into these holes according to the temper of the audience.

I am so sorry to have to leave you with all the weight of housekeeping on your shoulders—& at the same time I know that it is a blessing to you—for only wholesome care & work can make lonely people endure existence. I particularly hate to have to inflict on you the bore of answering my business letters. That is a hardship indeed.

I think Bliss has gotten up the prospectus book[7] with taste & skill. The selections are good, & judiciously arranged. He had a world of good matter to select from, though. This is a better book than the Innocents, & *much* better written. If the subject were less hackneyed it would be a great success. But when I come to write the Mississippi book, *then* look out! I will spend 2 months on the river & take notes, & I bet you I will make a standard work.

Well, it is late bedtime—so with a loving good night kiss, I send my deep love to my mother Olivia Langdon, & to my wife Olivia Langdon; to my niece Olivia Langdon; & to my future daughter Olivia Langdon.

SAML

His niece, christened Julia Olivia Langdon and called Julia, had been born on November 21, 1871, but his daughter, Olivia Susan Clemens and called Susy, was not born until the following March 19.

On November 28 Livy wrote wistfully: "I hope that I shall get a letter from you tomorrow morning, I do like to hear from you little man, because you know—well you know all about it—" A similar yearning is the dominant mood of her next letter.

HARTFORD *Dec.* 2nd 1871

MY DEAR HEART—It did me no good to wish for twenty letters, I did not get one—I have rec'd only one letter and one little note from you since you left home, they both came in the same mail—

7 For *Roughing It*, off the press in February 1872.

It is Saturday night, and I am homesick for you, not hearing from you makes me feel still more homesick—

The watches have come they are all nice and just the thing, Annie's is *lovely*, as prettie as can be—you have good taste Darling —I know she will be perfectly delighted with it—

I have heard nothing from Mrs Brooks, so do not know whether she is coming or not—

It is just after dinner, I guess I will not write more until bed time, perhaps I shall then write more cheerfully I am a little cross, beside wanting you so much and being disappointed about hearing from you—As you go further west it will take longer and longer for letters to reach me—

Bed time—

Have been drawing a plan of our house, and feel better than at dinner time—This will not go until Monday morning so will finish tomorrow—Good night, sweet sleep—

Sunday Evening

I tell you I am glad that tomorrow is Monday because I shall probably get letters—if I do not—well I do not know what I shall do, telegraph you I guess—

Mother and I went to church this morning, we found that we were the first people in the church, so went over to Mr Twichells and staid there until they were ready for church—

It is so long since I have been to church that I was mellowed by the very atmosphere I think, Mr Twitchells prayer touched me and made me cry, he prayed particularly for those who had fallen away and were longing to come back to God—Youth I am ashamed to go back, because I have fallen away so many times and gone back feeling that if I ever should grow cold again, it would be useless trying, because I never could have more earnest and prayerfull and even at times heart broken determination to keep by the truth and the right and strive for God's spirit—it would seem if I did not remain steadfast after such times, I never could—Mr. Twichell is such a good earnest man and gave us a good sermon, I think we shall enjoy our church there very much —If I was just a little stronger I would go into the Sunday school, I have a great mind too as it is, but I know Mother would not be willing to have me—and I have thought that I would be as careful as I know how during these coming six months—I hope not to have as delicate a child next time as little Langdon was—

How I do want you at home Darling, I am so thankful that I do want you—you are a dear little man—I am grateful that my heart is so filled with love for you—Mrs Warner was speaking this P.M. of lukewarmness toward God, she said she used to be greatly troubled about it, but lately she thinks that is of no consequence, our moods are different we do not always feel alike toward our husbands—I told her if I felt toward God as I did toward my husband I should never be in the least troubled—I did not tell her how almost perfectly cold I am toward God—

I think I have about decided what we shall do about building, I have *decided* so you will not have to decide you see, Dear Heart—

We will put if it is necessary the 29000. into house, grounds, and what new furniture we may need—If we wait to know whether we can afford it we shall wait eight years, because I do not believe we shall know whether we can afford to live in this way until the end of the Copartnership[8]—Charlie says I can perfectly well have from three to five hundred dollars a month—you may lecture *one month* in New England during the winter, that will give you 2000. so that will give you what money you want for me and other incidental matters—The three hundred dollars a month with what your regular work will bring you will be plenty—If after a time we find, that the estate is not worth a living to us we will change entirely our mode of living—That probably will not be discovered, for three or four or perhaps the eight years—we shall involve nobody and discomfort nobody, we will not be in debt for our house—The children will then be older and I shall not need so much help in the care of them, I shall then be stronger if I keep on increasing in strength as I have done—We will either board or live in a small cottage and keep one servant, will live near the horse cars so that I can get along without a horse and carriage—I *can not* and I *will not* think about your being away from me this way every year, it is not half living

8 Of Charles Langdon, J. D. F. Slee, and Theodore Crane, to operate the coal company.

—if in order to sustain our present mode of living you are obliged
to do that, then we will change our mode of living—

We need now the comfort of a convenient home, while our
babies are young and needing care—think if we wait two years
it is very likely that we shall not know any better than we do now
whether we can build or not—Charlie and all talk as if there was
no question about it—

I have not commenced French yet, Clara wants to study German
when she comes, and I know with Baby, house and all, both would
be more than it would be best for me to undertake—

Good night Darling—I do love our boy better and better
every day if that is possible—Richest blessings on you my youth
                                        Lovingly LIVY—
Ever and ever so much love to Ma, Pamela, Annie, Sammy—I
had forgotten that this letter was to reach you there[9]—

Did Pamela get my letter acknowledging the rec't of her prettie
bag?

Mark's itinerary shows that he had just completed a tour of
Michigan towns, ending with Kalamazoo, before he wrote the
next letter, prior to opening in Chicago on Monday the 18th for
a two-night stand. Here for the first time before a metropolitan
audience he gave his new lecture "Roughing It," mentioned in
this letter, and with great success. Much of the city's heart was a
desolation of ashes, thanks to the great fire that had broken out
on October 9.

                                        CHICAGO, *Dec.* 16 [1871]
My dear dear old darling, I went to bed considerably after mid,
night yesterday morning, got up again at 4 oclock & went down
(breakfastless) to the depot, & found, with unspeakable gladness
that there stood a sleeping car which I might have been occupying
all night—but as usual nobody about the hotel or among the
lecture committee knew anything *certain* about *any* train. I took
a berth—the train left immediately, & of course I couldn't go to
sleep. We were due here in two hours—we fooled along & got
here in *eleven* hours—3 P.M. Could get nothing to eat, all that

[9] The letter is directed to Fredonia.

time. Not a vehicle at the station, nor a man or a boy. Had to
carry my two satchels half a mile, to Mr. Robert Law's house, &
it did seem to me they weighed a couple of tons apiece before I
got through. I then ate a perfectly enormous dinner (a roast
turkey & 8 gallons of Oolong tea—well it was "long" something
—it was the longest tea that ever went down my throat—it was
hours in passing a given point).

Then Mr. Law & I immediately hopped into his buggy & for
2 steady hours we capered among the solemn ruins, on both sides
of the river—a crisp, bitter day, but all days are alike to my sealskin coat—I can only tell it is cold by my nose & by seeing other
people's actions. There is literally no Chicago *here,* that ever I
saw before.

We sat up & talked till 10 & all went to bed. I worked till after
midnight amending & altering my lecture, & then turned in &
slept like a log—I don't mean a brisk, fresh, *green* log, but an old
dead, soggy, *rotten* one, that never turns over or gives a yelp. All
night long. Awoke 20 minutes ago—it is now 11 A.M., & there is
a gentleman up yonder at the depot with a carriage, ready to
receive me as I step out of the cars from Kalamazoo. I telegraphed
him I would be in Chicago promptly at 11 oclock this morning,
& I have kept my word—here I *am.* But I can easily explain to
him that the reason he missed me was that I mean 11 oclock in a
general way, & not any particular way, & that I don't blame *him*
—particularly.

I shall now get up and go to Dr Jackson's house & be his guest
for 2 days. I feel perfectly *splendid.* One night's rest always renews
me, restores me, makes my life & vigor perfect. I wish I could see
my darling this morning, & rest her head on my breast & make her
forget this dismal lecture business & its long separations. But time
moves along, honey! Not so very many days yet!

With a world of love
SAML.

Mark's friend here mentioned was A. Reeves Jackson, the
"guide-destroying doctor" of *Innocents Abroad,* who in 1870
settled in Chicago and had already founded there the Woman's
Hospital of the state of Illinois, serving as its surgeon-in-chief.

CHAMPAIGN, ILL., *Dec.* 26, 1871

Livy Darling, it is almost lecture time, & I thought I would rattle off a line to tell you how dearly I love you, child—for I cannot abide this execrable hotel & shall leave for Tuscola after the lecture & see if I can't do better. My new lecture is about licked into shape, & this afternoon after trimming at it all day I memorized one-fourth of it. Shall commit another fourth tomorrow, maybe more—& shall begin talking it the moment I get out of the range of the cursed Chicago Tribune that printed my new lecture & so made it impossible for me to talk it with any spirit in Illinois. If these devils incarnate only appreciated what suffering they inflict with their infernal synopses, maybe they would try to have humanity enough to refrain.

I am *so* sorry you are so lonesome, honey, but keep bravely up till by & by. With ever so much love,

SAML

A telegram sent on January 7 from Clemens to William Dean Howells at the *Atlantic Monthly* explains the "sick & needy poet" mentioned in the next letter: "Please telegraph the following to Bret Harte immediately at my cost W A Kendall the poet writes that he is friendless & moneyless & is dying by inches as you know doctors say he must return to California & by sea wants to sail the fifteenth will you petition the steamship company for a pass for him & sign my name & Howells & the other boys to it & forward said pass to Kendall at three twenty three Van Buren street Brooklyn I will send him fifty dollars get him some money if you can I do not know him but I know he is a good fellow and has hard luck."

WOOSTER [OHIO], *Jan* 7 [1872]

Livy darling, did these clothes ever come? If so you ought to have informed me. If they did, forward the enclosed note to the tailors, along with the bill (have Orion get you a check for $89 & enclose that, too—I am out of money). If they *didn't* come, write & tell Redpath so (36 Bromfield st) & enclose my letter & the draft to *him* & let him see the tailors.

I hired a locomotive for $75 yesterday, to keep from having to get up at 2 in the morning; then I gave away $50 to a sick & needy poet, & so I am about out of cash.

I enclose a couple for Theodore—but both of them put together ain't as good as that child's-trumpet story.

I have been figuring. My lecture business, up to the end of January, yields about $10,000—& yet, when I preach Jan. 30, it is well I am so close to Hartford, for I would not have money enough to get home on. It has all gone & is going, for those necessaries of life—debts. Every night the question is, Well, who does *this* day's earnings belong to?—& away it goes. I *do* hate lecturing, & I shall try hard to have as little as possible of it to do hereafter. The rest of my earnings will go to Ma & Redpath, principally— & then what are *we* going to do, I don't reckon? *You* gave that $50 to the poet, honey, for that was the money I was going to buy you a Christmas present with. How do you like such conduct as those?

Lecturing is hateful, but it *must* come to an end yet, & *then* I'll see my darling, whom I love, love, *love.*

Love to all that jolly household & that dear old Susie.

SAML

STEUBENVILLE [OHIO] *Jan. 9* [1872]

Livy Darling, I am stopping at the Female Seminary—70 of the girls were at the lecture last night, & a mighty handsome lot they were.

These windows overlook the Ohio—once alive with steamboats & crowded with all manner of traffic; but now a deserted stream, victim of the railroads. Where lie the pilots. They were starchy boys, in my time, & greatly envied by the youth of the West. The same with the Mississippi pilots—though the Mobile & Ohio Railroad had already walked suddenly off with the passenger business in my day, & so it was the beginning of the end.

I am reading "The Member from Paris" a very bright, sharp, able French political novel, very happily translated. It is all so good & so Frenchy that I don't know where to mark! I have read & sent home the Golden Legend, the New England tragedies,

Edwin of Deira, Erling the Bold, & a novel by the author of John Halifax[10]—forgotten the name of it.

Did my canvassing book, full of lecture MSS reach you from Paris?[11] You do not mention it.

There is no life in me this morning—have slept too long & hard. Love to all those dear fellows under the roof, & cords & cords of love to you, Livy my darling.

SAML

KITTANNING [PA.], 12*th* [*Jan.* 1872]

Livy darling, this is a filthy, stupid, hateful Dutch village, like *all* Pennsylvania—& I have got to lecture to these leatherheads to night—but shall leave for Pittsburgh at 3 in the morning, & spend Sunday in that black but delightful town.

Am up for dinners & things there. I *love* you, Livy darling,

SAML

In early February Clemens closed "the most detestable lecture campaign that ever was," as he described it to Mrs. Fairbanks on the thirteenth, after returning to Hartford.

Shortly before Susy's birth in March, the Clemenses went to Elmira and remained with the Langdons and Cranes until the onset of summer. The best report of their growing family and activities is contained in a hitherto unpublished letter written by Clemens to their Hartford neighbor Charles Dudley Warner— whose "Back-log Studies," appearing serially, would be published before the end of the year as a volume.

Characteristically, on second thought Mark has canceled a facetious remark which he penned about Livy as a nursing mother, although the deletion can be read with difficulty.

ELMIRA, *Apl.* 22 [1872]

We have read two Back-logs aloud since we came here, and a thoroughly grateful audience have insisted both times that I write

[10] Jacobus de Voragine's *The Golden Legend*, endlessly reprinted; Longfellow's *The New England Tragedies* (1868); Alexander Smith's *Edwin of Deira* (1861); R. M. Ballantine's *Erling the Bold* (1869); Dinah Mulock Craik (*John Halifax*) spawned so many novels in this era that conjecture is profitless.

[11] He had lectured in Paris, Illinois, on December 30.

and cordially thank the author—a thing which I was glad enough to do. Mrs. C. reminded me of it again as I started to bed—hence my non-forgetfulness this time.

Livy desires me to write Mrs Warner in her place, too, since she has not "got down to her work" yet. I have no news save of the household. The new baby flourishes, and groweth strong and comely apace. She keeps one cow "humping herself" to supply the bread of life for her—and Livy is relieved from duty. [Livy is very inefficient in some respects.] Langdon has no appetite, but is brisk and strong. His teeth don't come—and neither does his language.

Livy drives out a little, sews a little, walks a little—is getting along pretty satisfactorily.

Peace be with you!

I write this note only on condition that it shall not inflict the duty of answering it. I fancy you have writing enough to do, Warner, without bothering with letters.

Yrs. Truly
S. L. CLEMENS

In early May the Clemenses, accompanied by Mark's mother, went out to Cleveland to spend a few days at "Fair Banks," Lake shore home of their friends of that name. To the infant Susy her father wrote as follows.

FAIR BANKS, May 9 [1872]

MY DEAR DAUGHTER: Your grandmother Fairbanks joins your mother & me in great love to yourself & your brother Langdon.

We are enjoying our stay here to an extent not expressible save in words of syllables beyond your strength. Part of our enjoyment is derived from sleeping tranquilly right along, & never listening to see if you have got the snuffles afresh or the grand duke upstairs has wakened & wants a wet rag. And yet no doubt *you*, both of you, prospered just as well all night long as if you had had your father & mother's usual anxious supervision. Many's the night I've lain awake till 2 oclock in the morning reading Dumas & drinking beer, listening for the slightest sound you might make, my daughter, & suffering as only a father can suffer, with anxiety for his child. Some day you will thank me for this.

Well, good bye to you & to all the loving ones who are trying to supply the paternal place.—My child be virtuous & you will be happy.

Yr father

SAML L. CLEMENS

Little Langdon, the white-faced baby with a chronic cough, succumbed to diphtheria and died on June 2, a few days after the Clemens' return to Hartford. Grief stricken, they left Orion and Mollie in charge of their house, and took the new baby to the shore at Saybrook for the summer.

CHAPTER NINE

Home Thoughts from Abroad

WITH Livy and the infant Susy in good health after a quiet summer at the shore, Mark Twain sailed for England on August 21, 1872. The purpose of his trip was threefold: to protect *Roughing It* against the notorious British pirate John Camden Hotten and other literary freebooters, to give lectures in London, and to collect notes (sent to Livy in the form of a journal) for a book on England and the English which Mark never got around to writing.

OFF QUEENSTOWN, IRELAND, *Aug.* 29/72

Livy darling, I have little or nothing to write, except that I love you & think of you night & day, & wonder where you are, & what you are doing, & how the Muggins comes on, & whether she ever speaks of me—& whether Mother is cheerful & happy. I hope & trust & pray that you are all well & enjoying yourselves—but I can't say that I have been enjoying myself, greatly, lost in a vast ship where our 40 or 50 passengers flit about in the great dim distances like vagrant spirits. But latterly our small clique *have* had a somewhat better time of it, though if one is absent there can be no whist.

I have given the purser a ten-dollar telegram of 3 words to send to you from Queenstown, & also my journal in 2 envelopes—& now I'll rush & give him this—consider, my dear, that I am standing high on the stern of the ship, looking westward, with my hands to my mouth, trumpet fashion, yelling across the tossing waste of waves, "I LOVE YOU, LIVY DARLING ! ! !"

SAML

His first ten days in Britain converted the romantic Clemens into a stout Anglophile, as the following letter attests.

THE BROADWAY, LUDGATE, LONDON, E. C.

Sept. 11, 1872

Livy darling, I was getting positively uneasy until this morning, when I got your two first letters (one dated Aug. 20 & one Aug. 28). I was going to telegraph you to day, to ask what the matter was. But now I am all right. You are well, Mother is with you & the Muggins is jolly & knows what her hands are made for. I would like very much to see you all just now.

Confound this town, time slips relentlessly away & I accomplish next to nothing. Too much company—too much dining—too much sociability. (But I would rather live in England than America—which is treason.) Made a speech at the Whitefriars Club—very good speech—but the shorthand reporters did not get it exactly right & so I do not forward it. No that is not it. I neglected to buy copies of the papers. The only places I have been to in this town are the Chrystal Palace, the Tower of London & Old St. Paul's. Have not even written in my journal for 4 days— don't get time. Real pleasant people here.

Left London day before yesterday with Osgood the Boston publisher & spent all day yesterday driving about Warwickshire in an open barouche. It is the loveliest land in its summer garb! We visited Kenilworth ruins, Warwick Castle (pronounce it *Warrick*) and the Shakespeare celebrities in & about Stratford-on-Avon— (pronounce that *a* just as you would the a in *Kate*). Go down to Brighton tomorrow with Tom Hood. (Tell Warner a Philadelphia paper, just arrived, abuses Hood for not separating his own feeble name from his father's great fame by calling himself "Thomas Hood the Younger"—& the joke of it is that the son's name is *not* Thomas, but simply *Tom*, & so there was no *Tom* Hood the *elder*.)

Indeed Charley's letter is in the last degree comforting—*isn't* it? Charley's a good brother, & I don't know how we ever could get along with our money matters without him.

I send all my love to you & our dear babies—& to Mother.

SAML

The day after printing his blast in The *Spectator* against "John Camden Hottentot," which won considerable British sympathy

for Mark Twain's copyright crusade, he wrote the following letter
to Livy.

The Turners here mentioned appear to be the wife and daughter of Chief Justice George Turner, known to Clemens a decade
earlier in the Nevada Territory—upon whose supreme bench he
sat.

LONDON, Sept. 22 [1872]

Livy darling, I am making tolerably fair progress, & am at last
getting my sight-seeing systematized. I am running the legs off
myself, but tomorrow & next day I am going to devote to my
diary. It will bring me up a good long way.

I have been carrying English paper money loosely in my pocket,
just as I always did with greenbacks, & I have come to grief. I
find I have lost it all out, sometime or other, don't know when
—only noticed it to-day. Lost anywhere from £30 to £40. Stupid
business.

Published that blast at Hotten yesterday. I met Mrs. George
Turner & Nellie on the stairs yesterday—wasn't expecting to see
them here.

This is no worn-out field. I can write up some of these things
in a more different way than they have been written before.

Made a speech at the Savage Club last night. Had a very good
time there.

Welly-well-well, I wish you were *here* instead of half a world
away, sweetheart. Tell me how you are. I love you Livy darling,
I do assure assure you, with all my heart.

SAML

Paine's biography, Appendix L, prints the Savage Club speech,
"About London," under the erroneous date of September 28. The
following letter shows that on this latter date Mark spoke at a
Guildhall dinner.

LONDON, *Saturday Night, Sept.* 28 [1872]

Livy darling, it has been a splendid night. I was at the installa-
tion in Guildhall, to-day of the new Sheriffs & Lord Mayor of

London. Tonight I was at the great dinner given by the new Sheriffs of London to the several guilds & liverymen of London. When I arrived nobody seemed to know me—so I passed modestly in, & took the seat assigned to me.—There was a vast crowd present at the dinner. In accordance with ancient custom, a man got up & called the names of all that immense mass of guests, beginning with the new Sheriff (a tremendous office in London) & called a horde of great names, one after another, which were received in respectful silence—but when he came to my name along with the rest, there was such a storm of applause as you never heard. The applause continued, & they could not go on with the list. I was never so taken aback in my life—never stricken so speechless—for it was totally unlooked for on my part. I thought I was the humblest in that great titled assemblage—& behold, mine was the *only* name in the long list that called forth this splendid compliment.

I did not know what to do, & so I sat still & did nothing. By & by the new sheriff, in his gorgeous robes of office, got up & proposed my health, & accompanied it with the longest & most extravagantly complimentary speech of the evening, & appointed me to respond to the toast to "literature."[1] Imagine my situation, before that great audience, without a single word of preparation —for I had expected nothing of this kind—I did not know I was a lion. I got up & said whatever came first, & made a good deal of a success—for I was the only man they consented to hear *clear through*—& they applauded handsomely. Indeed I wish I had known beforehand the good-will they had for me—I would have prepared a terrific speech. Even the fact that I was placed at the head of the table between Sir Antoine Baker[2] & Sir John Bennett had not prepared me for this ovation. I think it was a sort of lame speech I made, but it was splendidly received. I love you, Livy darling.

SAML

[1] Enclosed with this letter is the calling-card of Sir John Bennett, sheriff of London and Middlesex, on which is penciled: "Dear Twain—Will you stand for Literature if the Sheriff gives it? you can speak in your own language & the Press will understand every word. J.B."

[2] A Sir Antonio Brady was present (London *Times*, September 30, 1872), and Mark probably misunderstood the name.

Orion had lately lost his job with the Blisses. Mark's pet theory of job-getting here described—that is, working without pay until one became indispensable—was actually tried by Orion, as Mark recollected in his *Autobiography*.

Mark's comment upon Isabella Beecher Hooker's announced retirement from leadership in the feminist movement is in his choicest vein of irony.

LONDON, *Oct.* 3 [1872]

Livy darling, it is indeed pleasant to learn that Orion is happy & progressing. Now if he can only *keep* the place & continue to give satisfaction, all the better. It is no trouble for a man to get any situation he wants—by working at first for nothing—but of course to hold it firmly against all comers—after the wages begin —is the trick.

Somebody has sent me some Philadelphia papers whereby I see that poor old faithful Riley is dead.[3] It seems too bad.

Mrs. Hooker's solemn retirement from public life is news which is as grateful as it is humorous—but the tremendousness of her *reason* for retiring (because "her work is done" & her great end accomplished) surpasses the mere humanly humorous—it is the awful humor of the gods. For all these long months, this pleasant lady, under the impression that she was helping along a great & good cause, has been blandly pulling down the temple of Woman's Emancipation & shying the bricks at the builders; for all these long months she has moved sublimely among the conventions & congresses of the sex a very Spirit of Calamity; & whatsoever principle she breathed upon oratorically, perished; & whatsoever convert she took by the hand, that convert returned unto his sin again; & unto whatsoever political thing she lavished her love upon, there came sickness, & suffering, & speedy death; after all these long months, wherein she never rested from making enemies to her cause save when she was asleep, she retires serenely from her slaughter-house & says, in effect, Let the nations sing hosannah, let the spinning spheres applaud—my work is done!

She is a good woman—she *is* a good woman—but it is so like

---

[3] On the voyage home from the diamond fields he fell ill, and died apparently of blood-poisoning soon after landing.

her to do these things—she does derive such a satisfaction from everything her tangled brain conceives & her relentless hand demolishes. Well, anyway, I am glad she is out of "public life"—& I have no doubt that all of her best friends are, also.

Livy darling, I have been shopping & bought you a cloak, & if I don't lose it I will fetch it home to you. I shall probably buy no other present while here—they are too troublesome—but after hunting London over for a present for you, I found this thing & I liked it.

Been to Oxford for a day & a half—& if you *could* only see that piece of landscape (between here & Oxford) in its summer garb, you would have to confess that there is nothing even in New England that equals it for pure loveliness, & nothing outside of New England that even remotely approaches it. And if you could see the turf in the quadrangles of some of the colleges, & the Virginian creeper that pours its cataract of green & golden & crimson leaves down a quaint old gothic tower of Magdalen College— clear from the topmost pinnacle it comes flooding down over pointed windows & battered statues, & grotesque stone faces projecting from the wall—a wasteful, graceful, gorgeous little Niagara —& whosoever looks upon it will miss his train sure. That was the darlingest, loveliest picture I ever saw.

Good-bye sweethearts, good-bye. Good-bye sweetheart, goodbye. I love you.

SAML

P. S. Mr. Tyler of Hatch & Tyler, promised to send you your winter supply of coal—at $7 I think. Send to him when you need it.

LONDON, *Midnight. Nov.* 9, 1872

Livy darling, it was flattering, at the Lord Mayor's dinner, tonight, to have the nation's honored favorite, the Lord High Chancellor of England, in his vast wig & gown, with a splendid, sword-bearing lackey, following him & holding up his train, walk me arm-in-arm through the brilliant assemblage, & welcome me with all the enthusiasm of a girl, & tell me that when affairs of state oppress him & he can't sleep, he always has my books at hand & forgets his perplexities in reading them! And two other bewigged & gowned great state judges of England told me the very same thing.

And it was pleasant in such an illustrious assemblage to over-hear people talking about me at every step, & always compli-mentarily—& also to have these grandees come up & introduce themselves & apologize for it. You will heartily enjoy your English welcome when you come here. With a world of love,

SAML

Three days later he sailed for home, and remained in Hartford throughout the winter.

Early in 1873, chance dinner-table talk between the Clemenses and their neighbors, the Charles Dudley Warners, about the stu-pidity of current novels, led the wives to challenge their husbands to write a better one. In high glee and at top speed Clemens and Warner wrote *The Gilded Age,* the principal subject of this letter. The three Clemenses were going abroad in May, and while Mark remained in Hartford to revise his manuscript, Livy took Susy to Elmira for a brief visit in the old home.

Apl. 26th, 10.30 P M. [1873]

Livy darling, I have finished trimming & revamping all my MS, & to-day we began the work of critically reading the book, line by line & numbering the chapters & working them in together in their appropriate places. It is perfectly fascinating work. All of the first eleven chapters are mine, & when I came to read them right straight along without breaking, I got really interested; & when I got to Sellers' eye-water & his clock & his fireless stove & his turnip dinner, I could hardly read for laughing. The turnip dinner is powerful good—& is satisfactory now.

Warner failed on his description of Laura as a school-girl—as a *picture* of her, I mean. He had simply copied Miss Woolson's pretty description almost word for word—the plagiarism would have been detected in a moment. I told him so—he saw it & yet I'm hanged if he didn't hate to lose it because there was a "nip" & a pungency about that woman's phrases that he hated to lose —& so did I, only they weren't ours & we couldn't take them. So I set him to create a picture & he went at it. I finally took paper & pencil, had a thought, (as to phraseology) & scratched it down.

I had already told him what the *details* of the picture should be, & so only choice language was needed to dress them in. Then we read our two efforts, & mine being rather the best, we used it. And so it *ought* to have been the best. If I had been trying to describe a picture that was in *his* mind, I would have botched it.

We both think this is going to be no slouch of a novel, as Solomon said to the Hebrew Children.

Dined with Warner yesterday—at home today—lunch with Twichell noon tomorrow. The kitties are very frisky, now. They & the old cat sleep with me, nights, & have the run of the house. I wouldn't take thousands of dollars for them. Next to a wife whom I idolise, give me cat—an *old* cat, with kittens. How is the Muggins, now, by the way. It is very melancholy here, but I don't notice it. I'm pretty sad, but I'm used to it—it can't phaze *me*. I'm an old hand at grief. Grief makes me hump myself when I'm alone, but that is taking advantages. When my family is around I am superior to it.

But I am not grieving tonight, honey. I've pegged away all day till this hour & done a big day's work, & I feel as gay as a hymn.

Got a French version of the Jumping Frog—fun is no name for it. I am going to translate it *literally*, French construction & all (apologising in parenthesis where a word is too many for me) & publish it in the Atlantic as the grave effort of a man who does not know but what he is as good a French scholar as there is— & sign my name to it, without another word. It will be toothsome reading.

Goodbye my darling, I love you & I love the muggins.—It is bed time, now—I got to go down & roust out the cats.

SAML

While their new house in Hartford was building, the Clemenses took Livy's lifelong friend Clara Spaulding with them and spent the summer of 1873 in Britain and on the Continent. With the coming of autumn Livy grew homesick, and the pilgrims turned west. As soon as he had convoyed them across the Atlantic, Mark caught the next boat back to England, to meet a series of London lecture engagements.

Shortly after his return to Britain in mid-November he wrote the following letter, reporting the sights and sounds which all of them had relished only a few weeks before. "The Modoc" is his nickname for the infant Susy—in part because the cut of her hair suggested that Indian tribe currently waging. war in northern California, and in part because their London neighbor Joaquin Miller had just written his *Life among the Modocs.*

PARLOR 113, LANGHAM HOTEL, LONDON
Nov. 19 [1873]

Livy darling, it is close upon half past 9, now, the breakfast is on the table getting cold, & still you & Clara do not come. The Modoc amused me for a while with a distant sound, down the hall, of uncertain footsteps & abundance of *"Tah*-tah's" for the benefits conferred by somebody out there—but *she* is gone, now, & I have nothing now but the Times, with Mr. Lord Rector Disraeli's speech in it. I am not particularly hungry, but what I mind is the delay, & the lonesomeness of waiting. As far up Portland Place as I can see, the glittering Horse-Guards are filing in stately procession; out here on Langham Place that old "semi-detached" tooth-pick of a steeple stands up just as sharp & ugly as ever; that same beadle is behind a pillar "laying" for a tramp who has half a mind to venture inside the iron railings; that same one-legged crossing-sweeper is coming around the circle of the railings, & is humping himself too, to help a lady into a Hansom; that very same Punch & Judy man has arrived with a tap or two of his drum, a toot or two of his pipes & a wild, shrill remark from Punch himself—& the show is moving on again, the man taking off his hat humbly & beseechingly to people in various Langham Hotel windows—to no purpose. These sights are things that you & Clara always liked, heretofore, but now you do not [care for] come. Well, I will breakfast alone, then. Bacon, coffee & poached eggs are hardly worth sharing anyhow.

But I love you my sweetheart & would give a great deal to divide these refreshments with you & have your company.

SAML

The next letter refers to Mark's friend of San Francisco days, the poet and traveler Charles Warren Stoddard, now serving temporarily as Mark's secretary and album-paster.

Sunday, 23d [*November,* 1873]

Sweetheart, it is a rather handsome day for London—very sunny & bright & cheery, & I heartily wish you were here to enjoy it. Stoddard & I walked through Regent's Park & up on top of Primrose Hill & back again.

Stoddard has been spending some days at Oxford with the students, & they swear that if I will come there & lecture they will entertain me like a duke, & will also cram the largest hall in the town for me.—I would like it—& at a *lecture* they would come in evening dress & behave with the utmost decorum—with that thorough & complete decorum which noblemen's sons know so well how to practise when they choose—but at a common theatre what a queer lot they are!—& how they do behave, these scions of the bluest aristocratic blood of Great Britain! Stoddard attended the theatre there—a company of traveling actors. The house was full—both sexes—& all the students were there—or at least several hundred of them. They wore their hats all through the performance, & they all smoked pipes & cigars. Every individual devil of them had on an Ulster overcoat like mine, that came down to his heels; & every rascal of them brought a bull pup or a terrier pup under his arm, & they would set these creatures up on the broad-topped balustrades, & allow them to amuse themselves by barking at anybody or anything they chose to. Some Davenport Brothers tied themselves up with ropes, & people were requested to come on the stage & examine the trick; whereupon, several students, in their long coats, their hats on, their pups under their arms & their pipes in their mouths stepped out over the balustrades of private boxes, & gravely sauntered around & around the tied man on the stage examining the knots & expressing their opinions—& the audience never smiled or said a word but took the whole thing as a matter of course.

(Am called away, sweetheart,)

SAML

[LONDON] *Dec.* 11 [1873]

Livy my darling, I am just starting to the lecture hall, & O the dreadful fog still continues. The cattle are choking & dying in the great annual Cattle Show, & today they had to take some of the poor things out & haul them around on trucks to let them breathe the outside air & save their lives. I do wish it would let up.

If I'm not homesick to see you, no other lover ever *was* homesick to see his sweetheart.—[And when I get there, remember, "Expedition's the word!"]

Most *lovingly,*
SAML

2 A M. *Dec.* 12

My own dear little darling, it is 2 in the morning, & I had gone to my bedroom but I thought I will just go back to the parlor & look at Livy's picture once more before I go to bed. And so I am here, & your picture is before me (the same I have carried in my pocket so many many months) & I simply love it & I love you, Livy, my darling.

Tonight, after my lecture I went to the Scotch Morayshire dinner—the lord Viscount MacDuff was in the chair—& I made a speech which was received with prodigious applause—but I thought if Livy were only here, I would enjoy it a thousand times more. I do *love* you, Livy darling, & my last word is [(when I come) "Expedition's the word!"]

Most lovingly
SAML

This closing exclamation and the similar one above have been heavily inked out, at a later date and probably by another hand. Elsewhere Clemens uses the same phrase to express impatience; for example, to Bliss, November 28, 1870: "Say yes or no quick Bliss . . . Expedition's the word & I don't want any timidity or hesitancy now . . ."

LONDON, *Dec.* 14 [1873]

My own little darling, my peerless wife, I am simply mad to see you. *You* don't know how I love you—you never will. Because you do all the gushing yourself, when we are together, & so there is no use in two of us doing it—& one gusher usually silences another—but an ocean is between us, now, & I *have* to gush. I simply worship you, Livy dear. You are all in all, to me. I went

to Smalley's to-day, & in my secret heart I thanked Mrs. Smalley
for reminding me of you, in her soft, undulating, unstudied grace.
But she fell a long way short of you, after all. There is no woman
in the whole earth that is so lovely to me as you are, my child.
You must forgive me for not talking all I feel when I am at home,
honey. I *do* feel it, even if I don't talk it. Will you remember
that? Will you remember it & not feel harshly when I do not
utter it?

Finlay is my guest, for this week, & I warm up & am interested
as soon as he takes you for a topic. I do so wish I were with you,
my Livy.

SAML

[LONDON] *Dec.* 22 [1873]

Livy my darling, this is Monday. Yesterday I said it had been
more than a week since I had heard from you; Stoddard said, no,
just a week; but that letters would come today. When I woke this
morning & was going to turn over & take another nap, I remembered that there would doubtless be letters. So I got up at once &
dressed. There were two, my child—one about Dr. Browne's
"Margaret"⁴ & the other about Mrs. Cowan & the private theatri-
cals at the ladies club, & all that gossip—which is exactly what I
like. I have always contended that Ma was the best letter-writer
in the world, because she threw such an atmosphere of her locality
& her surroundings into her letters that her reader was transported
to her, & by the magic of her pen moved among creatures of living
flesh & blood,—talked with them, hoped & feared & suffered with
them.

I'll look up the Thackeray & Dickens. And as Finlay leaves for
Belfast tomorrow he shall take the order for the dragon, & then
I will get it when I lecture there.

I've got 7 razors all in one box, with the days of the week
marked on them. That is to give each razor a week's rest, which
is the next best thing to stropping it. Stoddard, Finlay & I are to

---

⁴ John Brown (1810-1882), Edinburgh physician who had greatly endeared himself to the Clemenses on their Scottish visit in the summer of 1873. The author of
Rab and His Friends wrote no book with the title here given; Mark probably means
his story of the precocious child called "Pet Marjorie" or "Marjorie Fleming,"
which Mark himself retold in *Europe and Elsewhere* (1923).

dine with the Dolby to-night at the Westminster Club & I reckon we'll have a pretty good time (now here's that Punch & Judy devil just struck up on his drum over by the church railings—but it is a dark, rainy day & he won't take a trick).

Another Tichborne[5] case—no, I mean a case of mistaken identity. Finlay & I started out for a walk yesterday afternoon—met a very young & very handsome [sic] within 5 steps of the door, who looked at me as if he knew me, & I looked at him, not expecting to know him, but instantly recognizing the fact that I had seen the face somewhere before.

Very well. I kept telling Finlay I knew that face—& by & by, when we were well up Portland Place, I said "Now I've got it!—it is the young Lord MacDuff who presided at a Morayshire Banquet in Regent street the other night."

Very good again. Half an hour later, in Regent's Park we met a lady whom Finlay knew—who was giving 3 or 4 of her children an airing. We walked with her an hour, then went to her house in Harley street (the "Long, unlovely street" of Tennyson In Memoriam) to drink a glass of wine—sat there half an hour, when in comes that same man we met before the hotel (Finlay nodded to me as much as to say, "Here he is again") & then, lo & behold you he was introduced to us as "Lord Arthur Hill" (and, in a whisper, "heir to the Marquis of Downshire"). I studied the fellow all over for more than half an hour, & there was *no* difference between the two men except that the hair of one was wavy & that of the other was not. The MacDuff is a Scotchman, but this chap is Irish, born close to Belfast & is heir to one of those mighty estates there that Finlay told us of, with 40 miles extent & 60,000 population. It was a curious case all around, considering the exceeding scarcity of lords.

I love you, my child.

SAML

[LONDON] Dec. 29 [1873]

Livy darling, I will only write a line, to accompany these enclosures. A moment ago I looked into the drawer & saw several

---

[5] The Tichborne trial, centering about the efforts of an almost illiterate claimant to capture a great English estate, so fascinated Mark that he hired Stoddard to fill six albums with clippings about it.

letters, addressed to me, in a familiar handwriting—yours; & they brought you before me. No, not that exactly, because nothing but *you*, yourself will do—but they so reminded me of you, & made me so long to see you & take you in my arms. Never mind the "gushing"; with one like me, that is nothing; I am not demonstrative, except at intervals—but I *always* love you—always admire you—am always your champion. In Salisbury when a gentleman remarked upon my taking the trouble to telegraph a Merry Christmas to my *wife*, saying it was the sort of thing to do with a *sweetheart*, I dosed him up very promptly, & said I did not allow any man to refer to my wife jestingly, however respectful he might intend to be. He apologized profusely—otherwise things would have been pretty unpleasant there, presently. I love you, my darling, whether I keep saying it or not—I *always* love you—*always*.

SAML

[LONDON] Jan. 1 *Midnight* [1874]

Livy darling! what an access of love, a bit of separation brings! I have such a longing for you these days; & the lesson it teaches, is, separate yourselves every now & then. When I have been away from you 2 days, I am wild to see you. So I mean to go away every now & then, just to renew that feeling—but never more than 48 hours. As long as we live I hope it will never be more than 48 hours that will intervene between our seeing each other. It seems that it will be a whole age before I see you again.

SAML

LONDON, *Jan.* 3, 2 A.M.

Livy darling, it is 2 in the morning here, & about 9 in the evening in Hartford, or half past 8. I am imagining you to be in the parlor, & the Modoc gone to bed. You are sitting by the table & the Warners are about to go home in the snow—& then you will go to bed too.—Well, I wish I were there with you. Here, Stoddard & I have been talking & keeping a lonely vigil for hours—but I won't talk of it any more. It is *so* unsatisfying. I want *you*—& nobody else. I do love you so.

SAML

LONDON, *Jan* 2 [1874]

Livy my darling, I want you to be sure & remember to have in
the bathroom, when I arrive, a bottle of Scotch whisky, a lemon,
some crushed sugar, & a bottle of *Angostura bitters*. Ever since I
have been in London I have taken in a wine-glass what is called
a cock-tail (made with those ingredients) before breakfast, before
dinner, & just before going to bed. It was recommended by the
surgeon of the "City of Chester"[6] & was a most happy thought.
To it I attribute the fact that up to this day my digestion has been
wonderful—simply *perfect*. It remains day after day & week after
week as regular as a clock. Now my dear, if you will give the
order *now*, to have those things put in the bath-room & left there
till I come, they will *be* there when I arrive. Will you? I love to
write about arriving—it seems as if it were to be tomorrow. And
I love to picture myself ringing the bell, at midnight—then a
pause of a second or two—then the turning of the bolt, & "Who
is it?"—then ever so many kisses—then you & I in the bath-room,
I drinking my cock-tail & undressing, & you standing by—then to
bed, and—everything happy & jolly as it should be. I *do* love &
honor you, my darling.

SAML

Nothing but *Angostura* Bitters will do.

While assuming Livy's unfamiliarity with the name and nature
of a cocktail, Mark himself clearly was no fresh initiate. For
example in a piece about notaries in the *Golden Era* for February
28, 1864, in describing his rendezvous with an old-timer he wrote:
"I went and gobbled a cocktail with him." The inference also
seems plain that Livy's opposition to spirituous liquors had relaxed since the early reformist days of courtship. No doubt four
years of marriage and intimate observation had convinced her
that Mark would never "fill a drunkard's grave," and she was
willing to settle for what he once called his policy of "temperate
temperance." In his *Autobiography* he wrote: "I doubt if God has
given us any refreshment which, taken in moderation, is unwhole-
some, except microbes. Yet there are people who strictly deprive

[6] Mark had returned to England on the Inman Line steamship of this name.

themselves of each and every eatable, drinkable, and smokable which has in any way earned a shady reputation. They pay this price for health. . . . It is like paying out your whole fortune for a cow that has gone dry."

On January 13, 1874, Mark Twain sailed from England and was soon reunited with Livy and "the Modoc." In June their second daughter Clara was born, and in this summer Mark began one of his greatest books, *Tom Sawyer*.

CHAPTER TEN

Hartford Days

THE most creative years for Mark Twain the artist, and the happiest for Clemens the man, were those that stretched from the mid-1870's until late in the next decade. He was busy, productive, prosperous, in good health, blessed with an adoring family and devoted friends.

Absences from home were not frequent, and hence during these years the letters written to Livy are scattered and few. A typical small series stems from an expedition he began on November 12, 1874, in company with Twichell, "to walk to Boston in 24 hours," as Mark announced to Redpath and the public generally. On the first leg of the trip he sent Livy a bulletin from Vernon, Connecticut, mirroring their high spirits: "Our jaws have wagged ceaselessly, & every now & then, our laughter does wake up the old woods—for there is nothing to restrain it, there being nobody to hear it."

They spent the first night in "a low tavern" at Westford, where Mark lay sleepless from a quantity of tea he had drunk, and set forth footsore at dawn. After six more miles they gave in, and found a tavernkeeper who drove them ten miles in a buggy to New Boston, where (as Twichell noted in his diary) "we got into a hot country store and rested—oh, how luxuriously!—from our labors." Here the following letter was written and a telegram dispatched to Redpath: "We have made thirty-five miles in less than five days. This demonstrates the thing can be done. Shall now finish by rail."

NEW BOSTON [CONN.], *Friday.*
[*November* 13, 1874]

Livy darling, it is bitter cold weather. We got up at half past 5 this morning, took breakfast & cleared out just as the dawn was breaking. It was a magnificent morning; the woods were white with frost, & our hands *wouldn't* keep warm—nor ourselves either. I supposed there was a flagstone pavement all the way to Boston, but I find there is nothing but wagon roads.

We shall take the train & be in Boston at 7 this evening. Wish we had accepted Howells's invitation.

Goodby my darling
SAML

They did telegraph Howells of changed plans, and he renewed his invitation to a literary party that evening, which the visitors reached at a latish hour. On a card Mark added a postscript.

Saturday

Livy darling, we had a royal time till midnight at Howells last night. Howells dines with us tonight & we lunch with him Monday. This hanky is for the Modoc with my great love. I bought it for 10 cents at Newton, eleven miles out of Hartford. You had a sentence in your letter that all the culture & all the genius & all the practice in the world could not improve. It was admirable. With *all* my heart,

Yours,
SAML

Twichell's diary supplies details. The Saturday supper given by Mark included Howells, Aldrich, Osgood the publisher, and Larkin Meade the sculptor. On Monday Twichell notes: "To Howells at 2 o'clock to lunch—disgracefully tardy—a most delightful afternoon. Late in the afternoon called on Prof. Lowell with Howells, and stayed a half-hour, which was mostly occupied with talk about Beecher. Lowell looked much as I had expected him to. But Dr. Holmes, to whom Mark introduced me on the street Saturday, looked older than I had imagined." That evening the quondam pedestrians took a train back to Hartford.

In the summer of 1875 Mark finished *Tom Sawyer*, and after his usual creative hibernation over the Hartford season began *Huckleberry Finn* the next summer at Quarry Farm.

In 1877 he wasted much time and temper over the production,

first in Washington and later on Broadway, of the comedy *Ah Sin,* which he had written in collaboration with Bret Harte. Harte's trickiness, shabby sponging, and flair for plagiarism—which led Mark to brand him to Howells as "the most abandoned thief that defiles the earth"—were more venial in Mark's eyes than Harte's sarcasms against the household in which he was a guest, and against Livy herself.

About the beginning of the last week in April Clemens went down to New York, preparatory to going on to Baltimore, where *Ah Sin* was in rehearsal prior to opening in Washington on May 7. The actor John T. Raymond, here bracketed with Harte as a target of Mark's wrath, in the dramatization of *The Gilded Age* had achieved considerable success in the role of Colonel Sellers. Praise went to his head and led him to treat the author as a negligible quantity—thus forfeiting the good will of Mark Twain, who was careful to see that the stellar role in the new play went to Charles Parsloe.

ST. JAMES [NEW YORK CITY]
Early Bedtime [circa April 23, 1877]

Livy darling, I am tired out—pretty completely fagged. So I'll only write a line. Since I reached here at 6 I have been talking with people all the time—Charley, Dan, Kingman, Fuller[1] & others—& now at 9 oclock, am dreadfully sleepy. I am ashamed that a trifling little railway trip should have so much effect upon me. But I had a delightful afternoon. I left behind me those 2 men who have not been absent an instant from my thoughts (& my hate) for months—Raymond & Harte—so I read Dumas & was serene & content. I move on in the morning. I love you darling— I love you all the time.

SAML

Mark's report to Howells on April 27, from Ford's Theater in Baltimore, gives a glimpse of the routine that followed: "I am needed every moment during these daily rehearsals, but I must

---

[1] Charles Langdon, Dan Slote, and Frank Fuller are readily identified; the fourth may be Captain Dan Kingman, ex-Mississippi River pilot who later wrote his recollections.

steal a second to wish you were here at this instant. There's a combat going on, of the most furious, & earnest nature, between two men in every-day clothes, who rave & roar & fell each other with imaginary chairs & shoot each other with imaginary pistols & *pretend* to fall & die in agony & be thrown into the Stanislaus river—& by George all the other actors & actresses sit within 6 feet of them & calmly converse about the reasonable price of board in Baltimore!"

After *Ah Sin* was launched with mild applause before theater-goers in Washington, Mark prepared to take Joe Twichell as his guest on a brief Bermuda holiday—a jaunt which Mark described six months later in the *Atlantic,* as "Some Rambling Notes of an Idle Excursion." On May 16 they took the night train to New York, whence Mark sent back the following letter.

[NEW YORK CITY] *Thursday* [*May* 17, 1877]

Livy darling, it is 8.30 AM and Joe & I have been wandering about for half an hour with satchels & overcoats, asking questions of policemen; at last we have found the eating house I was after. Joe's country aspect & the sealskin coat caused one policeman to follow us a few blocks. He talked to somebody then and disappeared—so I judge we are "shadowed" & shall be in the station-house presently.

I thought of you all night, my darling, on account of the lightning—and especially that time the thunder crashed so. When on my way to Joe's house I was sorry I did not leave instructions with Lizzie or Mary to go to your room in case it thundered. I do hope you are having a good rest this morning, and that dear old Sue will soon be with you.

We shall loaf around to Mr. Sage's business place presently.[2] O, the market! We have passed by such mountains of delicacies this morning. Breakfast is here, piping hot!—so good bye sweetheart—shall send another card by & by.

SAM

Home from his Bermuda ramble by the beginning of summer, Mark took Livy and the two children, Susy and Clara, to Quarry

[2] Dean Sage of Brooklyn, a particular friend of Twichell's.

Farm. On Saturday, July 14, he left them for a sojourn in New York and Hartford before the Broadway opening of *Ah Sin* on July 31. The following letter from Livy, addressed to him at the St. James Hotel, was almost certainly written the day after his departure.

[ELMIRA]
[probably Sunday, July 15, 1877]

YOUTH DARLING—We are all well and have had a most delightful Sunday, it would have been entirely perfect if you had been here—I made wreaths & crowns of Golden rod for the children this morning—This afternoon Susie and I had a rather sad time because she told me a lie—she felt very unhappy about it—This evening after her prayer I prayed that she might be forgiven for it, then I said "Susie don't you want to pray about it and ask for your self to be forgiven?" She said "Oh one is enough"—

Good night darling I will not write more for this may not reach you—

Lovingly yours
LIVY—

To his elder daughter, five years old, Clemens now wrote the first of many letters to his children; "Bay," a contraction of Baby, long served as a pet name for Clara, while Rosa of course was the nurse.

[NEW YORK CITY]
Monday AM. *[July 16, 1877]*

Susie dear, you & Rosa and Bay must keep a sharp lookout on the young birdlings up at the pond & see them begin life. They are ready to fly, now. Keep the squirrel supplied with nuts, if he comes around. If you have a very fine sunset, put a blanket over it & keep it till I come. Aunt Sue will give you one. I saw a lovely sunset yesterday, reflected in the water of New Jersey marshes. It was a beautiful, still evening—no sound but just one cow singing, and some frogs—(frosches).

There are some bells close here & a man who rings chimes. That man will die some day, & then he will wish he had behaved himself. I saw a cat yesterday, with 4 legs—& yet it was only a yellow cat, & rather small, too, for its size. They were not *all* fore legs—several of them were hind legs; indeed almost a majority of them were.

Write me.

PAPA

Rumors of a prowler about the Clemens place, inhabited during the summer by servants alone, led Mark to run up from New York and investigate. Having just finished a play called *Simon Wheeler, the Amateur Detective*, Mark attacked the mystery with special zest, soon discovering that the vagrant was a jobless mechanic and lover of the housemaid Lizzie. Patrick the Irish coachman, George the Negro butler, and Mary the cook figure as minor dramatis personae, in the graphic reports sent to Livy.

HARTFORD, Tuesday [July 17, 1877]

If you don't think this is a nice kettle of fish, you don't know anything about fish, Livy my darling. From 3 oclock yesterday till 12 last night I put in a good part of the time questioning & cross-questioning the servants (including Patrick & wife) & the Chief of Police. The chief of police & his detectives have a "theory," of course: to wit—George is preparing to gut the house & throw the crime upon imaginary burglars. I had done so much jaw & listened to so much jaw that when I went to bed I made two resolutions to make a choice from, & then dismissed the subject & took my whiskey. Now I have awakened refreshed & shall presently get up.

I find myself "set" in the opinion I went to bed with: there has been no burglar in the house, but only one or both of Lizzie's two loafers. Here is some of the testimony I have taken: The alarm went off very early one morning, before we went away; it was Lizzie's Willie going out of the basement door; George saw this. George, Patrick, & the two Marys & Rosa all believed Willy was sleeping with Lizzy occasionally here in the house before we went away. It is believed that he was the "burglar" of last Thursday night. (I believe the "burglar" of Friday, to be an imaginary one, invented by Lizzy.) Mrs. Perkins[3] has seen two persons

[3] Their neighbor Mrs. Charles Perkins.

resembling L's loafers, enter the house at noonday. Patrick & Mary have seen Lizzy sitting on the balcony of the N. E. room with her loafer in the daytime, & been scoffed at by them. The two loafers played billiards all day, 4th July, on my table. George hid the balls that night & Lizzy complained about it next day, accusing George of favoring his *own* friends with the game—the which George makes oath to be untrue. George testifies that he one day saw Patrick wearing my walking-shoes; asked where he got them; he said Lizzy gave them to him with the remark that I had ordered that they be given to a tramp or anybody that might want them.

I shall question Lizzy once more, privately, this morning; if she denies these things, I will confront her with all the witnesses. If she gives notice or I discharge her (the latter is what I would do if was sure you would approve), she must leave here before *I* do, & I shall search her trunk immediately after the conversation. I've got a special officer in the house nights till I get home & consult with you.

I believe in George & the cook, & Patrick, very thoroughly—but I haven't heard this morning's testimony yet, you see. George, Lizzy & Mary all agree that the 3 ruffians of July 4 who used insulting yells & cries with my name in them, did it from the *street* without provocation or any of our people being in sight; they kept it up half an hour; then George shot at them twice, but unluckily failed to get them; they threatened him, then, & he went down in the yard & very gallantly defied the gang.

I haven't had so much chin-chin for some years. I have enjoyed it very much; I am judge, jury, & lawyer for both sides. Moreover, the Court of Appeals being in Elmira, I have a pretty swinging jurisdiction here, & it sets me up & makes me feel my oats.

Had a pleasant short visit at the Perkins's yesterday evening, & a rattling time at Twichell's.

I love you my darling, ever so much I love you; I love you & I miss you—& yet it chuckles me with comfort to be in this big authority for once.

SAML.

A letter written to Livy at noon on Tuesday, and mailed separately from the foregoing and following letters, is omitted here because it adds little to the narrative. The present bulletin is labeled "Half an hour later."

Tuesday Afternoon

Have been to see Mrs. Perkins. She approves. Therefore Mary goes to her friends tomorrow to remain till we return (excuse bad writing, for I am in a horse-car—it has stopped on a switch now) home, & George stays in the house; at present with the policeman (whom we will soon send away).

I sent for Mary awhile ago & took her evidence. Then sent for Lizzy & said, "Lizzy, your friend slept with *you* the night he left this house so early in the morning." She confessed.

She had lied so valiantly, & carried her difficult part so well & with such excellent temper that I began to pity her, now, especially when she said she was lost irretrievably & her betrayer was manifestly never going to marry her.

I told her it was now of course necessary to discharge her at once & send her out of the house. She acknowledged that there could be no other course.

Then I laid a plan for her to follow during the next two hours, & tell nobody what it was. (I have been detective Simon Wheeler for 24 hours, now.)

Tuesday, Midnight, July 17

Then I walked part way down town & got some information I needed. Walked home, noted down some facts from Lizzy's lips; wrote a note & gave it to her, to be delivered in case of necessity, but not otherwise. Then took that street car & went down to the Court House & paid a man to do a few minutes' work for me (do you follow these detective maunderings, "Jany?"[4])

Then went to barber shop & got shaved. Then took a hack in a pouring rain & drove to telegraph office; then to the bank; then to Chief of Police. Concerted a plan, & said I would send him a note & a hack inside of 30 minutes. Drove home. Where's Lizzy? "Gone, 20 minutes ago, sir." Perdition! "George, jump into the hack & fly! Take this note & give it to the Chief of Police; take a detective, go to 575 Main Street, & from there get on Lizzy's track

[4] Jenny is Cap'n Simon Wheeler's wife, in Mark's play.

& give her this other note. Beware—don't fail!" (Ah, what a Simon Wheeler I was getting to be!)

Then I went down town to take dinner with a friend (told George where I should be). Sat there with him [ages & ages] chaffing & joking about things, & watching the clock.

At six, sharp, enter George. George: "They're on their way, by another conveyance; *your* hack's at the door."

Enter at the same moment, a domestic. Domestic: "Dinner is on the table."

I didn't wait for dinner. I said "Keep mine cool on a plate till I come."

Gave George some directions & then rushed home in the hack. —Went to N.E. room & watched, through the window, stroking & petting Stray Kit, but almost unconscious of it. One hack— another hack—a buggy—a grocer's wagon—another buggy, in the pouring rain. They all pass by. What in the notion *is* the matter? By & by a street car. Good!—No, it stops at Forest Street—lets out a man. I curse that horse-car & think something has failed somewhere—Now comes a man walking up the yard. Good! Don't know him, but *any* arrival promises something.

Enter Mary, excited: "They're here! Where shall I put them?" I—"Put them in the study—but let me get there first. You & George be within call—but out of sight. If you are in the kitchen, come a-booming at 3 taps of the study bell." They say they will be in the kitchen—(that was merely on account of the dramatic grandeur of those 3 bell-taps).

"Where shall we put the other man?" I—"Put him in the library & leave the door open."

I stand in the study. Enter Lizzy, with a tall, muscular, handsome fellow of 35. "This is my friend, Willie Taylor, Mr. Clemens."

I shake hands with a lying cordiality, shut the door, seat him, begin to talk; he ugly, wanting to quarrel, I sweet & calm, resolved beforehand that to lose my temper was to lose my game—& I had started in to *win*. He snarled: I looked him sweetly in the eye & rebuked him to gentleness, almost; fought shy of the subject; I gently brought him back to it; he talked of a "put-up job"; I said he could not mean *me*. He begged pardon, & said he did not.

I coaxed him, I argued, I pleaded, half an hour. I sprung a good joke on him. He *had* to laugh. I had a cigar in his hand & a lighted match under his nose before he was to the middle of his laugh. Lizzy had been crying straight along; now she laughed; *he* laughed again; I pretended to laugh—but I was deep in a serious business & it came hard. Four times I worked him almost up to the point I wanted him—made him choke & cry a little occasionally —& four times I failed—but the fifth time he said, hesitatingly, "I—I believe I'll do it—yes, I am willing, though—"

He never finished that sentence. I rang three bells (& *instantly* enter George & Mary!; I snatched the door leading to Mother's bath-room open & said "the Rev. Mr. Twichell will come in—here is the license"—(which I had procured in the afternoon).

Enter Joe & marries them, in presence of the witnesses—this bridegroom murmuring a moment later, "But it was a put-up job."

Lizzy cried through the service & the prayer, & then her husband put his arm about her neck & kissed her & shed a tear & said "Don't cry."

Enter George with champagne & glasses, places his waiter first before Lizzy & says, "Champagne if you please, *Mrs. Taylor*." Whereat, general jollity.

Then I drank long life & health to the couple, gave them a [hundred dollars apiece] trifle (for they'd only four dollars between them) told them to go to——any where that they could be happy, & then Joe & I marched back to his house & *he* ate dinner; but the strain was all over, now, & a dish of soup sufficed for me.

Then I read my play to Joe & Harmony (how like a Simon Wheeler I've been all day!) & then I came home & here I am in bed.

Do you see my plan? The man in the library was a detective in plain clothes. If persuasion had failed with Mr. Taylor, my purpose was to lock the door & say "you either leave this room a married man or you leave it with an officer, & charged with being in this house at midnight in March with a dishonest intent —take your choice."

But I *love* you, Livy dear, *any* way.

Now I go to sleep.   SAML.

Paine's biography, 600-602, tells this tale less vividly; Mark himself tried to work it up into a story called "Wapping Alice," which remains among the unpublished Mark Twain papers. At the Players Club he is said long afterwards to have told the incident, rounded off by his encounter some two years later with the bridegroom, who replied to a polite query by saying, "As to my family —there never was a baby, or any suspicion of any." (Walter Oettel, *Walter's Sketch Book* [New York, 1943], 54ff.)

The two next letters went to the children.

NEW YORK, *July* 19 [1877]

Bay Clemens, I have bought two bath tubs & two dolls & sent them by express—they are for you & Susie. One of the dolls is named Hosannah Maria & is in quite delicate health. She belongs to you.—She was out driving & got rained on, & caught a very severe cold. It settled on her mind. When she had partly recovered, she caught a new cold, which paralyzed the sounding-board of her ears & the wobbling nerve of her tongue. She has never heard or spoken since. I have consulted the best physicians. They say constant & complicated bathing will fetch her.

PAPA

NEW YORK, *July* 19 [1877]

Susie dear, *Your* doll is named Hallelujah Jennings. She early suffered a stroke of some sort, & since that day all efforts of the best physicians have failed to take the stiffening out of her legs.— They say incessant bathing is the only thing that can give her eventual relief. Her child, Glory Ann Jennings, is sickly & must never be bathed. She cries a good deal in a quiet way, but if you pinch her face together you can vary the expression and make her smile, after a sickly fashion.—Hosannah Marie's child (named Whoop-Jamboree) is similar. I send the children with their mothers. I kiss you all.

PAPA

Typical is this gently cautionary letter from Livy, fearful that her husband's ready boiling-point would betray him into utterances thoughtless and ungenerous about Bret Harte.

ELMIRA, *July 29th '77*

MY DARLING—Two letters came from you today and I assure you it was a *mighty* delight to get them—I am so thankful that all the arrangements about the play suit you so well, how I do wish that I was going to be with you on the opening night, I want to hear your speech and I want to *be with you*—I love you—We had such a wonderful evening last evening, beautiful cloud effects at sunset and then such a *beautiful* sky with the moon and clouds in the evening, I did wish so very much for you—

Youth I want to caution you about one thing, don't say harsh things about Mr. Harte, don't talk against Mr Harte to people, it is so much better that you be reticent about him, don't let anybody trap you into talking freely of him—We are so desperately happy, our paths lie in such pleasant places, and he is so miserable, we can easily afford to be magnanimus toward him—but I am afraid that my desire to have you quiet is not from generosity to him, but from my selfish desires toward you. I don't want you in the position of having talked against him—be careful my darling—

I am going to enclose you a letter from our policeman I hate to do it for fear it will worry you, but I think I better as you may want to do some thing about it before you leave N.Y. Perhaps your visit at home will have straightened matters up so that this letter will be unimportant. I hope so & that you will not be troubled by it, it has troubled me some what, I had a good letter from George today—I cannot understand his leaving the house that long alone, but if he left Augustus there I don't know but it was all right.

Today I had baby all undressed but her little under shirt—she said, "Oh if Susie see me she will say I am all legged"

Tonight I was reading to her that ever interesting story in Rollo, "Little Girl, *little girl*, you have left the gate open" &c when I read about the rooster I asked her if she would like to sleep up on a high pole, she said, "No, for the world, I wouldn't" —once afterward during our conversation she used that expression "for the world"—I spoke about our riding on the clouds the were so beautiful as we sat looking at them, she said in quite a fretful voice, "there isn't any chair up there on the clouds"—

Susie worked a long time today printing the letters to send to you at first she seemed to think that she was going to print the entire letter to you in a few minutes—but after she found how difficult it was she worked faithfully on it—

Sue & I had a letter from Clara[5] today, she is improving steadily will come home this week—If you come on Wednesday this is the last letter I shall send—Oh how glad I shall be to see you darling—Good night yours

I love you a bit   LIVY

A space of four years is lacking in important letters from Mark to Livy, save for those already published—namely four written during Mark's walking tour in August 1878 with Twichell in the Black Forest (*Letters*, 332-36), three from Chicago in November 1879, when he was a guest speaker at the reunion of the Army of the Tennessee (the same, 366-73), and one from Hartford in October 1880 describing the civic ovation to Grant (Paine's biography, 691-92).

In August 1881 Mark agreed to give a humorous address at Ashfield, Massachusetts, by invitation of Charles Eliot Norton, the Harvard scholar who made his summer home there. But after the shooting of President Garfield and his lingering between life and death for many weeks, Mark Twain canceled his speaking engagement. Yet as the result of his projected trip he found himself saddled with business commitments in Hartford and Boston that could not well be broken.

BOSTON, *Thursday* A.M. [*August 25*] 1881

Livy darling, I will write you just a line; then send down for my breakfast; then expect Osgood about 10 o'clock. I never saw Mr. Slee any more after I went to bed at midnight in the cars. I found, next morning, in Albany, that I could catch the Springfield train by rushing; so I rushed—in a hack—& was the last passenger that joined it.

Well, pretty soon I heard a couple of foreigners talking (it was in the smoking car) & they had exceedingly good faces—in fact one of them had a face strongly resembling Charles Kingsley's;

[5] Clara Spaulding.

& although he was evidently a laboring man, & was covered with cinders, his face was beautiful because of its sweetness.

Well, we hadn't gone many miles when it turned out that this one, being deceived by the chuckle-headed station-names (both having a *Boston* in its name,) was on the wrong road.—So his ticket wasn't good, & he must get off at the next station & go back & wait, &c. So I called the conductor aside & paid the man's fare to Boston & took his ticket. It had two days to run—so it is dead to-night. It was a "limited" ticket—second class. But what I started to say, was, getting interested in those people's faces, absorbed my attention & I just accepted, as final, the fact that there was no drawing room car when I came aboard, & never looked out of the window to see if a change was made—but sweated it manfully out, for 4 hours, in that filthy smoking car; & at last, when I stood in the Springfield depôt & the train I had just vacated glided by, I noticed that it had upwards of a million drawing room cars attached. So I said Darn those foreigners. But there's Osgood.

I love you, darling
S L C

On November 25 he left for a fortnight in Canada, to secure British copyright for *The Prince and the Pauper*, published December 1 in London. George Iles, mentioned below, was a Canadian author and snowshoe expert.

MONTREAL, Nov. 29/81.

Well, sweetheart, I have walked a few miles this morning with the same gentleman who took me to the mountain top (Mr. Iles) & inspected a lot of Catholic churches, French markets, shop windows, &c. But for the shame of it, the indignity to my pride, I would like to be a priest's slave, & glide in with my basket or my bundle, & duck my head & crook my knee at a painted image, & glide out again with my immortal part refreshed & strengthened for my day's burdens. But—I am not a priest's slave, & so it hurts me, hurts me all through, to recognize, by these exhibitions, what poor animals we are, what children, how easily fooled, beguiled, & by what cheap & trivial devices, by what thin & paltry lies. Which

reminds me—you must read about the early Jesuit missionaries
in Canada. Talk about self-abnegation! heroism! fidelity to a cause!
It was sublime, it was stupendous. Why what these men did &
suffered, in trying to rescue the insulting & atrocious savages
from the doom of hell, makes one adore & glorify human nature
as exemplified in those priests—yes, & despise it at the very same
time. In endurance & performance they were gods; in credulity,
& in obedience to their ecclesiastical chiefs, they were swine.

One is so carried out of his mind with enthusiasm over these
marvelous labors & sufferings & sacrifices, that for a moment he
is deceived into imagining that nothing but a religion can make
men do these things (& he is helped toward that delusion by his
life-long pulpit- & tract-teaching). But no—all that these men did
& suffered, the love of money, hatred of an enemy, affection for
a child, a wife, a betrothed, can make men do & suffer—yes, in-
fatuation for a filthy prostitute can make a man rival the Jesuit
missionaries at their grandest & finest.

But a friend waits to take me to luncheon—so I break off my
sermon. But I kiss you & Susie & Bay—& even Jean.[6]

Lovingly
SAML

[6] Jean Clemens, their fourth and last child, was born July 26, 1880.

CHAPTER ELEVEN

Back to the Mississippi

THE deepest, clearest springs of Mark Twain's inspiration
flowed always from his Missouri boyhood and his youth lived
upon the great River. In order to finish those sketches of pilot
days begun in the *Atlantic* as "Old Times on the Mississippi,"
and to complete a still greater project, *Huckleberry Finn*,
abandoned when the creator's "tank" had run dry, Mark decided
early in 1882 to renew his touch with enchanted ground.

On April 17 he left Hartford for a trip of nearly six weeks down
the Mississippi to New Orleans, then up the river again with his
old mentor the pilot Horace Bixby, to the head of navigation at
St. Paul. To protect his role of observer and private citizen, he
assumed the name of C. L. Samuels, but as the letters relate was
speedily unmasked. Mark's companions were the publisher Osgood
and a young Hartfordian, Roswell Phelps, engaged as stenog-
rapher for the field trip.

COLE'S LANDING, MENARD, ILL. 21*st*
[*April, 1882*]

Livy darling, I am in solitary possession of the pilot house of
the Steamer Gold Dust, with the familiar wheel & compass & bell
ropes around me. We are taking in coal. I came up here at a
quarter to 8 (½ hour ago,) while the dog watch was still on, &
before the regular watch began—consequently I've had a brief
acquaintanceship with both pilots. I'm all alone, now (the pilot
whose watch it is, told me to make myself entirely at home, &
I'm doing it!)

Thus far our fictitious names are a sufficient protection; but
we had to get out of St. Louis in a hurry, because I got to meeting

too many people who knew me. We swore them to secrecy, &
left by the first boat.

It is a magnificent day, & the hills & levels are masses of shining
green, with here & there a white-blossoming tree.

I love you, sweetheart.

SAML

Saturday Afternoon, ½ *way to* MEMPHIS
[*April* 22, 1882]

Livy darling, the swindle is all "up." Yesterday noon it came up
cold, & I was driven to the pilot house to get warm. Got to talking
with a little boy, son of a passenger, & presently felt the pilot's
eye on me. He had recognized my voice, after 21 years, though I
did not remember him or his name either. He waited a while for
confirmation of his suspicions; & presently when I raised my hat
& passed my fingers up through my hair, he had no further doubts,
& just called me by name. I confessed.

It would be nonsense to stop at Memphis, now, & fall a prey
to the newspapers; so we shall stick to this boat to the bottom
end of her voyage (Vicksburg), & then take a coast packet & go
on to New Orleans. We shall reach Memphis to-night, & if I had
the children along, we would turn out & hunt up Julia Kosh-
losky.[1]

We are having a powerful good time & picking up & setting
down volumes of literary stuff. I take a trick at the wheel occasionally, & find the mechanical work of steering a steamboat as
familiar as if I had never ceased from it. But the "Upper" river!
It was as new to me if I had never heard of it before. However,
I recognize the river below Cairo—I know it pretty fairly, though
some of the changes are marvelous. For instance Island No. 10 used
to be as close to shore as from our front door to Holbrook's; now
it lies away off across the water as far away as the Courant office.
Of course the island is where it *was*, but the shore has been eaten
away to that prodigious extent.

Telegraphed you from Cairo last night. Shall telegraph you
from Memphis to-morrow morning.

[1] No doubt a former domestic.

Good bye, my darling Livy & kiss everybody but Jean for me.

SAML.

P. S. Well, Jean too.

Susy began the following letter, which her mother finished. Katy Leary, here mentioned, served the Clemens family for thirty years, and furnished the material for Mary Lawton's book, *A Lifetime with Mark Twain* (1925).

HARTFORD, *April* 23rd 1882

DEAR PAPA—We all miss you very much, Jean calls for you almost every day, and mamma is very lonesome without you. Miss Murry has ben here, and she can play on the piano beaytifully, she played some pieces from Patience, and some of Scots. song. This morning Clara and I walked to Church with aunt Clara, and back with aunt Alice, the sermon was very good, and the organist did not play so badly. Just the day you went away Katie, Clara and I went to take a long walk, after awhile we went to a little boat near the river. Clara was Capt. first and I was Dr. I found an old pail and fild it with water, gave it to Katie (who was a passenger). We found an old cloth to and cleaned out the boat a little. After awhile we went home, and we thought we had had a very nice time.

April 27th 1882

Today mamma went to see Mrs. Warner and so we hope to see Daisy soon. We are lerning to play Eucher now, and we like it very much, today played with mamma, Rosa, Katie, Clara and Jaurge. We went to the mucical last Friday and we enjoyed it very much, I managed to get through with my pieces without one mistake. Dear papa you need not answer me my letter becouse I no you have not nearly enough time.

Your loveing dayghter
SUSIE CLEMENS.

[*Written on back of Susie's letter:*]

DEAR YOUTH—I hoped for a dispatch or letter today. I wonder if you have reached New Orleans safely—I surely hope so.

We are all well. The house seems pretty dull & quiet with no one in it, particularly after the children go to bed. but it is a pleasant change after the rush that we have been in—however I should like you to enjoy it with me.

Good night I love you and am so glad that you are having such a good time

With deepest love   yours

OLIVIA L. CLEMENS.

The zest of his old river days was returning upon Mark Twain, as his next letter to Livy shows.

On board Steamer GOLD DUST. *Apl.* 25/82

Well, Livy darling, we are working along down, slowly, landing every 2 or 3 miles, & having a most serene & enjoyable time. Osgood says he has never enjoyed any trip more. We were 6 hours & a quarter coming 23 miles, this morning, because we made so many landings. We are only 70 miles above Vicksburg, now (where we stop) but we shall be 12 or 14 hours making it.

I had myself called at 4 o'clock this morning, & came on with the morning watch. There was just a faint whitish suggestion in the east—the rest of the sky & the great river were wrapped in a sombre gloom. It was fascinating to see the day steal gradually upon this vast silent world; & when the edge of the shorn sun pushed itself above the line of forest, the marvels of shifting light & shade & color & dappled reflections, that followed, were bewitching to see. And the luxurious green walls of forest! & the jutting leafy capes! & the paling green of the far stretches! & the remote, shadowy, vanishing distances, away down the glistening highway under the horizon! *and* the riot of the singing birds!— it was all worth getting up for, I tell you. After this, I shall cease from rising at half past five, while on the river, & get up every morning at 4. (Been going to bed at 11 & 12 & rising at 5.30 & 6.)

Our present plan is to stay in Vicksburg all day to-morrow, & then go on to New Orleans—remain there a week & then go straight through to St. Louis on the great steamer "Baton Rouge," which is commanded by Horace Bixby, who taught me the river,

& to whom I owed & paid absolute obedience during a year & a half.

Good-bye for to-day, sweetheart—I'm getting pretty anxious for the letters I shall get at Vicksburg to-morrow morning. I love you, darling

SAML.

NEW ORLEANS, Saturday, 10 P M
[Apr. 29, 1882]

Livy darling, we are in the midst of a whirlpool of hospitality—breakfasts, dinners, lunches, cock-fights, Sunday schools, mule-races, lake-excursions, social gatherings, & all sorts of things. And I enjoy it, too, though it is powerfully taxing, both mentally & physically, & I shall be glad of a rest by & by. However, I go to bed early, sleep soundly, rise early, snatch a couple of hours' rest at noon, drink little or nothing, & consequently start out in a fresh & vigorous condition every morning. The weather is mighty hot, but I do not mind that. Called on a friend at 7:15 this morning; met an engagement at 9; breakfasted with some editors at a club at 10; met an appointment at 11; stripped & lay quiet till 1; drove with friends to the mule-races; returned at 5; dined with some new acquaintances; spent the evening at Cable's; have just reached home, now (10 P.M.), & am somewhat tired. So, with your permission I will stop writing & go to bed. But I miss you, & I love you; & it would delight me beyond measure to end this journey this moment, & step into our house & rout out you & Susie & Bay & Jean & give you all a hug or two.

Lovingly,
SAML.

George Washington Cable, story writer of old Creole days, and Joel Chandler Harris, creator of Uncle Remus, were the two most important friends made on this visit, as the next letter suggests.

NEW ORLEANS, Tuesday [May 2, 1882]

Livy darling, we are still booming along in the sociabilities, & find it a pretty energetic business & rather taxing to the strength.

However, we keep good hours, & are able to stand it. We spent yesterday afternoon & last night at Mr. Cable's house. Uncle Remus was there, but was too bashful to read; so the children of the neighborhood flocked in to look at him (& were grievously disappointed to find he was white & young) & I read Remus' stories & my own stuff to them, & Cable read from the Grandissimes & sketches. In the evening we all went to Mr. Guthrie's (brother to David Gray's wife) & had superb piano music by young ladies, & some excellent recitations by (myself) & others, & a song or two. Guthrie's little boy (aged 6) & little girl (aged 4) performed the balcony scene in Romeo & Juliet in the quaintest most captivating way, with good emphasis, elocution, earnestness, & perfect simplicity & unconsciousness. I never have seen anything that moved me more. They required prompting only once. There was an audience of twenty-five ladies & gentlemen.

We are reduced to lying, at last. We pretend to have engagements which we have not, in order to escape others which we want to avoid.

A big, fast steam-tug was offered us, & this morning we steamed up & down the river a couple of hours at a tremendous rate. I did the steering myself. There was a fine breeze blowing, the sun was bright, & orange groves & other trees about the plantation dwellings in full & sumptuous leaf. Splendid trip. I took along a couple of old-time pilots as our guests.

Mr. Hatch called, to-day, & invited us over to his house to see his daughter, but we had the usual engagements on hand & excused ourselves.

We dine with the editors to-night (& pretend to go down to the mouth of the river tomorrow, but shall lie abed & sleep, instead).

I have telegraphed St Louis for Howells's letter—I return his nice note to you.

We leave Saturday & shall be 5 days going up to St Louis. You can (& must) write to St Louis (Southern Hotel) as late as next Tuesday, but no later. With a whole world of love to you & them cubs.

SAML.

In reply to a greeting from Mark given largely in Paine's biography, 735, Howells wrote him from Boston on April 18; this letter is included with the above. Howells closes gaily: "Give my love to the young willows (but not widows) along the Mississippi River . . ."

On board BATON ROUGE, *May* 8 [1882]

We are moving along up the river pretty swiftly, Livy darling, & by Friday I expect to get a letter from you in St. Louis. It was a very genuine pleasure to receive such a nice long letter from you just before leaving New Orleans. I went to bed a trifle after midnight last night, & got up at 4 & was in the pilot house in a tolerably thick fog until breakfast. The dense foliage was beautiful in the fog. Every time we made a crossing we would be out of sight of land for some minutes, & then the great groves, like the faintest & filmiest spectres, would loom into view. They did not seem real, but only the spirits of trees. When we got closer—say within 600 yards—the reflections of the trees (where they stood on overflowed ground) in the glossy water, were stronger & darker than the trees themselves. We had a rattling nice storm yesterday afternoon: strong wind, blue-black sky, crawly white waves, vast sheets of driving rain, superb bursts of lightning, & a most inspiring cannonade of big thunder. And after it a couple of rainbows & the level rays of the sinking sun turning the Natchez hills into a kind of green-tinted conflagration. It was the kind of effect we get out of the low afternoon sun at home; & I thought of it shining on you loved ones at dinner & pouring a glory upon Emmaline & the gold walls of the library.

Goodbye, my darling, it's as hot as Hades——but I love you & the kids.

SAML.

"Emmaline" was the name given by the Clemenses to the head of a girl that hung among other pictures on the library walls, and along with an oil painting of a cat furnished the favorite theme for stories that the Clemens children demanded incessantly from their father.

[*near* ST. PAUL, MINNESOTA]
Saturday Eve [*May* 20, 1882]

We are in Lake Pepin, Livy darling, 80 or 90 miles below St Paul—where we shall arrive before breakfast if nothing happens. Among the passengers is a wretchedly poor & unkempt family on their way to the wilds of the Northwest—one of the new territories—out in the far wilderness. The man & his wagon take deck (steerage) passage, & his wife & five little children are allowed in the ladies' cabin by courtesy because there are no accommodations for such on deck. The woman looks worn out & miserable. She has slept two nights on a short sofa & her children on the cabin floor—all without pillows or covering, & it was mighty cold last night. This morning I got $5 from Osgood, added $10 myself, & got a lady to hand it privately to the woman, who was very glad to get it, the lady said. Afterward I found that they ate on deck, & of course had had nothing warm or nourishing; so I told the Chief Clerk to put them at the Cabin second table & charge to me. They were there this noon & evening at dinner & supper & ate like famished people. The woman stopped me afterward & asked if it was I that paid for their meals—& thanked me & broke down. They are all sound asleep on sofas, now (9 P M), but I notice that my interest in them has had an effect, for they all have pillows & coverings.

I have mightily enjoyed the children's letters, & even *Jean's* letter—(where she blotted a word for you). Well, I haven't seen any lady who is your equal—"taken by & large," as the sailors say—& none whom I could ever love half as well as I do you.

Goodbye, sweetheart, & kiss each of the children for me. I never forget them & they mustn't forget me. One of those little girls, about Bay's size, woke up, late last night & cried; & I comforted her & soothed her to sleep again—perhaps because she reminded me of Bay. I love you.

SAML.

I may not write again between this & home.

Arriving in St. Paul on May 21, he headed eastward by train. During a summer at Quarry Farm and an autumn in Hartford, Mark Twain completed *Life on the Mississippi.*

A flying visit to Canada in early May 1883, to protect his copyright of this new book, was followed by Mark's return trip to that country later in the month, to be the Governor-General's guest at a meeting of the Royal Literary and Scientific Society.

PRIVATE

GOVERNMENT HOUSE

OTTAWA

May 24, 1883

Livy darling, I must not attempt a scenery letter, it would seduce me into spinning out too long; & I must reserve my strength for the duties of these stirring times. I've had rattling good luck, as to blunders. True, the valet didn't ask for my shoes yesterday afternoon (had to remind him myself)—all was explained, in the evening when I observed that I was the only male creature in the drawing room who hadn't patent leathers on. Yes, that omission was a blunder, but I score a great success to make up for it: to-wit, although I had a burning desire to speak to her royal highess[2] about those unlucky shoes, I resisted it & didn't do it. And I had another lucky accident. Sitting at her right at dinner, I fell to delivering free but appreciative & admiring comments upon an oil portrait on the wall, & it so happened that God had allowed her to have painted it. As I hadn't suspected that, wasn't it a lucky stroke? I was saying I supposed it was a portrait, but that maybe it wasn't, because there was a grace & ease in the attitude & a deep & gracious something in the expression that suggested that it must be a composition. She called that a fine compliment; & when I asked "to the picture, or to the artist?" she said to the artist, which was herself. God was very good to me in this instance. But I was less fortunate earlier; when I had finished writing you, yesterday evening, I went down into the long corridor, & she was just entering a door. It was dim; I could not be sure it was she, but I thought I had better speak, for I was nearly sure; so I drew back respectfully, & said inquiringly, "Your royal highness?" Now you see, I should have been all right if I hadn't had the letter in my hand; but that, & my inquiring inflection, made her think I had been looking around the house for her, to ask how

[2] *Sic.* She was Queen Victoria's daughter, the Marchioness of Lorne.

I was to mail my letter. So she said she would show me; & she led the way down the corridor, & I was very sorry it proved so far. But I couldn't know it would be so far. It would have been further, but a soldier happened to cross our path & she gave the letter to him. So I was all right, again; & I remained right, at least until we had got back to where we had started from. Then, just as I was taking my leave & she had her hand on the door knob, I had the ill luck to intimate that I hadn't been able to find the smoking room. So she took me back over the same ground, & found the smoking room, & it was only about two rooms beyond where we had met the soldier. I believe I could have found it myself; for it was a perfectly straight line. She ordered a fire made; & then crossed the room & closed a door that was letting in some cold—but really she had done that before I could divine her purpose, so it was not possible for me to be quick enough to do it for her. O dear, it was a great pity that I should make all this trouble; & yet I was glad, in a way, too, because it showed what a human right heart a queen's daughter can have, in spite of the chances she has to get it spoiled. She sent me some magazines, presently—(upon my word & honor I never hinted to her that I wanted magazines) it was her own idea—do not blame me for at least the things I do not do—& I had a ten minute smoke before going to dress. I was all right, after that; I did not make another blunder between that & dinner, I think.

SAML.

His anxiety over proprieties of dress and behavior, beyond much doubt, was exaggerated to tease Livy. On May 28, for example, near the close of his visit to Government House, Mark reported: "I was provided with only 3 white neckties, & they were rather shabby ones, too. They are shabbier, now. My dress coat has a big moth hole between the shoulders; but I have blacked the white lining underneath with ink, & I suppose it hardly ever shows; in fact the wise Princess said—but dear me it is luncheon time."

HARTFORD, May 24th 1883

YOUTH DEAR—I rec'd today your letter from Montreal, and was glad to know that you had gotten that far safely, I was sorry you had not taken your own frock coat with you, so that you would have had no necessity to borrow.

We are all well. Katy seems just like herself now. Jean has had a very naughty cry this evening and needed you here very much to rap on the nursery door—my rapping was not the least use. She needed a whipping, but I was too cowardly to give it to her. I have had to give her one little spatting today and I thought that was enough.

I had a pleasant call from Joe today, he is anxious to have a walk with you to the tower before we go away.[3] I told him I thought you would undoubtedly be able to take it with him.

Susy said a sweet, lovely thing to me today. I took her to ride with me & we had a good time together. I have been a little worried at the much talking that there has been with Susy lately about mothers & daughters not agreeing. I think you will remember how many questions she asked Sue about Ida and her mother not getting on quite well together, she has been quite exercised on the subject and I have been afraid that she might begin to feel that it would be rather interesting not to get on quite well with me. Today as we rode she alluded again to mothers & daughters not getting on smoothly together, and I said "Susy I hope we shall always agree," she said "Mamma we can never disagree we think just alike about things, why Mamma we seem like *one* person." I was happy!

As it is after eleven, dear heart, I must say good night. We love you more than we can tell & miss you more than we can tell. So come home to us when you can. I hope you are having a pleasant, good, profitable experience.

Good night my darling
Your Livy

[3] The Talcott Tower outside Hartford was their favorite objective. Shortly after Mark's return, the Clemenses made their usual summer trek to Quarry Farm.

CHAPTER TWELVE

On Tour with a Sabbatarian

THE year 1884 saw the completion of *Huckleberry Finn*, and Mark Twain's vigorous personal campaign against the Republican nominee for President, James G. Blaine. Although Mark had briefly served as a Confederate soldier, his later allegiances rarely lay with the Democratic party. But a candidate so unsavory as Blaine provoked him to join the revolt of the mugwumps. Mark's postelection meeting in Albany with the successful nominee, Grover Cleveland, is described in one of the first letters that follow. Theirs was a friendship destined to ripen through the years. Long afterward, on June 19, 1908, Clemens wrote to his daughter Jean:

"Mr. Cleveland? Yes, he was a drinker in Buffalo, and loose morally. But *since* then? I have to doubt it. And of course I *want* to doubt it, for he has been a most noble public servant—& in that capacity he has been utterly without blemish. Of all our public men of today he stands first in my reverence & admiration, & the next one stands two-hundred-&-twenty-fifth. He is the only statesman we have, now. We had two, but Senator Hoar is dead. Drinks? No, I hope it is a mistake. However, Cleveland *drunk* is a more valuable asset to this country than the whole batch of the rest of our public men *sober*. He is high-minded; all his impulses are great & pure & fine. I wish we had another of this sort."

Meanwhile on November 5, 1884, Mark Twain began an ambitious joint reading tour with George Washington Cable, the story teller of Creole New Orleans. The two had met on Mark's river trip in 1882, as will be recalled, and in the winter of 1883-84 while giving public readings Cable came to visit the Clemenses in Hartford and promptly succumbed to a violent siege of the mumps. His convalescence, and an elaborate April Fool's Day joke which he concocted to amuse Clemens—swamping him with a hundred and fifty fantastic requests for his autograph—cemented their friendship. And so in the autumn Mark hired Cable at a fixed salary, $450 weekly and expenses, to share the spotlight on his program. All business arrangements were left in the hands of the impresario Major J. B. Pond, whose brother Ozias set out to accompany this strangely assorted pair: the generous, convivial, irascible Missourian, crested like a cockatoo with his shock of curly russet hair that the years were now graying, and by his side this small clerical figure in rusty black, heavily bearded and mousy in manner, Bible-reader and abstainer from tobacco, a notable miser and fanatic keeper of the Sabbath day. Both men obviously were egoists on tour, prima donnas in potential rivalry. Under the propinquity of a four months' association, the development of certain tensions between them might have been forecast.

To Livy went a report of their early appearances in Brooklyn.

N.Y., Nov. '84
Saturday, after midnight [i.e., Sunday the 23rd]

Livy dear, only a line to say we finished the *eighth* performance for this week in Brooklyn Academy of Music at 10 this evening, & then came over the Bridge & home. Tired to death, & hungry. Disposed of two great chops, 3 eggs, fried potatoes, & a bottle of ale. I eat a big breakfast every morning & a big supper every night, & am growing fat. We got up at 6 this morning, & have talked to two huge houses in Brooklyn to-day. Mr. Beecher & the Sages were there tonight & Dean came behind the scenes.

Thank those dear sweet children for me, for their welcome letters. I love them & their mother.

Saml.

Letters to their absent father from Susy and her younger sister Clara—whom her father often called by the pet name of Ben—drew replies like the following.

New York, Nov 23/84

Susie dear, I don't know how to sufficiently thank you & Ben for writing me such good letters & so faithfully. And I want to thank you both for making Jean say things to be sent to me, too. I called at Gen. Grant's the other morning, & when I saw all his swords, & medals, & collections of beautiful & rare things from Japan & China, I was so sorry I hadn't made Mamma go with me. And Mrs. Grant was sorry, too, & made me promise that I would bring Mamma there to luncheon, some time. Gen. Lew Wallace was there—he has an article in this month's Century about the great Victory of Fort Donelson—& when I told him Mamma was at the reading the other night & was sorry I didn't make her acquainted with the author of Ben Hur, he was very sorry I was so heedless himself. Mrs. Grant got up & stood between Gen Wallace & me, & said, "There, there's many a woman in this land that would like to be in my place & be able to tell her children that she had stood once elbow to elbow between two such great authors as Mark Twain & General Wallace." We all laughed & I said to Gen. Grant: "Don't look so cowed, General; you have written a book, too, & when it is published you can hold up your head & let on to be a person of consequence yourself."

Kiss 'em all for me, sweetheart—& I send love & kisses to you, too.

PAPA

The next letter to Livy is postmarked "NY & WASH FAST M[AIL]." After spending a night with Nast the cartoonist and his family at Morristown, N.J., Mark and Cable now took to the provinces.

On board the train, Nov. 28/84

We dined & stayed all night with Tom Nast & family, & had a most noble good time. I occupied his eldest daughter's room— Miss Julia Nast, aged about 20—the most remarkable I was ever in—a curious & inexhaustible museum. Not an inch of the four walls could be seen—all hidden under pictures, photographs, etchings, photographs, Christmas cards, menus, fans, statuettes, trinkets & knick-knacks in all metals—little brackets everywhere, with all imaginable dainty & pretty things massed upon them & hanging from them—the most astounding variety of inexpensive & interesting trifles that was ever huddled together upon four walls in this world. It took me an hour to undress, & another hour to dress, because my eyes were so busy & the new surprises were so constant & so engaging. She asked me this morning to give her a name for her room, & I told her to call it "Cesnola's Despair."[1] I would like to see Susie's room decorated in that way. The thing is easy, & occupies years: whenever you get hold of a new trifle, nail it to the wall with a pin. At a rough guess I should say there are 3,000 pretty trifles in Julia Nast's room. They didn't cost more than 3,000 dimes, perhaps, but they are worth twenty times the money to look at.

I love you my darling. I hope you had a good birthday[2]——& now I must stop, as the cars have started again.

SAML.

On the train, Dec. 3/84

We arrived at Albany at noon, & a person in authority met us & said Gov. Cleveland had expressed a strong desire to have me call, as he wanted to get acquainted with me. So as soon as we had fed ourselves the gentleman with some additional escort, took us in two barouches to the capitol, & we had a quite jolly & pleasant brief chat with the President-elect. He remembered me easily, have seen me often in Buffalo, but I didn't remember him, of course, & I didn't say I did. He had to meet the electors at a banquet in the evening, & expressed great regret that that must debar him from coming to the lecture. So I said if he would take my place on the platform I would run the banquet for him: but he said that that would be only a one-sided affair, because the lecture audience would be so disappointed. Then I sat down on four electrical bells at once (as the cats used to do at the farm), & summoned four pages whom nobody had any use for.

We were all over the capitol, which is a palace, & got acquainted with a lot of the State officers; then to the Senate Chamber & saw the beginning of the solemn ceremony of the casting of the electoral vote of the State of New York for President of the U. S.

[1] Luigi Palma di Cesnola (1832-1904), Italian soldier of fortune, veteran of the American Civil War, archaeologist and art collector, stormy director of New York's Metropolitan Museum.

[2] For this occasion he ordered from Tiffany "a diamond solitaire ring for Mrs. Clemens, to cost $250 or $300" (to Charles Webster, November 23).

At night it was an enormous audience.

I met young Smith of Elmira & got all the news about the Arnots —very sad news it is.

Kiss me the "chisn" as Jean used to say. I love you, my darling.

SAML.

ROCHESTER, *Sunday, Dec 7/84*

Livy darling, I got your letter enclosing Jean's 4^s—admirable child, cultivated child, how she is progressing! It is a sour, bleak, windy day, here, with trifling flurries of snow; but I have lain abed all day, reading & smoking, & having a restful & comfortable but rather homesick time. I miss you, & I miss the children & would so unspeakably like to be with you. The deluging rain played smash with us here. We should have had exceptionally good houses here, but for that. But I love you, sweetheart, that I know.

SAML.

ROCHESTER, *Sunday afternoon*

P. S. I have just seen a first sample of the Salvation Army. Across the street from my window I heard singing, & looked out & saw four very young men in military costume grouped upon the broad sidewalk, & they were swaying this way & that, about a gaudy banner, & making violent & absurd gestures with their hands, & singing unhymn-like hymns in loud voices. About them were grouped 12 or 15 women & girls in poor & faded attire. The singing presently drew a crowd of 50 men & boys—mainly street stragglers, & the bleak wind tugged at their worn overcoats & crippled umbrellas, & made a wintry & dreary spectacle of them, which had a most homeless aspect about it. Presently one of the uniformed youths took off his cap & made a prayer; then there was more fantastic singing; then a woman of 50 made an exhortation; then a lay youth did the like; then another old woman; then a man in poor clothes; then another youth in soldier clothes—all these performances sandwiched with singing. The service being ended, the standard bearer marched away with his flag, the uniformed youths followed him, two by two, the women followed these in double file, the ununiformed privates followed these in double rank, (in their midst a youth in blue navy cloth, with this legend in great white letters embroidered upon his back, *"Come to Jesus"*) & the mob brought up the rear.

I love you, sweetheart.

SAML.

GRAND RAPIDS, MICH. *Dec.* 13, 1884

Only one word, my darling, to say we have ridden the whole day in the train, & now I am in bed for an hour to rest me before going on the platform. You & the children have been in my mind all the day, & I have been very homesick & still am. I ate a lot of chestnuts that I found in my overcoat pockets, & that brought the children very near to me, for all three of them contributed to that stock. I love you, dear, & the time seems very long, that remains yet betwixt us & meeting.

SAML.

He returned to Hartford for a short Christmas recess, but was soon back on the road again, with a new excerpt from *Huckleberry Finn* added to his program.

PITTSBURGH, *Dec.* 29 [1884]

Well, mamma, dear, the child is born. To-night I read the new piece—the piece which Clara Spaulding's impassibility dashed & destroyed months ago—& it's the biggest card I've got in my whole repertoire. I always thought so. It went a-booming; & Cable's praises are not merely loud, they are boisterous. Says its literary quality is high & fine—& great; its truth to boy nature unchallengeable; its humor constant & delightful; & its dramatic close full of stir, & boom, & go. Well, he has stated it very correctly. It took me 45 minutes to recite it, (didn't use any notes) & it hadn't a doubtful place in it, or a silent spot. Ah, if it goes like that in its crude rude state, how *won't* it go when I get it well in hand? I make 2 separate readings of it, & Cable sings a couple of songs in the middle.

Come to think, I guess Clara never heard this—nor you either: I got disgusted, that night, before I got *to* this, I think. This is merely the episode where Tom & Huck stock Jim's cabin with

reptiles, & then set him free, in the night, with the crowd of
farmers after them with guns.

Heard a wonderful banjo player to-day. I love you, love you,
darling.

SAML.

According to the best available information, Jane Lampton,
born in 1803, spent her early girlhood in southern Kentucky, in
Adair county rather than in the north near Paris (Bourbon
county), as her son seems to imply in the next letter. He was
treating geography somewhat cavalierly.

PARIS, KY., New Year's '85

Livy darling, we have had a most pleasant evening here—in a
region familiar to Ma when she was a girl some seventy or eighty
years ago. Whenever we strike a Southern audience they laugh
themselves all to pieces. They catch a point before you can get it
out—& then, if you are not a muggins, you *don't* get it out; you
leave it unsaid. It is a great delight to talk to such folks.

At the hotel, before the reading, a large man introduced himself to me as "the big Kentuckian whom you have celebrated in
the Tramp Abroad, in your chapters about Heidelberg students"
—& showed me a huge scar extending from the bridge of his nose
clear across his face—a permanent memento of his stirring Heidelberg adventures. He said my account was correct. I got it from
Consul Smith, you remember. I asked him up to the room and had
a sociable good half hour with him.

Scrap of conversation overhead in the smoking car to-day:

"Well, I'd ben a keepin' school 6 or 7 years, & so I thought I'd
lay off a while & do some work. So I farmed it two or three yers,
& didn't no particular pains; & yit I raised one o' the likeliest
crops o' tobacker in the county. But I'm back keepin' school agin
—seemed like that uz what I uz made fur, you know, & so I kind
o' naturally sidled back into it agin. I've got a big school—45
scholars—& most uv 'em comes every day. They ain't *no* day that
30 or 35 uv 'em don't come. What's the *matter* uv you?"

"Well I'm a ailin' a little in a bad tooth I've got—aches right
smart, sometimes."

"Ought to have it out. *I* had one—'bout three yer ago: I jes' dismiss' school, & says I they ain't no two ways 'bout what *I'm* agoin' to do, & with that I jumps on my hoss and humps myself for the doctor; come acrost him on the road, 'fore I got more'n a mile or a mile & a half; & says I "Git right down off'n yo' hoss & pull this tooth." And he done it—right there on the road. An' I haint had no trouble sence, with that'n er any other tooth in my head."

I love you, my darling, & I send New Year's love to you & mother, & all the children.

SAML.

Mark Twain's superb ear for dialect was always most attentive when in the presence of Southern speech.

The next letter was written just after Clemens and Cable had left Louisville, and the hospitalities of its famous newspaper editor Colonel Henry Watterson, a distant cousin of Clemens on the Lampton side.

On the train, Jan 8/85

We were up at 7. this morning, with a 9-hour journey before us & no parlor car. But we are getting along all right. The train stops every half a mile. It is now 1 P.M., & this car has been filled & emptied with farmer-people some 300 times. They are a constant interest to me—their clothes, their manners, attitudes, aspect, expression—when they have any. A small country boy, a while ago, discussed a negro woman in her easy hearing distance, to his 17-year old sister. "Mighty good clothes for a nigger, *hain't* they? *I* never see a nigger dressed so fine before." She *was* thoroughly well & tastefully dressed, & had more brains & breeding than 7 generations of that boy's family will be able to show. I spent an hour, a while ago, re-writing a thing which is in the Tramp Abroad—speeches of a couple of bragging, loud-mouthed raftsmen.[3] I cut it up into single-sentence speeches—these sentences to be spoken alternately (a lively running-fire of brag & boast) by Cable & me, for Pond's amusement, nights, in our room. When

---

[3] Surely the boasting-match lifted from *Huckleberry Finn* to enrich *Life on the Mississippi*, chap. iii. *A Tramp Abroad* contains no such passage.

I had finished this bit of dramatization, I handed the MS over my shoulder to Cable & Pond, & as Cable began to read it to himself, a benevolent-looking middle-aged good-natured school-teacherish sort of an ass in the next seat behind stretched his long neck forward & began to read over Cable's shoulder with the most innocent eagerness you ever saw. I had to say twice to him, "It's *private*, sir," before he understood, so absorbed was he. Then he settled back to his place with a child's timid confusion.

3. P.M. DECATUR, ILL.

Here is the bulk of the day gone, & I have not noticed the flight of time—been busy & interested. We have been waiting here 20 or 30 minutes; & then jumped aboard the wrong train & made ourselves comfortable in a drawing room car bound for Niagara Falls, or up there somewhere. Learned our mistake only just time enough to snatch on our wraps & over shoes & skip aboard the right train.

Woman & 4 little children in one party crying, & another party of women & girls seeing them off & crying. Asked why the crying? Woman said she & her children were leaving their home here to go & live in Portland, Oregon, & these others were her young sisters, &c.

Blaine *did* betray his wife before marriage, & the child was born 3 months after the wedding. He then left her in Maine & returned West & engaged himself to marry one of the Marshall family of Kentucky; & after this girl learned the above things he *still* tried to persuade her (in letters which still exist, in his own hand & signed by himself) & assured her he would soon be able to get rid of "this woman" (his wife). The above facts are all beyond doubt or question, & would have been proven on the trial if Blaine had not withdrawn his libel suit. And he *knew* they would be proved. I talked with a perfectly trustworthy man who has had those letters in his hands & read them. I love you, darling. Goodbye

SAML.

With his cordial dislike of James G. Blaine, already noted, Clemens was not sorry to believe the worst of him. In 1850 this politician had married Harriet Stanwood, a Maine woman, in Kentucky. D. S. Muzzey's biography, *James G. Blaine* (1934), cites the "preposterous story that his marriage in Kentucky had been invalid, and that his eldest son Stanwood had been born out of wedlock," seeing this canard as a political reprisal for the Maria Halpin scandal about Cleveland. On August 14, 1884, Blaine had indignantly denied the story and brought suit for libel against an Indianapolis newspaper conspicuously fond of it.

Mark's next letter illustrates the sort of advice that a successful author was constantly invited to give beginners.

The postmark is (Monday) January 12, hence this must have been written on the 11th.

ST. LOUIS, *Jan.* 10 (?)/85.

Livy darling, it is a busy Sunday with me, although in bed. I have written you a bit of translation, read a young woman's (married, but a mere child), MS book through, & scribbled her a letter —which I must append here, to satisfy your curiosity:

My Dear Mrs. Whiteside:

I have read the story, & it has merit, but not enough to enable me to say the *strong* word necessary to rouse a publisher's interest & desire. I should have to be straightforward with him, & tell him the truth: that it is a moral essay, & an earnest & heartfelt essay, but more an essay than a story. And I should have to say it is crude, & betrays the unpractised hand all along; that it wants compression—is too wordy, too diffuse; that incidents & episodes & situations are hardly frequent enough, & when they occur are not successfully handled. I should have to say that with the exception of Malcolm's letter to his wife, the whole book ought to be carefully & painstakingly re-written. You know that after I should have said all these things—& I should have to say them, for my opinion would be asked—the publisher would be sure to decline to take the book.

You must try to forgive me for speaking so plainly—I mean no harm by it, but only good. I would not affront you with glozing speeches—& they would profit neither of us.

You must not be surprised at what must be pronounced a non-success—nor discouraged by it. Literature is an *art*, not an inspiration. It is a *trade*, so to speak, & must be *learned*—one cannot "pick it up." Neither can one learn it in a year, nor in five years. And its capital is *experience*—& you are too young, yet, to have much of that in your bank to draw from. When *you* shall have served on the stage a while (if you ever should), you will not send another heroine, unacquainted with the histrionic art, to ask a manager for a "star" part & *succeed* in her errand. And after you yourself shall have tried to descend a rain-water pipe, once, unencumbered, you will always know better, after that, than to let your hero descend one with a woman in his arms. Is it hypercriticism to notice these little blemishes? No—not in this case: for I wish to impress upon you this truth: that the moment you venture outside your *own* experience, you are in peril—don't ever do it. Grant that you are so young that your capital of experience is necessarily small: no matter, live within your literary means, & don't borrow. Whatever you have *lived*, you can write —& by hard work & a genuine apprenticeship, you can learn to write well; but what you have not lived you cannot write, you can only pretend to write it—you will merely issue a plausible-looking bill which will be pronounced spurious at the first counter.

These sound like harsh facts; but it is only the harsh facts that a body will listen to—& I want these to take hold, & make an impression.

Sincerely yours
S L CLEMENS

About two years earlier, his mother Jane Clemens had left Fredonia for Keokuk, to live the rest of her life with Orion, unsuccessful chicken-raiser, inventor, and lawyer in that Iowa community. Mark's visit with her and his earlier call at Hannibal powerfully stirred the depths of memory.

KEOKUK, Jan. 14/85

Livy darling, I'm *clear* behind!—With letters, I mean. Such slathers of ancient friends, & such worlds of talk, & such deep enjoyment of it! No time to turn around, for 2 or three days, now —no chance to even drop a line to say, I love you, sweetheart!

But wait—give me a chance—I will make it up. It is long past midnight. A beautiful evening with ma & she is her old beautiful self; a nature of pure gold—one of the purest & finest & highest this land has produced. The unconsciously pathetic is her talent —& how richly she is endowed with it—& how naturally eloquent she is when it is to the fore! What books she could have written! —& now the world has lost them.

This visit to Hannibal—you can never imagine the infinite great deeps of pathos that have rolled their tides over me. I shall never see another such day. I have carried my heart in my mouth for twenty-four hours. And at the last moment came Tom Nash —cradle-mate, baby-mate, little-boy mate—deaf & dumb, now, for near 40 years,[4] & nobody suspecting the deep & fine nature hidden behind his sealed lips—& hands me this letter, & wrings my hand, & gives me a devouring look or two, & walks shyly away. I kept it, & read it half an hour ago—& of course, although it was past midnight & I had not written to you yet, I sat down at once & answered it.

Goodbye, my darling—I love you, best of all; & those dear children next; & very, *very* soon, I am going to answer that precious Jean's letter & tell her about the wonderful bear I saw to day.

SAML.

Keep Tom's letter

No such letter from Tom Nash at this time is found in the Mark Twain Papers, but they do contain one from Nash on April 23, 1885, acknowledging Clemens' from Keokuk, and speaking of their boyhood together.

The infamous Mr. Wilson mentioned in the first paragraph of Mark's next letter to Livy seems to be unidentifiable; furthermore Mark probably confuses hemorrhages with hemorrhoids.

His reference to Ozias Pond under the Arthurian nickname of Sir Sagramore le Desirous is of special interest. At Rochester six weeks earlier Cable had introduced Mark to Malory's romance. On February 4 he explained further to Livy: "Some time ago, I

[4] Out skating on the frozen Mississippi with Sam Clemens, he fell into the icy water, and supposedly from the chill caught scarlet fever, which left him with these handicaps. (*Autobiography*, II, 97-98.)

gave [Ozias Pond] a full edition of the Morte d'Arthur, & addressed it to him as 'Sir Sagramore le Desirous'—a name which we have ever since called him by. We have all used the quaint language of the book in the cars & hotels . . ." From this atmosphere sprang the *Connecticut Yankee.*

CHICAGO, *Sat. night, Jan* 17/85

Livy darling, Mr. Wilson is a fraud & a liar. It is a satisfaction to know that he has got hemorrages.

Well, now I think the proofs are pretty good. They make you look too old & too care worn,—that is all the fault I find. You are not that old; so the look is only temporary. We will drive it away when I get home, & you shall be young again, my darling. The more I look at them the better I like them.

Sunday morning

No, I cannot have either of them. They reproach me so. They say "You have given these features this drawn look, & put the tired look into these eyes, with your desertion & absence." That is what they say, distinctly; & I feel the justness of the reproach.

My breakfast is arriving.

Noon

Sir Sagramore le Desirous (Pond), has just been in, & has received a few new dates from New York. They will be furnished you from New York (I gave strong orders the other day), but to make everything sure we also will telegraph them to you from here tonight.

We've had an immense time here with these three big audiences in this noble Central Music Hall. But for the fearful storms, we would have turned people away from the doors. It is a beautiful place, & you should have seen that alert & radiant mass of well-dressed humanity, rising tier on tier clear to the slope of the ceiling. Last night I was the greatest triumph we have ever made. I played my new bill, containing The Jumping Frog of Calaveras County (cut it down & told it in 13 minutes—quickest time on record) & Tom & Huck setting Jim free from prison—25 minutes —but it just went with a long roll of artillery-laughter all down the line, interspersed with Congreve rockets & bomb shell explosions, from the first word to the last—& then after a thrice-repeated crash of encores, I came back & talked a ten-minute yarn (Gov. Gardiner)—on the stage 35 minutes, you see, & no harm done— encored again *after* the encore, & came back & bowed. And mind I tell the old Jumping Frog swept the place like a conflagration. Nothing in this world can beat *that* yarn when one is feeling good & has the right audience in front of him.

We've got a new plan, & it *works*. Cable goes on at the very stroke of the hour, & talks 15 minutes to an *assembling* house, telling them not to be concerned about *him* & *he* won't be troubled. And so, with all the encores, we have in no instance been on the stage a minute over 2 hours. The good effect is beyond estimation. (And privately, *another* thing—only half the house hear C.'s first piece—so there isn't too much of C any more—whereas heretofore there has been a thundering sight too much of him.)

I *love* you, darling.

SAML.

P. S. Cable says the 3/4 face will be quite good in the finished & mounted photograph, & I begin to agree with him. So, then, let us have a dozen made from that negative—& sent me two of them, one for myself & one for the Garths. One or two of the rest I will send to Louisville, &c. (when I get home) where I have promised them, & the remainder we will keep.

S L C

Think of your rich position—you have the children with you! (Poor old Jean, & Clara's clattering clock!)

Mark's frank exultation in his success as public story teller hardly comports with Cable's recollections after the former's death, quoted in Paine's biography, on pages 785-86, "of Mark Twain's conscientious effort to do his best, to be worthy of himself." Cable remembered one evening when he had sat in the wings, waiting his turn, and hearing "the tides of laughter gather and roll forward and break against the footlights, time and time again, and how he had believed his colleague to be glorying in that triumph." But on the way back to the hotel in their carriage, Clemens had confessed with a groan, "Oh, Cable, I am demeaning myself. I am allowing myself to be a mere buffoon. It's ghastly. I can't endure it any longer." Mark Twain always had his moments of self-distrust, but this story suggests even more strongly the envy which his less popular traveling companion could not help feeling on many an occasion.

Mark's next letter, reflecting upon the gullibility of the human race, is highly characteristic.

ST PAUL, *Jan* 23/85.

No, Livy dear, I don't think Pond ever fails to mail my letters; but it was as I wrote you from Keokuk or from Chicago—between St Louis & Keokuk I was heavily driven, therefore did not write during 2 days; but that was all—2 days; but on many other days I wrote twice.

I wrote one letter in Keokuk, & Orion took it in his hand & insisted on carrying it at once to the street box a couple of blocks away. A couple of hours later, it transpired that he had the letter in his pocket; could remember going *to* the lamp-post box & coming back wondering vainly what his errand thither was for. I wanted to take the letter, then, but he begged for leave to try again; so I let him. But probably he failed again.

We walked 9 blocks through a heavy snowstorm to see the "ghost"—the mysterious something on a school-house window pane which from the street looked like a crayon drawing of a pretty girl, with ribbons & other proper decorations upon her hair & about her chin. But all *I* could see was a strong purple [stain in the] splash in or on the glass, the size of one's head, & resembling nothing in this so much as a ragged big bath-sponge with 2 or 3 of the usual round holes in it. By a strong effort I could imagine that it looked a little like the old-fashioned horned & distorted devils of the picture books, with an open mouth filled with tushes; but *no* stretch of my imagination was able to make anything much like a *human* face out of the thing. Lord, what a curious thing the imagination is! Do you know, there are people there who see in that shapeless purple blur a striking portrait of Martha Washington; & others who see in it a portrait of some distinguished *man* or other; Orion & others see in it all that goes to make up the head & face of a very pretty young girl; & there are a lot of idiot spiritualists who see a purpose of God in it, &

a spirit face sent from him to confound the disbeliever in their doctrine. If all the fools in this world should die, lordly God how lonely I should be.

In Quincy I saw—well, first it was an old man with bushy gray whiskers down to his breast, & farmer-like clothes on. When I saw him last, 35 years ago, he was a dandy, with plug hat tipped far forward & resting almost on his very nose; dark red, greasy hair, long, & rolled under at the bottom, down on his neck; red goatee; a most mincing, self-conceited gait—the most astonishing gait that ever I saw—a gait possible nowhere on earth but in our South & in that old day; & when his hat was off, a red roll of hair, a recumbent curl, was exposed (between two exact partings) which extended from his forehead rearward over the curve of his skull, & you could look into it as you would into a tunnel. But now— well, see O W Holmes's "The Last Leaf" for what he is now.

And there also I saw Wales McCormick, the giant printer-cub of 35 years ago—he & I were apprentices & the above dude, Pet McMurray, was the journeyman.

I *love* you, sweetheart.

Saml

Mark accompanies this description with a sketch of a goateed dandy in top-hat. In the *Autobiography*, volume II, he gives his further recollections of young McCormick, "a reckless, hilarious, admirable creature," and the "jour" printer McMurray.

"Fifteen years married sixteen years engaged," Livy wrote her husband on January 25. "And I do love you a scrap even now. I don't much fancy having you away on our anniversaries . . . Good bye Youth, *I love you with my whole heart*." On the anniversary itself he sent this little message to her.

Chicago, *Feb.* 2, 1885

This is the great day, my darling; the day that gave you to me fifteen years ago. You were very precious to me, then, you are still more precious to me now. In having each other then, we were well off; but poor, compared to what we are now, with the children.

I kiss you my darling wife—& those dear rascals.

Saml.

From time to time Clemens could not forbear telling Livy of
Cable's vagaries, on the twin scores of parsimony and fanatic
Sabbath observance. Sometimes he thinly disguised the identity
of his subject as "Mr. K." Thus on January 2 he noted: "When
we came to put out our washing in Cincin. Mr. K. piled out a
whole trunkful—all saved up since we were on the road last. I
called Pond's attention to it, & he said he would not permit that;
he would make K pay for that wash out of his own pocket. I speak
but the truth when I say I like K better & better; but his closeness
is a queer streak—the queerest he has got." A month later, on
February 5, this criticism of his other vice is typical: "I do not
believe that any vileness, any shame, any dishonor is too base for
Cable to do, provided by doing it he can save his despicable Sabbath from abrasion. In him this superstition is lunacy—no, idiotcy
—pure & unadulterated. Apart from this & his colossal self-conceit
& avarice, he is all great & fine: but *with* them as ballast, he aver-
ages as other men & floats upon an even keel with the rest." Four
days later Clemens returned *con amore* to this theme.

No place is given, but on February 8 he was in Indianapolis,
and set out next day for Columbus.

Feb. 9/85

Livy dear you cannot imagine anything like this idiotic Sunday-
superstition of Cable's. I would throttle a baby that had it. It is
the most beggarly disease, the pitiful, the most contemptible
mange that ever a grown creature was afflicted withal. The only
time the man ever grows nervous, the only time he ever shows
trepidation, is when some quarter of a minute of his detestable
Sabbath seems threatened. Saturday night a lady whom I seem
to have known as a little girl in Buffalo gave us a reception; as
midnight approached, I had gone upstairs with the gentlemen to
smoke. Suddenly Cable appeared in the door, & stopped, for all
were listening to an elaborate anecdote, & the speaker was spe-
cially addressing me. Cable saw that to interrupt would be a
bearish rudeness. He paused; then, the time being close to 12, he
cast manners aside & came & bent over me & whispered that *he*
must be going. I gave him curt warning to cease from his interruption (the anecdote was silenced & waiting); he held still a

moment, then bent down again & whispered, "I will take the carriage, & send it back for you from the hotel." I said aloud, "You will do nothing of the kind—simply *wait*." Ah, if I had but known it was his shabby and hateful Sunday that was moving him to this, he would have *walked* home through the slop. That was really it. It would be unholy to ride home in a hack after 12. It is perfectly loathsome. Since I have been with this paltry child, I have imbibed a venomous & unreasoning detestation of the very *name* of the Sabbath. Saturday he was out of linen & wanted a couple of shirts washed; & you should have seen the nervousness with which he questioned the call-boy as to whether they could be done & *brought up* by such & such hour. The boy was uncertain, as to 9 P.M., but finally said, "I know they can be done by half past eleven, or eleven, & I'll bring them up in the morning." "*No—No!*—I will not *have* them in the morning. Except they can certainly & *surely* come up this evening, I will not let them go at all!"

He is in many ways fine & great, & splendid; & in others paltriness itself. In Napoleon resided a god & a little [bit of] mere man.

I have modified Cable's insulting & insolent ways with servants, but have not cured them; may-be they cannot be cured. Pond says the servants of the Everett House all hate him. Says that when C. is paying his own expenses, he starves himself; & when somebody else is paying them his appetite is insatiable. O, do you know, that for a year or two he was longing to hear Beecher, but would not cross the river on Sunday? He wouldn't cross the *bridge* on Sunday.

Well, I love you, anyway, darling

SAML.

COLUMBUS, *Feb.* 10/85

Livy darling, rode all day in a smoking car, yesterday, stopping every 30 yards, arrived here in a rain storm about 2 hours after dark, jumped into evening dress in a desperate hurry & came before a full Opera House of the handsomest people you ever saw, & made them shout, & tore them all to pieces till half past 10, & not an individual deserted till the thing was over. I have been 3 months learning my trade, but I have *learned* it at last, & now I would rather stand before such an audience as that than play billiards. After the show (& a hot supper) Pond & I *did* play billiards until 2 A.M., & then I scoured myself in the bath, & read & smoked till 3, then slept till half past 9, had my breakfast in bed, & now have just finished that meal & am feeling as fine as a bird. My health is so superb, now, that I require an immense strain of exertion (and fatigue) to keep me refreshed & comfortable. Not for many many years have I been in such splendid condition physically. Sometimes I have to wonder if I am really the same person who used to feel weary after running up stairs to the billiard room.

Cover the C H I L D! Do you know, that infernal Night Ride of Mary's has grown from 6 minutes (in New Haven) to *fifteen*! And it is in *every* program. This pious ass allows an "entirely new program" to be announced from the stage & in the papers, & then comes out without a wince or an apology & jerks that same old Night Ride on the audience again. He did it 5 times in Chicago; but even that was not as bad as doing it 3 times in a little place like Indianapolis. He keeps his program strung out to one hour, in spite of all I can do. I am thinking of cutting another of his pieces out of the program.

I love you darling—goodbye. Be sure to give *my* love to Gen Franklin when you see him.

SAML

"Mary's Night Ride," the reading of a sentimental episode near the end of Cable's novel *Dr. Sevier*, described Mary Richling's crossing of the Confederate lines to reach her dying husband. To Clemens, soon surfeited with this anecdote, it remained a perennial touchstone of the comic. Thus on his trip down the Rhone, to Livy on September 24, 1891, he described a mooring which they had barely achieved in the dusk: "Cover the child! cover the che-ild! lay on! lay on! *you*'ll make it! YOU'LL make it!—and—we—*did* make it! Just by the skin of our teeth."

The abrasion wrought upon Mark Twain's temper by Cable's peculiarities continued through the letters that Livy received during the later weeks of their reading tour. Her transmission of a hint by some Hartford charity that Cable appear in a benefit performance led Mark to write her:

DETROIT, *February* 13 [1885]

Livy darling, if they want Cable they must apply to him themselves—as for me, I wouldn't even vaguely suggest it to him for any money. He *might* & *may* say yes, if they ask him, but I'll never believe it till I see it. He is one of the most spoiled men, by success in life, you ever saw. I imagine that if a charity wants his in-his-opinion-almighty-aid, that charity will have to pay dollars for it. I don't believe he would do *any*thing for nothing. I don't believe he 'lays over,' Sundays, gratis: I believe he keeps an account against God. Of course I may be all mistaken, but no matter, I *think* these things. And he would be quite right to decline to read in Hartford for nothing. It is not his town; he owes nothing to its charities. Don't you allow yourself to be in any way, directly or indirectly, concerned in the applying to him.

Hang it, I believe he did read for a ladies' charity in New Orleans for nothing. And so, after all—

No—I've ransacked my memory, & I was wrong—he told the ladies he would charge his regular price—& he did, & collected it. No, *he* wouldn't read in Hartford for nothing; he wouldn't read in Heaven for nothing.

A few days later, after Cable had borrowed Mark's writing pad and used up all the paper, the aggrieved victim informed Livy on February 17: "He has never bought one single sheet of paper or an envelop in all these 3½ months—sponges all his stationery (for literature as well as stationery) from the hotels. His body is small, but it is much too large for his soul. He is the pitifulest human louse I have ever known."

Between Ottawa and Montreal Mark wrote to Livy in high spirits.

On board the train, Feb. 18/85

This is a most superb winter morning—snow up to the fence tops, splendid sunshine, no wind, white smoke floating up in lazy columns from the scattered log houses, the distances vague & soft in a haze that is lightly tinted with blue. A beautiful French Canadian girl came along, a minute ago at a station, clothed in a picturesque short dress made of heavy white blanket with the red & blue stripes of the blanket running around the lower half of the skirt, the body trimmed with blue, a broad blue belt, deerskin moccasins, a blue-&-red tuque[5] on her head—a most picturesque & captivating spectacle. The youth with her was in a blanket-costume, also, adorned with strong bright colors; had tight blanket pants on, broad blue belt & tuque & moccasins. Doubtless they had been snowshoeing, as these are snowshoeing costumes.

Several gentlemen were indignant that the Governor General didn't come to the reading or offer me any hospitalities of any kind; & said the town would by no means like it; for something was due me from the Marquis of Lansdowne, since everybody knows I was a guest of his predecessor & liked by him & the princess. I had wit enough to not divulge the fact that I hadn't *had* wit enough to invite the Governor to the show—& doubtless that was a politeness which was distinctly due from me. I don't know —but anyway I ought to have done it.

That poor Jean!—& poor mamma, too, who has to be up nights, & take care of her. I do hope Jean is well by this time.

I love you, darling.

SAML

P. S. Feb. 19. Talked here in Montreal last night, sweetheart. Shall write to-day.

From Toronto on February 15 he wrote Livy of going tobogganing in subzero weather with seventy-four students from "a Young Ladies' College" who had sought his autograph: "It is a tremendous sport, and no danger. You sit in the midst of a row of girls on a long broad board with its front end curled up, and away you go, like lightning." His experience probably prompted his purchase of a toboggan for the Clemens children, mentioned in the next letter.

On train, Feb. 20/85

Ah, my darling, if you could only be along, to-day. Never, never never *was* such a marvelous winter journey! For an hour or two

5 "Tuque" is Canadian French for toque.

we have been skirting Lake Champlain, & the landscape is too divinely beautiful for language to describe. You look miles & miles out over the frozen snow-white floor of the lake, with the dazzling sun upon it, & huge blanket-shadows of the clouds gliding over it, & here & yonder a black speck on the remote level (a sleigh), & away on the far further shore a dim & dreamy range of mountains rises gradually up & disappears in a ragged, low-hanging leaden curtain of clouds.

We have left the lake, now, & are among rolling farms, clothed to the fence-tops with the blindingest white snow, & on every hand in the distance rise rugged mountains mottled with dark forest-patches & frothy fields of snow, all softened & enriched with a purple haze—& then the mountain summits! They are as vague & spectral, away up there in the sky, as if you saw them through a veil of summer rain.

I sent a toboggan for the children. They better not try to use it till I come.

I will send a pasteboard box, to-night which must remain closed till I come. It is for the children. I bring you something myself by hand—I *may* possibly send it by express.

I love you, sweetheart.

SAML

Two lectures in Washington on February 28 ended his four months' tour. From that city he wrote to her in that rough and ready German which they had learned together in Heidelberg and Munich in 1878-79—an idiom whose amusing possibilities fascinated Clemens for the rest of his life.

WASHINGTON, den 2ten März [1885]

MEINE LIEBSTEN—Die Aehnlichkeit Zwischen Washington und anderen Städten existirt wohl nicht. Die Verschiedenheiten sind fast unzählbar. Die Stadt ist gross; sie ist auch klein; sie ist breit, sie ist eng; theils theils ist sie nass, theils ist sie von Staub umgewölkt. Am frühem Tage geht die Sonne auf, lächerlos, leicht verschleiert, und kalt; später brennt sie wie der Hölle; noch später steigen die Wolken auf, und schon auf einmal findet man sich im Finsterniss verschlungen, von Regen durchnässt—und, im volgedessen—seine moralische Stimme wohl gar umge-

worfen. Ehe man sein Regenschirm ausbreiten mag, ist das Un-
wetter wieder verschwunden und Alles liegt im hellen Sonnen-
schein. Man schliesst seine Augen zu, ausliefert eine feierliches
"Gott sei Dank," öffnet wieder seine Augen, und beim heiligen
Moses, es schneit!

Lass' das sein!

Ich liebe dich.

SAML

A translation follows:

"MY DEAREST ONES—A similarity between Washington and
other cities probably does not exist. The differences are almost
innumerable. The city is big; it is also small; it is large, it is
narrow; it is partly wet, partly enveloped in clouds of dust. In the
early morning the sun rises, unsmiling, somewhat veiled, and
cold; later it burns like an inferno; even later the clouds rise, and
suddenly one finds oneself surrounded by darkness, drenched with
rain, and, as a result, one's mood is probably upset. Before one is
able to open one's umbrella, the bad weather has disappeared,
and every thing is bathed in clear sunshine. One closes one's eyes,
renders a solemn 'Thank God,' opens one's eyes, and, Holy
Moses, it snows!

"Let it be!

"I love you.

"SAML"

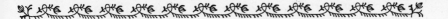

CHAPTER THIRTEEN

Grant's Memoirs and Other Schemes

DURING the rest of the year 1885 Clemens' absorbing interest lay not in his own work but in the *Memoirs* which
ailing Ulysses S. Grant had agreed to write so that his widow
might not be left impoverished, following the general's recent
indiscretions among the bucket-shops of Wall Street. Mark had
obtained this book for the new publishing house of Charles L.
Webster & Company, named for and nominally headed by the
young husband of Mark's niece Annie Moffett. Charles Webster,
a surveyor from Fredonia, New York, was as ignorant of the sub-
scription-publishing business as was his financial backer Samuel
Clemens, whose chronic suspicion of commercial publishers had
started the whole enterprise. But in the beginning the new firm
had the great good luck to publish *Huckleberry Finn* and then
the best-selling *Memoirs* of Grant.

In the spring and early summer of 1885 the old general was
dying stubbornly from cancer of the throat, and Mark's best
efforts went into encouraging him to finish the job in hand. On
his way to Philadelphia in early April, to appear at a benefit performance for the Actors' Fund, Mark called upon the Grants
before writing his nightly letter to Livy.

NEW YORK, *Apl.* 8/85

Livy darling, this is a dull trip, for I was fully expecting to have
you along, & I don't seem to reconcile myself to making the trip
alone. I am disappointed; & yet I knew it could not be well for
you to travel with such a cold & headache, & so I was bould[1] you
shouldn't come. This is a pleasant parlor (181) & well lighted;
& if you were here with a pack of cards I would be well satisfied

---

[1] *Sic;* probably error for "bound."

& not dreary. If you were well, I would wish you *were* here; but as you are not, I dont—you are better there with the best children in the land.

General Grant's book is not in type—indeed, the work on it is only fairly begun, & not a scrap of advertising has been done; & yet 20,000 sets are already in effect sold—they have been ordered by two responsible general agents; 20,000 sets is 40,000 volumes, for it is a 2-volume work. This affords a clear profit to *us* of $13,000—& over $26,000 to Mrs. Grant. You were a little afraid to have me venture on the book & take all the risks for so small a share as 30 per cent of the profits. I did not think there was any risk. These 40,000 books are ordered for only 2 States—Michigan & Iowa—wait till you hear from the other 37!

I was out at Gen. Grant's this evening. Col. Fred said the General was restful, & very happy, exceedingly pleased, over the inflowing expressions of sympathy from rebel soldiers of all ranks in the South. His last hours are among the happiest of all his life.

I kiss you darling, & all the babies.

SAML

Grant had a relapse on April 3 but rallied, and Colonel Fred Grant urged Clemens to encourage his father's perseverance on the book. With the coming of warm weather, the dying man was carried to Mt. McGregor, New York, where as reported in the next letter Mark visited him, just after the Clemens family had moved on June 27 to Quarry Farm.

MT. McGREGOR, *June 30*

Livy darling, what a journey it was!—sneaking along all day in accommodation trains, till half past 6: then I snatched a bite in Saratoga, then jumped into a buggy at 7.20 & reached here at 8.40—after dark. I shall have to remain here all day, but I can get away tomorrow I hope—& expect.

One looks out on a most lovely valley from this height—wide & level, & green, & checkered with farms & splotched with groves like cushions of moss—remember how the Rhein valley used to look from the Kaiser-Stuhl?

Good-bye my darling, I am in a great hurry to get out of bed, for it is already 8:15. I dearly love you—& I dearly love you *all*.

SAML

Karl Gerhardt, mentioned in the following day's letter, was a Hartford mechanic with aspirations to be a sculptor, whom Clemens had subsidized for three years' study in the ateliers of Paris. At this time, presuming on Mark's friendship he had taken Grant as his subject. A death mask which he made of the General three weeks later and refused to surrender to the widow unless he were paid handsomely, caused Mark a few days of intense embarrassment in mid-December 1885.

MT. McGREGOR, *July* 1/85

Livy darling, I shall no doubt leave for Hartford at noon tomorrow, as I telegraphed you this afternoon.

The photograph of the General which Gerhardt got taken is a most impressive & pathetic picture. Gerhardt's bust of Jesse Grant's little child is a very successful thing, & they are all pleased with it.

I think they are all full of apprehension with regard to the General; & I think that from what I hear, the apprehensions are just; yet the General is as placid, serene, & self-possessed as ever, & his eye has the same old humorous twinkle in it, & his frequent smile is still the smile of pleasantness & peace. Manifestly, dying is nothing to a really great & brave man.

I do most powerfully love you, sweetheart. I believe I dated this morning's letter June 30—or did I write it last night? Please kiss some of those children for me—all of them, except Kiditchin.[2]

SAML

Clemens soon returned to his family at Quarry Farm, but left promptly for New York on July 23, after getting news of Grant's death. He wrote to Livy the next day: "The second volume was finished last week, to the last detail; & was formally delivered to Charley Webster at Mt. McGregor last Saturday. General Grant having not another interest in this world to live for, died. He would have died three months ago if his book had been com-

2 Jean's donkey.

pleted. I am satisfied of that." After three days in New York, Mark went back to Quarry Farm, but shortly revisited the city for Grant's funeral.

NEW YORK, *Aug* 4/85

Livy darling, New York was well draped when Garfield died, but in the matter of cost & elaboration the present occasion is a long way ahead. Some of these vast stone & brick fronts are almost hidden in swathings of black drapery. The artistic *way* in which it is done is a remarkable feature, too—it makes the effect beautiful to the eye. White marble fronts make the handsomest show. In some cases no more of the marble is seen than of the black. Where there are columned porticos, the columns & their capitals are *solid black*, unmarred by a single touch of black [*sic*]. The effect is very striking—& also exceedingly handsome. I think I have seen a thousand big portraits of the General set in the centre of a desert of black, on stone-fronts.

I love you, my darling, & I love the children, too. Good-bye, sweetheart.

SAML

[NEW YORK CITY]
Wednesday-Thursday, Midnight, Aug. 5-6 [1885]

Livy darling, I have eaten but 3 meals since the night before I left the farm—consequently I am in perfect condition physically. If I could get your permission I would eat only once a day for the rest of my life.

I sat in the Lotos Club this afternoon & saw the procession pass on its way to the City Hall with Gen. Grant's body. It was very grand & impressive. The Catafalque was drawn by quite a procession of black horses clothed in a most graceful black network. The procession on the day of the funeral will be a memorable spectacle & I shall be glad to be here, since the General *must* be buried.[3] I wish you were with me; & at the same time I *don't* wish it, since it would involve a couple of exhausting railway journeys.

I got your letter, & shall obey your orders if I go to Hartford;

[3] Mark's letter to the New York *Sun* urging the metropolis as the place of his burial carried some weight in that decision; see *Letters,* 456-57.

but there is no certainty of my going there. I very much doubt if I go.

> Good-bye—I love you, darling.
> Kiss the children & Sour Mash[4] for me.
>
> SAML

Autumn saw the Clemens family back in Hartford. The *Memoirs* still claimed top priority for Mark Twain. Having gone to New York to read proof, he wrote Livy on November 17: "I am afraid I can't go home Saturday, because they want me to go to Washington the end of this week & talk international copyright to the President. One must not refuse an office of that kind, when asked—a man who prides himself on his citizenship *can't* refuse it. . . . In the circumstances, you will not object, & so I don't need to holler for pardon."

His next letter describes a small dinner given by William M. Laffan, Irish-American journalist, currently publisher and later proprietor of the New York *Sun*. He was a friend and art adviser to J. P. Morgan, and something of a man of mystery to most of his associates. He had various business dealings with C. L. Webster & Company, and many sociable times with Mark Twain. A caricature self-portrait which Mark inscribed for Laffan in 1902, "To the pleasant barrels we've drunk together!" is now in the Berg Collection in the New York Public Library.

NEW YORK, *Nov.* 18 1885

Livy dear, I suppose I shall leave for Washington at 8 in the morning, arriving at the Ebbitt House there about a quarter before 2 in the afternoon.

I dined last night with Laffan in a private room at a restaurant, in company with Osgood & two young Harpers. Well, Laffan's dinner consisted of but 3 courses, but I tell you it was a marvel. By each man's foot stood a quart of champagne in a silver cooler —& an extra one on a sideboard—there was no other wine.

1st course—Very small raw oysters—just that moment opened, & swimming in their own sea-water. Delicious.

2d course. Terrapin stew, in dainty little covered pots, with

---

[4] Their favorite cat.

curious little gold & silver terrapin spoons from Tiffany's. Sublime. There never was such terrapin before. It was unspeakable.

3d course. Before *each* man was set an entire canvass-back duck, red hot from the oven, & on his plate was laid a carving knife & fork.—he must do his own carving. These ducks were just simply divine.

So ended the dinner. No coffee, desert, cheese—*nothing.* Not a scrap of the 3 courses was left. Five skeletons represented the ducks; 6 empty bottles represented the champagne. A memorable dinner.

Then the young Harpers forced Laffan to match half dollars with them, & in 15 minutes they hadn't a cent, & Laffan had won enough to pay for the dinner.

Then we went to a private room connected with a great billiard saloon & had champagne (which I did not touch) & billiards; & at 1.30 A.M. (billiard-room bill $7) as we were leaving & Laffan about to pay, I said, "I know nothing about matching half-dollars, but I'll match you for that bill." We uncovered the coins & looked —result, *I* paid the seven dollars & went home to bed.

I love you darling.

SAML

Livy's fortieth birthday and his approaching fiftieth led him to write thus tenderly.

HARTFORD, *Nov.* 27/85

We have reached another milestone, my darling, & a very very remote one from the place whence we started; but we look back over a pleasant landscape—valleys that are still green, plains that still bear flowers, hills that still sleep in the soft light of that far morning of blessed memory. And here we have company on the journey—ah, such precious company, such inspiring, such lovely, & gracious company! & how they lighten the march! Our faces are toward the sunset, now, but these are with us, to hold our hands, & stay our feet, & while they abide, & our old love grows & never diminishes, our march shall still be through flowers & green fields, & the evening light as pleasant as that old soft morning glow yonder behind.

Your HUSBAND

The winter and spring that followed were jubilant with the success of Grant's *Memoirs*, a profit of nearly six hundred thousand dollars remaining to be divided between the publisher and the General's family. "I am frightened at the proportions of my prosperity," Clemens is said to have told a friend. "It seems to me that whatever I touch turns to gold." His illusion would turn out to be as disastrous as that of King Midas, but while it lasted it tempted him still further to neglect writing his own books for sake of promoting others'. One of his most grandiose schemes which turned out a total flop was a life of the reigning Pope, Leo XIII, by Bernard O'Reilly, D.D., LL.D., which with Protestant naïveté Clemens and Webster expected every Catholic to buy, under pain of damnation.

Shortly before Charles Webster went abroad to interview His Holiness in person, Livy wrote her nephew that she hesitated to order an expensive sofa unless "the contract for the Pope's book is signed." Hence the point of the next letter, still further elucidated by Twichell's diary for May 5-7, 1886: "To West Point with M. T.—just to see a little more of the Academy than we were able to last month, or at our previous visit in 1881. On the way, at New York, M. learned that the contract for the 'Pope's Book,' which, as publisher, he had been for some months negotiating with high Roman Catholic authorities about, was signed. The issue of this book will be the greatest event in the way of book publishing that ever occurred; and it seems certain, M. T. will make a vast amount of money by it." Long afterward Twichell subjoined: "(P.S.—Proved quite otherwise in the event.)"

On the cars, May 5 [1886] 4.30 P.M.

It was good news I sent you, Livy darling. I thought it would reconcile you to your costly sofa. You can order 1000 such sofas now, if you want to—the future bank account will foot the bill & never miss it. The Pope's book is ours, & we'll sell a fleet load of copies.

I love you, sweetheart, deeply, fondly, & always.

SAML

Can't write any more till tomorrow, at West Point—whither we are bound now.

The next letter was written late that summer, while Mark was on his way to Philadelphia to attend the trial of a damage suit he had brought against a distributor for selling Grant's *Memoirs* below cost for advertising purposes. The defendant, as he informed Howells on July 15, was "that unco-pious butter-mouthed Sunday-school slobbering sneak-thief John Wannemaker, now of Philadelphia, presently of hell." Before the litigation was over Mark learned how to spell his adversary's name, but he lost the suit.

NEW YORK, *July* 30/86

Livy darling, I have arrived, & am just out of the bathtub, & in bed & ready for immediate sleep, for it has been a long day, & pretty warm & fatiguing. I have a note from Laffan asking me to go down & stay over Sunday with him.[5]

Met George Warner in the lobby of the hotel, but only stopped to shake hands with him.

I thought of you people all along, to-day, naturally enough: "Now they're at supper"—"now they're out on the porch, & Theodore sitting in the roadway"—"now the children & the pony are at it"—"now Jean is kissing good-night"—"now the children are playing the piano for Theodore"—"now *they're* off for bed" —"& now Aunt Sue is taking advantage of the absence of their natural protector to set out the Mash family an hour ahead of time"—"& finally all hands are off for early bed, & Mamma & Jean are bunking together, & all is quiet, all is still but the dog."

I love you, sweetheart.

SAML

In the summer of 1886 he began *A Connecticut Yankee at King Arthur's Court*, and after a busy but unproductive winter in Hartford—with speeches, social life, and speculative enterprises making inroads upon his time—Mark returned the next season to Quarry Farm and again fell to work upon the *Yankee*. The next letter went to Livy from the midst of a routine trip begrudged because it tore him away from the growing fascination of that tale. From the hilltop he wrote to Mollie Clemens on July 24: "But I have to lose the present week, in New York & Hartford,

[5] An undated note written to Livy a day or two later reveals that he had gone to Laffan's house near Lawrence, Long Island, for a week-end of surf bathing.

on business. If I could buy said week, & remain at work here, I could afford to pay $3,000 for it." His comment to Livy upon the ill-health of Charles Webster is significant, because Webster's excruciating pain forced him to retire from the firm a few months later, and foreshadowed his death in 1891.

ST. JAMES HOTEL [NEW YORK], *July 26/87*

Livy darling, I have finished up what I had to do here, & shall start to Hartford at 4:30. Charley is a constant sufferer from his neuralgia, but has lately found a doctor who gives him several hours' relief per day.

I read the 4th volume of Metternich's memoirs all the way down in the cars yesterday—& last night. Apparently no narrative that tells the facts of a man's life in the man's own words, can be uninteresting. Even this man's State papers are after a fashion interesting, when read by the light of his private remarks & comments. And this difference between him & Gen. McClellan is conspicuous. Metternich's book removes the obloquy from his name, but McClellan's deepens that upon *his,* & justifies it.[6]

Ich liebe Dich, ich liebe Dich.

SAML

The concerns of his publishing house, plus the friends and club life of New York, drew Clemens with increasing frequency for short visits to the metropolis. Thus on Saturday March 10, 1888, he went down for Charles A. Dana's dinner in honor of the great actor Henry Irving. According to plan Livy would join him four days later for a trip to Washington, to visit their old Hartford neighbor General Hawley, now senator from Connecticut, and his wife. But the Great Blizzard interposed. On the envelope of the following letter Mark has whimsically altered the return address: "If not delivered within 5 years . . ."

MURRAY HILL HOTEL, NEW YORK
March 16, 1888. Noon

Livy darling, I have only just this moment given you up. All these years since the blizzard ceased I have expected you "next day," & next day, & next day—until now. I give it up. I no longer

6 *McClellan's Own Story* was published in 1887 by the Webster concern.

expect you. It is perfectly manifest that that road will not be open for one or two—or possibly 30 days yet. So I will go along to Washington this afternoon in the special car with the rest of the menagerie, & be rested-up & fresh for Mrs. Hawley's dinner tomorrow night.

I was going to wait here for you till Monday—I have had no other plan recently—but after declining, a half hour ago, to go with the menagerie to-day, it suddenly occurred to me that you would regard it as simply criminal for both of us to be absent from the dinner when one of us could be present. To be present, one must go *to-day*—for only an ass attends a dinner party after 6 hours' railway travel.

And so, after all my labor & persuasion to get you to at last promise to take a week's holiday & go off with me on a lark, this is what Providence has gone & done about it. It does seem to me the oddest thing—the way Providence manages. A mere simple *request* to you to stay at home would have been entirely sufficient; but no, that is not big enough, picturesque enough—a blizzard's the idea: pour down all the snow in stock, turn loose all the winds, bring a whole continent to a stand-still: that is Providence's idea of the correct way to trump a person's trick. Dear me, if I had known it was going to make all this trouble & cost all these millions, I never would have said anything *about* your going to Washington. Now in the light of this revelation of the methods of Providence, consider Noah's flood—I wish I knew the *real* reason for playing that cataclysm on the public: like enough, somebody that liked dry weather wanted to take a walk. That is probably the whole thing—& nothing more *to* it.

Blast that blasted dinner party at Dana's! But for that, I—ah! well, I'm tired; tired calling myself names. Why, I could have been at home all this time. Whereas, here I have been, Crusoing on a desert hotel—out of wife, out of children, out of linen, and out of cigars, out of every blamed thing in the world that I've any use for. Great Scott!

However, I will pack, now, & then go down town & make one more attempt to get a word to you—by long-distance telephone or somehow; though of course it will be the same old story & I shan't succeed.

But I love you my darling, & I am sharply disappointed. Blast the blasted reading, I wish it were in Jericho. Please to kiss those unmatchable jewels for me, & assert that I love them. I kiss you again, sweetheart.

SAML

Livy's forty-third birthday evoked a characteristic billet-doux of devotion.

HARTFORD, *Nov.* 27/88

Livy darling, I am grateful—gratefuler than ever before—that you were born, & that your love is mine & our two lives woven & welded together!

S.L.C.

In the autumn of 1888 Theodore Crane was stricken with partial paralysis, but made sufficient recovery to spend part of the winter with the Clemenses in Hartford, nursed by his wife Sue and by Livy. But in the following summer, when they were all back at Quarry Farm, he failed rapidly and died on July 3. An egotistic mediocrity, Theodore Crane had never been a favorite of, and was occasionally a positive irritant to, his famous brother-in-law. But his long illness and death readily erased that score, and the thoughts of mortality awakened by this recent event are reflected in the second letter which follows. Both were written to Livy from the Clemens house in Hartford, where Mark had returned for a midsummer visit of about twelve days.

The first letter mentions their Nook Farm neighbor Harriet Beecher Stowe, now in her erratic old age. She would run about the premises like an animal on the prowl, raid the Clemens greenhouse for fistfuls of blossoms, and sometimes slip up behind a person reading or meditating and (as Mark recalled in his *Autobiography*) "fetch a war whoop that would jump that person out of his clothes."

HOME, July 12/89

It is lovely & cool & nice & twilighty & still, here in the home after breakfast; & I can see the dog-house down the slope, & past its roof a burnished square yard or two of river with rich foliage-reflections in it; & this way a little, by the dog-house, is a grassy swale, the half of which is deeply shaded & the other half glares with sun; & at my right—among some ferns to the right of the tree that has Sue's old squirrel-boot nailed to it—is the peaceful picture of Satan & her child,[7] blinking up devout & drowsy, praising God for the weather.

I stepped to the front door a few minutes ago, & immediately encountered Mrs. Stowe, coming with her gray head bare, & welcoming smile in her eye, & her welcoming hand held out. She took a turn through the library & hall & went away, cheerful & happy, as always. But there's a pleasant change: she was not noisy, she didn't sing, & a stranger would have supposed she was a neighborly old friend who was knocking around quite *at* herself.

They had a disaster there night before last. Their cook, a young Irish girl (22 years) was taken sick in the morning; away in the night, that night, her mother, who was watching by her, went down stairs for something, & when she came back the girl was on the floor—& dying. She hardly lived long enough for Dr. Porter to get in there. He can't account for it, Katy says; thinks she must have had an internal abscess, & ruptured it falling out of bed, & choked to death.

Good bye & love & kisses to all of you.

SAML

"I shall be here ten days yet, and all alone; nobody in the house but the servants," he wrote Howells on July 13. ". . . can't you come and stay with me?" Although Howells seems not to have come, the neighbors kept Mark from getting too lonely. Three days after the above letter, for example, he wrote to Livy: "I asked Cousin Susy Warner to play the Seventh Symphony for me, & she done it. Also she played that other deep, rich, noble Beethoven piece—the one where, all along & all along, half a dozen of the bass notes keep rolling back down-stairs a little way—only to the first landing; & then get up again & roll down again, & are the darling of the piece & the charm of it."

Letters between Mark Twain and Howells were passing fre-

[7] Clemens cats.

quently at this time—the latter in mourning for his daughter Winnie, lost after a long tragic illness. These two Victorian skeptics were led to compare notes about the solace of faith—if possible. The opening sentence of Mark's next letter to Livy refers to a remark lately made by Howells: "I read something in a strange book, *The Physical Theory of Another Life,* that consoles a little; namely, we see and feel the power of Deity in such fullness that we ought to infer the infinite Justice and Goodness which we do not see or feel."

HARTFORD, *July* 17/89

Livy darling, this that Howells speaks of appeals to one's reason; it sounds like sense. We do see & feel the *power* of what we call God; we do see it & feel it in such measureless fulness, that we "ought to infer"—*not* Justice & Goodness from *that*; but we may from another thing, namely: the fact that there is a large element of Justice & Goodness in His creature, man; & we may also infer that He has in Him Injustice & Ungoodness, because he has put *those* into man, too. Next I am privileged to infer that there is *far* more goodness than ungoodness in man, for if it were not so man would have exterminated himself before this; & I may also infer this supremacy (in quality) of goodness over ungoodness in man by calling up in my mind the various servants whom I know; the various mechanics whom I know; the various merchants, military men, the various Tom-Dick & Harrys of *all* walks, whom I know—in this long list I find goodness the rule & ungoodness the exception. I should still find this the case among all tribes of savages in all parts of the earth & in all the centuries of history. I detest Man, but nevertheless this is true of him. Well, since what we call God made that preponderance of Goodness, he must have done it because he admired it, & he must have admired it because he discovered it to be his own principal feature. At this point, then, I draw another inference: that he is as good & as just as Man is (to place the [possibi] likelihood at its lowest term). And if that is so, I arrive at this result. I am plenty safe enough in *his* hands; I am not in any danger from that kind of a Deity. The one that *I* want to keep out of the reach of, is the caricature of him which one finds in the Bible. We (that one & I) could never respect each other, never get along together. I have met his superior a hundred times—in fact I amount to that myself.[8]

I don't *know* anything about the hereafter, but I am not afraid of it. The further I get away from the superstitions in which I was born & mis-trained, the more the idea of a hereafter commends itself to me & the more I am persuaded I shall find things comfortable when I get there.

I have seen a charming machine to-day. You could put it in my study at the farm & have room around it for chairs for the spectators. It makes envelops—9,000 an hour. You place 500 sheets of paper in its grip, & then stand aside & let it alone. That is *all* you ever have to do. It gums them, prints them, counts them, & passes them out in packages of 25 with a paper band around them. It oils itself, it attends to its own glue & ink. If you steal an envelop from it, it won't count that one. I enclose a specimen of its work.

I love you, love you, *love* you, sweetheart, & its mighty lonesome here.

SAML

[8] To Pamela he wrote, in an undated fragment in the Webster Collection: "I love you, & I am sorry for every time I have ever hurt you; but God Almighty knows I should keep on hurting you just the same, if I were around; for I am built so, being made merely in the image of God, but not otherwise resembling him enough to be mistaken by anybody but a very near-sighted person."

CHAPTER FOURTEEN

The Infernal Machine

CLEMENS' fascination with an envelope-making machine, described in his last letter to Livy, discloses one aspect of his character that had already begun to rule his destiny and wreck his fortunes. An amateur inventor himself, ex-printer, tinkerer and incurable optimist, he had begun quite casually in 1880 to take a small interest in a typesetting machine being built at the Colt Arms factory in Hartford. Visits to the plant and the persuasive words of its inventor, one James W. Paige, gradually lured Mark into heavier and heavier subsidies, until by the latter eighties it was devouring funds at the rate of three thousand dollars a month, to pay for materials and the wages of a small staff of mechanics to tend it, in its more elaborate nursery at the Pratt & Whitney works. Its twenty thousand delicately adjusted parts were in a constant state of construction and dismemberment, for Paige was a perfectionist who never finished anything.

In the palmy days of Charles L. Webster & Company, Clemens had begun to milk the firm's cash resources, along with his personal income and savings and his wife's estate, to feed the insatiable monster. Rightly believing that there were millions in an automatic typesetter, he blandly refused to exchange a half-interest with the Mergenthaler backers, and pledged himself not only to see this rival machine through to completion but also finance its promotion and marketing.

He had planned a trip abroad for the summer of 1890, partly for the children's cultural advantage, but abandoned it as the future of the Paige typesetter and his commitments to it grew steadily more complicated. In search of other "angels" as trusting as himself, Clemens made a series of futile trips to New York and Washington. "Youth don't let the thought of Europe worry you

one bit because we will give that all up," Livy wrote about May
2, 1890, on one of his first such expeditions. "I want to see you
happy *much* more than I want any thing else even the childrens
lessons. Oh darling it goes to my very heart to see you worried."
Far from reproaching him for undermining the financial security
of their family, Livy at first shared Mark's great expectations—
and then, with the dream fading, set herself quietly to retrench
on their lavish expenditures.

In June, Clemens' loyal Nevada newspaper crony Joe Goodman
joined him in the search for financial backing. They went down
to Washington together, their sights trained upon Senator John
P. Jones from Nevada, a wealthy friend from the old Comstock
days. He had recently expressed a curiosity to see the machine,
but Paige chose that juncture to dismantle it for improvements—
and, as it turned out, not even the present pilgrimage to Washington could revive the senator's flagging interest.

WASHINGTON, *June* 14/90

Livy darling, I got your letter a little while ago—just before
breakfast—and was sorry I had nothing to write you that first
day. I *did* write, of course—just a scrap; but there was nothing
to write the next day; & yesterday we came down here, arriving
at night, with still nothing to write; & we ate an enormous supper
& went right to bed & to sleep; & now I have had two nights of
almost unbroken sleep; & after a cold bath & a breakfast I am
feeling more like myself, bodily & mentally than I have felt before
for three months.

Joe has gone to call at Senator Jones's & make a business
appointment, & I am utilizing the interval to write to you. We
had a delightful journey down. The water & the woods & the
grass employed the eye untiringly for 6 hours, the general smoking car was cool & comfortable, the train was swift & the movement exhilarating, & I didn't read a line on the way. Once we cut
a horse entirely in two, slightly injured the driver's arm, & whirled
the carriage entirely around without damaging it in the least.
When we got to the next station, men appeared with stretchers,
ready to be conveyed back, with physicians to care for the
wounded—for the telephone had been at work.

In New York Joe & I went to a ten-cent dive where we saw a variety performance which Jean ought to have shared with us. It lasted 2 hours: there was Punch & Judy; & a very small dwarf; & some Zulus in native lack of costume (from Baxter Street, I reckon); & a girl who had 25 alligators & crocodiles for pets, & they crawled all over her, & a sweet little girl of ten years who played delightfully on the harmonicon; also on a row of common bottles; on a concertina; on a violin; on a curious & rich-noted little instrument like a mussel (shell); on a cornet; & a banjo. Very wonderful. And there was a Jap juggler who did the most extraordinary things I ever saw.

Well, I am loving you all the time, sweetheart, & thinking of you & honoring you every minute. Kiss them for me.

SAML

Instead of going abroad, the Clemenses spent the summer at the Onteora Club at Tannersville, New York. Mark Twain briefly revisited Hartford, at the time of the following letter to his daughter Clara, largely to talk with Howard Taylor, another friend from *Territorial Enterprise* days in Virginia City, Nevada, about the latter's inept dramatization of the *Connecticut Yankee* which never reached production.

HOME, *Sunday, July some-thing-or-other,* 1890 [July 20]

Clara dear, I hope your piano has arrived as you hoped, & that you are satisfied with it & having a good time—a better time than I have been having today. It's a secret that isn't to be breathed outside of the family—the new play, the Yankee in Arthur's Court, has bored the very soul out of me. Four level hours I listened, today, in misery. Taylor has made a rattling, stirring, & spectacular, & perhaps taking play, & has shown dramatic talent & training; *but* his handling of archaic English is as ignorant & dreadful as poor Mrs. Richardson's[1]; & he has captured but one side of the Yankee's character—his rude animal side, his circus side; the good heart & the high intent are left out of him; he is a mere boisterous clown, & oozes slang from every pore. I told Taylor he had degraded a natural gentleman to a low-down

---

[1] Abby Sage Richardson's similar try with *The Prince and the Pauper,* despite efforts by Belasco and Frohman in the winter of 1889-1890, proved distinctly a failure.

blackguard. He thinks he can modify him & refine him—but I
doubt it. However, the awful ordeal is over & Taylor is gone. He
is a very old friend of mine, & a good fellow; so I was careful to
say nothing harsh about his work; but if he had been a stranger
I should have said things that would have hurt. This is the very
last play that I ever mean to have anything to do with.

Don't let Mr. Howells get away before I come. I don't know,
yet, when I can come, but keep him there, anyway. Why the
nation didn't he come sooner!

Goodnight, sweetheart, & be good like

Your
PAPA

In the autumn Susy entered Bryn Mawr as a freshman. On
October 12 her father wrote to his sister Pamela: "The last time
I saw her was a week ago on the platform at Bryn Mawr. Our
train was moving away, & she was drifting collegeward afoot, her
figure blurred & dim in the rain & fog, & she was crying." Mark
and Clara soon returned to solace the homesick girl.

SUMMIT GROVE INN, BRYN MAWR, Oct. 24 [1890]

Livy darling, it is 20 minutes to 11, I've been dancing with the
College girls till a minute ago—the children have just left in the
omnibus for the College.

We left Hartford at 12:25; got out at New Haven & waited 10
minutes, then took a Shore Line parlor car & never got out of it
till it pulled up in the Broad Street station, Phila. Mighty lovely
trip. Dining room on the boat, skirting around New York, & an
hour & ten minutes to eat (a poor) dinner in. Ben ate two buttered
rolls at New Haven & nearly a thimble full of baked potato on
that boat.

When we drew into the Broad-st station we were 15 minutes
late, and the 7:15 Bryn Mawr train was ready to leave; but our
conductor sent his brakeman on a run, & a porter with our baggage without removing the Phila. checks, and when they saw us
coming they held the train & we got aboard with our baggage, &
paid our fares on board. Next instant we were sailing out of the
station again.

Reached B. M. 8:15; walked to the College—no Susy there—

gone to a dance, some girls said. But in a moment Susy burst in—
she had heard of our arrival. She was for going straight & hospitably to her room & giving up the dance; but I wouldn't allow
that. Clara didn't seem tired, & I wasn't, & had been free from
rheumatism all day & was feeling like a bird; so I joined the
crowd.

To my joy it turned out that the dance was *here*—right at
home. I danced two Virginia reels & another dance, & looked on
& talked the rest of the time. It was very jolly & pleasant, & everybody asked after you & was disappointed when I said you hadn't
come.

Got to write to Brusnahan, now. Good night, sweetheart, we
all love you & Jean.

SAML

A few scattered letters to Livy represent brief absences in the
autumn and winter of 1890-91. One of them closes with the
waggish postscript: "So *many* people adore you. But it is only
on my account."

Susy continued miserably homesick and ill-adjusted at Bryn
Mawr, until at length in the spring Livy went down to help her
pack up and withdraw from college.

HOME, Sunday, Apr. 19/91

Well, sweetheart, I hope you & Susy are satisfied with yourselves, going away & leaving people this way. *I* don't think much
of it.

Still, I will write you a line—just a line, to say all are well. I
am vaguely conscious that young girls by twos & threes flit in &
out, & sit around & chat & laugh, & sometimes I am conscious of
Clara's voice & catch the remark, "G'*won*, Weeja!"[2] Jean & I go
bicycling evenings. She runs beside the machine, & picks it up
when I plunge off. I am progressing all the time. Yesterday I
learned a new way to fall off. But, it's the cussedest thing to tame I
ever saw—twice as difficult as the old high wheel.

With lots of love & kisses,

SAML

[2] Perhaps a reference to the ouija board, the latest parlor amusement.

About this time his struggles with that contraption inspired Mark to write "Taming the Bicycle," which appears in *What Is Man? and Other Essays*, published posthumously in 1917.

In 1891 in order to save money the Clemenses closed their expensive Hartford house, never to live there again nor to find another real home. On June 6 they sailed for Europe, seeking first the benefit which Aix-les-Bains might give to Clemens' rheumatic right arm. While Jean accompanied her parents to the spa, Susy and Clara entered a boarding-school in Geneva. The following letter, addressed by Mark to these absent ones, is undated, but other letters to the children supply roughly its place in the sequence.

[AIX-LES-BAINS, *circa June* 28, 1891]

DEAR CHILDREN—I love you both, and when I shall have finished learning to write with my left hand, I will communicate with you more frequently.

C'est mon premier leçon, et je ne suis pas encore maitre de l'art. Je la trouve un peu plus difficile qu'a ecrire de la main droit. (Ah, grace à Dieu, ces dernieres mots sont fait à merveille!)

Adieu, mignonnes.

PAPA

From this "paradise of rheumatics" the Clemens family went to the Wagner festival at Bayreuth, and then pretty extensively through Central Europe—their itinerary supplying "copy" for a series of travel letters that Mark had agreed to write for his old friend William M. Laffan's *New York Sun*.

On September 19, leaving his family at Lausanne, Clemens as an old river hand undertook a more strenuous side trip which could also be turned into copy, although the narrative was not published until after his death, as "Down the Rhone," in *Europe and Elsewhere* (1923). He hired a courier, a flatboat and boatman for a ten days' descent of that river. Frequent bulletins of his progress went back to Livy; the following is typical.

HOTEL BERTRAND, LA VOULT, *Saturday nightfall*
[*September* 26, 1891]

Land, Livy darling, but I am tired! I got up at 7:30 in Valence & drove ½ hour to the foot of a mountain, climbed it on foot (very steep), & spent an hour or more in wandering among the acres of ruins of a seldom-visited castle nine or ten hundred years old, perched on that lofty pinnacle & overlooking a vast landscape of plain & river. Returned to the city & spent a long time examing two most curious & ornate dwellings of the Middle Ages! then, at 1:15 set sail, but the Mistral (the stormwind of the Midi—the Midi is "the south") struck us & kept us back; at 4 we had made but 18 kilometres & I was tuckered out & sleepy; so we landed at this village, & ever since I have been prowling through its maze of steep & narrow alleys—mere stone stairways 6 feet wide which turn & turn & never arrive at any place, but are sufficiently interesting as a peculiarly first-class remnant of the Middle Ages; & we also prowled through the huge ancient castle that rises out of & above the village & dominates it; & so at last I am in my room & shan't wait for pitch-dark to come, but shall get immediately to bed & to sleep.

I wish you all a happy goodnight & I do assure you that I love you & miss you all the time. It's a lovely trip.

SAML

The Clemenses spent the winter of 1891-92 in Berlin. After more Continental travel by the family in the spring and summer of 1892, and a month's business trip to America by Mark Twain, they settled for the next winter at the Villa Viviani, Florence. Clara soon left them for study in Berlin at Mrs. Willard's school. Among many letters to her reflecting Clemens' anxieties over her mother's failing health, the following may be chosen here.

Miss Phelps, mentioned in this letter, was the daughter of W. W. Phelps, American Minister to Germany. Soon afterward she married an undersecretary of the interior in the Imperial government, who, as Mark noted to Livy on June 3, 1895, shortly found himself relegated to a professorship at Bonn and "is drinking himself to death in that fortunate obscurity. . . . Separately, foreign marriages and whisky are bad; mixed, they are fatal."

Wednesday [November 16, 1892]

DEAR OLD BEN—Now didn't you give us a start, this morning! —with your grippe? It is well you were able to say you were about to climb out of bed & get around again—I suppose Mamma would have been for getting out of bed herself & flying to Berlin. Well, we are most glad & grateful that you are coming out of it all right. Take care of yourself—grippe is a mean thing for backsets —one gets them easily.

Mamma is still ailing along, & it is just heart-breaking to see her. She is patient & uncomplaining—just as always—but she is very weak & all wasted away. She is in the best place there is— that is all the comfort we have.

The Willards have been very lovely to you, & we are thankful to them. And it was nice of Miss Phelps to remember you. She is a lovely girl & I think ever so much of her. Do give my warm regards to her & my warm love to her father when you see them.

I'm at work on the twins again.[3] It is half the size of the Prince & Pauper, now, & going right along.

We all send slathers of love to you, Ben dear.

PAPA

P. S. Ned Bunce[4] wants your address.

[3] Eventually the sub-plot in *The Tragedy of Pudd'nhead Wilson and the Comedy of Those Extraordinary Twins* (1894).

[4] An old Hartford friend, currently in Italy with the Laurence Huttons.

CHAPTER FIFTEEN

Downward Spiral

THE Paige machine, with its complicated build and inventor who took it apart every few weeks in quest of perfection, proved to be a financial quagmire into which Mark Twain sank deeper and deeper through his frantic efforts to win liberation and solvency. Furthermore, the publishing house of Webster & Company, drained to support the machine and also managed wholly by amateurs of less and less ability, as Charles Webster yielded to his underling Fred Hall, found itself badly over-extended. By the beginning of 1893 both ventures were inter-acting to push Mark Twain into debt, along a descending track soon greased by the panic of that summer.

Tardily returning to the craft he had long neglected, Mark began to write furiously during this season of economical exile in Europe. (A villa in Florence with a full staff of servants includ-ing a coachman, or a Paris apartment with a cook and two maids, at first constituted the Clemenses' idea of paring expenses to the bone. There were also boarding-school bills for the girls, along with interminable doctors' bills and interludes at spas—for rare were the times when but a single member of the family was receiving costly medical treatment.) Haunted by these anxieties and the specter of "the poorhouse," Mark tried to make up in industry what he lacked of the old creative fire. By January 1893 he had *Pudd'nhead Wilson* ready for the printer, and laying aside the long project that was the apple of his eye, *Joan of Arc*, he plunged into the writing of stories and articles for a market of high pay and quick returns.

Ever jealous for his prestige, Livy could not hide occasional misgivings. From Florence she wrote on April 16, early in a six-weeks' trip which Mark made to New York and Chicago in worried search of a patron for the typesetter: "You did not tell me anything about sending an article or articles to the Cosmopolitan. Why did you do that? I should greatly prefer appearing in the Century or Harpers. What made you do it?" Yet her deepest concern was to save him from desperation and self-reproach. In the same letter she added: "My dear darling child you *must not* blame yourself as you do. I love you to death, and I would rather have you for mine than all the other husbands in the world and you take as good care of me as any one could do."

On this journey, after landing in New York, Mark hastened on to Chicago, where Paige had now set up the machine. A severe cold laid Clemens low, and most of the activity had to be assumed by his traveling companion Fred Hall, manager of the Webster concern. The letter to Livy which follows reports a call from Eugene Field, well-known poet and columnist of the *Chicago Record*, who brought the invalid a copy of Mrs. Gaskell's sedentary novel *Cranford*, which in his subnormal mood Mark found tolerable. Contacts between Mark Twain and Field were few, although their common Missouri origin and training in the school of newspaper humor supplied a bond. Field died two years later, and on Mark's last visit to St. Louis in 1902 he unveiled a tablet at the poet's supposed birthplace.

CHICAGO, *Apl.* 18/93

Dear old Sweetheart, this is only a note to kiss you & say good-night—for I tear up the matter of a couple of good-length letters because I have not told my tale well & will leave it for my tongue to do when I get home.

The doctor is done with me but requires Mr. Hall to keep me in bed a day longer, & maybe two. I do not mind it, for the reading & smoke is (are) pleasant—*but!* Yesterday the calling was like a levèe. No respite, no rest. To-day we are wiser.

Eugene Field brought me "Cranford"—I never could read it before; but this time I blasted my determined way through the obstructing granite, slate & clay walls, not giving up till I reached the vein—since then I have been taking out pay ore right along.

I love you all, every one—Susy, Ben, Jean—& mamma at the head of the procession & also at the foot of it.

SAML.

I was afraid to have my letters sent out here—I feel mighty newsless.

Meanwhile a bulletin of premature optimism from her absent husband sent Livy into a mood of rejoicing.

[FLORENCE, ITALY] *April 23ʳᵈ 1893*

YOUTH DARLING: Your letters rec'd this morning made me just about wild with pleasurable excitement. It does not seem credible that we are really again to have money to *spend*.

I rec'd this morning the check for nine hundred odd dollars from Mr Hall. I have not needed to use the last check of 100 x 500 dollars [*sic*] that he sent me. Of course it was made out to you so if I had desired to use it I could not have done so very well, but I have not needed it. I have still nearly 1500. dollars with Charley. Well I tell you I think I will jump around and spend money just for fun, and give a little away if we really get some.

You are so good to write me so often and I do thank you more than I can tell. Now I suppose as your last letter was written from Albany and you were moving westward that it will be some little time, that is some few days before I receive another.

I do love you so my darling! What should we do and how should we feel if we had no bright prospects before us and yet how many people are situated in that way. Aren't you glad that we did not sell any royalties. Always I have wanted them kept. Now I suppose you will send Sue's back to her.

The weather here is lovely. But the farmers greatly need rain and say if it does not soon come the crops will be ruined. Prof. Fiske[1] said on Friday that it began to look very serious.

The common people call it Queens weather and are very anxious to have the queen leave Florence for they think it will remain pleasant while she stays.

It is astonishing to think that perhaps there is not yet a very long time for us to keep up this economy. I find already that it does not seem to me so important whether the house bills are 350 or 375 francs a week.

---

[1] Willard Fiske, through whose friendly interest they had rented the Villa Viviani in his neighborhood.

Good bye my darling I love you with my whole heart

Yours always

LIVY

P. S. Will you please tell Mr Hall that I rec'd the check Darling do send some message to M*lle*

This trip, ended by his sailing back to Europe on May 13, on the whole proved a disappointment to Clemens. "I was ill in bed eleven days in Chicago, a week in Elmira & 3 months in New York (seemingly) & accomplished nothing that I went home to do," he wrote Twichell on June 9, from the Villa Viviani.

Leaving Florence in mid-June, the Clemenses went to Franzensbad, Germany, for the baths. But the typesetter continued to haunt Mark's thoughts. "That is unquestionably the boss machine of the world," he wrote to Hall in early August, "but is the toughest one on prophets when it is in an incomplete state that has ever seen the light." That Paige could not or would not finish it Clemens was still unready to concede. Anxiety about business led him to sail again for New York, accompanied by Clara, from the port of Bremen on August 29. A report of cholera in European cities added to his worries at leaving Livy behind at Franzensbad; after the scare was over, she settled in Paris for the winter.

THE PALMBAUM, LEIPZIG, *Aug.* 28 [1893]

Livy darling, it has just occurred to me that possibly you would detect faults at every turn in this hotel—maybe Clara is detecting them too—but to me it's all satisfactory.

I do not feel very *very* cheerful this morning, leaving you homeless & no home selected or possible of selection until the cholera shall have exhibited its plans. It would be a crime to leave some women as you are being left; but with your grit & intelligence & unapproachable good sense *you* are better off than if you had two or three husbands to help you & confuse you & make your efforts abortive.

I am at late breakfast (Clara has had hers in her room)—& in a little while we shall leave for the train. I love you, sweetheart.

SAML.

When you come in this direction they examine your baggage at Franzensbad before you leave—if you get to the station in time. *We* did.

The Panic of '93 had been taking shape in the United States that summer, with a growing toll of bank failures, runs on banks, and in August the admitted insolvency of the Erie and Northern Pacific railroads. A poorer time for Clemens to raise money in aid of his sinking enterprises could hardly have been chosen.

MURRAY HILL HOTEL, NEW YORK CITY, MONDAY, *Sept.* 7/93

My darling, your dear letter was waiting for me when I reached the office this morning, & I was very glad to get it. I wonder if you are troubled about the cholera? This morning's news shows that it is well scattered around the continent, but not alarmingly so, & not in your neighborhood. There is no cholera alarm on this side at all (Unberufen!)

Commercial matters are still very stringent here, but everybody is growing hopeful now. Mr. Hall feels sure we shall pull through, & by & by pay all the money owing to you & me & the rest. We are to have a thorough talk tomorrow.

The whole United States stopped work two or three weeks ago, the machine along with the rest. It still lacked *3 weeks* of being done. Of course! When there's anything more to tell about it I will let you know, dearheart.

I've sold the Esquimaux Girl's Romance to the Cosmopolitan,[2] for eight hundred dollars (which I will keep to live on here), & Pudd'nhead Wilson to the Century for six thousand five hundred, which will go to you by & by—first payment after Nov. 1—for it is even hard for the Century to get money. Story will begin in December number, & be made the "feature."

Gilder and Johnson are vastly pleased with the story, & they say Roxy is a great & dramatic & well-drawn character. I am going to dine with Johnson & Dr Rice at the Players, to-night, & am sending Clara & Jervis[3] to the theatre. I've bought some big handsome peaches for Clara—my, but you ought to see the fruit-

---

[2] "The Esquimau Maiden's Romance" appeared in the November issue.
[3] Son of Charles and Ida Langdon.

stalls here!—the peaches, pears, plums, apples—dear me, how pitiful and shabby are the fruit stalls of Europe by comparison! And I saw 1200 noble watermelons in a pile down on the pier. I bit into a peach & the juice squirted across the street and drowned a dog.

I left my watch with the best watchmaker in town—it has refused to run, of late. He examined it & said he would have to keep it two weeks to get it straightened up again.

Jervis & Clara will go to Elmira day after tomorrow, & I will then take board & lodging at the Lotos Club, for economy's sake. I shall stay right here until this business cyclone abates. I experience great satisfaction in being on the spot in these troublous times. I could even be light & cheerful if I felt no uneasiness about you three. I force myself to feel approximately restful about you, but it is pure compulsion.

Time for that dinner! I love you, darling.

S L C

He actually moved into temporary bachelor quarters with his physician and friend Dr. Clarence C. Rice, on East 19th Street, but before the end of the month had taken "a cheap room" at The Players.

NEW YORK *Sept.* 13 1893

Livy darling it is mighty sorrowful work writing daily uncheerful letters to you & yet concealing my reasons for being measurably cheerful & hopeful myself. But my reasons are so uncertain & intangible that they are not worth putting on paper; & they might be only a preparation for disappointment anyway. These are certainly terrific times, & no one can foresee the outcome yet; still, they are improving, everybody concedes that.

To-day I haven't a thing to report, except that I love you & think of you all the time, & do immensely admire you—your mind as much as your person; your character & spirit far & away above these qualities as existent in any other person whom I have ever known. I am notorious, but you are great—that is the difference between *us*.

Dr. Rice & I went to Harrigan's[4] last night for an hour. Saw one of his old pieces, where the nigger ball is broken up by the fire—by all odds the funniest scene that was ever put on the stage I think. You & I saw it together once, I guess.

I am so grateful to hear (unberufen!) that the dear old Jean is out of the doctor's hands again. I hope you are all having a comfortable good time. Our stay here is indefinite—I daren't stir from here while our affairs are in doubt.

I dearly love you, & Susy, & also Jean. Good-bye for to-day.

SAML

Mark's next letter was written at the "model farm" near Madison, New Jersey, of his old Western friend, Frank Fuller, whose brief day as acting governor of Utah Territory had invested him with a lifelong title. He now owned the Health Food Company in New York, but fancied his life as a country squire at Chemmiwink, which included not only the house "in barbarous taste" here mentioned, but also "a bowling alley & a beautiful little theatre . . . all yellow pine . . . lavishly lit with electricity," as he informed Clara on the same date.

Most important, however, is Mark's reference to help in his financial straits that was just beginning to come through Dr. Rice from "a rich friend of his who was an admirer of mine." This friend was Henry Huttleston Rogers (1840-1909). To Clara on September 15 her father wrote: "The best new acquaintance I've ever seen has helped us over Monday's bridge. I got acquainted with him on a yacht two years ago."

Henry H. Rogers was a self-made millionaire of Standard Oil. To his rivals in commerce he was a man of cold steel, whose blue eyes and arrogantly handsome port were the hallmark of a ruthless will. But to his few intimates—soon embracing this innocent in business, whose books had stirred Rogers' memories of his own small-town boyhood, and whose wit came to enliven his dinner table and yachting parties—the magnate turned a different face. With ready sympathy he offered to pull this self-styled "ass" from the slough where he was floundering.

[4] Edward Harrigan's Theater, west of Broadway on 35th Street.

SUNDAY, 7 A.M., *in bed at* GOV. FULLER'S FARM
out in NEW JERSEY, *Sept.* 17/93

The billows of hell have been rolling over me. I have never lived any such days as those beginning last Monday & ending at 4 Friday afternoon. Our affairs are really in good & handsome condition—as confessed by all bankers & others who understand balance sheets—& yet it looked for days together as if we must go under, for lack of $8,000 to meet notes coming due to morrow, Monday. I raced up to Hartford & back again—couldn't get it. At Hartford I wrote Sue[5] telling her I had no shame, for the boat was sinking—send me $5,000 if she possibly could. Mr. Halsey, Mr. Hall & I raced around Wall Street Thursday, assailing banks & brokers—couldn't get anything. When I fell on the bed at 8 that evening, ruin seemed inevitable, but I was physically so exhausted that mental misery had no chance & I was asleep in a moment.

Next morning I was up at 7 (as usual all that dreadful week), & at it again. By noon all schemes of Hall & Halsey (who worked for us like a beaver) had failed, yet we must live or die on that day. Sue's letter came, saying she had no money, & no bonds or other securities salable in New York, but that she had exchanged securities with Ida & would send $5,000 worth of negociable bonds if I would telegraph. Mr. Hall said it wouldn't save us, for it was $8,000 we wanted, not $5,000. Then a messenger came from Dr. Rice to call me back there, & he told me he had ventured to speak to a rich friend of his who was an admirer of mine about our straits. I was very glad. Mr. Hall was to be at this gentleman's office away down Broadway at 4 yesterday afternoon, with his statements; & in six minutes we had the check & our worries were over till the 28th. I telegraphed thanking Sue & Ida & saying everything was all right, at present. Mr. Hall wanted me to write Charley that we should probably pass the 28th without trouble & would be able to excuse him from endorsing that $15,000 for us—& I did it.

I came out here at noon, yesterday, but was still so tired that I went right to bed at 3 o'clock & rested till half past 6; & went

[5] Susan Crane.

to bed again at 9. At last I am over the fatigue, and feel fresh &
vigorous this morning.

When I pack my satchel to leave New York—it may be weeks
& it may be months yet, dearest!—my share of Webster & Co will
belong to somebody else. I am going to get out of that. I mean to
stick to the neighborhood of New York till it is accomplished.
If I hadn't come the concern would have gone under—I do not
want to be so necessary to any business again.

The Fullers look as they always did, except that he has laid
off his glasses after wearing them 30 years. They are as cordial
& breezy as ever, & have no gray hairs. This is a charming place
of theirs, with dense groves & wide levels of grass; & the house
is large, & furnished rather expensively & in barbarous taste.

On the table at dinner there was roast beef, potatoe soup,
green corn, sliced tomatoes, succotash, Lima beans, cucumbers,
boiled potatoes with the jackets on, radishes, apple pie, cake, ice
cream, home-made cheese, milk, beer, cider, & oceans of thick
rich cream—with grapes, peaches, apples, pears & so on—& I
believe there was nothing on the table except the sugar, salt, &c.,
that the farm didn't furnish.

I return to Dr. Rice's in the morning. They are finishing
breakfast down stairs; I must rush. I love you dear people very
very much—I do indeed.

SAML

The following letter was begun in one of those self-reproachful
moods which often overtook Samuel Clemens. He suddenly
recalled a stormy night when he and Livy were driving on the
hill road between Elmira and Quarry Farm, and her fear of
lightning led her to propose their stopping at "the Water Cure,"
a local spa run by their neighbors the Gleasons. His refusal is
doubtless played up by a conscience that now reproved him for
jeopardizing Livy's security in other ways.

[THE PLAYERS, NEW YORK CITY]
Thursday, Sept. 21/93

Sweetheart, I am waiting patiently to see what is going to
happen. If there had been any news of a cabling sort you would

have had a cable before this, of course. I should not have forgotten; I would not lose any time in sharing good news with you
if I had any.

Late last night I was smitten suddenly with shame & remorse
in remembering how I forced you to drive through the thunder
& lightning & rain that night that you were so frightened & wanted
to stop at the Water Cure. I have remembered that brutality
many a time since, & cursed myself for it. It is at times like these
that I also visit with deep & honest curses the memory of those
various people who plucked me from the water when I was a lad
& drowning.[6]

I called on Charley & Ida again yesterday morning at 9:30 and
waited half an hour for the call-boy to return & report—a delay
which made the clerks uncomfortable, inasmuch as they had been
telling me what a perfection of a hotel their Waldorf was. Finally
they sent out a search expedition after the call-boy, & one clerk
& I went on a search to the breakfast room after C & I. Well, we
never found them, though both were in the house the whole
time.

Ida sent me a note in the afternoon saying Charley's time was
pretty well absorbed by his physician, & asking me to make another attempt. Which I did at 5:30 P.M., in morning clothes.
They arrived from driving at that moment, & we had a pleasant
half hour together. Charley can't eat anything—all he took
yesterday was a trifle of Koumiss—& Dr. Fuller has taken hold of
him vigorously, with massage & all sorts of things, & says he can't
budge from his hands for a week.

They speak ever so fondly of Clara; that witch has witched her
way into their & the other folks's admiration & affection & is
having a good time. Why *didn't* you all come with us! I do wish,
wish, *wish* you had. The farm would be such a magnificently effective health resort, such a darling change from unspeakable Europe;
then we could go back to the baths in the spring.

I had no letter from any of you yesterday—a circumstance
which would not usually disturb me but *did*, this time, for your

[6] He used to speak of "nine narrow escapes from drowning" in Hannibal's Bear
Creek and the Mississippi.

last you were just over your first attack, & I of course expect it to
be followed by fifteen others.

Good-bye, sweetheart, I must go over to the Century & read
some proof (for December) on the story which they continually
& everlastingly glorify & shout about.

SAML

[NEW YORK] Sept. 21 1893

My darling, I've been in a fine fury since I wrote you from
the Players three or four hours ago! I went to the Century, took
my Pudd'nhead proofs, & sat down & began my corrections.
Presently it began to seem to me that there was something very
odd about the punctuation—was it possible that some impertinent
puppy had been trying to improve it? Pretty soon I came across a
"d——" —a pitiful & sneaking modification which I well knew
I *couldn't* have put upon paper, drunk or sober. I asked for the
copy—in a most unsteady voice, for I was suffocating with passion.
When it came, it was fairly small-poxed with corrections of my
punctuation—my punctuation, which I had deeply thought out,
& laboriously perfected! Then my volcano turned itself loose, &
the exhibition was not suited to any Sunday school. Johnson said
that the criminal was De Vinne's peerless imported proof-reader,
from Oxford University, & that whatever he did was sacred in De
Vinne's eyes—sacred, final, immutable. I said I didn't care if he
was an Archangel imported from Heaven, he couldn't puke his
ignorant impudence over *my* punctuation, I wouldn't allow it for
a moment. I said I couldn't read this proof, I couldn't sit in the
presence of a proof-sheet where that blatherskite had left his
tracks; so Johnson wrote a note to De Vinne telling him the laws
of his printing office must be modified, this time; that this stuff
must be set up again & my punctuation restored, to the minutest
detail, & always be followed hereafter throughout the story. So
I'm to return there tomorow & read the deodorized proof.

They showed me some of the advertisements they are preparing, & a white-clad "process" from the Onteora picture (it is to
go in the Century, I think).[7] I asked them to send the things to

---

[7] A photograph by James Mapes Dodge, showing Clemens in his famous white
clothes lounging on the veranda at Onteora (*Century*, XLVII, 232).

you. I like the Century people, & am glad I'm back there again.

Mrs. Johnson came in, looking plump & young & pretty, & wanted to be warmly remembered to you & the rest.

With lots & lots of love,

SAML

[NEW YORK] *Sept.* 28, 1893

My darling, I wonder where you are & *how* you are. You are at Botzen I suppose, & I do hope you are well & cheerful. I am well, & measurably cheerful; but it is very difficult to be cheerful in my circumstances. This concern, as you know, is in a bad way. I have been trying for three weeks to get rid of all or part of it, & so escape disaster, but thus far we have had no bid that we can accept. By hard work & much trouble I have got extensions on the most pressing debts, & this gives us a little breathing spell & a chance to look around & try further. The times are desperately hard.

As for the Machine Co., it is at a standstill, & they are feeling dismal & disheartened. They are trying to join the Chicago & New York companies together & on a better & more business-like basis. It may be that they can accomplish this—in fact it is only in times like these that it *could* be done. But now everybody is humble; everybody is willing to come down a little & make sacrifices & so be so proud & confident. Thank goodness I don't have to help run *that* concern. We will wait & see what happens.

Sometimes I seem to foresee that I have *got* to go on the dreadful platform again. If I must, I must—but nothing short of absolute necessity will drive me. If I have to go, I would rather begin with India & Australia, & not reach the American platform till times are better. Do you think you could go with me? I do hope it will not have to be, but often it seems to me that there is going to be no other way out.

The whole trouble comes of Mr. Hall's unspeakable stupidity (& mine) in not seeing 3 years ago, that we were not strong enough to carry L. A. L.[8] A child should have seen it. He should have been trying to get us rid of that burden a good 3 years ago.

As I have intimated, we have an offer for L. A. L. which we cannot accept. We must look around & see what we can do.

[8] The Library of American Literature, the heaviest incubus of the Webster firm.

It breaks my heart to write these things to you, & I kept still as long as there was nothing definite to say; for as long as the offer was *going* to be made but the size of it not named, there was hope that it might be large enough to enable us to get out of our horrible hole alive. It may be that the offer will be enlarged a little, but I don't expect it.

I do love you so, & it does *hurt* me so to send you such news when you are away off there, lonely among strangers. I love you deep deep down.

SAML

NEW YORK, Sept. 28/93

Livy darling, only a line, to-day, to say I have engaged to try to write an article in a great hurry, for the Cosmopolitan. I will get at it at once.

I do miss you so! Every day the separation becomes harder & harder to bear. Yet I know it must continue a good while yet; for things *must* be straightened out here, & something captured out of that type-setter if possible, & these things will take time.

I do hope you are happy. *Don't* get sick again—do please take every possible care of yourself.

SAML

Sept. 30. I forgot to mail my letters of yesterday & day before. By Jackson a body forgets pretty much everything, these days, except his visions of the poor-house. But I'm doing my best, dear heart—& you are my stay & my courage. Without you I should be nothing.

His solicitude for Livy's health was matched by his secretiveness in disclosing his private ills. To Clara on September 23 he wrote: "Dear heart, don't you let Mamma find out that I've got this cough, or have had it. Day before yesterday Dr. Rice told me I coughed too violently, & that there was no need of it; that if I would try, I could repress the cough almost entirely. I find it true. I cough very little, now. But he told me too late to save me—I had already ruptured myself. There is no inflammation & no pain, & he did not tell me to put on a truss; but uncle Charley says I *must* put one on, & wear it the rest of my life."

His eldest daughter Susy he charged with special responsibility
for protecting her mother from worry, as this letter testifies.

THE PLAYERS, *Nov.* 6/93

I will drop a line to the dearest of all the dear Susies to say,
bear up mamma's hands and help her to endure our long separation as patiently as she can, for I absolutely must not budge
one step from this place *until we are safe from the poorhouse.*

That I shall succeed, I have not the slightest doubt—if I don't
go rushing across the ocean again too soon. If I budge too soon,
I shall fail.

I believe I could run over to France now, for a couple of
weeks, but I am not absolutely sure; therefore I am going to wait
until I am sure.

We are millionaires if we hold the royalties 12 months.[9] And
we shall hold them if I stand by until they are safe from getting
into trouble through Webster & Co's debts. And that I mean to do.

I have wasted not a moment in America: I am wasting no
moments now. I have four irons in the fire and I take vigilant
care of *all* of them.[10]

I will see to it that we have twelve or fifteen thousand dollars
to live on for the next ten or twelve months; and if more should
be necessary I will turn out and earn it. Make Mamma believe
these things. She will believe me anyway, but you *help.* It is
necessary to her health that she be kept free from money-anxieties.
We must all look sharp to that. We must never let her be low-
spirited for one moment if we can help it. She is my only anxiety;
I have no other. When I get that out of my mind I am buoyant,
and destitute of forebodings.

My new book that I am writing makes me jolly. I live in it.
But when I think of Joan of Arc, how I long to get at that again!
I should be fixed just right if I could have both books to work
on month-about.

But I lost most of to-day, because I got to work late, and then
Joe Jefferson arrived and sent up for me and we spent the rest
of the afternoon talking.

[9] So-called advance royalties from the machine.
[10] Probably the typesetter, the publishing house, the serialization of *Pudd'nhead
Wilson,* and writing of the "new book" mentioned below.

I dined with the Laffans last night; dine with the Huttons tomorrow night; Dr. Rice's Wednesday night; with him and Mr. Huntington Thursday night; Lotos banquet in my honor Saturday night; Booth Memorial Service with Mrs. Rice next Monday afternoon and dine with the Huttons and Irving etc., that night. By then I hope to know if I can cross the water for a fortnight.

Be good to Mamma, child! Love her and pet her and make her just as happy as you know how.

I kiss you, dear heart.

PAPA

When the next letter to Livy was written, Mark had plunged into what seems to be an early draft of "Tom Sawyer Detective," an ingenious but uninspired yarn not published until August and September 1896 in *Harper's Magazine*.

Nov. 10/93

Dear Sweetheart, it is getting toward noon & my day's work not begun yet. How the time does get away from a body! Still, with all the interruptions, I am making good progress with "Tom Sawyer's Mystery," for I have written 10,000 words, which is one-seventh of a book like Huck Finn or Prince & Pauper. The last two days I have written very slowly & cautiously, & made my steps sure. It is delightful work & a delightful subject. The story tells itself.

The election last Tuesday was a whirlwind! It swept the Democratic party off its feet just in the same tremendous way that the Republican party was swept off its feet a year ago. It is curious to see both great parties in turn turning Mugwump. Yet both abuse the Mugwumps all through the off-months.

The Democratic party had everything their own way & could have remained steadily in power, but they had no sense, & *haven't* had any for forty years. They had not a single leader in Congress with any ability; their majority in the Senate was made up of cowards, & their President of the Senate was a wax figure. By consequence the country was left in a state of intolerable commercial congestion 3 months while those idiots sat pottering in the Senate. Evidently the whole country has taken the alarm, &

is aghast at the idea of leaving itself longer at the mercy of these blockheads & poltroons.

In this State Dave Hill put up a convicted thief for one of the loftiest places in the Judiciary. The people rose with lightnings and thunder & tempest and snowed him under—buried him past resurrection under whole mountain-ranges of ballots. *Now* you understand why our system of government is the *only* rational one that was ever invented. When we are not satisfied we can *change* things.

You are *most precious* to me.   SAML

The political background of the above letter deserves a word. Voters who had elected Cleveland to a second term in 1892 were led by the Panic of '93 to stampede in large numbers to the Republican Party—which won eight out of eleven state elections on November 7. The "President of the Senate" whom Mark dismisses as a wax figure was Adlai E. Stevenson of Chicago. Upon election to the vice-presidency he found himself presiding over a Senate which, out of political pique, had lately refused to confirm him for a minor office. David Hill at this time was Senator from New York. In 1893 he had put up for Judge of the Court of Appeals one Isaac H. Maynard, who had been arraigned by the New York City bar association for election frauds; but he lost by more than a hundred thousand votes.

Mark's next letter to Livy encloses a note that he had received from the famous actor Henry Irving. Incidentally Irving had turned over $500 to Clemens for investment in the typesetter.

PLAZA HOTEL, NEW YORK, 17 *Nov.* 1893

MY DEAR CLEMENS—Will you give me the pleasure of dining with me on Sunday week 26th Nov. at Delmonicos at half past seven oclock

Believe me

Yours very sincerely

HENRY IRVING

Dear old sweetheart, I accepted this invitation of Henry Irving's last night behind the scenes at the theatre.

I am desperately disappointed because my photograph is not ready for your birthday. I was going to send it to Susy & have her put it with the other tokens of love & remembrance Nov. 27th. But I see I can't manage it now. I went there & sat 7 times & got one or two very good negatives. Sarony should have had the pictures here two days ago but he has failed me.

The Century people misunderstood me about the money; but they will send part of it to you Dec. 1st. They feel the hard times like the rest. And bless your life they're *bitter* hard times! You have never seen anything to remotely compare with them.

I love you deeply, my Livy, & I wish I could be with you on your birthday, but it cannot be & I am sorry for that. But I hope you will be light-hearted & happy, & that you will have all the children around you to bless you.

SAML

The next letter concerns John Mackay, poor Irish immigrant who laid the foundations of his fortune in Gold Hill and Virginia City during Mark's newspaper days there, and a few years later became greatest of the bonanza kings, and still later founder of Postal Telegraph. As a mine superintendent on the Comstock he is said to have declined Mark's facetious offer to swap jobs, saying "My business is not worth as much as yours. I have never swindled anybody, and I don't intend to begin now."

NEW YORK, *Nov.* 28 [1893]

I wonder if I sent John Mackay's letter to you. However, it invited me to talk with you over his cable. You see two old Californians were giving him a supper at the Players the other night, which I could not attend because I had an engagement; but when I returned at midnight they sent for me & I helped do the talking (in my usual modest proportion, perhaps) till 1:30; & I did a still better service: I took the restraints off of Mackay & made things easy for him—for the others, a dozen guests, couldn't well do it, they being new acquaintances. I have always had a warm feeling for him & he has had the same for me. He said I promised to send him a book, & didn't. So I sent it a couple of days ago (ought to have done it immediately—'twould have saved a lot of cabling expense); & I wrote in it, "To John Mackay from Mark Twain, in affectionate remembrance of a friendship which has stood the wear of 31 years & is not out of repair yet"—&

John Russell Young said he was as pleased as a child with it. I
went to his office at noon, yesterday, & he sent for all his Chiefs
of departments—6—& introduced me in great style & with much
swearing. "Now Sam, you sit down there & take the pencil &
understand that you're in Paris & Mrs. Clemens will hear what you
say in two minutes. Say all you want to—make yourself at home.
And whenever you want to send her a message, put it on a piece
of paper & send it right over to my house in Fifth Avenue & I'll
attend to it."

Dinner last night at Dana's. Mr. & Mrs. Dana, Dr. & Mrs.
Brannan, Laffan & wife, General Wilson (who captured Jeff
Davis) & me. Jolly & pleasant. Mrs. Laffan had been hunting for
more Paris addresses for you & is to send me one to-day; but I'll
go over there from the Murray Hill talk & tell her you are settled.
I can't imagine a person's taking a more warm and loving interest
in anything than she has taken in this matter of finding shelter
for you. She has been brim full of it—it was no sleepy interest.

Good-day again, sweetheart. SAML

[NEW YORK] *Dec.* 4/93

Livy darling, we had our meeting at the Murray Hill last night.
Webster (of Chicago) & Charley Davis were both there. Mr.
Rogers mapped out a reformed contract & Webster will have it
drawn by a lawyer here & submitted to Mr. Rogers for approval.
Then he will take it to Chicago & see if he can get Paige to sign.
If it shall seem best, Mr. Rogers & I will go out there.

Then Mr. Rogers mapped out a plan for absorbing the royalties
which is worth a dozen of the one devised by Webster. A singularly clear-headed man is Mr. Rogers—this appears at every
meeting. And no grass grows under his feet. He takes his steps
swiftly, yet no step is bungled or has to be taken over again. If
nothing comes of all this work, nobody will be to blame but Paige.
The proposed amended contract is absolutely fair & just & honorable to every person concerned. Therefore Paige will never sign
it unless hunger compels him. And hunger may; for he had but
a thousand & five dollars in the world four weeks ago, & of this
only seven dollars were left in his pocket six days ago.

The more I think of the contract I took upon myself Sunday,

the more I am surprised at my stupidity. Without any reflection or any estimating of distances, my plan as mapped out in my head was this:

To *walk* from here to 127th Street in 30 minutes—111 blocks;
To walk back in 30 minutes—111 blocks;
To walk to Howells's—44 blocks;
To walk home from there—44 "

111
111
44
44

Total—310 block = *31 miles.*

I failed to accomplish it.

Good-bye, sweetheart, Mr. Webster calls for me.

Lots of love to all of you.

SAML

Dear Jean, I'm ashamed about that St. Nicholas business & am trying to think of ways to atone. I have just been ordering the "Cosmopolitan" to be sent regularly to you & the cost charged to Mr. Walker, the editor. If it fails to reach you let me know. Walker *told* me to do this.

PAPA

In an earlier letter on this same day he had written: "Dear me, I started at 11:45 to meet that noon breakfast engagement yesterday, & soon saw I must take a horse-car. Even then I was an hour late when I arrived. Nobody seemed surprised. They merely told the cook to go to cooking breakfast. A slow process—it was served at 3 P.M. I had to leave at 5, before it was over in order to get to Howells's on time. From here to that breakfast place is 110 blocks! And I was idiotically proposing to *walk* it—both ways!—22 miles in snow & slush."

While John Brisben Walker's *Cosmopolitan* was publishing Mark Twain sketches in its September, November, and December issues of this year, the *St. Nicholas Magazine* was running "Tom Sawyer Abroad" in installments from November to January; Clemens had probably forgotten to supply copies for Jean.

The following letter reveals the shrewd disingenuousness of

Henry Rogers in action—a guilefulness which Mark could admire but despair to imitate. The Connecticut Company, with an office on Broadway, whose letterhead this message bears, was one of several mushroom concerns hastily formed and shakily financed, to market the typesetter. The Farnham Company of Hartford, mentioned still later in this letter, held advance royalties upon the machine, and was an object of special annoyance to Clemens. Of its representative Bill Hamersley, an old Hartford neighbor, he wrote Livy on January 27, 1894: "I will strip to his skin that fat fraud, that cask of rancid guts."

NEW YORK, *Dec.* 9, 1 P.M. 1893

Well, Livy darling, it is better than a circus. But it is fearfully fatiguing. After the 2-hour session the other evening amending the contract, we met next day (yesterday) at 4 P.M. (Mr. Rogers & I holding a private preliminary meeting at 3:45, to agree upon a detail or two belonging to this stage of the campaign). It was beautiful to see Mr. Rogers apply his probe & his bung-starter & remorselessly let out the wind & the water from the so-called "assets" of these companies. And he did it so sweetly & courteously —but he stripped away all the rubbish & laid bare the fact that their whole gaudy property consisted of just $276,000 & no more! Then he said, "Now we know where we stand, gentlemen. I am prepared to listen to a proposition from you to furnish capital." There was a deep, long silence. Then their spokesman proposed a basis of 50 cents on the dollar. Mr. Rogers said, "We will all think, to-night, & come together in the morning—early. Shall we say 9?" That was agreed to, & he & I went away. Along the street he said, "They ask 50, & would be glad to get 12. But we will not take advantage of their necessities. I know exactly what it is worth, to a farthing. I will offer them that in the morning; they will accept, & try not to look as glad as they feel. When that business is settled you will go at once to the President of the Connecticut Co & claim the block of stock which you, conspiring against me, two months ago, required & were to get in case you succeeded in beguiling me into taking hold of this swindle; & you want to magnify the trouble you've had with it, & how hard you've had. to work to keep me from squeezing them down to 12 cents. And another thing. Let them get options on North's & the Farnham royalties, but don't you give them any option on yours. When they have secured those options & you know the terms, then you can say you are ready to listen to a proposition, but that it must be at considerably higher rates than those others get, & that on the whole you think you will leave your wife's royalties undisturbed." (I've got 95 of them in your name—& they're sound & safe, too—can't be siezed for any debt of mine. I will tell you how I managed that, by & by.)

So we met at 9 this morning, & everything came out as Mr. Rogers said it would. He pays 20 when they only hoped for 12 or at the very most 15—therefore there is rejoicing in their camp, now. Then we broke up, to meet again in four hours, & I went with him away down in the Elevated because he wanted to talk & laugh. He said, "Once when you were out of the room I said 'Please hurry this matter, gentlemen; you understand I am not going into this thing for any rational reason, but because I don't see any other way of getting rid of Clemens. I feel sure I ought not to pay 20, but when a person is harried as I am he loses a good share of his judgment.'"

I saw him clear down to Rector Street & then he said I had better go right back & catch Ward & nail him in writing to give me the block of stock I was to get in case I bunco-steered Mr. Rogers into the scheme.

He isn't here, & I mustn't wait any longer, because Mr. R. & I have a private meeting at 2:45—the general meeting is at 3. I love you!

SLC

Dec. 15, Night [1893]

Dear heart, they say there is another newspaper report that I am sick. It is a lie. Pay no attention to such things. They aggravate me beyond expression. I promised, the other day, to talk to a Workingmen's Society last night. But I told Clarence Buel at the time, that I had a cold, & would not talk unless I got rid of it in the meantime. Well, I could have gone, last night, if it had been reasonable weather, but is wasnt; it was fearful weather, snowing & blowing & bitter cold. So I sent & had the thing postponed till the weather improves.

I acted as I did for your sake. For myself, I would have gone.

If you had been here you would have sent me; but in the circumstances I refused to take *any* chance, even the triflingest.

Everybody had a cold until I took one. I was the last. The whole State is supplied, now. Mine does not trouble me, nor interfere with my hearty eating, nor with my billiards. The weather being atrocious, I have staid indoors & played all day.

I won't talk to anybody or *for* anybody, after this. One only gets himself in the papers trying to be accommodating. I am very angry—but I love *you*, dear old sweetheart, nevertheless.

SAML

Once more Livy kindled prematurely to some spark of optimism in her husband's letters; the desperation of both schemes they long refused to admit, to each other or themselves.

Dec. 17th 1893

YOUTH MY DARLING: Your dispatch reached me last night and greatly rejoiced my heart because it does look as if perhaps you were going to be able to come here some day. Thank you so much for sending it. It also seems as if perhaps you were beginning to see your way through financially. How is Webster & Co. situated now? Are they working out of debt?

You should have been here today to see Clara imitate you telling them stories and eating at the same time, it was just as funny as it could be. She bit a piece of bread exactly as you bite it. She said "I don't know what it is but Papa always seems to be having a quarrel with his piece of bread to make it let go."

We have just had a visit from our new doctor. He has examined Susy most thoroughly, he says there is some extension of the cells of the lungs, he thinks it comes from enemia and will not long resist treatment. I like him exceedingly. He says that one great trouble with her is that she is not sufficiently develloped, particularly her chest he is going to have her take gymnastics for developing that, and also masage. I hope now she will soon be on the road to health. It has been very pitiful to see her look so miserable. And sometimes it has been hard to keep cheerful with her so down hearted.

Can it be that pretty soon I shall have a cable stating *when* you are coming wont that be glorious!

Good night, many kisses and hugs and may the sense of my great love for you, give you comfort

Yours always

LIVY L. C.

On this same day he was writing Livy: "And do find that Christian Scientist for Susy." The subject of mental healing began about that time keenly to interest the Clemenses, as the following letter still further suggests, with its account of Mark's visit to a "mind curist" recommended by George Warner, brother of Charles Dudley Warner, and an old Hartford friend.

To Livy next day he gave a fuller account: "Then to Dr. Whipple's arriving on time, & took half an hour's treatment. He sits silent in the corner with his face to the wall, & I walk the floor & smoke. . . . A cough followed [a recent cold], & Mr. Rogers has been buying homeopathic powders & feeding them to me ever since. They kept the cough down & moderated it, but didn't remove it. I tried the mind-cure out of curiosity. That was yesterday. I have coughed only two or three times since. Maybe it was the mind-cure, maybe it was the powders."

His letter next day to Livy notes that "the mind-cure Whipple cured the [Perkins] boy, & now he is a prominent athlete at Yale & plays in the football team . . . These things are mighty interesting."

[THE PLAYERS, NEW YORK CITY] *Dec.* 29/93

Dear old sweetheart, I hope I'll be left alone fifteen minutes so that I can write you a line. My land, what crowded days these are! Two business calls while I was putting on my shirt—had to attend to them before putting on any more clothes. Then when I got down stairs to my coffee George Warner was there waiting to tell me about Dr. Whipple, mind curist, & take me to see him. We went—328 Madison ave. He could tell me of no mind-curist in Europe; said they would be jailed promptly if they attempted to practice in France.

Mighty sorry—unspeakably sorry; for George says Dr. Whipple's cures of Mrs. Edward Perkins & of her son (heart disease & given up by the doctors) have all the aspect of miracles.

Well, I have a project (Unberufen!) I will reveal it to you after some days.

Went then to the Conn. Co. office to read a letter containing the latest developments from Chicago & to warn them against intimating in any letter or telegram that Mr. Rogers & I will yield any inch or half an inch of our requirements. It heavily taxes their nerve & staying power, but they have to stand it.

I must be back there half an hour from now to conduct a disagreeable business interview with a royalty-holder—a function which I have insisted on performing myself with no others present —& they have yielded the privilege to me with a good deal of alacrity.

Saw Mr. Potter in the horsecar. He is just as majestic & handsome & young-looking as ever—but spoke of taking his grandson to the opera the other night. He asked with warm interest after you & the children.

A fine & intelligent society young lady of 30 at dinner last night, noticing that I sent up for my overcoat & put it over my shoulders at table, said she had taken a course of mind-cure lessons & had got *one* profit out of it; to-wit, that she no longer minds drafts, whereas she used to have a terror of them. She sits in them now, when overheated in the ballroom, & suffers no damage. Well, I must go. I love you, dear heart, all the time.

SAML

On October 17, 1893 he began a true-story narrative for Livy's entertainment called "Tale of the Dime-Novel Maiden," about the daughter of a millionaire tyrant who persecuted her for having fallen in love with her music teacher, but she remained "a resolute grenadier" and supported herself by working for the S.P.C.A., the only organization which refused to be intimidated by her father. On December 17 Mark continued the story. Although the girl is not called Benny in the letters now preserved this is probably the story alluded to in the first paragraph below.

[NEW YORK] *Jan.* 4/94

No, dear sweetheart, I am not acquainted with the girl yet, & therefore cannot say what sort of a person she is going to be until I find out. I called her Benny because I liked the name. I guess you know a little more about the story by this time, for I judge you had not received the second batch when you wrote. I haven't added anything to the second batch. It is a long time since I have had an idle hour—or allowed Mr. Rogers to have one, for that matter.

Mr. Archbold of the Standard Oil got tickets for us & he & Mr. Rogers & Dr. Rice & I went to the Athletic Club last Saturday night & saw the Coffee Cooler dress off another prize fighter in great style. There were to be 10 rounds; but at the end of the fifth the Coffee Cooler knocked the white man down & he couldn't get up any more. A round consists of only 3 minutes; then the men retire to their corners & sit down & lean their heads back against a post & gasp & pant like fishes, while one man fans them with a fan, another with a table-cloth, another rubs their legs & sponges off their faces & shoulders & blows sprays of water in their faces from his own mouth. Only one minute is allowed for this; then time is called & they jump up & go to fighting again. It is absorbingly interesting.

I am glad you are to have electrical treatment. I hope you will get hold of an operator who is *thoroughly* competent. I hear of almost miraculous cures performed by electricity.

I am glad Jean is to have her teeth put in order. I would do the like with mine if I could get time. I am already away behind again with my correspondence—which consists mainly of declining all conceivable kinds of entertainments. Dr. Rice said last night that my welcome to New York has been phenomenal, & that the manifest affection of the people for me was the sort of fame that was worth having; & Mr. Rogers said the other day to Rice or to Archbold that other people's successes in this world were made over broken hearts or at the cost of other people's feelings or food, but that my fame had cost no one a pang or a penny. And this morning down stairs some one read a remark in an English magazine that there was a curious fact that had been observed—to wit, that the most fleetest & evanescent of fames was that of the second-rate humorist, while the most substantial & permanent was that of the first-rate humorist; & said *he* believed I was a first-rate. All this is pleasant. I can stand considerable petting. Born so, Jean.

To-day is like the days of weeks ago. It is a waiting day. I was

to be up & dressed & breakfasted by 9, & then wait here until sent
for. If needed in the conference I must come & play my hand—
not otherwise. It is now a quarter to 2 & no news yet. At 10:45
the conference was still at work, with no result. If they send for
me Mr. Rogers knows the card I will play, & I guess it will be
effective. But I judge they think they can get along without that.
This is the last of the games in the long tournament. Mr. Rogers
& I have not lost a single one, thus far, & we think we are equal
to this occasion. If we can hang this last remaining scalp at our
belt the victory will be complete, all along the line.

Recognizing, yesterday noon, that the campaign was ended,
barring to-day's assault, & that in it I was not likely to take part,
I experienced a sudden collapse of interest & a deep drowsiness,
an overwhelming desire to stretch out & take a nap. So I went to
bed & napped the whole afternoon away; then had some supper
brought up. Rice came in & made a long visit, but by 11:30 I was
asleep again & didn't wake till called at 8:30. I've caught up, now,
& am rested & vigorous. I have spent the day walking the sidewalk
out in front taking the brisk air & keeping watch for messengers.

Poor old Brer Rogers gets so tuckered out through having this
additional business added to his immense burden that he has to
get to bed earlier than usual. When the enclosed telegram arrived
showing that we had at last got Paige where we wanted him, I
went to that conference & when it was over & we had telegraphed
Chicago to go ahead & prepare the contracts, Mr. Rogers said, as
we walked toward his horse-car, "To-morrow is to be a blank day
—the fight is as good as won—it is time for us both to catch a
little rest. I will be in bed & asleep before 8 o'clock and get three
extra hours in that way & you'd better do the same." We were at
the perfunctory conference next morning at nine—but he had
been up until one o'clock with his wife, who had had a savage
attack of her heart trouble. She is a cheerful person & goes to
dinner parties and theatres—Mr. Rogers carries her up the steps
in his arms—& she violates the doctor's commands pretty regularly. Still, she gets along very well until she tries to climb three
or four stair-steps—then the throes of pain come & for a few hours
they think she is not going to pull through. In her own house
they watch her & make her use the elevator always, but away from

home she sometimes tries to climb the steps of a stoop, & then disaster ensues.

Dear—dear, I couldn't pay my dinner calls yesterday because I had to sleep, & to-day I can't pay them because I must wait here & watch. I believe I will not accept any more dinners where a dinner call is necessary. I'm going down stairs, now, & hunt up a game of billiards. I don't reckon I could tell you how I love you & how dear your letters are to me & how glad I was to get the cable saying our Susy is improving—so I won't try.

SAML

On December 30 he disclosed his social technique to Livy: "I am very prompt about paying my dinner calls. I mean I am going to be. I always explain to those people. I have a system. I do not pay any call for a *first* dinner, but the next time I go to that place to dine I go in & make my dinner-call first & then come back in 5 minutes to dinner. Then the next time & the succeeding times, I repeat the process. It saves a deal of time, & they all say it is an elegant idea & perfectly satisfactory."

Between this and the next letter Clemens had run up to Hartford to see a play staged by members of The Saturday Morning Club, which he had founded two decades earlier, for 'teen age girls. He returned on the same train with Rudyard Kipling and Laurence Hutton.

20 EAST 23rd STREET, NEW YORK

Jan. 12/94

Waiting here for telegrams from Chicago.

I have just received 3 letters from you, my darling, & my heart is sore with the realization that my long deferred coming is wearing upon you. But you must not doubt that I am delaying because it is pure necessity. So long as the contract is not signed in Chicago, I should die at sea if I started. Upon that contract depends our very bread & meat. If it fails we are ruined—[ruined past hope or help] badly crippled, at least. If it is signed, it means the banishment of the wolf from the door permanently. Every night I say to myself "I *must* see the wife & the children, if only for one day"—but have to follow it with "Hold your grip & don't be a fool—you've *got* to stay here till this thing is settled."

This morning Mr. Rogers was pretty restive—his stock of patience is running low. After he left the conference I was glad to see that all hands had noticed this. It had also been noticed at the conference held Wednesday evening during my absence in [Chicago] Hartford, & still more noticeably at yesterday morning's conference.

Charley Davis & I are here together waiting for telegrams, & he has just told me in confidence that he sent a telegram to Chicago early this morning saying that Rogers is plainly getting sick of the whole business & that his stepping down & out is a disaster to be looked for at any moment, now.

I was glad of that. An hour ago the conference sent a telegram saying in effect that things are looking gloomy at this end, & that Mr. Rogers had promised to send a telegram later. Mr. Rogers then prepared his telegram & read it. It was courteous but firm. It as good as said that the final concession required must be granted or—

He made no threat, but the inference was clear. The others wanted the apparent positiveness of it softened, but I insisted on having it go unmodified, & it did. There is only one way to deal with Paige, & that is to take a stand & keep it. I do hope I can cable you, the 15th, that the contract is signed. That is the time I set in my cablegram of Jan. 5 saying I believed you would hear good news in 10 days. Nobody can tell—but, I strongly *hope*.

It does distress me so, that you & Susy are ill. If I could only send you that cablegram maybe it would help you both. I am sure it would help you, & Susy & Ben, & Jean, all & every of you, as the ancient law-forms say—every darling I've got.

Joe & Harmony[11] want Susy to come & live with them many months—they say the young Hartford life will set her up mentally & physically, & Hartford is full of delightful girls of her age. *That* part of it is sound (but privately the table would not nourish Susy).

Joe is just as darling & delicious as ever, & oh, you ought to hear Harmony when Isa[12] is the text! It's nuts! Also when Charley

[11] Mrs. Joseph Twichell, born Harmony Cushman.
[12] Isabella Beecher Hooker.

Warner is her text, with Isa as sub-text. Harmony doesn't believe that the relations between Annie T. & Isa are intimate & tender. She argues that Annie is not a fool, & therefore couldn't choose a fool (& a humbug) for comrade.[13]

Not since Innocents Abroad have I heard so much talk about a book of mine as I now hear about Pudd'nhead. [And I don't try to answer all the letters I get.]

In a lecture on "Politics from 1781 to 1815," in New York last night, by Professor Powell of the University of Pennsylvania, where Mr. Hall was present, he had considerable to say about the serious deeps underlying the humor in my several books, & then said that Pudd'nhead was clearly & powerfully drawn & would live & take his place as one of the great creations of American fiction. Isn't that pleasant—& unexpected! For I have never thought of Pudd'nhead as a *character*, but only as a piece of machinery—a button or a crank or a lever, with a useful function to perform in a machine, but with no dignity above that. I think we all so regarded him at home. Well, oddly enough, other people have spoken of him to me much as Prof. Powell has spoken.

I enclose the "Masque" program. In the "Convention" there were a lot of my Club girls whose names do not appear—among them one of those lovely Knight Cheney girls.[13a] Annie & the rest beckoned to me through the crack of the curtain as soon as it was down, & I swarmed toward them & they toward me, & we had the grand hand-shake in front of what would be a stage-box if they had such things there—& it was great & congratulatory times, I tell you! It wasn't the single hand-shake of commerce, but the shake with both hands—the shake of measureless approval and welcome. I was proud to be the father & sole male member of a club that could write & play plays like that. The more I think of that evening the more I want to see the play again. (P.S. One of you write Annie T. & tell her how much I was delighted, won't you?)

When I go anywhere to dinner on *invitation*, I go in evening dress, of course. When I drop in at either of three places—Rice's,

[13] Annie Eliot Trumbull, daughter of the Hartford philologist and historian James Hammond Trumbull. Witty and lively, she was a favorite of the Clemenses.
[13a] The Cheneys belonged to the family of silk manufacturers.

Laffan's & Hutton's on my own invitation, it is always on a sudden notion & there's no time to dress. I go as I am. It is the clear understanding. My place is ready for me—to occupy when I please. I have never dropped in at Hutton's in this way—it is only *accident* that I haven't—but various times Mrs. Hutton has ordered Larry to bring me & he has done it & there was no other guest there & no occasion for evening dress & we didn't wear it.

Now while I think of it I'll run out & leave cards at Chas. A. Dana's. I declined a dinner there for day before yesterday. I love you with all my heart, & I keep your commandments better than I give myself credit for, my darling.

SAML

P.S. Mind you, it rains invitations, but I don't accept them. I am attending strictly to business, & to private dinners where there are no speeches. To-night, dinner at R. U. Johnson's—don't want to go, but can't properly decline; Tuesday, 1 P.M., at Mrs. Carroll Beckwith's—luncheon—she's playing me as a card, & will have a large company—but she has been treating me very handsomely, & so I'm perfectly willing to spin yarns if her guests want them; Monday 7.30 P.M., dinner with Stanford White the architect, up in his quarters in the Tower of Madison Square Garden—Abbey the artist & other artists are to be there. I shall enjoy it. But I decline *all* of the banquets, now. I made such a big hit at Brander Matthews' banquet—without expecting it—that I'm going to keep what I've gained, & make no more speeches.[14]

I'll tell Howells what you say, if I ever get a chance to get out there again.

No telegrams from Chicago—I must start right out to Dana's.

Dearheart, there are days when I can't get a shadow of a chance to write—but I try to make up by piling two or three days' indebtedness into a single long letter.

Premature jubilation over the refinancing of the Paige machine inspired his next letter. To Livy on January 27 he alludes to "the details of Mr. Rogers's new arrangement with the C[onnecticut] C[ompany] to aid them in corraling the outstanding royalties."

[14] On December 20, 1893, at a dinner honoring the Columbia professor Mark gave a happy toast in which he made the name of "B-r-r-ander Mat-thews" sound like the roll of stately profanity. It is given in Clara Clemens' *My Father Mark Twain*, 132-34.

His two disastrous enterprises were still linked together; on "Feb. 7 or 8" he wrote Livy: "You understand, dear heart, don't you, that my presence here is absolutely necessary until I float a big block of stock & thus capture my half of the pool & also fix Websterco's bank-debt so it can't jump on my back in some sudden panic—fix it by *paying* it."

[NEW YORK] *Midnight, Jan. 15/94*

Livy darling, when I came in, an hour ago, & found this letter, it did not move me or produce any quickening of the blood, because I was days & days ago prepared for such news & reasonably confident that it was coming. I at once wrote a telegram to you & dispatched it by a messenger, so that it would be delivered to you as soon as you were up in the morning: "Look out for good news." I played billiards till 1:15—it is really 2 A M now though I have headed this "Midnight"—you see I wanted to preserve the date, Jan. 15, it being the date I had appointed ten days before for "good news."

I came up to my room & began to undress, & then, suddenly & without warning the realization burst upon me & overwhelmed me: I and mine, who were paupers an hour ago, are rich now & our troubles are over!

I walked the floor for half and hour in a storm of excitement. Once or twice I wanted to sit down & cry. You see, the intense strain of three months & a half of daily & nightly work & thought & hope & fear had been suddenly taken away, & the sense of release & delivery & joy knew no way to express itself.

There, now, I will write no more to-night. Kiss me, all my darlings, & I will go to sleep.

THE PLAYERS, *Feb* [9]/94

Ah, Sweetheart, confound the heedless clerk downstairs who told me the Gascogne was to sail *Thursday*. It gave me another day; so I waited, in order to have a word to say after Shoemaker's visit.[15] Of course when I brought my bulky letter down, Wednesday evening to have it weighed & the stamps plastered on, another clerk proved to me by book that no ship touching at Southampton

[15] Other letters speak of him as "the representative of the Standard Oil company in the Elmira region" whom Clemens had lately interested in selling stock in Webster & Co.

or a French port sails on Thursdays. Formerly this would be a matter of no consequence—when I wrote & mailed one or two letters every day—but now that I gradually build up a large letter twice a week, it's an ugly piece of ill luck, for the gap that is going to occur may make you uneasy. But I hope not. You will already have noticed that I am mailing only twice a week, & will infer that I have missed a mail.

I met Walker of the Cosmopolitan that evening & explained that the reason I hadn't come in the day was that I was writing you. He considered *that* an explanation that didn't explain—until I told him the size of my 2 weekly letters. Then he said:

"My! this is the last possibility of unwisdom! it is the last extravagance of wastefulness, of unthinking prodigality. Two such letters a week flung across the ocean to Mrs. Clemens, who—who —oh, stop it & send them to *me*—I'll give you fifteen hundred dollars for them!"[16]

Ben & Susy must read "A Study of Indian Music" in the Feb. Century.[17] I think it will interest them

I wrote a magazine article yesterday for the Youth's Companion.[18] At 6 I went to Richard Harding Davis's 5 o'clock tea, in his bachelor quarters which he occupies in 5th Ave. with young Howard Russell. Mrs. Stanford White was there to receive & matronize young ladies. A splendid grand creature to look at! Of course I had forgotten her—I should forget Satan—but she immediately told me her name. The daily thing happened—I was greeted by fifty people who knew me, & who hardly ever mentioned their names. I could have killed them!

I had a very pleasant time, nevertheless. Among others, Barnes (that adorable mimic) was there, & I siezed the chance to get better acquainted. A mighty nice man. I like Harding Davis, too. This was the third tea to which I had been invited there & twice had failed to arrive; & so he said he would telegraph me several hours before the tea, & then I couldn't possibly forget. He did so—but I wasn't going to forget anyway: I had a note of it pinned

[16] "The Cosmopolitan pays me $150 a page," he wrote Livy on February 11. ". . . Authors are too much given to (commercially) undervaluing their wares."
[17] By John Comfort Fillmore.
[18] "How to Tell a Story," published in the issue of October 3, 1895, is Mark's only contribution to that magazine listed in Johnson's *Bibliography*.

to my bed-canopy. He was almost embarrassingly hearty in thanking me for coming. Think of it! Lord, that we vanishing poor things should be *thanked* for enjoying ourselves—*thanked* for privileges bestowed—thanked for coming & buzzing in one's garden.

At 7 I went von dannen to dinner in 1 E 19th Street, at Mr. Olin's. Present, Olin, Millet, Dwight, & another gentleman; Mrs. (wife of that other & cousin to the host) Mrs. Millet, Miss Frelinghuysen, Miss Minturn. Four times during the evening Millet told me the name of the couple who were related to the host, but I was never able to keep it 5 minutes. I took out Miss Frelinghuysen (whom I knew in Washington when her father was Secretary of State) & sat between her & Mrs. Millet. Miss F. is sterling in character and high & fine in breeding, & she has read everything & knows how to discriminate between best & second-best. Mrs. Millet was as prodigious an improvement upon herself as—well there isn't *any* comparison that will describe it. She was pretty, she was unstunningly dressed, hardly the top of the crevice between her breasts was exposed, she was dignified & reposeful, her feverish eagerness to jabber & jabber & jabber was gone, she said many rational things & got badly caught out only once. I was glorifying Aldrich as being the one man in this earth who was *always* witty, *always* brilliant. It was Mrs. Millet's opportunity to expose herself, & she said with large calm superiority:

"I think you cannot have met him *very* often. My experience differs from yours. I have met him at dinners often & over again when he was dull, monosyllabic—yes, & even *silent* during long intervals."

I saw poor Millet wince! And yet nevertheless I was not mollified, but said (gently & without emphasis, but *said* it)—

"Yes, there *are* dinner companies that do even that miracle."

Even Mrs. M. herself joined in the laugh & with an apparent heartiness that was full of tact & did her infinite credit. Miss Frelinghuysen said, privately:

"I didn't see how that speech of hers could fail to bring trouble upon her, but she has come as well out of it as the circumstances would allow."

People ask me every day—

"What is the secret of your extraordinary health?"

"Six hours of *sound* sleep instead of nine broken and interrupted."

Oh my darling, I do so long to see you! What an exile it is! I love you dearly, & I kiss you.

SAML

Mark Twain's quickness of retort is again illustrated in his account to Livy on February 23 of his attendance in Fairhaven, Massachusetts, at the dedication of a family memorial given by Henry Rogers. The state dignitaries were drinking champagne toasts in the dining-car of the special train that had brought them:

The Governor, who is as bald as Theodore Crane, raised a laugh by bowing in a courtly way & saying—

"But before you begin, Mr. Clemens, I shall have to ask you to take off your wig."

I said—

"All right, I will, when you put yours on."

Which bowled his Excellency out & turned the laugh the other way. Clark whispered to Rogers—

"The Governor forgot that the wise man doesn't monkey with the buzz-saw."

His allusion in the next letter to memorizing the famous blue-jay story from *A Tramp Abroad* indicates probably a postponement of the engagement mentioned to Livy on February 20: "I finally yielded to Carey's urgings & said yes I would read with James Whitcomb Riley Feb. 26 & 27 at $250 a night, on condition that Riley leave all of the humorous part to me & restrict himself to the serious. And so, ever since I have been memorizing stuff for those readings—memorizing it along the street, going from one business to another; memorizing it in horse-cars & the elevated; in momentary intervals at dinner parties & other social life; & in bed. I am all right, now—and ready."

NEW YORK, MCH. 2 [1894] 3.40 P.M.

Dear sweetheart, I was up at 8 & down at my office at 9, & Hall Rogers & I put in a quarter of an hour talking & arranging for

Mr. R.'s afternoon campaign with the Century people. Then I walked up town half a mile & bought 3 Yaeger shirts & a camels hair rug for shipboard. Then I carried some Pudd'nhead proofs to the Century. Then I answered some letters in my room. Next I went to memorizing the Bluejay for my Saturday reading. Then Frank Bliss arrived, 1 P.M., from Hartford in answer to my telegram & we talked an hour over the Century proposition to issue my books in a uniform set of 14 or 15 volumes. Then he went away to think it over, & I went on with my memorizing, which I have now successfully finished. And now I must go & find Frank Mayo & sign contract for the Pudd'nhead Wilson drama.[19] In the meantime I have added an appointment to tomorrow's list—to let the electrician Tesla do my photograph again for the Century.[20]

I'll go out to Mr. R's tonight & see what he has done.

To-morrow (Saturday) is full. Appointment on the Webster business at 9; meet Frank Bliss at 10; later, make some steamer arrangements; probably meet Bliss & Century people about 2:30; fuss over that photo from 4 to 6; read from 8:10 to 9; meet Bram Stoker[21] here at 10:30; supper at Mr. Cowdin's, with music & doubtless dancing, until 1 A.M.; then be fetched by a carriage & attend the annual round-up of the Aldine Club (Story-Tellers' Night), & help the able story-tellers spin yarns & make speeches indefinitely.

But next Wednesday!—then I'm out of it all & on shipboard, bound for you & the chicks!

Good-bye again, sweetheart,

SAML

I am getting uneasy. No letters from you for a whole week. But it is only another failure of the mails—I won't allow myself to dream of it's being anything else.

Sailing on March 7, he was at last reunited with Livy in Paris eight days later, after the longest separation of their married life.

[19] First produced in Hartford on April 8, 1895.
[20] The well-known Serbian inventor Nikola Tesla (1857-1943).
[21] The author of *Dracula* had invested $100 in the Paige machine, for which Clemens reimbursed him when that project ran hopelessly aground.

CHAPTER SIXTEEN

Bankruptcy

AFTER only three weeks of reunion with his family, Clemens found himself dragged back to New York by the imminent collapse of Webster & Company. Rogers helped to convince him that the stark admission of insolvency was the only rock bottom from which an upward step could be taken. Mark returned in time for the last gasp of the Webster concern, which on April 18 executed assignment papers, carrying Samuel Clemens into voluntary bankruptcy with it. A little later Rogers persuaded him to abandon all hope in the Paige machine, and the last remnants of a fool's paradise crumbled.

One of the most remorseless of the so-called robber barons, Rogers advised his friend that the ethics of literature were higher than those of business, telling him that "you must earn the cent per cent" and repay all his creditors. And this Mark was able eventually to do, at considerable cost to his flagging strength.

While these decisions trembled in the scales, Livy offered all her personal fortune that remained and her moral suasion over Mark in anxiety that he do the scrupulously honorable thing— more than a little fearful, as her letters disclose, that Rogers with his business cunning and her husband under his burden of debt, family insecurity, and a kind of automatic irritation against his creditors, might cut some of the corners. Her solicitude that he do and say the right thing was never more earnest than in those dark days.

Above all, their letters prove that the love which had grown through all those golden years when he was fortune's darling and she the little heiress of Elmira, could stand the test of adversity —a disaster still more galling to them because the fame of Mark Twain guaranteed that the news of his bankruptcy would echo around the world.

The first letter here published was written immediately after the blow fell; its cancelations, marked as always by brackets, are as revealing as the rest concerning his state of mind.

[NEW YORK] *7 a.m. Apl. 19/94*

Dear old sweetheart, I leave in an hour for Hartford on business —returning this afternoon. Mr. Rogers is [delighted] perfectly satisfied that our course was right—[al] absolutely right & wise. Cheer up—the [worst is] best is yet to come. Goodby, dear heart, I love you, don't you b'lieve me when I says dat, Chambers?

SAML

In *Pudd'nhead Wilson* "Chambers" is the son of Roxy the slave, whose adoration of him leads her to change him and his little white master in the cradle.

[NEW YORK] *April 20/94*

Well, dear heart, I read everything the newspapers had to say about it yesterday on my way to Hartford, & discovered not one unkind or unpleasant or fault-finding remark. As I hadn't done anything to be ashamed of, I wasn't ashamed; so I didnt avoid anybody, but talked with everybody I knew on the train. The same, coming back. All my friends say I was wisely advised, & did right. I think your desires made Mr. Rogers think, for a while, that he wanted the assignment prevented—but I haven't a doubt that that was merely a momentary weakness on his part; the moment he saw the rigorous attitude of the Mt. Morris Bank his sanity returned to him & we precipitated the assignment. I feel an immense sense of relief today; & so does Hall, though when he signed the assignment he could hardly keep from crying, & I half thought he would go off & drown himself. I have seldom been so out of patience with a person as I was with Mr. Hall. He was stubbornly determined to consider it dishonorable to sign without first notifying Whitford.[1] Nothing that I & my lawyers could say could make him see the crass stupidity of his position.—In all my days I have never seen so dull a fool. Then he was in a perfect

[1] Representing the Mount Morris Bank, which had made substantial loans to Fred Hall and the Webster company, and proved the most inflexible creditor.

fever to run to Whitford the moment he had signed. Whitford laughed at him, of course.

Even *now* Hall can't understand why his act doesn't make Whitford his enemy & fill his mouth with upbraidings & charges of treachery. Dull? He is as dull as a tadpole. It was not even a question, in his mind, as to where his loyalty was due: it was due to *Whitford's bank* because W. had procured favors there for him. It was not due to you, who had done rather more than that. He amazed the lawyers—apparently he was the first of his species that they had encountered. To-day Hall is as happy as a child—and prattles like one.

I hope you have all gotten acquainted with Mrs. Duff & Miss May before this.[2] There aren't any better girls than *they* are; *that* I know. I am eating their meals for them while they are away.

I love you, darling.

SAML

NEW YORK *Friday May* 4/94

Well, dear heart, I've been to Elmira & had a glimpse of the folks, including the Stanchfields.[3] Sue reminded me of the lace & I sent it to her as soon as I got back. I have had a sort of notion to run up to Hartford for an hour, but I don't get the chance. We had a meeting with the Mt. Morris bank yesterday afternoon, but nothing came of it. President Paine was pleasant & courteous & we got on well together, he using persuasions & I answering that I was ready to do anything my counsel might advise. Whitford began to bluster & threaten, but I smiled on him & he did not continue. It seems pretty evident that the business can pay its debts if allowed to go on; so all the creditors but the bank are quite willing to take that chance & release me & set me free of all legal obligations to make up any deficit—& of course I don't ask or *want* them to free me from the *moral* obligation to pay.

Apparently we owe the bank $29,500—but I have a strong suspicion that a good half of it is bogus paper & that we don't really owe it more than $15,000. The accountants are hard at work; if they ferret out the evidence that a part of our debt is on bogus

[2] Daughters of H. H. Rogers.
[3] Livy's old friend Clara Spaulding was now Mrs. John Stanchfield.

paper, then I shall be very frank with Whitford & the bank. Their time for bluster will have gone by. I have a kind of notion that President Paine doesn't know about that bogus paper. If he knew of it he surely wouldn't be quite so intractable as he is.

I was instructed to be quiet & composed at the conference; be courteous & polite; parry all attempts to get me excited or angry; make no admissions; answer no arguments; & let Paine & Whitford go away empty at last. Hard conditions; but the lawyers said I carried them out, in letter & spirit. Only one attempt was made to bully me & anger me—that was Whitford's—& it fell so effectless & flat that he was ashamed of it himself.

I don't know what the outcome is going to be—I mean I don't know what decision is going to be arrived at—but I am indifferent. It will be best for all of us if the concern is allowed to go on under a trusteeship—otherwise nobody is seriously hurt but the bank. If the bank forces an auction of the effects, the result will be some little money to each creditor, & in time you & I can pay the rest—*excluding* the bank. I shall be a very old person before I pay the bank any more than half of their claim unless it can be clearly shown that I *owe* more.

Nobody finds the slightest fault with my paying you with all my property. There is nothing shady or improper about it. We make no concealment of it. The bank wanted to cable you & ask your permission to take the royalties of my books during a certain period, but my lawyer said—

"What! & get no concession in return for it? We will by no means allow it. She is in no way concerned in these affairs. Her property is her own & [lawfully] legally and morally acquired, & although she has a right to impair its value if she so elects, you cannot expect *us* to advise her to such a course. To release her husband—who owns nothing in the world—from his obligations, in return for the temporary use of certain of her copyrights—*that* is a suggestion which she might consider; but to *give* away such a thing for nothing, is a thing not to be thought of."

It was confoundedly difficult at first for me to be always saying "Mrs. Clemens's books," Mrs. Clemens's copyrights," "Mrs. Clemens's type-setter stock," & so on; but it was necessary to do this, & I got the hang of it presently. I was even able to say with gravity, "My wife has two unfinished books, but I am not able to say when they will be completed or where she will elect to publish them when they are done."

Once Mr. Paine said—

"Mr. Clemens, if you could let us have Pudd'nhead Wilson—"

"So far as I know, she has formed no plans as to that book yet, Mr. Paine"—he took the hint & corrected his phraseology.

I love you, dear old sweetheart, & shall soon see you now, I guess. This is my last letter, I guess.

SAML

Sailing promptly from New York, Clemens remained with his family in France from mid-May until early July. Albert Bigelow Paine's biography, page 987, asserts that although Rogers urged Clemens to return for a summer consultation, the latter declined. Letters to Livy, however, show that he did sail on July 7 and remained absent in the United States until about the middle of August. With the onset of hot weather, the family moved from the south of France to Etretat in the north.

S. S. *Paris. At Sea*, July 13/94

Livy darling, we shall arrive early tomorrow morning—Saturday. It has been an astonishing voyage, as regards weather: warm brilliant, smooth—the sea a millpond, all the way over.

I have worked every day, but have accomplished nothing; what I have written is not satisfactory & must be thrown away. However my time was put in most pleasantly; without the work I should have been worrying about you & Susy all the time; with it I have worried only a part of the time.

Part of my work was not lost, for I have revised Joan of Arc & made some good corrections & reductions. Also I have discovered that the introduction is incomplete. I will complete it on shore.

We have 200 first cabin passengers; very pleasant people, & considerably above the quality of folk who travel by the German ships. Our American lady is from South Africa—Mrs. Hammond; she met Clara at Sibyl Sanderson's. Her husband is employed by the British Government; he has charge of all the vast mining interests in South Africa, at a salary of $60,000 a year, with emoluments amounting to $40,000 more.

Mrs. P. T. Barnum is on board. She was an invalid 8 years, with nervous & other troubles, & spent most of the time in hospitals. She said her case was apparently hopeless, but she fell into Dr. Playfair's hands in London & in 5 months he has made a well woman of her. She thinks Susy ought to go to him.

Morse is on board—our Consul-General in Paris. We sit at table together. I find him very pleasant company.

Mrs. Horwitz & her daughter & her daughter's engagè are on board. Mrs. H. has kept her room the whole way. Also that Mrs. Smith is on board—the one who met me on the street in Paris.

I wonder where you are. I hope you are still at La Bourboule, but I hardly expect it. It is a weary and doleful place for you & I guess you have flown it before this. Well, all right—be happy; that is the main thing—you deserve it. But wherever you are, I love you dearly, dearly, & always shall.

Saml

Mark's mention in the above letter of meeting on shipboard Mrs. John Hays Hammond is of particular interest. He saw her again in Pretoria, South Africa, in late May 1896, during his global tour, and with her went to the jail to visit her husband, the American mining engineer imprisoned for his share in the Jameson Raid. On "the Queen's Birthday/96" he wrote Livy: "Found I had met Hammond when he was a Yale senior, & been introduced by Gen. Franklin. . . . Made a talk (or speech—sitting—) to the prisoners; explained to them why they were better off in jail than they would be any where else; that they would eventually have gotten into jail anyhow, by the look of their countenances; that if they got out they would get in again; that it would be better all around if they remained quietly where they are & made the best of it; that after a few months they would prefer the jail & its luxurious indolence to the sordid struggle for bread outside; & that I would go & see Pres. Kruger & do everything I could, short of bribery, to double their jail-terms." On June 4 he informed Livy that "the Four are released from prison, with banishment & £5,000 fine each."

To return to the present sequence, the following letter begins

by alluding to a sum of money mislaid by Clara, then recalls the
grief that had lately overtaken Henry Rogers, with the death on
May 21, 1894, of his long-ailing wife.

THE PLAYERS, NEW YORK
July 17/94

Livy dear, I deposited some money with Drexel to cover Clara's
loss, but I don't remember how much—it was $100 anyway; it was
either that or it was $200—but I *think* the former. I didn't wait
to get a receipt. I meant to write you about it but I reckon I
forgot it.

Mr. Rogers tried to tell me about the last days of Mrs. Rogers
this morning, but it was finally too hard for him & his voice broke
& he could not go on. She was suffering intolerable pain (from
the unsuspected tumour, which was as big as a man's fist) & was
glad to undertake the surgical operation. It was to take ¾ of an
hour, but it took an hour & three-quarters. Before it she made
various arrangements: wrote a cablegram to be sent to Mrs. Duff
saying the operation had been successfully performed & all was
well. She called for some bills & her check-book & signed checks
for them. Mrs. Benjamin suggested that she sign some more in
blank, but she said no, there would be no occasion for that. She
[joked] told Mr. Rogers & the doctors that soon she would have
the advantage of them—she could eat grapes without fear, & they
couldn't. Then the surgery began; after its completion she began
to sink & never rallied. Mrs. Duff says all the family were depend-
ent on her & rested in her, & that in losing her they have lost more
than can be described. Mr. Rogers says his hardest time is when
he gets up every morning—for, coming out of sleep he is expecting to see her, & then comes the daily shock & the new realization.

Let us be spared this, my darling. May we die together.

SAML

"Rev. Sam Jones's Reception in Heaven," mentioned in the
next letter as a private reading for friends, was a variant upon
the theme which also inspired "Captain Stormfield's Visit to
Heaven." The manuscript about Sam Jones still exists among the
Mark Twain Papers with the notation "not published—forbidden
by Mrs. Clemens, S. L. C."

However, it should be 23, for it is past midnight. The band doesn't play Sunday nights, so Mrs. Duff asked me to take its place, & I said I would if we could find a small, private corner. We got a small dining room away at the end of the house a hundred yards from the main entrance, & put about 20 chairs in it & invited as many personal friends, & I read Rev. Sam Jones's Reception in Heaven, & we had a gay time over it. Then shandy-gaff for the gentlemen & buttermilk & seltzer-lemonades for the ladies; then a literary chat & smoke with the landlord till midnight; then to my room.

I had to run up to New York to get "Sam Jones," & it was raining & storming hard; but it was very pleasant, both on the water & in the trains. I left at 4 & was back at 8 P.M. I do wish you were with me. Sometimes there are 500 guests in the hotel, & they are very nice people. The verandahs are very broad & very long, & accommodate a multitude of people without crowding or inconvenience. All day the ships flit by in front, & at night one has the stars & the moon & the distant winking of the light-houses.

It has been cold all day, but is warmer now. Good-night all you darlings. I love you.

SAML

Livy's anxiety over the strict integrity of his dealings with the creditors set the theme for his next. As a proud and sensitive man he could not help wincing under the lash of bankruptcy. Two days later he wrote: "Dear Sweetheart, tomorrow Jean will be 14! My land, how time flies! Give the child my deep strong love— I am a bankrupt & haven't any other present. But we are rich, although we haven't any money, & by & by we will make up to the children all the lacking presents."

My darling, I note carefully everything you say in yours of the 12th; I note it reverently & lovingly, honoring you & loving you for what you say & for the high position which you take. *You* can take no other position; I would not wish you to take any other, I could not bear to have you take any other.

My own position must necessarily differ from yours in one or two details. My first duty is to you & the children—my second is to those others. I must protect you first—protect you against yourself. That accomplished I mean to take the fullest possible care of those others. And at the right moment I shall tell them so.

They are all acting handsomely—even the bank. Everything is agreed upon except your royalty for Pudd'nhead. I mean to see to it that if they strenuously object to 20 per cent, they shall have the book for less. That detail arranged I am free from legal persecution for one year. In that time I hope to make them perfectly safe, & ourselves also. Mr. Rogers is still detained in Washington. He expects to get back tonight. Then I hope the papers can be signed tomorrow. I think nothing is wanting but his signature. After the papers are signed I will ask him to let me tell the creditors—but he won't. He will probably say: "It could make them lax; let them alone—they'll work the harder; a year hence will be time enough."

Mind you, dearheart, nobody can charge me with dishonorable conduct; I have not been guilty of any; I shall *not* be guilty of any until I desert my family to take care of those others. Whenever I do that, it will be time for people to call me names; up to that time they *can't* call me names. Those creditors *forced* me to make an assignment—goodness knows *I* didn't want to do it. They must stand part of the hardship of their own act. They did me a very great kindness, & I am grateful to them for it & shall try & see that they lose no penny by it.

Suppose father had been here in Mr. Rogers's place? Would he have advised me differently? Indeed, no. He would have said "If you let your property fall into the hands of those creditors it will be rushed upon the market & *nobody* will get his due. If you keep it & handle it yourself everybody will get a hundred cents on the dollar."

My very dearest, I love you, I honor you, & I am not going to do a single dishonorable thing. I am not going to wrong anybody. If ever I should, I am not going to begin with *you*.

Nothing that any newspaper can say will give me a single pang until they try to insinuate that I made no distinction between you & the other creditors. Then they will hear from me.

The moment Mr. Rogers signs the papers my campaign will begin. I will get right to work & do my best in the selling of stock. I have to keep still until then. People are out of town, but I can find them. Dr. Rice's brother is to be my agent. I am to see him Wednesday morning. He is not able to come down to New York sooner.

I am going to rush over now & get a glimpse of Mrs. Rice, who will pass through at 1:15 PM.—which is now.

I *am* so gladly Susy is going to finish the cure!

With worlds of love,

SAML

26 BROADWAY, *July* 26/94

Good-morning & I wish you well, my darling! I am very cheerful, & can't help it; & I hope you & the rest of you are also very cheerful & can't help it.

I like my lawyers very much. Mr. Stern says our case will not be handled as he would handle the case of an ordinary bankrupt, but that my world-wide reputation will be considered all the time, & no move made which can be open to any man's criticism as a departure from the highest standard of honor; that my children's & grand-children's & great-grand-children's heritage in my reputation will be considered, & regarded as the most important interest involved; that we will pay 100 cents on the dollar, but will adopt the wisest & best way to accomplish this.

However, that isn't what makes me so extravagantly cheerful; but another thing: an offer from Harpers for Joan which is pretty nearly satisfactory. I shall think it over, & I may end by accepting it. The Century would give more, I think.

We are just leaving, now, for Fairhaven.

With lots of love, my darling—

SAML

P. S. Mr. Rogers inclines to want the Harper offer accepted.

Mark's very human inclination to interpret the whole episode of the bankruptcy as a tug-of-war or game of wits between himself and his masterful champion, Henry Rogers, on the one side, and the creditors on the other, deeply troubled Livy. The following letter clearly explains her attitude, particularly when she writes, with an irony so dry as to be almost unconscious: "You say Mr Rogers has said some caustic and telling things to the creditors. . . . I should think it was the creditors place to say caustic things to us."

HOTEL BRIGHTON, 218 RUE DE RIVOLI. PARIS.

July 31st 1894

YOUTH DARLING: We came back from Fontainbleau today. We did hate to leav that lovely spot. It was simply charming there. Susy enjoyed it very much. She has rather dreaded having our travels end, and so have I, for that matter still I believe I shall be glad to get settled in Etretat.

We arrived here a little before one today. We went out this afternoon to get our cup of tea and while we were taking it Miss Dater came into the Café where we were. She had just returned from Etretat, and she told Susy it was perfectly lovely down there. I have been careful not to say one single encouraging thing about the place, but have put forward every-thing that could strike one unpleasantly. The loneliness of the situation of the cottage &c. Thinking it better to let all that was agreable be unexpected to her.

Oh darling, I hope you will be able to come soon. Is this going to be an unadvantageous time for you to do business? I do pray not. Is the weather so hot that every one is out of town. I feel that I can not wait while you are waiting for other people. Couldn't you put the work in Mr. Geo. Warner's hands. That is if you find that now is not a good time for you to do it.

In a letter which I rec'd today Sue says that they do not yet know whether you are in America or not.

You say that Mr Rogers wanted to ask the creditors 25 cents and that you felt that .20 was enough for Puddin' head Wilson. In that case if I were over there I should probably ask them .10 or .15 What we want is to have those creditors get all their money out of Webster & Co. and surely we want to aid them all that is possible. Oh my darling we want those debts paid and we want to treat them all not only honestly but we want to help them in every possible way. It is money honestly owed and I cannot quite understand the tone which both you & Mr Rogers seem to take— in fact I cannot understand it at all. You say Mr Rogers has said some caustic and telling things to the creditors. (I do not know what your wording was) I should think it was the creditors place to say caustic things to us.

My darling I cannot have any thing done in my name that I should not approve. I feel that we owe those creditors not only the money but our most sincere apologies that we are not able to pay their bills when they fall due. When these bills are all paid, as they of course will be, I do not want the creditors to feel that we have in any way acted sharply or unjustly or ungenerously with them. I want them to realize & know, that we had their interest at heart, more, much more than we had our own. You know my darling, *now* is the time for you to add to or mar the good name that you have made. Do not for one moment [let] your sense of our need of money get advantage of your sense of justice & generosity. Dear sweet darling heart! You will not throw this asside thinking that I do not understand will you? You will always consider at every proposition whether it is one that I would approve will you not?

How fine the mention is of your defense of Hariet Shelly. I am *delighted* that it has rec'd its merrited praise. I like it so *very* much. The magazine has come to Susy & now tonight I am going to reread the article.[4]

Mr Warner's Golden House I like very much. It will and[5] tellingly I think. We bought a cope of the magazine as ours did not come. I hope the Eng. number will soon be here. Will you make inquiries about it? Come back soon my own darling: you are unspeakably dear to me—So is your honor above every thing else. Don't fail to write me freely about everything, machine & all.

We start for Etretat at noon tomorrow.

[4] "In Defence of Harriet Shelley" appeared in the *North American Review*, July, September 1894. The praise here mentioned must have been quoted in a letter now lost, but to a second letter of July 26 he appended: "P.S. My! but I get lots of nice compliments upon the Shelley article. Even from hardened politicians, like the Secretary of the Navy."

[5] *Sic.* Charles Dudley Warner's *The Golden House* appeared in book form in 1895.

Good night yours in the deepest love of my heart

LIVY L. C.

P.S. This poem which was in the "Critic" the other day ex-
presses exactly what I feel for you and more finely & truly than
I can ever hope to do it.

> The night has a thousand eyes
> And the day but one
> But the light of the whole world dies
> With the setting sun.
>
> The mind has a thousand eyes
> And the heart but one
> But the light of the whole life dies
> When love is done.

This was the well-known poem "Light" by Francis W. Bour-
dillon, first published in 1878.

The following letter to Livy concerns Mark's dealings with the
House of Harper respecting the publication of *Joan of Arc.*
J. Henry Harper ("Harry") later set down his memories of Mark
Twain in the autobiographical *I Remember,* in 1934. Henry Mills
Alden was the veteran editor of *Harper's Magazine.* To Livy on
July 31 her husband wrote: "Their offer was $5,000 for this first
part of Joan (in case I carried the work no further before next
April.) That would be only $75 per 1,000 words. I told them
frankly that I thought it rather a slim price; so they urged me to
appoint day & place & Harry Harper would come & see me & dis-
cuss the matter; but I couldn't make an appointment, but said I
would call on *him* when I got a chance." This then was the
expected meeting.

THE PLAYERS, NEW YORK. *Aug.* 5/94.

Livy darling, I went to Harper's Friday afternoon to take Joan
away, but I found Harry Harper there; & he is a very lovely man
& we came to an understanding in five minutes. Then he wanted
me to go home with him—down on the seashore on Long Island
—& I have been there ever since till a few minutes ago. It is a

charming family, & I am to let them know when you come, so that they can know you. They are very fond of the Huttons. They have several children; among them a daughter 18 or 20 years old & a son about to enter Harvard. I have work to do or I would have staid a day or two longer. Besides, I want to be in reach of Mr. Rogers; for I have a strong hope that if Broughton arrives to-night (as is expected), we can get through in time for me to sail next Saturday.

When I sail, a Harper artist will be cabled to come down from Paris to Etretat & get my (your views) views about the illustrations for Joan.

Harry Harper is open & honest & frank; & was not afraid to tell me (after I said I couldn't quite afford to let the book go at the terms offered) that he was charmed with the book & that Alden would be deeply disappointed if it was allowed to slip out of his hands.

I said the terms were plenty liberal enough if we succeeded in keeping the authorship secret; but that if the secret got out & my name had to go to it, I thought 25 or 30 per cent ought to be added to the price (Puddn'head Wilson terms). So we settled on that, without any trouble. He wants me to write some articles.

And now I've come back here & there ain't no letter from you— which I am disappointed; but I ain't complaining, dearheart. I love you too well; it is my only fault.

SAML

On August 28 Clemens joined his family at Etretat, in Normandy; with the coming of autumn they migrated to Paris. That winter saw the completion of *Joan*, and the final interment of all hopes for the typesetter. In early March Clemens was back in the United States—looking after the shattered fragments of his fortune, closing arrangements with Major Pond for the worldwide lecture tour by which he hoped to repay the creditors, and briefly revisiting the old home in Hartford, pungent with memories of happier days. The upsurge of national pride which Clemens always felt when he first set foot on American soil is worth remarking.

AT HOME, HARTFORD, *Mch.* 20/95

Livy darling, when I arrived in town I did not want to go near the house, & I didn't want to go anywhere or see anybody. I said to myself, "If I may be spared it I will never live in Hartford again."

But as soon as I entered this front door I was siezed with a furious desire to have us all in this house again & right away, & never go outside the grounds any more forever—certainly never again to Europe.

How ugly, tasteless, repulsive, are all the domestic interiors I have ever seen in Europe compared with the perfect taste of this ground floor, with its delicious dream of harmonious color, & its all-pervading spirit of peace & serenity & deep contentment. You did it all, & it speaks of you & praises you eloquently & unceasingly. It is the loveliest home that ever was. I had no faintest idea of what it was like. I *supposed* I had, for I have seen it in its wraps & disguises several times in the past three years; but it was a mistake; I had wholly forgotten its olden aspect. And so, when I stepped in at the front door & was suddenly confronted by all its richness & beauty minus wraps & concealments, it almost took my breath away. Katy had every rug & picture and ornament & chair exactly where they had always belonged, the place was bewitchingly bright & splendid & homelike & natural, & it seemed as if I had burst awake out of a hellish dream, & had never been away, & that you would come drifting down out of those dainty upper regions with the little children tagging after you.

Your rocking chair (formerly Mother's) was in its place, & Mrs. Alice[6] tried to say something about it but broke down.

March 21 (Uncle Joe's)

I was to dine there at 6:30—& did. It was their first day, & their first meal. I was there first, & received them. Then John sent in the roses & your card, which touched Mrs. Alice to the depths. Good-bye dear sweetheart, good-bye.

SAML

[6] Alice Day, who with her husband John had leased the Clemens house. Livy's mother had died in 1890.

P.S. Hartford is resounding with a thundering roar of welcome for you & the children—for I have spread it around that you are coming to America in May. Words cannot describe how worshipfully & enthusiastically you are loved in this town; & the wash of the wave reaches even to me, because I belong to you; it would wash to your dog, if you had a dog. I avoid everybody. I traveled from Joe's to Main street in the electric car with Sam Dunham & never let on that I saw him. Some hours later I returned over the whole distance with him & never let on. He & a lady & I were the last ones left in the car, & as I was following them out he turned & recognized me. Why, his touching & flooding outpouring of welcome & delight was the most moving thing I ever saw. And his beaming face—& his caressing great hands—well, you should have seen it, if you like being overcome.

I have made up my mind to one thing: if we go around the world we will move into our house when we get back; if we don't go around the world we will move in when the Days' time is up.

I can't describe to you how poor & empty & offensive [Europe] France is, compared to America—in my eyes. The minute I strike America I seem to wake out of an odious dream.

The Twichells are lovely—but you knew that. They claim Susy & Clara for a limitless visit; they even want them to go to the Adirondacks with them. The Days require a visit, too. I say *you* can't visit anybody, but they may have the elder girls. You will stay in New York till that doctor leaves in July. He has got to cure you.

Good-bye my darling, I shall leave for New York now. This is nearly the last letter I'll write you—possibly the last—don't know.

SAML

The Twichells send worlds of love; Mrs. Whitmore also. Our Katy is the same old Katy. She won't stay with the Days, because with "the family" not here she would be so homesick she couldn't stand it.

At the end of the month Clemens sailed back, to fetch his family home in May. Helen Keller, the marvelous blind girl now fourteen years old, wrote on her new script typewriter to her friend Mrs. Dodge, March 29, that on the previous Sunday in company with her teacher, at Laurence Hutton's she had met for the first time Mark Twain and William Dean Howells: "Mr. Clemens told us many entertaining stories, & made us laugh till we cried. He told us he was going back to Europe this week to bring his wife & daughter back to America because his daughter, who is a schoolgirl in Paris, had learned so much in three years & a half that if he did not bring her home she would soon know more than he did. I think 'Mark Twain' is a very appropriate nom de plume for Mr. Clemens because it has a funny & quaint sound that goes well with his amusing writings, & its nautical significance suggests the deep & beautiful things he has written."

CHAPTER SEVENTEEN

Heartbreak

SAILING for home in May 1895, the Clemenses spent the early
summer at Quarry Farm, preparing for the world lecture tour
that Mark Twain had dreaded so long but foreseen as necessary
to clear his debts. In mid-July the parents accompanied by Clara,
set forth for Vancouver and thence to Australia, New Zealand,
India, and South Africa. According to plan, Susy and Jean would
rejoin the family in England a year and a month later, in August
1896.

Susy, now aged twenty-three, decided to stay behind at Quarry
Farm because an Italian singing teacher had advised her "to live
on a hill . . . and gather vigor of body," preparatory to studying
for grand opera in Paris, and it was decided that Jean as the
youngest would keep her company and go to school. Though
intensely proud of being "Mark Twain's daughter," Susy was
driven by ambition to become a celebrity in her own right, and
European teachers had flattered her by praising a good soprano
voice. Beyond doubt she was a girl of considerable talent, much
adored, petted, encouraged by this singularly affectionate and
loyal family—both parents and sisters always casting her in the
role of youthful star. In her teens she had written and acted in
neighborhood plays, composed verse, carried around "a vast
Shakespeare," and begun a precocious biography of her father
which years later he interwove lovingly with his *Autobiography*.

Volatile, charming, impractical about time and money, averse
to routine and steady habits, she had pined under the first
separation from her family as a freshman at Bryn Mawr, and
developed thenceforth a state of poor health which Clemens
ascribed to those six months of tearful homesickness. From both
parents she inherited a precarious nervous balance. In old age

her father, ever prompt in self-accusation, is reported to have said gloomily to a friend that two such hypersensitive people should never have had children.

Recognizing that Susy's malady had roots which in today's vocabulary would be called psychosomatic, Clemens sought to interest her in mental healing. He had hopes that the same therapy might benefit Livy. In 1894, as has been seen, at instigation largely of George Warner, he invoked a New York practitioner to cure a persistent cough and also *pour encourager les autres*. And so in the winter of 1895-96, when threatened apparently by another of those illnesses which visited Susy when she was separated from her family, she resorted determinedly to the mind cure. Her father wrote approvingly to her, alluding by contrast to some of his own recent mishaps:

CALCUTTA, *February 7, 1896*

Mamma is busy with my pen, declining invitations. And all because we haven't you or Miss Foote or Miss Davis here to argue some of our stupid foolishnesses out of us and replace them with healthy thoughts—and by consequence physical soundness. I caught cold last night, coming from Benares, and am shut up in the hotel starving it out; and so, instead of river parties and dinners and things, all three of us must decline and stay at home. It is too bad—yes, and too ridiculous. I am perfectly certain that the exasperating colds and the carbuncles came from a diseased mind, and that your mental science could drive them away, if we only had one of you three here to properly apply it. I have no language to say how glad and grateful I am that you are a convert to that rational and noble philosophy. Stick to it; don't let anybody talk you out of it. Of all earthly fortune it is the best, and most enriches the possessor. I always believed, in Paris, that if you could only get back to America and examine that system with your clear intellect you would see its truth and be saved—permanently saved from the ills which persecute life and make it a burden. Do convey my deep gratitude to Miss Davis and Miss Foote—I owe them a debt which would beggar my vocabulary in the expression and still leave the debt nine-tenth unpaid.

Miss Davis, Lilly Foote, and George and Lilly Warner were the chief enthusiasts whose disciple Susy quickly became, the latter chiefly after she went to Hartford in the summer of 1896 for a long visit with George's brother and sister-in-law, the Charles Dudley Warners.

Shortly before time for Susy and Jean and their faithful maid Katy Leary to sail for England to meet the senior Clemenses and Clara arriving there the first of August, Susy fell gravely ill, with high fever, prostration, and a distraught manner forecasting the onset of delirium. Overriding at last her stubborn refusal to see a doctor, Katy summoned the family physician, Dr. Porter, who diagnosed spinal meningitis. The first intimation by letter of her illness alarmed the Clemenses, and when an exchange of cablegrams failed completely to reassure, Livy and Clara sailed from Southampton on August 15, leaving Mark behind. He had rented a small house at Guildford, but was dissatisfied with it and hoped to find better quarters against their return. The next day he wrote anxiously to Livy.

GUILDFORD, *Sunday noon, Aug.* 16/96

My darling, you were in my mind till I went to sleep last night, & there when I woke this morning, & you have been there ever since—you have not been out of it a single waking moment since you disappeared from my vision. I hope you are not sad to-day but I am afraid you are. You & Clara are making the only sad voyage of all the round-the-world trip. I am not demonstrative; I am always hiding my feelings; but my heart was wrung yesterday. I could not tell you how deeply I loved you nor how grieved I was for you, nor how I pitied you in this awful trouble that my mistakes have brought upon you. You forgive me, I know, but I shall never forgive myself while the life is in me. If you find our poor little Susie in the state I seem to foresee, your dear head will be grayer when I see it next. (Be good and get well, Susy dear, don't break your mother's heart.) I was thinking in bed this morning, that the calamity that comes [is always the last] is never the one we had prepared ourselves for.

I took Mr. Smythe to luncheon at the hotel; & we left for Guildford at 2. I was so fagged & so distraught that I forgot to send the cablegram; but that was no matter. We walked to the P. O. here & got it off before 4; and besides I wanted to see about my cable address anyway—which I did; in future it is simply *"Clemens Guildford."*

I sent a postcard to Chatto[1] saying Come Monday as arranged; & one to the agents at Weybridge saying I was remaining here & would watch for the table-ware. I will send a line to the terrible Miss Hawdon today to say you are gone [&]—I don't know what else.

I told Emily about that little bill that is to be paid; she knew the name. (I am writing on my knee.) I wore my slippers last night in tramping about in my shirt. Mr. Smythe & I played billiards till midnight, & I gave him the pyjamas that had not been worn. He has gone to London and will be back at 6:30 with his things. Satan (the cat) came in early by the window & took a nap. Package of photos arrived from France this morning for Clara. Emily has the key of the trunk room. Your note from the ship came this morning. I will remember, dear heart, about Emily's day out, Thursday 26th.

Monday noon. Chatto is evidently off on his vacation. I do not hear from him.

I enclose a letter received this morning, about the photos. It has no signature, but I suppose it is from Miss Blood—so I have answered it.

The maids are excellent. They do everything necessary for Mr. Smythe & me, & keep the house in nice order.

(Susy dear I hope you are well [this day] & in no pain; that will make Mamma happy. You have had a bitter affliction, poor child.)

It was very cold last night. I had to get an extra blanket & close the window. The extra blanket was your fancy cloak that you left hanging on the bath-room door. I am sorry you left that & the gray shawl—you would need them at sea.

This pen was leaking through the barrel, but I have pasted postage-stamp borders around it & I think it is cured.

Livy darling, you are so good & dear & steadfast & fine—the highest & finest & loveliest character I have ever known; & I was never worthy of you. You should have been the prize of a better

---

[1] His London publisher.

man—a man up nearer your own level. But I love you with all
my heart, from my proper place at your feet.

SAML

P. P. S. *Chatto has come.*

P. S. I mail this to-day for the New York, & will mail another
line tomorrow for the Wednesday steamer.

In Hartford meanwhile Susy had been moved to the Clemens'
old home on Farmington Avenue, and there she paced the floor
in a raging fever, often taking pen and paper to scribble those
notes in a large sometimes incoherent hand which her father
mentions poignantly in the letter below. She fancied that her
companion was La Malibran, famous Parisian mezzo-soprano who
had died sixty years before, at only little more than Susy's age—
after days of terrible suffering from an accident in which she had
been thrown by a horse. "My benefactress Mme Malibran Now
I can better hold you," wrote the dying girl in Hartford. ". . . In
strength I bow to Mme Malibran Mr. Clemens Mr. Zola . . . to
me darkness must remain from everlasting to everlasting. Forever
sometimes less painful darkness but darkness is the complement of
light yes tell her to say she trusts you child of great darkness and
light to me who can keep the darkness universal and free from
sensual taint and lead her on to strength & power & peace. . . .
You will never follow far enough in her footsteps artistically to
dominate the artistic world with light. Would exclude you therefore from all dominance? This is the arrogance which the Lord
alone may hold." And then the infection crept deeper into her
brain and she could no longer see. "I am blind, Uncle Charlie,
and you are blind," she told her uncle at the bedside. Feeling
for Katy Leary's face she put her burning hands upon it and
said, "Mamma." But her mother was still in midocean on the
evening of August 18 when Susy died. Clemens was told immediately by cable; his wife and Clara sailed on for three more
days in newsless anxiety.

Brooding over his almost insupportable loss, Clemens' mind
played him some strange tricks. A passage early in the next letter
suggests that by a fantastic chain of logic he saw Annie Moffett's
marriage twenty years before to Charles L. Webster as having led

to creation of the Webster publishing company, thence to the
bankruptcy of 1894, and that in turn to the global lecture tour—
which left Susy behind (at her own request) and presumably
neglected. Thus the concatenation of disaster.

Aug. 19–6 P.M.

I have spent the day alone—thinking; sometimes bitter
thoughts, sometimes only sad ones. Reproaching myself for laying
the foundation of all our troubles and this final disaster in oppos-
ing Pamela when she did not want Annie to marry that Webster
adventurer. Reproaching myself for a million things whereby I
have brought misfortune & sorrow to this family. And I have been
re-reading Sue's[2] letter received day before yesterday, & written
three days & a half after Susy's attack of mania; reading it and
feeling so thankful that you & Clara went; for I read it with a
new light, now & perceive that it has warnings in it that were not
before apparent. Yes, & I have been searching for letters—fruit-
lessly. I have no letter that Susy wrote me—oh, not so much as a
line. Sue says that in our house after they took her there she was
up & dressed and writing all the time—poor troubled head! I
hope they have kept every scrap; for they must often have suspected that these were the last things that would flow from that
subtle brain. I know that if they are there you will find them. I
wish she had written something to me—but I did not deserve it.
You did, but I did not. You always wrote her, over burdened
with labors as you were—you the most faithful, the most loyal
wife, mother, friend in the earth—but I neglected her as I neglect
everybody in my selfishness. Everybody but you. I have always
written to you; for you are always in my heart, always in my mind.

Think of it—if she had lived & *remained* demented. For Dr.
Stearns once told me that for a person whose reason is once
really dethroned there is no recovery, no restoration. Poor child,
her [calamity] stroke was brief, not lingering & awful like Winny
Howells's.[3] The beautiful fabric of her mind did not crumble to
slow ruin, its light was not smothered in slow darkness, but passed

---

[2] Susan Crane.
[3] Winifred Howells, daughter of Mark Twain's friend, had died in March 1889
after protracted illness and confinement in a sanitarium.

swiftly out in a disordered splendor. These are mercies. They will help us to bear what has befallen.

It rains all day—no, drizzles, & is sombre & dark. I would not have it otherwise. I could not welcome the sun today.

Shall I write again to you, I wonder. The letter would not reach you; for now there is no need to stay in America; there is but one thing to do—hide in an English village away from the sight of the human face. I think you will sail Sept. 2. I shall know presently. Though I do wish you would see that doctor in New York & take his treatment.

If I were only with you—to be near with my breast and my sheltering arms when the ship lands & Charley's [sobs] tears reveal all without his speaking.

I love you, my darling—I wish you could have been spared this unutterable sorrow.

SAMUEL

P. S.

Aug. 19.

Oh, my heart-broken darling—no, not heart-broken yet, for you still do not know—but what tidings are in store for you! What a bitter world, what a shameful world it is. Yesterday we were playing billiards, here, & laughing & chatting; & you & Clara at sea were planning to take this or that or the other Hartford train according to possibilities, & conjecturing & forecasting as to how soon you could get our poor little Susy out of Hartford & on board a ship; & at the very same hour that we four were doing these things Sue and Charley were saying in whispers, "She is passing away"—and presently, "All is over." O my God! My darling I will not say to you the things that are in my heart & on my tongue—they are better left unsaid. [Why are *you* visited with this calamity]

Later. I had just sent away a cheerful letter to you about the Joan reviews & such light matters when the cablegram was put into my hands in which Charley and Sue said our poor child had been "released." It was a shock. I was not dreaming of it. It seemed to make me reel. I loved Susy, loved her dearly; but I did not know how deeply, before. But—while the tears gushed

I was still able to say "My grief is for the mother—for myself I am thankful; my selfish love aside, I would not have it otherwise."

You will see her. Oh, I wish I could see her, and caress the unconscious face & kiss the unresponding lips—but I would not bring her back—no, not for the riches of a thousand worlds. She has found the richest gift that this world can offer; I would not rob her of it.

Be comforted, my darling—we shall have *our* release in time. Be comforted, remembering how much hardship, grief, pain, she is spared; & that her heart can never be broken, now, for the loss of a child.

How you wrought for her! how you gave yourself to her, night & day, at cost of strength & sleep; how faithful you were to her; you did all for her that a mother could do for a child, you were all to her that a mother could be; let it assuage your grief to know that you have nothing to reproach yourself with.

I seem to see her in her coffin—I do not know in which room. In the library, I hope; for there she & Ben & I mostly played when we were children together & happy. I wish there were five of the coffins, side by side; out of my heart of hearts I wish it. You & Jean & Charley & Sue & all of you will be in that room together next Sunday, with our released & happy Susy (& no unrelated person but Katy)—& I not there in the body—but in the spirit, yes. How lovely is death; & how niggardly it is doled out.

She died in our own house—not in another's; died where every little thing was familiar & beloved; died where she had spent all her life till my crimes made her a pauper & an exile. How good it is that she got home again.

The maids [know] seem to suspect that something is the matter, & they pursue me with gentle offers of service; & with tenders of luncheon; & so on; & Emily has been in here again, after all these declinations, & mutely set a decanter of port wine & some biscuits close in front of me. And I think Smythe suspects, because I would not go to luncheon. I am shut up in the morning room. I will go to dinner this evening I think.

Livy darling I do pity you—& you have all my love. But how fortunate is our poor Susy.

SAML

GUILDFORD, *Friday Aug.* 21 [1896]

Oh, poor Livy darling, at 8 tomorrow morning your heart will break, the Lord God knows I am pitying you. Smythe & I have done what we could—cabled Mr. Rogers to have Dr. Rice at the ship & keep all other friends prudently out of sight—for if you saw them on the dock you would *know*; and you would swoon before Rice could get to you to help you.

Hour by hour my sense of the calamity that has over-taken us closes down heavier & heavier upon me; & now for 48 hours there is a form of words that runs in my head with ceaseless iteration—without stop or pause—"I shall never see her again, I shall never see her again." *You* will see the sacred face once more—I am so thankful for that.

But though my heart *break* I will still say she was fortunate; & I would not call her back if I could.

I eat—because you wish it; I go on living—because you wish it; I play billiards, and billiards, & billiards, till I am ready to drop—to keep from going mad with grief & with resentful thinkings.

You will find my health perfect—for your sake—when you come.

I know where you will be, tomorrow and Sunday, & in spirit I shall be at your side & taking step by step with you.

Give my love to Clara & Jean. We have that much of our fortune left.

I love you with all my whole heart.

SAML

GUILDFORD, *Aug.* 25/96

Livy darling, Your cablegram came yesterday asking after my health. I was unspeakably glad to get it, for it swept away a fast-growing burden of apprehension concerning your own state; I judged that its inner meaning was a message to me to say "Do not be uneasy about me."

I meant to write you a line yesterday, but we were house-hunting; & my heart was to heavy to write. And then there was an incident that smote me hard. One of the examined houses pleased me very greatly because of its *neighborhood*—the cheery & bright

& homy look of the dwellings. Unconsciously I was saying to myself "There will be plenty of young life here for Susy." That
thought was singing & purring in my head for half an hour—not
articulate, you understand, but the unformulated thought—
before it burst upon me "Oh, my God, *she* will never need it."

I will not write more now, Mr. Smythe is waiting; we are going
to Godalming to look at a house. I love you with all my whole
heart, darling.

SAML

P. S. Take the heart-treatment in N. Y.—& cable me that you
are doing it.

This new sorrow brought back to mind his grief nearly forty
years ago, when his favorite brother Henry was scalded to death
in the *Pennsylvania* steamboat explosion.

GUILDFORD, Aug. 26/96

I know what misery is, at last, my darling. I know what I shall
suffer when you die. I see, now, that I have never known sorrow
before, but only some poor modification of it. In Henry's case
I would not allow myself to think of my loss, lest the burden be
too heavy to bear; but in poor Susy's case I have no disposition or
desire to put it out of my mind—I seem to want to think of it
all the time. For the present the zest of life is gone from me, which
is natural. I have *hated* life before—from the time I was 18—but I
was not indifferent to it. Mind, I am not always dully indifferent
now, in these heavy days. No, my mood changes; changes to fury,
& I [vomit blasphemies] rage until I get a sort of relief.

Only eight days ago she was a part of us; and now—

If I suffer so much, what *must* it be with you; for my capacity
for suffering bears no comparison to yours.

No letters have come—not a line since Jean's of the 8th and 9th
& Sue's of the 11th. They *must* have written after that & before
you sailed; & surely they would write *me* after you sailed. I was
sure I should get letters yesterday or to-day—surely I shall not
be disappointed tomorrow.

Our daily life goes on by unchanging routine. Mr. Smythe
takes his bath at 8; I take mine at 8:30 & shave; breakfast (with

fish or meat) at 9; the newspaper for a quarter of an hour; then
a walk of miles through the town & the beautiful outskirts, from
two to three hours, & get back at lunch-time or a shade later;
after lunch, billiards & reading—my reading being the letters,
often—the letters that came from Sue & Jean & Charley, and
which *now* mean so much, so *much*! after dinner, billiards till
1 A.M., or a trifle earlier if Smythe finds he is no longer able to
stand up. I get so tired that in bed if I drive poor Susy out of
my mind I go to sleep at once. I do not wake until I am called.
O, I love you, dear heart.

SAML

After dinner—8:45. Mr. Smythe has gone up to lie down & try
to get rid of a headache, & I am alone with my memories of the
Light that Failed. I enclose a paragraph which Mr. Smythe told
you he would send you. It gave me a pang to read it, because it
reminded me that in all these years I have never wholly ceased
to hope that some day Susy would take up my biography again.
That is, I kept up a vague hope that she might take to making
occasional notes and that my death would bring back the lost
interest in the matter & that she would then write the book. So
another of my ambitions is laid to rest. It has gone the way of all
the others.

I find I cannot write. It is so soon after dinner that my words
clog and will not flow.

Noon, Friday. There is yet time to add a line before posting
this for tomorrow's steamer.

No letter from Hartford yesterday, from any relative or friend!
I do not know how to describe my disappointment. Sue, & Jean,
& Lilly Warner all believed, up to noon of Saturday the 15th, that
you were going to remain here. Did they imagine that you would
be content with a letter a week? I am amazed. Letters written
any day for [six] 7 days—those tremendous days!—from Sue's last
letter (11th) to the evening of the 18th—that disastrous day, that
day of imperishable memory!—would all have been in my hands
by now. *But there is not one line.* Forasmuch as you had sailed,
did those friends think none was left behind who would care to

know the pathetic details of those last days? I get a cablegram which I am wholly unprepared for—a message which strikes like a sword: "Susy could not stand brain congestion and meningitis and was peacefully released to-day"—& I sit back & try to believe that there are any human beings in the world, friends or foes, civilized or savage, who would close their lips *there*, & leave me these many, many, many days eating my heart out with longings for the tidings that never come.

Only one individual in all America has sent me a line, either of news or regret. It is a word of sympathy from—Harper & Brothers. It came this morning when I was watching for the postman. I thank *them*—& out of my heart I do it.

I have not a word of blame for aunt Sue—her heart & her hands were full. I have only gratitude for her. But I think that Jean could have remembered me. Or Katy, or Twichell, or somebody.

I love you with all my heart, my darling.

SAML

GUILDFORD, *Aug.* 29/96

I wonder if she left any little message for me, any little mention, showing that she thought of me. I was not deserving of it, I had not earned it, but if there was any such word left behind for me, I hope it was saved up in its exact terms & that I shall get it.

My remorse does not deceive me. I know that if she were back I should soon be as neglectful of her as I was before—it is our way. We think we would do better, because of our lesson. But it is a fallacy. Our natures would go back to what they had always been, & our conduct would obey their commands. My selfishness & indolence would resume their power & I should be no better father to her, no more obliging friend and encourager & helper than I was before. If I could call up a single instance where I laid aside my own projects & desires & put myself to real inconvenience to procure a pleasure for her I would forget all things else to remember that. How *you* gave your whole self to her! how you thought for her, planned for her, worked for her, lavished your capital of physical and mental strength upon her; & did it with

such loving interest in it. Oh, yes, and resumed the service again
& again, when it had apparently failed of its due reward. You
were the best friend she ever had, dear heart, & the steadfastest.
Keep the thought of it in mind, & get from it the solace you have
earned, dear Livy.

Sunday, mid-afternoon, 30th. Not a line yet, not a single line.
It seems as if I cannot bear it.

It is a bleak day, cold and silent—Sundaylike & mournful. I am
by myself, for the long walk has tired Smythe & he went to his
room after luncheon.

Poor Susy, it is now eleven days. "After life's fitful fever she
sleeps well."[4] And will wake no more for me.

> "O for the touch of a vanished hand
> And the sound of a voice that is still."

What a year of disaster it has been. Such a little time ago we had
three daughters, now we have lost two. Susy goes out of our life
to something better; Clara goes out of it to a doubtful change—
and one which I would have prevented if I could have done it.[5]

Day before yesterday we went to the Castle; & it seemed kins-
man to me, for I am a ruin, too. But there was solace for me there,
& healing: for all that danced & were happy in those once sumptuous halls a thousand years ago, & danced & were light of heart,
have gone the way of all that dance & are happy, & in my time I
also shall be set free.

> "And the name of that isle is the Long Ago,
>   And we bury our treasures there:
> There are brows of beauty & bosoms of snow,
> There are heaps of dust—but we loved them so!
>   There are trinkets, and tresses of hair.
> There are fragments of song that nobody sings,
>   And a part of an infant's prayer;
> There are broken vows & pieces of rings,
> There's a lute unswept & a harp without strings,
>   And the garments that *she* used to wear."[6]

[4] These lines adapted from *Macbeth*, III, ii, later were chosen by the grieving
father for Jean Clemens' epitaph.

[5] Probably her intention to study for the concert stage.

[6] Quoted with slight changes from Benjamin F. Taylor's "The Long Ago."

It is an odious world, a horrible world—it is Hell; the true one, not the lying invention of the superstitious; and we have come to it from elsewhere to expiate our sins.

And now what can we do? Where can we go & hide ourselves till we earn release? For what have we further to do with the world?

Within a few days after Susy's funeral in Elmira, the mother and two daughters accompanied by Katy Leary set sail for England. Giving up the house in Guildford, they found a hideaway for the winter in Tedworth Square, Chelsea. Refusing to be comforted, the parents ceased to celebrate Thanksgiving, birthdays, Christmas, and other feast days—not only in the first poignant months of sorrow, but for years afterwards—and never tarried again in Hartford, which to them had become "the city of Heartbreak." This letter written upon a once-joyous anniversary is typical.

LONDON, *Nov.* 27/96

We have lost her, & our life is bitter. We may find her again—let us not despair of it. God knows how much poorer we are by this loss than we were before; but we still have the others, & that is much; & also we have each other, my darling, and this is riches.

This is the blackest birthday you have ever seen: may you never see its mate, dear heart.

With worlds of love,

SAML

During the next four years Mark and Livy were together almost constantly, and always in the shadow of a common grief—which, even by the standards of a devoted family and loss of a favorite child, seems extravagant. These were seasons, spent largely in Vienna and near London, of productivity for Clemens the writer. He told Howells that incessant work was his best medicine "because of the deadness which invaded me when Susy died." But sadly enough his old creative strength was failing, and despite an occasional effort lifted to greatness because it fitted his mood of pessimism—like "The Man that Corrupted Hadleyburg" and drafts of *The Mysterious Stranger*—the margin of unpublishable waste grew enormous.

With the commercial success of *Joan* and *Following the Equator*, Mark's last debts were paid early in 1898 and his prosperity re-established. An incurable speculator, he would promptly have sunk another fortune in an Austrian carpet-pattern machine and a British skim-milk compound called plasmon save for the restraining hand of Henry H. Rogers.

The Clemenses returned to New York in the autumn of 1900 and took a house at 14 West Tenth Street—for a winter season signalizing Mark's return to metropolitan life as a great public figure, speaker and diner-out, perennial guest of honor at the Lotos Club, introducer of young Winston Churchill up from the Boer War, anti-imperialist and single-handed foe of the American Board of Foreign Missions. In June 1901 he moved his family to Ampersand for a summer on Saranac Lake, and in early August left them there to cruise up to Nova Scotia on Henry Rogers' steam yacht the *Kanawha*. But this month was dogged by memories of tragedy.

(*near* BAR HARBOR) BASS'S BAY—*Aug.* 14 [1901]
10 P.M: *at anchor*

Livy darling, I am with you in spirit every hour, now, & I know how you are feeling as these sad anniversaries dawn & drag their course & decay. To-day is one of them—& *I remember*. Your mother-instinct warned you that there was danger & you went to the tragedy fearing it; but I was suspecting nothing, & the awful cablegram found me unprepared, & struck with force unmitigated. I wish I could be with you these days; I know what you are suffering, & although I could do nothing to relieve your pain by words, neighborhood & sympathy would be a help for us both.

Even my speaking these things upon paper may add to your sorrow, & I will refrain & say no more upon the sacred subject—I shall only think, & brood, sending my thoughts through the air & receiving yours in return—as I am doing now.

Goodnight, my darling, with love & kisses.

SAML

In the autumn of 1901 the Clemenses settled in the old Appleton house at Riverdale-on-the-Hudson, meanwhile putting up the
Hartford place for sale. On October 20, in connection with the
Yale Bicentennial, that university conferred honorary doctorates
in letters upon Mark Twain and William Dean Howells.

NEW HAVEN, *Oct.* 22/01

I didn't write last night, Livy darling, for it was 11 when I went
to bed, & I was part tired & part lazy. Breakfast was to be served at
8:45, & I thought I would have plenty of time to write before that
meal, but I slept until 9—then I rushed down unshaven, & was just
in time. The reason I didn't shave was because there was no razor
among my traps. Immediately after breakfast I borrowed the razor
of my fellow-guest, Professor Walton, who is here to represent
Edinburgh University.

The Stokeses are charming. There are three tall unmarried
daughters; the Ilsenberg Stokes is the oldest son—he will be here
tomorrow morning.[7]

The function at 3 yesterday afternoon was the first one requir-
ing gowns & hoods, & is described as being a splendid display of
brilliant colors.

The second one was at 10, this morning; there were to be a lot
of formidable orations, & I didn't go; Walton, his wife, the Stokes
girls & I made a tour of the University buildings, covering two
hours very pleasantly. In the campus a great crowd of students
thundered the Yale cry, closing with "M-a-r-k T-w-a-i-n—Mark
Twain!" & I took off my hat & bowed.

When we got back to the house (12:05) Choate had arrived, &
we went & left cards at President Hadley's house—nobody at
home. So that's done, & I'm glad, because of course I missed his
guest-reception yesterday, & am intending to leave before his
guest-farewell tomorrow, though it may be that I can't do it. The
reception to the President of the U.S. is tomorrow evening, 9 to 10.
Etiquette may require that I remain to that; in which case I shall
not reach Riverdale until some time day after tomorrow (Wednesday) afternoon.

[7] I. N. Phelps Stokes, architect and future author of *The Iconography of Manhattan Island.* He had studied in Germany, living briefly at Ilsenberg in the Harz
mountains in 1891, and may have met the Clemenses during this *wanderjahr.*

Mr. Stokes and Wm. E. Dodge[8] are cousins.

The town is very gay with decorations. The procession last night was prodigiously long, & was picturesque & interesting, but of course not comparable in the latter regard with 1000th anniversary of Heidelberg University—which I didn't see, because of laziness.

I love you dearly, dear heart, & I miss you & the children & Blennerhasset.[9]

SAML

From the windows I see dozens of brilliant gowns walking up & down the street. Some of the foreign ones are like pillars of fire.

The second major grief of the Clemenses came to light shortly after the blow of Susy's death. Jean's erratic behavior and moodiness since her mid-teens was discovered to be a symptom of epilepsy. Repeated attempts at a cure, including a stay in 1899 at the Kellgren sanitarium in Sweden, proved fruitless. A corroding anxiety had come to dwell within the household's daily life. "I wish to learn . . . to keep constantly in mind that she is heavily afflicted by that unearned, undeserved & hellish disease," her father told Clara on October 20, 1905, "& is not strictly responsible for her disposition, & her acts when she is under its influence (if there is ever a time when she is really free from its influence— which is doubtful)." The next letter, addressing the one daughter who increasingly had come to share these family cares, was written home to her at Riverdale while the others visited Susan Crane on the hilltop above Elmira.

QUARRY FARM, *Jan.* 20, 9 P.M. [1902]

Clara dear, Mrs. Clemens is pretty well fagged out, & is lying on the sofa here in the parlor gossiping with Mrs. S. Crane, & has instructed me to write you & say Jean was bad all day long, & until the middle of dinner this evening. She lay in the stateroom on the train all the journey, & was persistently absent. The day's anxiety —not the journey—is what has made your mother so tired; for the day was beautiful & bright, the spread of fields & hills pure

---

[8] Head of Phelps, Dodge & Co., the large mining concern.
[9] Current favorite among the cats.

white with unmarred snow, the car nearly empty, & delightfully quiet. Jean is very nearly herself, now, & is out talking with the servants. The pallor in her face has been replaced by color. She is out there talking about the dog. She has no commerce with me —I am not yet forgiven about the dog.

This region is sumptuously clothed in snow, & is very beautiful under the moonlight; the town-lights make as fine a picture as ever. This yard glows with intense sparks, fascinating to the eye & the spirit—facets of snow smitten by the moonbeams. Mrs. Crane & Mrs. Clemens your mother are still gossiping & happy—skinning the Elmirians.

Uncle Cholley & Aunt Ida received us at the station with a very heart-warming welcome. We came up the hill in gubernatorial style in fine sleighs.

[*postscript by Olivia Clemens*]

Jan 21st

Good morning Clara darling I shall write you today.

Jean is better but not well

I *adore* you

        Yours

                MOTHER

Letters from Livy in these last years are very few. Among the Mark Twain Papers is a single sheet, written on both sides in pencil as if in haste. It is exceedingly characteristic of what Livy's critics call her exercise of censorship and her partisans regard as her loving solicitude that in all public relations he put his best foot forward. The date is lacking; it was probably left on his desk or work-table as a reminder more earnest than spoken words. The occasion also seems unknown to Mark Twain biography. About Marie Van Vorst (1867-1936) Mark seems to have written—and probably at Livy's instance suppressed—an unkind letter to the newspapers. She was a prolific lightweight American poet, novelist, and feature writer for magazines. Her first publication was a poem in *Scribner's Magazine* in 1893, but she did not become well known until some years later, after publishing in 1901 (with Bessie Van Vorst) *Bagsby's Daughter,* an independent effort in 1902 called *Philip Longstreth,* and in the following year a serial report

on the working girl, "The Woman Who Toils," which ran in
Everybody's Magazine before appearing as a book. Whatever
Mark's quarrel with her, it probably boiled up quickly and spent
itself with the catharsis of self-expression, as was his tempera-
mental habit. And Livy's message mirroring her distress over the
incident could not but have been a powerful deterrent.

Youth darling, have you forgotten your promise to me? You said
that I was constantly in your mind and that you knew what I would
like & you *would not* publish what I would disapprove. Did you
think I would approve the letter to Marie van Vorst?

I am absolutely wretched today on account of your state of
mind—your state of intellect. Why don't you let the better side of
you work? Your present attitude will do more harm than good.
You go too far, much too far in all you say, & if you write in the
same way as you have in this letter people forget the cause for it &
remember only the hateful manner in which it was said. *Do* darling
change your mental attitude, *try to change* it. The trouble is you
don't want to. When you asked me to try mental science I tried it
& I keep trying it. Where is the mind that wrote the Prince & P.
Jeanne d'Arc, The Yankee &c &c &c. Bring it back! You can if you
will—if you wish to. Think of the side I know, the sweet dear,
tender side—that I love so. Why not show this more to the world?
Does it help the world to always rail at it? There is great & noble
work being done, why not sometimes recognize that? Why always
dwell on the evil until those who live beside you are crushed to
the earth & you seem almost like a monomaniac. Oh! I love you
so & wish you would listen & take heed. Yours

LIVY

In the years following Susy's death Mark's interest in mental
healing continued, and he was still willing under many conditions
to grant its efficacy. But between the date of his bantering articles
on Christian Science in the *Cosmopolitan* in 1899 and his book
on that subject in 1907 his attitude toward Mrs. Eddy and her
methods hardened into hostility and so remained until his death.
For what seems to be his final word on this controversial subject,
see his letter of August 7, 1909, to J. Wylie Smith, first correctly
printed by De Voto, *The Portable Mark Twain* (1946), p. 786.

The next few months, from spring through early summer, were the last tranquil ones enjoyed by the Clemens household. Jean's condition grew no worse, and Livy's always precarious health appeared to hold its own. Prosperity continued, and the Hudson River place they liked—for its country aspect, and easy access to New York, inviting a steady stream of old friends for dinner and week-ends. On March 13 Clemens left New York for Florida, by train, in order to take a Caribbean cruise on Rogers's yacht the *Kanawha* with his fellow-Missourian the politician "Czar" Reed, Dr. Rice, Laurence Hutton and others.

ROYAL POINCIANA, PALM BEACH, FLA.
Sunday, March 16/02

Livy darling, the whole multitude in this vast hotel wear Panama hats—& there isn't one among them that is as fine as the one I left at Riverdale. I did not remember that I had such a thing until Rice inquired after it. He has lent me a nice soft hat to use until I can buy a straw.

Yesterday was a most trying day; from 9:30 A.M. until 6 P.M. through midsummer weather of an exhausting sort. We got the trunks right away; & as every room has a bath we were soon scoured-up and refreshed; dressed for dinner & went down in a body, we 7, & sat at one round table. There were 150 similar round tables in *our part* of the dining room, & more than 200 glimpsable in the other part of it. When the dining room is full there are 2,500 persons present. The hotel corridors afford fine perspectives —in fact about three times that of St. Peters at Rome, where the people furthest away look like children. One of these corridors, they say, is 1700 feet long. Of course this is the largest hotel in the world.

After dinner I went at once to bed & to sleep. Joe Jefferson sent up his card & a note this forenoon, & presently followed in person & visited half an hour with us. We are to go on an excursion with him in a steam launch at 3 this afternoon. He is a dear. You might send his card to Miss Harrison;[10] it is an autograph, but not a signature.

We are just back (1:30 P.M.), from a two-hour excursion in wheel-chairs of willow, driven by negro power—the negro

[10] Henry Rogers' secretary.

is behind you, & the thing is a 3-wheeled, rubber-tyred bicycle. It makes great speed. We visited the crocodile pools & the ostrich farm—& saw an ostrich sit down & lay an egg. Few tourists have seen *that*. One ostrich is named for Mr. Cleveland, & another for me. It was Mrs. Cleveland that laid the egg.

We saw no country around the world whose aspects & vegetation are more tropical than this.

It is expected that the yacht will reach Miami to-night. As soon as she reports by telegram, we shall join her. It is even possible that she may come to *this* place, & get us.

Livy dear, send letters to me

 % H. H. Rogers,
 The West India Oil Refining Co.
 Havana, Cuba.

That seems the only way thus far discovered, to reach us.

I do hope you are not lonely, dear heart, & that life & the world are not all black to you. It seems a century since I left home. Children! make your mother's days a pleasure to her.

 With great love to you all

 SAML.

I'm inquiring about the Hot Springs. We will go there when I get back.

P.S. I sent you a telegram from the Ponce de Leon, & hoped for a wire from you here, but it hasn't come yet.

 [*off* MIAMI, FLORIDA]
 March 19? [1902]
 At Anchor—waiting

Livy darling, we did not get away this morning, but are lying far out in a brilliant & beautiful light green sea, the loveliest color imaginable. It was stormy outside, but is no longer so, & the pilot says he will sail, now, in a little while.

You give me no chance to forget you; I find your thoughtful & loving hand everywhere & at every turn among my traps & belongings. In the night I was cold, & wished I had my brown dressing-gown which you bought for me & which has been so useful to me a thousand times. I turned on the light, & there it hung, on the wall! It seemed for a moment as if you had heard me and answered

—as you always do when I am in need. I wish I could be as thoughtful for you as you are for me.

It is not dull, lying here in the marvelous sea, this flashing & sparkling & luminous sea. I sit out on the cushioned deck & read up on the West Indies, & sometimes try to write. It is a delightful holiday & I wish you were in it; then it would be perfect.

I will get this into the pilot's hands, now; I have already given him a telegram saying we are to sail toward evening.

Love to all of you, & goodbye.

SAML

NASSAU, *Apl.* 2/02

Livy dear, it is decided that we sail tomorrow for Jacksonville, reaching there on the 5th; then run up the St Johns river & take a look at it; then to Charleston & the Fair; stop next at a point in Virginia & take coal; then to New York. So it looks now as if we can hardly fail to be home by the 12th—& I do hope there won't be any failure.

I have telegraphed you to-day to write to Charleston; slow as the mails are, *that* gives time enough for a letter to arrive before we get there. I have written Havana to send my letters to Riverdale.

I hope you are well of your cold; I wanted to ask you to telegraph me, to-day, but I couldn't, as we were likely to leave here before night. It is a long time since I got those letters from you & Jean—it seems weeks.

It is cool & pleasant tonight, & we are wearing our coats & vests once more; the heat has been very oppressive ever since we were here before.

We went out of our road yesterday & lost a day to call on a West Indian native woman who served in Mr. Rogers's family 22 years ago. It was a lonesome little out-of-the way island called Rum Cay, with a population of 3 whites & 500 blacks—all very poor; a wretched & unattractive little solitude in the sea, & seldom visited. Our coming was a vast event, & the English magistrate (the sole official & he has nothing to do) said it would be the talk of the place for months. The negro clergyman was as glad to see me as if I had been his long-lost son—said he "couldn't *believe* he was actually looking at me & seeing me in the flesh—was talking about me *this very morning*—why it's just as if you are God-sent, sir!"

Good-night, dear sweetheart, I kiss you & the girls.

SAML

Shortly after his return to Riverdale, Clemens received an invitation from the University of Missouri to attend the June commencement and receive the degree of LL. D. Leaving home in late May he went first to Hannibal, always an intoxicant to him with its heady memories of boyhood. Robertus Love of the *Post Dispatch* accompanied him during much of this visit.

HANNIBAL, Friday, After midnight
[Saturday, May 31, 1902]

Livy darling, I slept pretty well the second night on the train, & was up at 6 in the morning well rested; shaved & put on a white shirt; breakfasted in my room & was at the same time interviewed by a St. Louis reporter who had mounted the train after midnight.

Jim Clemens[11] & his cousin a Mr. Cates met me at the station & took me to the Planters, where I stood in the lobby from 8 till noon talking with reporters & hundreds of people; then went to the Pilots' Rooms with Bixby & talked half an hour with the old stagers—several of whom I knew [55] 45 years ago; then to the Merchants' Exchange with its President, & made a 5-minute speech.

Then back to the hotel & sat or stood & talked with people (& Bryan Clemens) until 2:15; then to the station with Jim & Cates, & started for Hannibal. In the train was accosted by a lady who required me to name her. I said I was *sure* I could do it. But I had the wit to say that if she would tell me her name I would tell her whether I had guessed correctly or not. It was the widow of Mr. Lakenan.[12] I had know her as a child. We talked 3 hours.

Arrived at Hannibal 5:30, P.M., I went to the hotel & was in bed

[11] Probably James Ross Clemens, St. Louis physician, whose acquaintance Mark had made in London in 1896, and whose illness soon afterward furnished the occasion when Mark declared reports of his own death "grossly exaggerated."

[12] R. F. Lakenan, lawyer and co-sponsor of the Hannibal & St. Joseph Railroad with Samuel Clemens' father in 1846, later became the town's richest man. In 1854 he married young Mary Moss, a match always believed by Clemens to have been loveless and cruel.

in an hour—leaving word that I was not to be disturbed. I read & smoked until 10:30; then to sleep; awoke at 8 this morning; got a hot bath; shaved; put on a fresh white shirt & the lightest gray suit; breakfasted; went & stood in the door of the old house I lived in when I whitewashed the fence 53 years ago; [a big crowd] was photographed, with a crowd looking on.

Then drove with Mrs. Garth[13] & her daughter to the Cemetery & visited the graves of my people.

Back to the hotel by 12:30; rested till 2:15 & was driven to the Presbyterian Church & sat on the platform 3½ hours listening to Decoration-Day addresses; made a speech myself.

Back to the hotel & jumped into evening dress & a fresh white shirt, & was at Mrs. Garth's before 6:30, in time to dine. Laura Hawkins present (schoolmate 62 years ago).[14] Smoked & talked, & was ready at 8 to go to the Opera House & deliver diplomas. (It was High-School Commencement.) Entered by the stage door & sat at the base of a great pyramid of girls dressed in white (the audience not visible, the curtain being down.) When it went up, it rose upon a packed house, & there was great enthusiasm. I listened to the essays 3 hours; then spoke 15 minutes; delivered the diplomas, & shook hands with that crowd of girls & other people an hour—then home.

In the afternoon (forgot to mention it) the church was crowded; I was speaker No. 3, & when I stepped forward the entire house rose; & they applauded so heartily & kept it up so long, that when they finished I had to stand silent a long minute till I could speak without my voice breaking. At the close I shook hands with everybody. It has been a rushing day, but I have felt no fatigue & feel none now. I love you dearly.

SAML

Returning from his native state in early June, Clemens engaged a cottage for the summer at York Harbor, Maine. Henry Rogers' yacht, taking the family aboard at the foot of their Riverdale garden, carried them up by sea. There on August 12 Livy fell gravely

[13] Helen Kercheval Garth, his schoolmate.
[14] Laura Hawkins Frazer, celebrated in fiction as Becky Thatcher.

ill, her long suffering with goiter and heart disease having an adverse effect, one condition upon the other—"nervous prostration," the family called it. In mid-October, with the oncoming of winter, she was moved in easy stages back to Riverdale. From this attack until her death twenty-two months later she was bedridden and often critically ill.

During these days the abiding concern of the Clemens family was to insulate her against fatigue, worry, or shock. The exciting effect of Mark Twain's presence in her room, tender and thoughtful though he was, caused his company to be rationed severely by the doctor—often to a few minutes each day. Clara became her mother's chief nurse and protector—hence the admonition to her standing at the head of this letter. Clemens had just been to New York to attend a sixty-seventh birthday dinner given in his honor a little ahead of time, on November 27, at the Metropolitan Club, then gone to Elmira for the wedding on the 29th of his niece Julia Olivia Langdon to Edward Loomis, vice-president of the Lackawanna Railroad.

Clara dear, this is to your mother, but you must not risk showing it to her without reading it first yourself.

ELMIRA, *Nov.* 30/02

Dearheart, it was a beautiful wedding, beautiful; & I was [thoughtful] careful, & watchful of my conduct & manners, & was the first to hug the new wife, & was greatly pleased with myself until Ida came & asked for a chance. After the supper I stood a little beyond the couple & received the wash of the reception-file as it broke upon them & flowed my way, just as any authorized & accredited bridesmaid would have done—& this was all volunteer-work on my part, & unasked. I suppose near [a thousand] 500 people—no, more than 500—passed along—everybody I had ever seen in the town in all the years. (To return to the wedding):

When the bride came marching on her father's arm through the parted sea of faces—marching to the same old Wedding March & through the same faces— (a little faded, a little wrinkled)—33 years blew away from my life, & it was our wedding over again.

And all the evening there was the same joy, the same excitement

& hilarity, taken right out of 33 years ago & reproduced unchanged under the same ceilings—lord God, what a sad thing a wedding is!

* * *

But I must say a word about my birthday banquet. It was very grand & flattersome, & finely successful. All the speakers preceded me: Howells, Reed, Depew, Wayne MacVeagh, St. Clair McKelway, Hamilton Mabie, Bangs, Dr. Van Dyke (with long introductions of each by Col. Harvey)[15]; so it was probably well after midnight before I got on my feet. All through the various speeches there had been fine bursts of applausive approval; but it was the last name & the last praise (yours) uttered that night that brought the *mighty* burst—when I explained, in closing, what you had been to me—briefly, but in definite & dignified words—& said only half of the chief guest was present in the body, the other & best half absent but present in the spirit—"& so, we both, by my mouth & out of our one heart, do most gratefully thank you gentlemen." (I told them already "Yesterday was her birthday.")

Howells said "It's the best speech you've ever made"—that, or something like it—"& it was splendid to close, like that, with Mrs. Clemens." He, & John Hay, being closest to me, began it; & the others flocked by & they all said it—& many had to work their way half round the great room to say it, but they were *bound* to say it. It would have shriveled Clara with jealousy.

I'm—loving you with all my might,

YOUTH

It was a private dinner—no reporters—there is to be no mention of it in the papers.

Livy's birthday was the twenty-seventh and hence in addressing the diners after midnight he spoke of its having been "yesterday." Of Livy herself he said, with a shade less scruple for the larger chronology: "I knew her for the first time just in the same year that I first knew John Hay and Tom Reed and Mr. Twichell—thirty-six years ago—and she has been the best friend I have ever

[15] Howells, Thomas B. Reed, and Chauncey Depew were old friends; Wayne MacVeagh was the well-known lawyer and diplomat, St. Clair McKelway editor, H. W. Mabie editor and critic, John Kendrick Bangs author, Henry Van Dyke clergyman and essayist, and Colonel George Harvey publicist and publisher.

had, and that is saying a good deal—she has reared me—she and Twichell together—and what I am I owe to them." John Hay, also mentioned in the letter above, had become Mark's good friend in early New York newspaper days; he was now Theodore Roosevelt's Secretary of State.

On Christmas Eve Jean came down with pneumonia, and to shield the mother from fretting it was necessary to enact within the household a conspiracy of benevolent lying such as Mark Twain had described by coincidence in his story "Was it Heaven? or Hell?" in the current number of *Harper's*. As her mother's constant companion Clara had to weave an elaborate tissue of deception about Jean and her activities, which Mark in his brief span of daily visiting did his best to keep intact. Eventually Jean grew better, only to fall prey to measles.

Meanwhile the mother showed dishearteningly few signs of improvement. "Mr. Clemens could only see her two minutes at a time every day, and oh! he was always waiting at her door long, long before he could get in," Katy Leary is quoted as saying in the book *A Lifetime with Mark Twain*. ". . . And sometimes when he couldn't stand it any longer, he used to write little notes and push them under her door. That seemed to comfort him a little." Most of these jottings are impossible to date with precision, but apparently belong to the late winter and early spring of 1903. On February 2 he wrote in his Notebook: "33d wedding anniversary. I was allowed to see Livy five minutes this morning in honor of the day."

Jan. 14

Livy dear, there's a new effect—the sea has come ashore. Water, blown by the wind in crinkling curves & long lines, is frozen white, & a stretch of it up the slope of the grassy hill gives the aspect of a section of green sea with wimpling white-caps chasing each other over it.

I love you dearheart, I love you dearly.

Y.

Rice was lovely, and (as Henry Robinson said about Charley Clark) "as funny as a frog."[16]

[16] Dr. Clarence C. Rice is familiar; the others were old Hartford friends.

Jan. 25.

Dearest sweetheart, it is a most fine & delicate snowfall & beautiful to watch as it sifts down through the naked branches. And Blennerhasset is enjoying it—goes tearing along the high limbs like a shuttle, & carrying on most gaily. Good-morning, dearest dearheart, I love you dearly.

Y.

On the back of the following note are penciled the squares of a ticktacktoe game and the date February 16, 1903. About this time Mark himself was ill abed with bronchitis.

Honey, I's gwyne take de res' you tole me to take, en I ain' gwyne git up in de mawnin' ontwel I done feel fust-rate en ker-*blunkety* blunk. I love you darling old-young sweetheart of my youth & my age, & I kiss you good-night.

Y.

"Ashcat" was his pet name for Clara, here also including Jean as well.

Feb. 27—P.M. The ashcats have gone to their rooms, I have come to mine; the day is done, it is time for reading, smoking, reflection, sleep—with you for text & undertone, dear sweetheart, whom I love—& so with a kiss, & another, & others, beside, Good night & pleasant dreams.

Y.

Good morning, dear heart, & thank you for your dear greeting. I think of you all the time, & it was for you that I was awake till after midnight arranging for this snow-storm & trying to get it at fair & honest rates—which I couldn't, but if you will take a handful of the snow & examine it you will realize that you have never seen any that could approach this for fineness of quality, & peculiar delicacy of make & finish, and unqualified whiteness, except in the Emperor's back-yard in Vienna.

I love you most dearly and continuously & constantly, Livy dearest.

Y.

I can't find that about Father Gerard.[17] Will look again, later.

I am not stirring, yet, Livy dear; I hate to wake up, because sleep feels so comfortable & restful; so I shall not wake at all until I've finished a dream that I'm dreaming, wherein are persons drowning & I wish to see it—so, good morning my darling, I shall call upon you when I wake.

Y.

With the coming of spring a mild improvement in Livy's condition cheered them, and by the first of July she was strong enough to be carried by yacht and rail to Elmira, to spend her last summer at Quarry Farm. Clara stayed behind at Riverdale, to undergo a minor operation upon which her father comments in the next letter.

QUARRY FARM, ELMIRA
July 17/03

You dear little rat, the reason I was troubled was because your mother was very miserable for several days & I dreaded the effects of your revelations. Why, dear me, it almost gave *me* a collapse to read about the surgical butcheries you were undergoing & contemplating. But you're forgiven. You can tell everything, from this out—your mother is bound to have it so.

She says go ahead & pay those holiday-visits, by all means, if you are strong enough & the heat isn't too great.

I am so thankful you are going to pull out of that slaughter-house & come along home with the remains of your throat. The air is divine here, & will set you right up. There is no medicine to equal it.

Now that the weather is getting warm enough to permit it, your mother will begin to sleep out in the open, to-night as an experiment. *That* will be effective medicine, too. She sleeps but poorly & brokenly in the house.

She drove out with Aunt Sue & Miss Sherry[18] yesterday. Last night we wheeled her almost to Jean's trough in the chair.[19]

---

[17] Father John Gerard (1840-1912) wrote books of Catholic apologetics and church history.

[18] Margaret Sherry, trained nurse, later accompanied them abroad.

[19] Along the road up the hill to Quarry Farm a series of stone troughs still remains, placed there at the request of the Clemens children and named for all of them (including little Langdon), so that passing horses could drink.

We shall take the villa Papiniano to-morrow by cable.[20]

We sail for Genoa October 24 in a great & fine ship, the "Princess Irene"—rooms on the promenade deck.

With lots of love to you & Jean

FATHER

Clemens' desire to be near the invalid almost extinguished his social life and public appearances during these months. In the late summer, on one of his rare and brief visits to New York, Livy wrote him from Quarry Farm, on August 5:

Oh how I love you & how deeply I thank you for your dear letter. I am more grateful than I can express for your unceasing love. I am much better than the early part of the week: really a different creature. I don't expect to die today, as I felt that I might on Tuesday. With the deepest love of my heart, your

LIVY

He was again in New York in late September, to make preparations for their going to Italy. He set down his latest reflections upon a subject they had pondered together myriads of times since those earnest evangelical letters written in their early courtship days—personal immortality. He could not help wishing for her the solace found by millions in the hope of a life beyond life. Only a few months earlier he had written in his Notebook: "One of the proofs of the immortality of the soul is that myriads have believed in it. They also believed the world was flat."

GROSVENOR HOTEL, NEW YORK.
Night, Sept. 20/03

Dear, dear sweetheart, I have been thinking & examining, & searching & analyzing, for many days, & am vexed to find that I more believe in the immortality of the soul than misbelieve in it. Is this inborn, instinctive, & ineradicable, indestructible? Perhaps so. I will put it out of my mind. Not that I object to being im-

---

[20] These negotiations broke off, as he wrote to Jean on August 12. "I proposed to send a cable saying 'Take your Papiniano & go to hell with it,' but Clara & I could not agree. She wanted to insert 'dam' in front of Papiniano, but I felt that your mother would not approve of that . . ."

mortal, but that I do not know how to accommodate the thought, nor how to give it welcome. As to what to do with it—well, that I will not bother about, it must take care of itself. It at least cannot appal me, for I will not allow myself to believe that there is disaster connected with it. In fact, no one, at bottom, believes that; not even the priests that preach it.

I could not telephone you from the station before leaving, or I would have sent you my love & another good-bye; then I wrote a note on a card, & found that *that* would not go, at least for about a day. So I had to put in my half hour unprofitably.

I shall hunt up Ben.[21] Don't you wish you could see her? I wish you could. But you have Jean & Aunt Sue, & that's a plenty.

Livy darling, I love you dearly & worship you.

Y.

I opened a newspaper of Jean's to see what it was, but I have remailed it.

Their discussion of personal immortality at this late date is almost certainly the same incident which Howells describes in *My Mark Twain:* "After they had both ceased to be formal Christians, she was still grieved by his denial of immortality, so grieved that he resolved upon one of those heroic lies, which for love's sake he held above even the truth, and he went to her, saying that he had been thinking the whole matter over, and now he was convinced that the soul did live after death. It was too late. Her keen vision pierced through his ruse . . ."

Her answer to the letter above, however, suggests pleasure and acquiescence in his will to believe, rather than doubts of his candor. That Howells was right in calling Mark's profession a ruse, nevertheless, is suggested by the cryptic epigram which Mark has penciled on the back of the envelope containing Livy's letter: "In the bitterness of death it was G. W.'s chiefest solace that he had never told a lie except this one."

QUARRY FARM, *Sept 23rd* 1903

YOUTH DARLING: I was so glad to get your letters yesterday morning. I am truly thankful that you "more believe in the immortal-

[21] Clara.

ity of the soul than disbelieve in it." Why are you "vexed" at this I should think you would be most pleased, now that you believe or do not disbelieve, that there is so much that is interesting to work for. An immortality already begun seems to make it worth while to train oneself. However you don't need to "bother about" it, "it" will "take care of itself."

How your reading did move me Sunday night. How sweet & fine you are! How much of immortality you have in your dear blessed self.

Dear heart will you ask them at the hotel to have a box of Buffalo Lythia water for me if they do not keep it? Also I would like you to ask them about their milk, whether it is certified &c. If we are not sure about it we better have Briarcliff leave us a quart a day. Will they (the hotel people) get in our Echo Farm whole wheat bread or shall we order it sent? Darling with all my heart— I love you. I hope yesterday was a satisfactory day & that business is going on to your mind. I am glad Mr Fairchild could say a good word about the machine. In deepest love

LIVY

To Clara Clemens at 249 East 32nd Street, New York City, her father wrote as follows:

[NEW YORK, *September* 24, 1903]

Benny dear, I am very sorry I missed you—it was too bad that you had your trip for nothing. You mustn't do that. You must step to the nearest telephone station & pay 10 cents & ask the hotel if I am in.

I am not expecting to get away for a day or two yet. I may be mistaken—I hope & pray I am. I hope to get up to see you.

At the Century Club the other night I had an hour's talk with the loveliest man. It was the same clergyman that taught us to sing—

"By the humping jumping J——
What the hell is that to you?"

He sent you his love. And I send mine.

GRENOUILLE

It is evening. I have this moment arrived, & am going out to dinner.

A month later all the Clemenses, with Katy and the nurse, sailed for Genoa, and were soon settled in Florence at the Villa di Quarto, a picturesque but uncomfortable Renaissance palace that had been rented sight unseen. Its owner was a fellow-American, Countess Massiglia, who continued to live on the premises and immediately plunged into a spirited feud with her tenants. These battles, joined to a damp and cloudy winter unlike that sunny Tuscan season remembered by the Clemenses from a decade before, were only disagreeable outriders accompanying their daily dread. Livy grew physically weaker, through a mingling of some good spells with bad.

"He only could see her once a day," Katy Leary remembered, "and it almost killed him. His room was right next to hers, and he could hear any little sound she made. . . . He was only allowed to come in every night to bid her good night, but he broke the rules pretty often and he'd slip in sometimes during the day, just for a glimpse of her. She'd put her arms around his neck the first thing, and he'd hold her soft, and give her one of them tender kisses. . . . It was a great love, I tell you."

The following note, marked by Paine "1904," was written during one of Clemens' attacks of bronchitis. The allusion to war pictures refers doubtless to those coming from the Russo-Japanese struggle, begun in February of that year.

Livy darling I am sending you my love & Harper's Weekly, both by the same female. There's war pictures—not very interesting ones, but maybe you will think different. I have heard good news from you every time to-day—oh, it's splendid (unbe).[22] As for my cough it [is] was hardly even worth cussing, all day, but now it is quite cussable, & threatens to become more so. The room is now being aired & the stink-pot prepared. I send you a kiss right away, so that it won't carry the odor. And lots & lots of love I send, too, to my dearest darling.

Y.

[22] Abbreviating the old German charm to ward off the ill-effects of boasting. To Richard Watson Gilder on May 12, 1904, he wrote: "For two days now we have not been anxious about Mrs. Clemens (unberufen)."

The long companionship of Samuel and Olivia Clemens ended on June 5, 1904. Three days later he wrote to the old friend who had joined them in marriage, Joe Twichell.

Wednesday afternoon (Clara's birthday).
VILLA DI QUARTO, *June 8/04*

Dear Joe: We were eager to serve her, all these piteous months. She couldn't devise a plan, howsoever staggering, that we didn't applaud, & do our best to bring it to fruitage. Every day, for weeks & weeks, we went out armed with the enclosed paper, hunting for a villa—to rent for a year, but always with an option to *buy* at a specified figure within the year: & yet, deep down in our hearts we believed she would never get out of her bed again.

Only last Sunday evening, with death flying toward her, & due in one hour & a quarter, she was full of interest in that matter, & asked me if I had heard of any more villas for sale. And many a time, these months, she said she wanted a *home*—a home of her own; that she was tired & wanted rest, & could not rest & be in comfort & peace while she was homeless. And now she is at rest, poor worn heart! Joe, she was so lovely, so patient—never a murmur at her hard fate; yet—but I *can't* put her sufferings on paper, it breaks any heart to think of them. She sat up in bed 6 months, night & day, & was always in bodily misery, & could get but little sleep, & then only by resting her forehead against a support—think of those lonely nights in the gloom of a taper, with Katy sleeping, & with no company but her fearsome thought & her pathetic longings; it makes my heart bleed, it makes me blaspheme, to think of the gratuitous devilishness of it.

How sweet she was in death, how young, how beautiful, how like her dear girlish self of thirty years ago. Not a gray hair showing. This rejuvenescence was noticeable within 2 hours after death; that was at 11:30; when I went down again (2:30) it was complete; the same at 4, 5, 7, 8—& so remained the whole of the day till the embalmers came at 5; & then I saw her no more. In all that night & all that day she never noticed my caressing hand—it seemed strange.

She so dreaded death, poor timid little prisoner; for it promised to be by strangulation. Five times in 4 months she went through that choking horror for an hour & more, & came out of it white, haggard, exhausted, & quivering with fright. Then cursing failed me; there was no language bitter enough whereby to curse the cowardly invention of those wanton tortures. But when death came, she did not know it. Nor did we. She was chatting cheerfully only a moment before. We were all present, I was stooping over her; we saw no change—yet she was gone from us! Why am I required to linger here?

SLC

On June 12 Clemens wrote a letter to Howells, which has been published by Paine save for the last griefstricken paragraph:

It was too pitiful, these late weeks, to see the haunting fear in her eyes, fixed wistfully upon mine, & hear her say, as pleading for denial & heartening, "You don't think I am going to die, do you? Oh, I don't want to die." For she loved her life, & so wanted to keep it.

On June 28 the father and his two daughters sailed from Naples with their burden. "In these 34 years we have made many voyages together, Livy dear, and now we are making our last," he wrote in his Notebook. "You down below & lonely. I above with the crowd and lonely." On July 14 she was buried in Elmira, in the family plot where the body of Jean would be brought to lie beside her at Christmas, 1909, and that of Samuel Clemens four months later.

A week after Livy's funeral Mark wrote from a cottage in the Berkshires to his Yale friend Professor Thomas R. Lounsbury.

LEE, MASS., *July* 21/04

DEAR MR. LOUNSBURY: I know you are right. I know that my loss will never be made up to me in the slightest. The family's relation to her was peculiar & unusual, & could not exist toward another. Our love for her was the ordinary love, but added to it was a reverent & quite conscious worship. Perhaps it was nearly like a subject's feeling for his sovereign—a something which he does not have to reason out, or nurse, or study about, but which comes natural. It was an influence which proceeded from the grace, &

purity, & sweetness, & simplicity, & charity, & magnanimity & dignity of her character. That & the frailty of her body, which made us nurse her, & tend her, & watch over her & hover about her with all ministries which might help out the poverty of her strength by riches drawn from our abundance. It was the attitude of more than one of her friends toward her, it was the common attitude of her servants toward her. Her servants stayed with her till death or marriage intervened: 12 years, 16, 19, 20, 22—that is a part of the record. And one is still with us who served her 23 years, & closed her eyes when death came, & prepared the body for burial.[23] One that served her 20 years sent five dollars from his small savings to buy white roses for her coffin.[24] Letters have come to me from shop-girl, postman, & all ranks in life, down to the humblest. And how moving is the eloquence of the untaught when it is the heart that is speaking! Our black George came, a stranger, to wash a set of windows, & stayed 18 years. Mrs. Clemens discharged him every now & then, but she was never able to get him to pack his satchel. He always explained that "You couldn't get along without me, Mrs. Clemens, & I ain't going to try to get along without you." He had faults, but his worship of her was perfect, & made the rest of us blind to them. When we became bankrupt he was determined to serve her without wages, & would have done it if she had allowed it.

I thank you, Lounsbury, for remembering her.

Joe Twichell married us in Elmira 34 years ago, in her father's house; & on the spot where she stood as a happy young bride then, she lay in her coffin seven days ago, & over it Twichell spread his hands in benediction & farewell, & in a breaking voice commended her spirit to the peace of God.

Sincerely & gratefully

S. L. Clemens

[23] Katy Leary.
[24] Their old coachman Patrick McAleer.

ACKNOWLEDGEMENTS

By kind permission of Mr. Samuel C. Webster, son of Mark Twain's niece Annie Moffett Webster, several family letters in his possession are here quoted. Miss Mary Barton has courteously agreed to publication of Clemens' letter to Warner on April 22, 1872, and Mrs. Ruth Wilcox Wheeler to the publication of his letter to her aunt, Hattie Lewis Paff, as well as Mrs. Paff's own recollections of Mark Twain. Miss Helen Keller has kindly consented to publication of an excerpt from her letter of March 29, 1895 to Mrs. Dodge. The Yale University Library has helpfully granted permission for use of Clemens' letter of July 21, 1904 to Thomas R. Lounsbury. To all the Editor offers his thanks. In the preparation of this manuscript he acknowledges gratefully the assistance of Mrs. Edna Fotsch and Mrs. Ursula Bond, of the Huntington Library, and of Miss Marianne Gregory.

LIST OF PERSONS

This list includes those persons mentioned in the letters who are not otherwise identified in the text.

ABBEY, EDWIN A. (1852-1911). Painter, illustrator, good friend of Mark Twain.

AMES, OAKES (1804-1873). Union Pacific Railroad financier in the thick of the Crédit Mobilier; the storm of that scandal broke upon his head in 1872. Unfastidious in business ethics, he was a neo-Puritan and aggressive teetotaler.

AMES, OLIVER (1831-1895). Son of Oakes Ames, who took an early interest in the family railroad interests and shovel manufactory, later governor of Massachusetts.

ARCHBOLD, JOHN D. (1848-1916). From about 1882 the spokesman and dominant spirit of Standard Oil.

ARNOTS, the. The family of a rich Scotch banker, neighbors of the Langdons in Elmira.

BATEMAN, KATE (1843-1917). Well-known actress who played in New York. She spent her girlhood years between 1855 and 1859 in St. Louis, where her father was manager of a theater, and where Sam Clemens as river pilot made his home from 1857 to 1861.

BECKWITH, CARROLL (1852-1917). Portraitist, was the second most famous citizen of Hannibal, Missouri.

BEECHER, JULIA JONES. Thomas Beecher's second wife. He called her "my strong, courageous, energetic Julia," but in reply to a friend's inquiry about his health, Beecher once answered, "As well as anyone married to a steam engine can be." (Eva Taylor, *A History of the Park Church* [Elmira, 1946], p. 20.)

BOWLES, SAMUEL (1826-1878). Built the Springfield *Republican* into the greatest American provincial newspaper of its heyday. Irritable and sharp-tongued, he made many enemies.

BRANNAN, JOHN W. (1853-1936). Consultant at Bellevue and other Manhattan hospitals; son-in-law of Charles Dana.

BROOKS, MRS. HENRY. Her house at 675 Fifth Avenue was almost a New York home to the Langdons.

BRUSNAHAN, JOHN. Of Brooklyn. In the publishing business, and an interested observer of the Paige typesetter.

BUEL, CLARENCE C. (1850-1933). Longtime assistant editor of the *Century Magazine.*

BURLINGAME, ANSON (1820-1870). Befriended Mark in Honolulu in 1866; late in 1867 he resigned as American minister to China.

CHOATE, JOSEPH (1832-1917). Noted lawyer, ambassador to England, rival to Mark Twain and Chauncey Depew as best after-dinner speaker of their generation.

CLEMENS, HENRY (1838-1858). Mark's younger brother, fatally burned in the explosion of the steamboat *Pennsylvania.*

COIT, LILY HITCHCOCK (*ca.* 1842-1929). Daughter of an army surgeon and of a San Francisco bluestocking who wrote for the *Alta* and *Overland Monthly* and was friend of Bret Harte and Joaquin Miller. The daughter, a San Francisco madcap, honorary member of Knickerbocker Engine Company No. 5, spoke fluent French, spent the early Civil War years with her mother abroad because of their Confederate sympathies, adored hunting and coaching, and in November 1868 contracted a none-too-happy marriage with Howard Coit, "caller" of the San Francisco Mining Exchange, poker player and *bon vivant.*

COLLYER, ROBERT (1823-1912). English blacksmith turned liberal minister, pastor of Chicago's Unity Church.

CONNESS, JOHN. Elected to the Senate in 1863 from California, a great devotee of pull and preferment.

CRANE, ANNA. Spinster sister of Theodore Crane, inhabitant of Elmira.

CRANE, MRS. THEODORE (Susan Langdon). Livy's sister by adoption.

DANA, CHARLES (1819-1897). Famous editor of the New York *Sun.*

DE VINNE, THEODORE (1828-1914). Manhattan printer.

DICKINSON, ANNA (1842-1932). Abolitionist orator, actress, playwright, and egoist. Hattie Lewis's recollections speak of the Clemens's hospitality in Hartford: "Anna Dickinson came before she had the insane idea that she was a tragedian. She and Mr. C. did not get along well together. They seemed to be always trying to test each other's right to be famous."

DOLBY, GEORGE (d. 1900). Best remembered as the lecture manager of Charles Dickens. He handled Mark Twain's English bookings.

DOUGLASS, FREDERICK (*ca.* 1817-1895). Son of an unknown white father and Negro-Indian mother, ex-slave and famous abolitionist orator. Douglass was once a guest of the Langdons at Elmira (*Mark Twain Business Man,* p. 108).

FINLAY, FRANK (d. 1917). Irish Whig newspaperman who met the Clemenses abroad and visited them in Hartford in October 1889.

FRANKLIN, GENERAL WILLIAM B. (1823-1903). Civil War veteran and manager of Colt's firearms factory in Hartford.

FRELINGHUYSEN, FREDERICK T. (1817-1885). Secretary of State under President Arthur.

FULLER, FRANK. Sometime acting governor of Utah, convivial friend of Mark's Western years who had managed the humorist's Cooper Union lecture of May 6, 1867.

GARTH, HELEN and JOHN. Lifelong Hannibal friends of Clemens.

GILDER, RICHARD WATSON (1844-1909). Editor, poet, civic crusader.

GOODMAN, JOSEPH T. Able newspaperman and chief editor of the Virginia City *Territorial Enterprise* from whom Mark got his start in Western journalism. In Washoe he was regarded as a poetic genius as well; Mark wrote Livy on January 10, 1870: "He *could* have been so honored of men, and so loved by all for whom poetry has a charm but for the dead weight and clog upon his winged genius of a wife whose soul could have no companionship save with things of the dull earth."

HADLEY, ARTHUR TWINING (1856-1930). Economist and president of Yale.

HAWLEY, JOSEPH R. (1826-1905). Civil War general, governor of Connecticut, editor of the Hartford *Courant*—a newspaper into which Mark as a new-comer in 1869 hoped to buy his way, only to be rebuffed by Hawley and his partner, Charles Dudley Warner. Later they became good friends.

HITCHCOCK, LILY. See COIT, LILY HITCHCOCK.

HOOD, TOM (1835-1874). Humorous poet and artist.

HOUSE, EDWARD H. (1836-1901). Newspaper crony of Mark's early days in New York, noted Japanophile, who later quarreled bitterly with Mark Twain over dramatization of *The Prince and the Pauper*.

HUBBARD, GARDINER G. (1822-1897). Washington and Boston lawyer, organizer of the Bell Telephone system.

IRWIN, RICHARD B. Assistant adjutant general of Civil War days and author of military reminiscences.

JOHNSON, ROBERT UNDERWOOD (1853-1937). Associate editor of the *Century*; he and Mark had worked together to induce Grant to write his memoirs.

LAW, ROBERT. Chicago financier and sometime alderman from the ninth ward.

LESLIE, FRANK (1821-1880). Pioneer in the field of pictorial journals, in 1855 he launched *Frank Leslie's Illustrated Weekly*.

LEWIS, EDWIN. Brother of Hattie Lewis, Livy's cousin.

LOGAN, OLIVE (1839-1909). Erratic lecturer, actress, and playwright. In 1870, in Amenia, N. Y., she signed a guest book, "Yours ever, for God and Woman." As Clemens informed Livy, he followed with his signature and the legend: "Yours, always, without regard to parties and without specifying individuals."

MILLET, ELIZABETH GREELY MERRILL. Married Frank Millet, painter and war correspondent, in Paris in 1879. The Clemenses attended the wedding breakfast in Millet's studio.

NASBY, PETROLEUM V. (1833-1888). Mark's fellow-humorist David Ross Locke, owner of the Toledo *Blade*.

POMEROY, SAMUEL C. (1816-1891). U. S. senator from Kansas who figures as the corrupt Dilworthy in *The Gilded Age*.

POTTER, EDWARD. Architect of the Clemens house in Hartford.

REDPATH, JAMES (1833-1891). Manager of the famous Boston lecture bureau.

RICHARDSON, ABBY SAGE. Widow of the journalist A. D. Richardson and an amateur playwright.

SLEE, J. D. F. Agent of the Langdon coal interests in Buffalo, who after the founder's death in 1870 became manager of J. Langdon & Company.

SMALLEY, GEORGE (1833-1916). Overseas journalist, essayist and book collector, a good friend of Mark Twain's.

SMYTHE, R. S. Clemens's manager during his lecture tour through the British Empire.

SWISSHELM, JANE GREY CANNON (1815-1884), feminist reformer and editor, inhabitant of "Swissvale," near Pittsburgh.

TRAIN, GEORGE FRANCIS (1829-1904). Eccentric promoter, agitator for the Fenians and Communists, jailed for disturbing public meetings. Mark "blackguarded" him briefly in his speech on "Woman" at the Washington Correspondents' Club in January 1868 (Paine's biography, Appendix G), widely reprinted in the press, and probably derided him elsewhere.

TRUMBULL, HENRY CLAY (1830-1903). Sunday-school missionary living in Hartford.

WHITMORE, FRANKLIN. Mark's secretary and business agent in Hartford.

WILEYS, the GEORGE WASHINGTON. St. Louis and Hannibal neighbors of the Clemenses. Their son George later married Livy's New York friend Josephine Polhemus.

WILSON, GENERAL JAMES H. (1837-1925). Federal commander in Macon, Georgia, who received Jefferson Davis from the hands of his real captor, Colonel Pritchard.

WOOLSON, CONSTANCE FENIMORE (1840-1894). A prolific writer of novels and stories.

YOUNG, JOHN RUSSELL (1840-1899). Irish-American journalist, American minister to China and librarian of Congress.

Almost all the letters written by Mark Twain to his wife have passed into the personal possession of their daughter, Clara Clemens Samossoud, although a few were used by Albert Bigelow Paine and thus found their way into the Mark Twain Papers, now at the University of California.

In the following list, an attempt to record every known letter from Mark to Livy, all unpublished items are in the Samossoud collection unless otherwise indicated. These are the letters of which synopses are given here; no note is supplied regarding the content of letters printed in full or in large part, now or in earlier collections. Save for occasional excerpts used for annotative purpose, all letters contained in the present volume are published in their entirety.

Most of the letters quoted by Paine in his biography and in his *Letters* remain in the Mark Twain Papers, although a few originals are missing. Those printed by Mrs. Samossoud in *My Father Mark Twain* are still in her custody, as are the manuscripts from which the present editor prepared a three-part series in the *Altantic* in 1947-48, and drew some extracts quoted in his volume *Mark Twain to Mrs. Fairbanks* (1949).

Letters written during courtship days were carefully numbered by the recipient herself. To indicate the gaps left by missing letters, these endorsements are given in the inventory that follows. Letters written after marriage bear no numbers, and hence the form here used changes at that point.

In the preparation of this list the assistance of Mr. Edwin H. Carpenter, Jr. is acknowledged with thanks.

Place	Date	Endorsement Number
[Elmira, New York]	[Sept. 7, 1868]	1
St. Louis	Sept. 21, 1868	2
Hartford, Conn.	Oct. 18 [1868]	4
His "repentant" mood after writing a letter overstepping the brother-sister relationship; his week-old friendship with Twichell, and visit with him to "preach & sing" at the almshouse.		
Hartford	Oct. 30 [1868]	5
Reconciliation; his attempts to pray; encouragement and thoughtfulness of Twichell; plans to visit New York and Cleveland in next fortnight. (Last letter to use "Sister" as term of address.)		
New York	Nov. 28 [1868]	6
New York	Dec. 4 [1868]	8
Love "is born of both heart & brain." Portion printed in *My Father Mark Twain*, 13.		
New York	Dec. 4 [1868]	9
She must not be afraid of love; he has told their secret to his sister, Mrs. Fairbanks, Twichell, and Dan Slote; confession of moodiness in writing this long letter "so happily begun, so sadly ended."		

Place	Date	Endorsement Number
[New York]	Dec. 5, 1868	10

Reflections on prayer; his reading of Dinah Mulock's *Life for a Life* at her recommendation; Livy as a "Paragon."

New York	Dec. 9 [1868]	11

He and Twichell pray together for Livy; a letter from her inspired him to do his best "before a great audience in Newark."

Norwich [New York]	Dec. 12 [1868]	12

Jubilation at approaching visit on the 17th; he preaches a little sermon from the text "Wait on the Lord."

Fort Plain [New York]	Dec. 19 [1868]	13

Portion in *MFMT*, 22-23; remainder tells of his being the guest of poet-editor George Elliott and his wife, original of "Bonnie Eloise."

Detroit	Dec. 21 [1868]	14

Fatigue, disgust with hotel life; a call on Emma Nye; begs a picture.

Lansing, Mich.	Dec. 23 [1868]	15

Portion printed in *MFMT*, 20-21; remainder describes success of his lecture; their possible settling in Cleveland.

[Lansing, Mich.]	Dec. 24-25 1868	16

Christmas greetings; impatience for her daguerreotype.

Tecumseh [Mich.]	Dec. 27 [1868]	17

Printed with minor omissions in *Atlantic*, Nov. 1947, 34-35.

Cleveland [Ohio]	Dec. 30 [1868]	18

His worry that "a chilly apathy" possesses his religious life; begs Livy to lie abed late and conserve strength; his happy visit with Fairbankses.

Cleveland	Dec. 31 [1868]	19

A jolly dancing party at Akron; Elmira gossip speculates about their betrothal; he bids farewell to the Old Year which has brought love to his "barren loveless" life.

Fort Wayne [Ind.]	Jan. 2, 1869	20

Despite local grievance at misdated lecture announcement he captured his audience here; gratitude to Langdons for friendly letters. Very small portion in *MFMT*, 21.

Rockford [Ill.]	Jan. 6, 1869	22

Part in *Atlantic*, Nov. 1947, 37.

Chicago	Jan. 7 [1869]	23

Exhausting lecture schedule but high spirits.

El Paso, Ill.	Jan. 12 [1869]	25

Largely printed in *Atlantic*, Nov. 1947, 37-38.

Place	*Date*	*Endorsement Number*
Ottawa, Ill.	Jan. 13 [1869]	26
Davenport [Iowa]	Jan. 14 [1869]	27

His itinerary and activities; smoking and reading in bed his relaxation; women-haters are "unimportant whelps with vast self-conceit."

Chicago	Jan. 16, 1869	28

Largely printed in *Atlantic*, Nov. 1947, 38.

Cleveland	Jan. 19 [1869]	29
Toledo	Jan. 20 [1869]	30

Partially printed in *Atlantic*, Nov. 1947, 38-39.

Norwalk, Ohio	Jan. 21 [1869]	31

Dreams frequently of her; regrets "the distress & despondency those California letters plunged you into."

Cleveland	Jan. 22 [1869]	32

Her porcelaintype received; rhapsody of devotion. Small portion in *MFMT*, 19-20.

Cleveland	Jan. 23 [1869]	33

Teases Livy about her literal-mindedness, and the innocent vanity with which she accepts his judgment of her faultlessness.

Cleveland	Jan. 24 [1869]	34
Batavia, Ill.	Jan. 26 [1869]	35

Kisses her picture; demands she always wear blue, "because its language is Purity."

Galena [Ill.]	Jan. 29, 1869	37

Plans to reach Elmira next Thursday.

Cleveland	Feb. 13, 1869	38

Lecture engagement missed through ineptness of Mr. Fairbanks; vexation now spent; Mrs. Fairbanks will have Livy's engagement ring made.

Ravenna, Ohio	Feb. 13, 1869	39

Has heard Congregational sermon today, but preacher "incoherent"; business plans turning from Cleveland toward Hartford.

Ravenna, Ohio	Feb. 15 [1869]	40

"Both of us . . . would prefer the quiet, moral atmosphere of Hartford to the driving, ambitious ways of Cleveland."

Titusville, Pa.	Feb. 17, 1869	41

A lecture-committee spoiled his sleep; he feels unwell and cannot concentrate on this letter.

Stuyvesant [New York]	Feb. 26 [1869]	43

Adverse condition for writing letters—visitors, cold room, a smoking stove, and fatigue.

Lockport [New York]	Feb. 27 [1869]	44
Rochester, New York	Feb. 28 [1869]	45

Severe storm causes his first cancellation of a lecture; asks Livy to keep a file of all his articles in print.

Place	Date	Endorsement Number
Rochester	Mar. 1 [1869]	46
Lockport	Mar. 4 [1869]	47

Lecture tour completed, visit from old Hannibal preacher, Mr. Bennett.

| Hartford | Mar. 5 [1869] | 48 |

Everybody who knows Livy thinks she is too perfect for him—as he agrees.

| Hartford | Mar. 6 [1869] | 49 |

Describes illustrations for *Innocents Abroad*; "You are my very ideal of a wife, 'healthy' or not healthy"; he cares little for acquaintances (i.e., the Hookers) as against friends (Langdons and Fairbankses).

| Hartford | Mar. 6 [1869] | 50 |
| Hartford | [Mar.] 8 [1869] | 51 |

Reading *Autocrat of the Breakfast Table*.

| Hartford | Mar. 8 & 9 [1869] | 52 |

Having defended the sowing of wild oats, he now yields to her and Twichell. Apparently the first letter mailed to her directly, not through her brother Charles.

| Hartford | Mar. 10 [1869] | 53 |

Liking for his rival and new acquaintance Nasby.

| Hartford | Mar. 12 [1869] | 54 |

Having been "pointedly snubbed, & slighted many & many a time" through life, he has misgivings about the Hookers; a dream of Livy's snubbing him; he will bring proof of the book for them to read together five days hence; meanwhile he goes to Boston and New York.

| Hartford | Mar. 13 [1869] | 56 |

Invites her to open packages of proof and "plunge your dainty fingers into my affairs just as much as you want to."

| New York | [May] 8 [1869] | 61 |
| Hartford | May 8, 1869 | 62 |

Written just after return from New York; this morning's New York *Tribune* carries his "squib . . . about the Wilson murder case."

| Hartford | [May] 9 [1869] | 64 |

Thoughts on permanence of their troth, evoked by broken engagement of friends; has read 50 pages of *Innocents* proof this morning.

| Hartford | May 12 [1869] | 67 |
| Hartford | [May] 13, 1869] | 68 |

Her slowness to see jokes; dream that he had lost her; proofs of *Innocents*; reading Victor Hugo.

| Hartford | [May 14, 1869] | 69 |

Last night wrote the "Private Habits of the Siamese Twins"; 20,000 copies of *Innocents* to be printed

immediately; doubts he will go to California with
J. H. Riley and James R. Young; hopes that C. D.
Warner will look favorably upon Clemens's desire
to join the Hartford *Courant*.

Hartford   [May 14, 1869]   70
"General disagreeableness of mixing infants into
grown people's entertainments" as shown at the
Trumbulls. He dates this "Thursday" but internal
evidence shows it was written after No. 69 but the
same day, namely Friday, May 14.

Hartford   [May 15, 1869]   71
Broken engagement of her friend Emma Sayles to
Dr. Greeves. Small portion in *MFMT*, 17.

Hartford   [May 15, 1869]   72
Portions printed in *Atlantic*, Dec. 1947, 68-69.

Hartford   [May 17, 1869]   73
Portions printed in *Atlantic* Dec. 1947, 68-69.

Hartford   [May 19, 1869]   75
East Windsor Hill [Conn.]   May 24, 1869   81
Is guest at country house of aged novelist Azel
Stevens Roe, whose son is "my old Nevada & Cali-
fornia friend."

[Elmira]   June 8, [1869]   82
Portion in *MFMT*, 16-17.

Hartford   June 21, [1869]   83
[New York]   [June 22, 1869]   84
Urging her to take care of herself; plans for shopping trip next day; his visit to Academy of Design,
wishing she could have enjoyed pictures with him.
Delivered by hand to the Brooks house where she
was staying.

Buffalo   [Aug. 8, 1869]   90
Self-incrimination for having offended her the day
before; attendance at a church service, with summary of sermon; his debt of gratitude to her father.

[Buffalo]   [Aug. 19, 1869]   101
Buffalo   Aug. 21, 1869   104
Buffalo   [Aug. 25, 1869]   108
Clemens and two friends in a boat caught in "heavy
sea" on Lake; will visit her two days hence.

Buffalo   Sept. 2 [1869]   110
Their plans after marriage, whether to start housekeeping or to live in a boarding house; Mrs. Fairbanks' proposed visit to Elmira.

Buffalo   [Sept. 3] 1869   113
[Buffalo]   [Sept. 6, 1869]   115½
Tirade against the editor-poetaster Elliott, who
"passionately admires every sick rhyme his putrid

Place	Date	Endorsement Number

brain throws up in its convulsions of literary nausea," a troublesome correspondent of Clemens.

Buffalo　　　　　　　　　　Sept. 7, 1869　　　116
His loneliness without her; is collecting reviews of
Innocents for publicity purposes; sends her his
maiden effort from the *Express*.

Buffalo　　　　　　　　　　Sept. 8, 1869　　　117
Portion printed in *MFMT*, 17-18 and *Atlantic*, Dec.
1947, 69.

Pittsburgh　　　　　　　　Oct. 30-31, [1869]　　128
Portions printed in *Atlantic*, Dec. 1947, 69-71.

Boston　　　　　　　　　　Nov. 10, [1869]　　133
Progress of his lecture tour.

Boston　　　　　　　　　　Nov. 10-11, [1869]　　134
Success of his Boston lecture; has been buying wedding
clothes.

Clinton, Mass.　　　　　　Nov. 15, [1869]　　138
and
Holyoke, Mass.　　　　　　Nov. 16, [1869]
Two letters in one; the later (not printed) devoted
to endearments and his itinerary.

Boston　　　　　　　　　　[Nov.] 19, [1869]　　141
Summary of his schedule for a few days, written on
back of a *carte-de-visite* photograph.

Hartford　　　　　　　　　Nov. 24, 1869　　147
Boston　　　　　　　　　　[Nov.] 25 [1869]　　148
Nasby has relieved him of a lecture at Rutland, Vt.;
missed chance to see Livy in New York; has had an
evening's visit from Josh Billings.

Boston　　　　　　　　　　[Nov. 27, 1869]　　149
A "big house" last night; encloses two photographs
of self, Nasby, and Billings, "The American Humorists."

Boston　　　　　　　　　　[Nov. 28, 1869]　　150
[Boston]　　　　　　　　　[Nov. 29, 1869]
Copy of his lecture schedule from Dec. 1, 1869 to
Jan. 17, 1870, on which he has written a brief endorsement
to Livy.

Springfield, Mass.　　　　　Dec. 14, [1869]　　[155?]
His platform technique; calls *Jumping Frog* "best
humorous sketch that America has produced";
dream of losing her to a rival. Small portion in
MFMT, 46.

Pawtucket, R. I.　　　　　[Dec.] 14, [1869]　　156
Boston　　　　　　　　　　Dec. 18, [1869]　　159
Joe Goodman's visit in East; recovering from a cold;
Mrs. William Barstow continues to seek jobs for
"her well-meaning but useless husband."

Boston　　　　　　　　　　Dec. 21, 1869　　160

Place	Date	Endorsement Number
Boston	Dec. 25, 1869	163
New Haven [Conn.]	Dec. 27, [1869]	166
[New York]	[Jan. 6, 1870]	168

Is reading *Robinson Crusoe*, but has left his much-prized *Don Quixote* with Susan Crane.

Troy [New York]	Jan. 7 [1870]	169
Troy	Jan. 8 [1870]	170
Albany	Jan. 10 [1870]	172

Apologies for having asked her not to attend his lecture at Owego, knowing it would be a poor one; upbraids himself as incurably selfish; satirical synopsis of *Ivanhoe*.

Albany	Jan. 10 [1870]	173

Largely printed in *MFMT*, 209-10.

Cambridge [New York]	Jan. 13 [1870]	176

In *Atlantic*, Dec. 1947, 71-72, except last paragraph.

Troy	Jan. 14 [1870]	177
Utica	Jan. 15, 1870	178

Apologies for his irritation over her sermon against smoking; highly successful lecture tonight; glad Livy likes his gift of a Milton.

Hornellsville [N.Y.]	[Jan.] 20 [1870]	184

Last letter before marriage. Portion in *Atlantic*, Dec. 1947, 72.

Place	Date	Contents
Washington	July 6 [1870]	Lobbying activities in Washington.
Washington	July 8 [1870]	
[Cleveland]	[Jan. 12, 1871]	Description of Alice Fairbanks' wedding.
[Hartford]	[c. Aug. 9, 1871]	
Hartford	[Aug.] 10 [1871]	
[Hartford]	[Aug. 18, 1871]	Hopes some day to write "an Autobiography of Old Parr," against background of English history.
Washington	Sept. 8, 1871	His search of patent records in relation to an invention.
[New York]	Oct. 14 [1871]	Billiards and theater in New York.
Bethlehem [Pa.]	[Oct. 15, 1871]	Description of the town and its cemetery. In part in *MFMT*, 50.
Bethlehem	[Oct. 16, 1871]	Intends to try lecture with no notes.

Place	Date	Contents
Allentown [Pa.]	[Oct. 17, 1871]	
Wilkes Barre [Pa.]	Oct. 18 [1871]	Dissatisfaction with lecture; hard at work on a new one.
Milford, Mass.	[Oct.] 31 [1871]	
Boston	Nov. 1 [1871]	Success of his Boston appearance.
Worcester [Mass.]	[Nov. 10, 1871]	Printed almost entirely in *MFMT*, 45.
Boston	[Nov. 11, 1871]	Lecture at Randolph was jolly, but hotel roused him too early.
Boston	[Nov. 12, 1871]	Printed in full, *Atlantic*, Jan. 1948, 84.
Haverhill [Mass.]	[Nov. 15, 1871]	Printed in part in *Atlantic*, Jan. 1948, 84, under date of postmark.
Portland, Maine	[Nov.] 16 [1871]	Brief note on successful lecture.
Bennington [Vt.]	[Nov. 27, 1871]	
Homer [N. Y.]	Dec. 3 [1871]	Details of mail, money, etc.
Geneva [N. Y.]	Dec. 4 [1871]	A "lovable" Episcopal minister he had met on train; Hannibal friends encountered at lecture.
Auburn [N. Y.]	Dec. 5 [1871]	Acknowledging birthday note.
Chicago	Dec. 16 [1871]	In full in *Atlantic*, Jan. 1948, 84-85.
Chicago	Dec. 25, 1871	Largely in *MFMT*, 53.
Champaign, Ill.	Dec. 26, 1871	
Tuscola [Ill.]	[Dec.] 27 [1871]	Part in *MFMT*, 48-49.
Danville [Ill.]	Dec. 28 [1871]	Anxiety for wife and baby.
Paris [Ill.]	Dec. 31 [1871]	Given almost entirely in *MFMT*, 9-12.
Dayton	[Jan.] 4 [1872]	Almost entirely in *MFMT*, 52.
Wooster [Ohio]	Jan. 7 [1872]	Part in *MFMT*, 46, as belonging to another letter.
Salem [Ohio]	Jan. 8 [1872]	Is tired of tour.
Steubenville [Ohio]	Jan. 9 [1872]	
Wheeling [W. Va.] & Pittsburgh	[Jan.] 10-11 [1872]	Success in both places; her social life; his "fat-Cholley Aithens" reading.
Kittanning [Pa.]	[Jan.] 12 [1872]	
Pittsburgh	Jan. 13 [1872]	Brief note sending Pittsburgh clippings.
[Pittsburgh]	[Jan.] 16 [1872]	Never wants to tour again.

Place	Date	Contents
Harrisburg [Pa.]	[Jan.] 20 [1872]	Success in Lancaster; he defends Longfellow against plagiarism; hopes that he has finally sold his interest in Buffalo *Express*.
[New York]	[Aug. 20, 1872]	Arrangements for trip to England; meetings with John Hay and Bret Harte.
Off Queenstown, Ireland	Aug. 29, 1872	
Liverpool [Eng.]	[Sept. 1, 1872]	Nostalgia for family, his journal, etc.
London	Sept. 11, 1872	
London	Sept. 15, 1872	Printed in *Letters*, 199.
[London]	[Sept. 15, 1872]	Stanley's reception by Queen Victoria; zoological gardens; visit to Brighton with Hood; tribute to Henry Lee; Brighton aquarium.
London	Sept. 22 [1872]	
London	Sept. 25 [1872]	Concert at Albert Hall; invitation to the Sheriff's dinner.
London	Sept. 28 [1872]	
London	Oct. 3 [1872]	Printed almost wholly in *Atlantic*, Jan. 1948, 85-86.
London	Oct. 25 [1872]	More interested in people than in sight-seeing; Sir Henry Stanley not a gentleman; Royal Geographical Society Dinner.
London	Nov. 9, 1872	
[New York]	[Feb. 2, 1873]	Comments on their wedding anniversary; reviews of *Roughing It*; partially in *MFMT*, 47.
[Hartford]	April 26 [1873]	In *Atlantic*, Jan. 1948, 86-87.
At Sea	[Nov. 1873]	Description of "City of Chester" and its accommodations.
At Sea	[Nov. 1873]	Description of storm.
London	Nov. 19 [1873] (Date of "20" has been superimposed.)	
[London?]	Nov. 21 [1873]	Purchases of wardrobe in London; arrangements for her not to spend nights alone in Hartford house during his absence.
[London]	[Nov.] 23 [1873]	Printed in *Atlantic*, Jan. '48, 87.

Place	Date	Contents
London	Nov. 24 [1873]	Oxford student audiences.
London	Nov. 26 [1873]	Birthday greetings, enclosing letter from Charles Kingsley.
[London]	Dec. 3 [1873]	Busy revamping and memorizing "Roughing It" lecture.
[London]	Dec. 6 [1873]	"Unspeakably sick of the Sandwich Islands as a topic to lecture on."
[London]	Dec. 7 [1873]	Has just rehearsed new lecture.
[London]	Dec. 9 [1873]	New lecture a great success; London fog.
[London]	Dec. 11-12 [1873]	
[London]	Dec. 13 [1873]	Fog's adverse effect on his audiences; proofreading Gilded Age; Lord Mayor's forthcoming dinner.
London	Dec. 14 [1873]	
[London]	Dec. 16 [1873]	Responsive audiences; letter from Tennyson.
[London]	Dec. 20 [1873]	Last London appearance; new lecture ("Roughing It") much better than old.
[London]	Dec. 21 [1873]	Dinner party at Smalley's.
[London]	Dec. 22 [1873]	
London	Dec. 23 [1873]	A reading by Burnand, at which Mark was the observed of all observers.
[London]	Dec. 25 [1873]	Salisbury Cathedral; Stonehenge.
[London]	Dec. 29 [1873]	
London	Dec. 31 [1873]	Thirteen more days in England.
[London]	Jan. 1 [1874]	Note about an address.
London	Jan. 1 & 3 [1874]	
London	Jan. 2 [1874]	In Atlantic, Jan. 1948, 87.
London	Jan. 4 [1874]	Dinner party at Dolby's.
London	Jan. 4 & 5 [1874]	Endearments; impending return.
Vernon [Conn.]	[Nov. 12, 1874]	Progress of walking tour.
New Boston [Conn.]	[Nov. 13, 1874] [and enclosure of 14th in Boston.]	
Boston	Nov. 16, "1935" [i.e. 1874]	Really intended for Howells, Aldrich, etc. Printed in Letters, 231-4. Original in Berg Collection, N.Y.P.L.

Place	Date	Contents
Cambridge	[c. Apr. 18, 1875]	Visit with Howells family.
Hartford	Nov. 27, 1874	In *Letters*, 268-9.
[New York]	[Dec. 3, 1876]	Brief note about his activities in New York.
[New York]	[c. Apr. 23, 1877]	
Baltimore	Apr. 26, 1877	Long letter describing visit to Ross Winans house, full of mechanical gadgets.
[Baltimore]	[Apr. 27, 1877]	Visit to Maryland State Prison.
[New York]	[May 17, 1877]	
[New York]	[July 15, 1877]	Trip from Elmira.
Hartford	[July 17, 1877]	This and the two letters following deal with Lizzie, the errant housemaid.
[Hartford]	[July 17, 1877]	
[Hartford]	[July 17, 1877]	
[New York]	[July 27, 1877]	Description of rehearsals for *Ah Sin*.
[New York]	[July 30, 1877]	Tribulations of *Ah Sin*.
Allerheiligen [Württenberg]	Aug. 5, 1878	In *Letters*, 332-4.
[Rhone ?]	[Aug. 1878]	*Letters*, 334.
Gemmi Pass [Switzerland]	Aug. 24, 1878	*Letters*, 334-5.
St. Nicholas [St. Niklaus, Switzerland]	Aug. 26, 1878	*Letters*, 335-6.
Chicago	Nov. 11 [1879]	In *Letters*, 366-8.
Chicago	Nov. 12, 1879	*Letters*, 368-69, and somewhat garbled in Paine, biography, 653-4.
Chicago	Nov. 14, 1879	In *Letters*, 370-3.
[Hartford]	[October 1880]	Portion in Paine, biography, 691-2.
Boston	[Aug. 25] 1881	
Montreal	[Nov.] 27, 1881	In *Letters*, 407-8.
Montreal	Nov. 28, 1881	In *Letters*, 407.
Montreal	Nov. 29, 1881	
Montreal	Dec. 1, 1881	Hospitalities to Clemens and Osgood in Canada; publication of *Prince and Pauper*.
Quebec	Dec. 2 [1881]	Dislike of hotel in Quebec.
Quebec	[Dec. 4] 1881	In *Letters*, 409-10.
[Boston]	[March 12, 1882?]	Clemens working with Howells over a play about "Orm" (Orion Clemens).
[Near Indianapolis]	[April 19, 1882]	Brief note written on train.
Menard, Ill.	[April 21, 1882]	

Place	Date	Contents
"½ way to Memphis" Steamer *Gold Dust*	[April 22, 1882]	
[near Vicksburg]	April 25, 1882	
New Orleans	April 29, 1882	
New Orleans	[May 2, 1882]	
New Orleans	[May 4, 1882]	"Enthusiastic meeting" with Horace Bixby.
New Orleans	[May 6, 1882]	Plans for return trip; visit to an ice plant.
Steamer *Baton Rouge*	May 8, [1882]	
Quincy, Ill.	May 17, 1882	In *Letters*, 419.
[Lake Pepin, Minn.]	[May 20, 1882]	
New York	March 2, 1883	Billiards in New York.
Boston	[May 8, 1883]	Plans for another Canadian trip.
Montreal	[May 22, 1883]	Business contacts in Canada.
Ottawa	May 23, 1883	Arrival at Government House.
Ottawa	May 24, 1883	
Ottawa	May 28 [1883]	Country walks, billiards, and late hours with Governor General.
Ottawa	May 28 [1883]	Leaving for return trip.
Lowell [Mass.]	Nov. 12, 1884	Reports poor performance at Springfield.
Philadelphia	Nov. 21 [1884]	Good reading in Philadelphia.
New York	Nov. [23] 1884	
Washington	Nov. 24, 1884	Successful appearance in Washington.
"On board the train"	Nov. 28, 1884	
Baltimore	Nov. 29, 1884	Social contacts (Winans, Gilman, etc.)
Adams, Mass.	Dec. 1, 1884	Short letter after having seen her *en route*.
"On the train" [Between Albany and Rochester]	Dec. 3, 1884	
Rochester	Dec. 6, 1884	Progress of tour.
Rochester	Dec. 6, 1884	His lecture costume.
Rochester	Dec. 7, 1884	
Toronto	Dec. 8, 1884	Excerpts printed in *MFMT*, 51-2.
Toronto	Dec. 9, 1884	Short letter about meeting Frank Hall on train.
Ann Arbor [Mich.]	Dec. 12, 1884	Social contacts in Buffalo.
Grand Rapids	Dec. 13, 1884	
Grand Rapids	Dec. 14, 1884	Rugged schedule.
Toledo	Dec. 15, 1884	First snowfall.

Place	*Date*	*Contents*
Toledo	Dec. 15, 1885	Desire not to see people at his Christmas return home, in order to work harder on his readings.
New York	Dec. 27, 1884	Visits with Langdons.
Pittsburgh	Dec. 28, 1884	Large part in *MFMT*, 55-6.
Pittsburgh	Dec. 29 [1884]	
Dayton	Dec. 30, 1884	Excellent banjo performance attended; letter partly in German.
Paris, Ky.	Jan. 1, 1885	
Paris, Ky.	Jan. 2, 1885	Cable's parsimony about his laundry.
Cincinnati	Jan. 3 [1885]	Large part in *MFMT*, 47-8.
Cincinnati	Jan. [4] 1885 [dated by SLC "3 or 4"]	Visits in Cincinnati, description of a pottery factory.
"On cars"	Jan. 7 [1885]	Southern audiences bring out his best.
"On the train"	Jan. 8, 1885	
St. Louis	Jan. [11] 1885 [Dated 10 with ?]	
St. Louis	Jan. 11, 1885	Sending partial translation of Pied Piper of Hamelin.
Keokuk	Jan. 14, 1885	
Chicago	Jan. 17, 1885	Is suing Estes and Lauriat for selling his books at cut rates.
Chicago	Jan. 17-18, 1885	
Chicago	Jan. 19, 1885	Brief note about mail address.
Madison, Wis.	Jan. 21, 1885	Is using sleeping-bag in bed to keep warm.
St. Paul	Jan. 23, 1885	
Davenport [Iowa]	Jan. 31, 1885	Visits with friends and relatives *en route*.
Chicago	Feb. 1, 1885	Successful appearance in Davenport; schedule.
Chicago	Feb. 2, 1885	
Chicago	Feb. 3, 1885	Try-outs of new lecture pieces; Cable's "greatness."
Chicago	Feb. 4, 1885	Success in Chicago; O. W. Pond's illness.
South Bend	Feb. 5, 1885	Lecture at South Bend; sees C. W. Stoddard; Cable's "lunacy" about Sabbath observance.
Lafayette [Ind.]	Feb. 6, 1885	Cable's "petty magnificence."
"On the train" [Near Indianapolis]	Feb. 7, 1885	Finds little food and much black coffee beneficial.

Place	Date	Contents
Indianapolis	Feb. 8, 1885	Cable "has hogged so much of the platform time" that Clemens often hurries disastrously.
[Between Indianapolis and Columbus]	Feb. 9, 1885	
Columbus	Feb. 10, 1885	
Detroit	Feb. 13, 1885	Cable "wouldn't read in Heaven for nothing."
Toronto	Feb. 15, 1885	Large part in *Atlantic*, Jan. 1948, 88.
"On the train" [in Ontario]	Feb. 17, 1885	Additional irritation with Cable.
"On board the train" [Between Ottawa and Montreal]	Feb. 18, 1885	
Montreal	Feb. 19, 1885	Inquiry about a lecture invitation from "the Union for Home Work ladies."
"On train"	Feb. 20, 1885	
Washington	Mar. 2 [1885]	
New York	Mar. 4, 1885	Telegram. In *Letters*, 451.
New York	Apr. 8, 1885	
Philadelphia	Apr. 9 [1885]	Actors' Fund benefit performance.
Mt. McGregor [N. Y.]	June 30 [1885]	
Mt. McGregor	July 1, 1885	
New York	July 24, 1885	Grant's death.
New York	Aug. 4, 1885	
[New York]	Aug. 5-6 [1885]	
New York	Aug. 6, 1885	Visit with Grant family, General Sherman, Watterson, and others.
New York	Nov. 17, 1885	Proofreading; leaves for Washington to "talk international copyright to the President."
New York	Nov. 18, 1885	
New York	Nov. 21, 1885	Brief note on plans and train schedule.
New York	Nov. 25, 1885	Typesetter explorations; visit with the Danas.
Hartford	Nov. 27, 1885	Printed in full, *Atlantic*, Jan. 1948, 88.
New York	Dec. 3, 1885	Calls upon Mrs. Grant.
New York	Jan. 26, 1886	Visits Mrs. Grant on her birthday.
Washington	Jan. 28, 1886	Copyright business; constantly "lionized."

Place	*Date*	*Contents*
"On the cars"	May 5 [1886]	
West Point	May 6, 1886	Visit to the Academy.
Boston	May 10, 1886	Consultation with Howells for "improving the play."
New York	July 30, 1886	
[New York]	[Aug. 1?, 1886]	On Long Island with Laffans.
New York	[Aug. 2, 1886]	Leaving for Philadelphia.
New York	[Oct. 26, 1886]	Trip to Washington to see General Sheridan.
New York	Feb. 10 [1887]	Has just given two lectures.
New York	July 26, 1887	
[New York]	Oct. 4, 1887	Domestic tragedies of the Joseph Choates.
New York	Mar. 16, 1888	In part in *MFMT*, 54.
Hartford	Nov. 27, 1888	
Hartford	July 12, 1889	
Hartford	July 17, 1889	Printed, with names deleted, in *MFMT*, 85-6.
Hartford	July 17, 1889	
New York	May 21, 1890	Going yachting on Hudson with Laffan.
Washington	June 14, 1890	
Hartford	[July 21? 1890]	Fragment; refers to her eye trouble.
Washington	Aug. 28, 1890	Hurrying to Philadelphia with Hall.
Bryn Mawr	Oct. 24, [1890]	
[Hartford]	Nov. 29 [1890]	Kind offices of Mrs. Taft.
Washington	Jan. 13, 1891	Efforts to interest Senator John P. Jones in typesetter.
Washington	Jan. 14, 1891	Reading *Cymbeline* with admiration.
Hartford	Apr. 18, 1891	Jean's dancing class; Clemens is "pretty well battered up with bicycling."
Hartford	Apr. 19, 1891	
Hartford	Apr. 21, 1891	Homesick to see Livy.
[On Lake Bourget & the Rhone]	Sept. 20, 1891	In *Letters*, 549-50 and in part in Paine, biography, 924.
On the Rhone	[Sept. 20, 1891]	Extract in biography, 924, and in *Letters*, 550.
Port-de Groslèe	[Sept. 21, 1891]	In *Letters*, 550.
On the Rhone [near Villebois]	[Sept. 22, 1891]	In *Letters*, 551, and biography, 925.
On the Rhone [near Vienne]	[Sept. 24-25, 1891]	In *Letters*, 552; the two paragraphs at top of 553 also belong here.

Place	Date	Contents
"Afloat" [On Rhone near Tournon]	[Sept. 25, 1891]	Partially printed in *Letters*, 552 (the passage on 553 is not from the same letter). An additional portion in biography, 924-5.
La Voult[e-sur-Rhone, Ardèche]	[Sept. 26, 1891]	
On the Rhone [near Bourg-St-Andèol]	Sept. 28 [1891]	In *Letters*, 553-4.
Avignon	Sept. 28 [1891]	In *Letters*, 554-6, and excerpt in biography, 927.
Arles	Sept. 30 [1891]	In *Letters*, 557-8.
Nimes	[Oct. 3, 1891]	Very brief greeting.

NOTE: Although SLC made a trip to the U. S. in June and July, 1892, no letters to OLC from this period seem to have survived.

New York	Apr. 4, 1893	In part in *MFMT*, 101-2.
Chicago	Apr. 18, 1893	
Elmira	May 6, 1893	Appreciation of Langdon family.
Elmira	May 8, 1893	Almost in full in *MFMT*, 177.
Leipzig	Aug. 28 [1893]	
New York	Sept. 7, 1893	
Hartford	Sept. 13, 1893	Attempts to borrow money in Hartford.
New York	Sept. 13, 1893	
[Madison, N. J.]	Sept. 17, 1893	
[New York]	Sept. 19, 1893	Business details; "we skinned through" yesterday.
New York	Sept. 21, 1893	
[New York]	Sept. 21, 1893	
[New York]	Sept. 28, 1893	
New York	Sept. 28 & 30, 1893	
[New York]	Oct. 3, 1893	Returns from visiting Clara.
[New York]	Oct. 18, 1893	In *Letters*, 595-6 and biography, 971.
[New York]	Nov. 8, 1893	Family plans.
[New York]	Nov. 10, 1893	
New York	Nov. 14, 1893	Edwin Booth memorial service.
New York	Nov. 17, 1893	
[New York]	[c. Nov. 27, 1893]	Fragment, social comment.
New York	Nov. 28 [1893]	
[New York]	Dec. 2, 1893	In *Letters*, 597-8, and excerpt in biography, 976.
[New York]	Dec. 4, 1893	Family and social details.
[New York]	Dec. 4, 1893	
[New York]	Dec. 8, 1893	Business conferences.

Place	Date	Contents
[New York]	[Dec. 8?, 1893]	Written on Frank Millet's letter to SLC, Dec. 8, '93; confusion over social engagement.
New York	Dec. 9, 1893	
[New York]	Dec. 15 [1893]	
[New York]	Dec. 17, 1893	"Tale of the Dime-Novel Maiden," a sketch based on real life, begun two months earlier.
New York	Dec. 19, 1893	Meetings with Huttons and Richard Harding Davis.
[New York]	[c. Dec. 20, 1893]	In large part in *MFMT*, 132-34.
New York	Dec. 25, 1893	In part in *Letters*, 598-600.
[New York]	[Dec. 28-29, 1893]	Notes on business and social matters penciled on H. H. Rogers' letter to SLC, Dec. 28, 1893.
New York	Dec. 29, 1893	
[New York]	Dec. 30 [1893]	Business matters; mind cure.
[New York]	Jan. 4, 1894	
Hartford	[Jan.] 11, 1894	Amateur theatricals.
	(Erroneously dated Dec.)	
New York	Jan. 12, 1894	In *Letters*, 601-02.
New York	Jan. 12, 1894	
New York	Jan. 13, 1894	Business negotiations; Twichell's edition of the Winthrop love letters.
New York	Jan. 15, 1894	Business; Twichell's offer to take Susy into home. MT Papers.
[New York]	Jan. 15, 1894	Bits printed in *MFMT*, 135.
Boston	Jan. 25, 1894	Printed, with minor omission, in *Letters*, 602-3.
New York	Jan. 27, 1894	In part in *Letters*, 603-8 and biography, 974-5.
[New York]	Feb. 7 or 8, [1894]	In part in *Letters*, 609-11 and biography, 977.
New York	Feb. [9] 1894	
New York	Feb. 11-12-13, 1894	Brief extract printed in *MFMT*, 134, as postscript to a different letter. Business; prices offered for his magazine appearances; dinner at Danas' and other social affairs.
New York	Feb. 15, 1894	Printed with some omissions in *Letters*, 611-13, and an excerpt in biography, 793.

Place	Date	Contents
[New York]	[Feb. 20, 1894]	Fragment, crowded schedule.
Fairhaven [Mass.]	Feb. 23, 1894	Opening of Millicent Library. MT Papers.
New York	Feb. 25-26-27, 1894	Visit from Mrs. Fairbanks; family health; business and social details. MT Papers.
[New York]	[Mar. 1, 1894]	Fragment; amused that a mechanic in elevated train told him he resembled Mark Twain.
[New York]	Mar. 2 [1894]	
New York	Mar. 2 [1894]	Heavy business loss in view; imminent return to Europe. Actually written early morning March 3.
New York	April 14 [1894]	Return voyage; arrival; visit with Howells. MT Papers.
New York	April 15, 1894	Chat with Poultney Bigelow. MT Papers.
New York	April 16, 1894	Business affairs a little brighter; high hopes for *Joan*; *Tom Sawyer Abroad* is published today. MT Papers.
[New York]	April 19, 1894	
[New York]	April 20, 1894	
New York	April 22, 1894	In part in *Letters,* 613-14.
New York	May 4, 1894	
[Paris]	July 6, 1894	Plans for voyage to New York.
"At Sea" [near New York]	July 13, 1894	
New York	July 17, 1894	
New York	July 20, 1894	Visit with Rogers at Manhattan Beach.
Manhattan Beach [N. Y.]	July 22, 1894 [Actually written on 23rd]	
New York	July 23, 1894	
New York	July 25, 1894	Lingering hopes for the Paige machine in a forthcoming "test."
New York	July 26, 1894	Business delays.
New York	July 26, 1894	
New York	July 29, 1894	Yachting with Harry Rogers.
New York	July 31, 1894	Negotiating with Harpers for *Joan*.

Place	*Date*	*Contents*
New York	Aug. 3, 1894	Brief excerpt in *MFMT*, 132. Hartford news gleaned in visiting the Whitmores.
New York	Aug. 5, 1894	
New York	Aug. 9, 1894	Tedious legalities over bankruptcy.
New York	[c. Mar. 11, 1895]	Scraps in *MFMT*, 99-100.
Hartford	Mar. 20-21, 1895	

NOTE: Since his wife accompanied him on his around-the-world lecture tour in 1895 and 1896, Clemens was not writing to her except in South Africa, where she did not visit every city with him.

Pietermaritzburg [Natal]	May 15, 1896	Tour details.
Pietermaritzburg	May 16, 1896	Excerpts in *MFMT*, 168-9.
Johannesburg	May 19, 1896	Fatigue and rehearsals.
Johannesburg	May 19, 1896	Calls on the governor.
Johannesburg	May 20-21, 1896	Almost entirely in *MFMT*, 167-8.
Pretoria	May 23, 1896	Visit to Hammond and other political prisoners.
Pretoria	May 25, 1896	Rhodes clearly meant to overturn government.
Pretoria	May 27, 1896	Note about a delayed telegram.
Johannesburg	May 29 [1896]	Arrival of Poultney Bigelow.
Bloemfontein	June 1, 1896	The veld "just as beautiful as Paradise."
[Bloemfontein?]	June 3, 1896 [dated 1895 by error]	Tour details.
Queenstown	June 4, 1896	Release of Pretoria prisoners.
King William's Town	June 7, 1896	In full in *MFMT*, 166-7.
King William's Town	June 8, 1896	Thinks he might like to be consul at Johannesburg.
King William's Town	June 10 [1896]	With m i n o r changes in *MFMT*, 169-70.
East London	June 12, 1896	Extract in *MFMT*, 167.
Guildford [Surrey]	Aug. 16-17, 1896	
[Guildford]	Aug. 19 [1896]	Postscript, with minor omissions, in *MFMT*, 172-4.
Guildford	Aug. 21 [1896]	
Guildford	Aug. 25, 1896	
Guildford	Aug. 26 & 28, 1896	
Guildford	Aug. 29-30, 1896	With m i n o r changes in *MFMT*, 175-6.
London	Nov. 27, 1896	
New York	Aug. 2 [1901]	Family finances, inspection of a new house for the family.

Place	Date	Contents
[New York]	Aug. 3 [1901]	Seagoing wardrobe bought; has boarded Rogers' yacht.
New London	[Aug. 4, 1901]	Farewell from yacht.
"Off Cape Cod, at sea."	[Aug. 6, 1901]	Fellow guests.
Bar Harbor	[Aug. 7, 1901]	Sends report by captain to attest Clemens' superior behavior.
St. Johns, New Brunswick	Aug. 9, 1901	Some changes in *MFMT*, 221.
[At Sea]	[Aug. 11, 1901]	"Even the others are behaving well."
Yarmouth [Nova Scotia]	Aug. 13, 1901	Ashore for a drive.
"At Sea"	Aug. 14, 1901	Fog partially cleared.
Bass's Bay [Maine]	Aug. 14 [1901]	
"Nearing Bath"	Aug. 16 [1901]	Fascination of the sea.
New Haven	Oct. 22, 1901	
[On train]	Mar. 14, 1902	Carolina and Georgia swamps as seen from train.
"Below Savannah"		
St. Augustine	Mar. 15, 1902	Note while waiting for breakfast.
Palm Beach	Mar. 16, 1902	
Palm Beach	Mar. 17, 1902	Plans to board yacht.
[Miami]	Mar. 19, 1902	
Nassau, Bahamas	Mar. 21, 1902	Swimming and sightseeing.
"At Sea"	Mar. 22, 1902	In *MFMT*, 238.
[Havana]	Mar. [24, 1902] [dated "23" with ?]	Visit to Havana.
Bowden, Jamaica	Mar. 29, 1902	Sightseeing in Jamaica.
"At Sea"	Apr. 1, 1902	Itinerary for return trip.
Nassau	Apr. 2, 1902	
"At Sea"	Apr. 4, 1902	Color effects of tropical seas.
"At Sea"	Apr. 5, 1902	Off Hatteras after visit to Charleston.
Hannibal	[May 31, 1902]	
Elmira	Nov. 30, 1902	
[New Bedford, Mass.]	[May 17, 1903]	A visit with Rogers family.
[New York]	Sept. 20, 1903	

NOTE: Of billets-doux sent to Mrs. Clemens' sickroom during illnesses in the winters of 1902-3 in Riverdale and 1903-4 in Italy, twenty-eight have survived in the Samossoud collection and three in the Mark Twain Papers, including those printed herein and in *MFMT*.

Set in Linotype Baskerville
Format by A. W. Rushmore
Manufactured by The Haddon Craftsmen
Published by HARPER & BROTHERS, *New York*